Oskar Panizza and
The Love Council

D1567426

Oskar Panizza and
The Love Council

*A History of the Scandalous Play on
Stage and in Court, with the
Complete Text in English and
a Biography of the Author*

PETER D. G. BROWN

McFarland & Company, Inc., Publishers
Jefferson, North Carolina, and London

LIBRARY OF CONGRESS CATALOGUING-IN-PUBLICATION DATA

Brown, Peter D.G., 1943–
Oskar Panizza and the love council : a history of the scandalous
play on stage and in court, with the complete text in English
and a biography of the author / Peter D.G. Brown.
p.   cm.
Includes bibliographical references and index.

ISBN 978-0-7864-4273-7
softcover: 50# alkaline paper ∞

1. Panizza, Oskar, 1853–1921. Liebeskonzil.
2. Panizza, Oskar, 1853–1921— Stage history.
3. Panizza, Oskar, 1853–1921— Trials, litigation, etc.
4. Trials (Blasphemy)— Germany.   5. Panizza, Oskar, 1853–1921.
6. Authors, German —19th century — Biography.
I. Panizza, Oskar, 1853–1921. Liebeskonzil. English.   II. Title.
PT2631.A5L535 2010   832'.912 — dc22   2009054317

British Library cataloguing data are available

Front cover: program cover design by Leonor Fini for Le Concile d'Amour
at the Théâtre de Paris, 1969 (courtesy of Richard Overstreet, La Galerie Minsky, Paris,
and Neil Zukerman, CFM Gallery, New York. Copyright © Leonor Fini Estate)

Manufactured in the United States of America

*McFarland & Company, Inc., Publishers
Box 611, Jefferson, North Carolina 28640
www.mcfarlandpub.com*

Contents

I always thought about the possibility of a performance...
— Oskar Panizza, *My Defense in the Matter of* The Love Council, 1895

Preface

Oskar Panizza's play, *Das Liebeskonzil. Eine Himmelstragödie in fünf Aufzügen* (*The Love Council: A Heavenly Tragedy in Five Acts*), exploded like a bombshell in the middle of the tumultuous 1890s. Before publication of this play, the 41-year-old author from Bad Kissingen was virtually unknown outside a small circle of "moderns," mostly Protestant avant-garde literati from southern Germany who had clustered in the predominantly Catholic Bavarian capital of Munich. Panizza's notoriety was established not so much by his play as by the fact that he was charged with 93 counts of blasphemy for "distributing" a dozen copies of the work within the German Empire. His place in literary history was assured when he was indeed convicted, arrested on the spot and sent off to serve his one-year prison sentence for writing a satire lampooning the Trinity, Mary, the Pope, the entire Catholic Church hierarchy and everything held dear and sacred by Christians.

In addition to a new English translation of *The Love Council* from Panizza's original handwritten manuscript, the present book contains extensive and updated biographical material to aid in understanding the man and the times that brought forth this play. All the key materials relating to Panizza and his *magnum opus*, written by the playwright as well as by his contemporaries, have been collected and presented for the first time in English. Among other things, this book gives readers the means to compare the reception of the play in book form during the 1890s with the reviews of scores of different productions staged around the world a century later.

The genesis of this book goes back forty years. I was a graduate student in the department of Germanic Languages and Literatures at Columbia University in New York when, in the spring of 1969, my parents wrote me that they had just seen a spectacular performance of *Le Concile d'amour* in Paris. My mother wanted to know what I thought of the play's author, a certain Oskar Panizza from Bad Kissingen. My father was equally enthusiastic about the play, which was rather unusual for him. Not unlike graduate students everywhere, I routinely ignored most of what my parents had to say. At the time, I was preoccupied with writing my dissertation on Gottfried Benn and had never heard of this author who, I assumed, was probably Italian and not German, anyway. When my parents replied that they had just come back from seeing the play for a *second* time, insisting that Panizza was indeed German and that the original title was *Das Liebeskonzil*, I checked out Hans Prescher's edition of the play from the Columbia library and devoured it in one sitting.

From that day forward I was hooked, enthralled by a virtually unknown dramatic work that was almost too outrageous to be true. The fascination has not waned in the intervening years, and I am almost ashamed to admit that this bizarre love affair has outlived two marriages and still endures undiminished after four decades.

Later that spring, I abandoned my work on Benn and began what would be the first ever dissertation devoted to this "madman" from Bad Kissingen. During the summer of 1969, I translated the entire play, which remained unpublished as I sought first to secure a theatrical production of my translation. Then Oreste Pucciani's translation, *The Council of Love*, was published by Viking in 1973. Even though Pucciani's work had evidently been based on Jean Bréjoux' French translation of 1960 and not on Panizza's original German text, there was little justification for a second English version, so mine was relegated to a desk drawer. After completing my dissertation, *Doghouse, Jailhouse, Madhouse: A Study of Oskar Panizza's Life and Literature*, I moved to New Paltz in 1971 to pursue a career as a professor of German at the State University of New York.

Work on Panizza was pushed aside for a while as I pursued other projects, but eventually I returned to "Uncle Oskar" and published the first critical monograph devoted to this author in 1983, titled *Oskar Panizza: His Life and Works*. The following year, Michael Bauer published his revised Munich dissertation, *Oskar Panizza: Ein literarisches Porträt*. Thanks to Bauer's extensive use of primary source material obtained from a variety of archives, our picture of Oskar Panizza has become considerably clearer and more complete. Panizza scholarship is also indebted to Jürgen Müller, whose study of *The Love Council*'s author is based on a wealth of official medical documents and psychiatric evaluations. Müller's book, *Der Pazjent als Psychiater. Oskar Panizzas Weg vom Irrenarzt zum Insassen* (1999, *The Patient as Psychiatrist: Oskar Panizza's Journey from Insane Asylum Physician to Inmate*), contains some important correctives and additions to Bauer's work.

Now that Pucciani's version has long since gone out of print, there is indeed a need to make *Das Liebeskonzil* available in English once more. My current translation of *The Love Council* presented here is completely new. It is the first edition in *any* language to be based on Panizza's 1893 hand-written manuscript of *Das Liebeskonzil*, which I acquired from a French collector and subsequently published in a large-format facsimile edition with facing transcript (Munich: Belleville, 2005). I will always be grateful to my publisher, Michael Farin, who generously gave of his time and resources to publish that lavish facsimile edition and who also variously contributed to this current volume.

Preceding the text of the play in Part I of the current book is an initial chapter introducing Panizza and his heavenly tragedy. Following the play, I have included all the additions that appeared in the second (1896) and third edition (1897) of *Das Liebeskonzil*, which are here assembled for the first time in one volume. Part II includes Panizza's brief *Autobiographical Sketch* of 1904, preceded by several chapters outlining his life and literary career in greater detail. Portions of this biographical material appeared in different form in my previous book, *Oskar Panizza: His Life and Works* (1983). Part III focuses on Panizza's trial of 1895 and on subsequent legal battles surrounding *The Love Council* that continued for another hundred years. An earlier version of this section is contained in an article I wrote for the *German Studies Review*, "The Continuing Trials of Oskar Panizza: A Century of Artistic Censorship in Germany, Austria and Beyond" (Vol. 24, no. 3, October 2001).

Part IV, dealing with the play's reception and performance, presents all new material. M.G. Conrad's 1895 evaluation of the play appears here for the first time in English, as do the "Critical Responses" from contemporaries, which Panizza appended to the third edition of his work. The final chapter provides the first overview ever undertaken to survey the scores of productions of *The Love Council* that have been staged worldwide in the past five decades.

As a scholar writing for what is hoped will be a wider audience of readers with diverse backgrounds and interests, I have chosen to dispense with footnotes, except for those that Panizza himself inserted into *The Love Council* and a few of his other writings reproduced here. Instead of footnotes, I use abbreviated parenthetical notations to document the sources of all citations. Fuller information regarding sources can be found in the extensive bibliography. Precise page numbers for the hundreds of newspaper and magazine articles are provided whenever readily available.

I use the titles *Das Liebeskonzil* and *The Love Council* interchangeably and, unless otherwise indicated, all the translations throughout this book are my own. Beginning in 1893, Panizza developed his own idiosyncratic system of German spelling and punctuation. No attempt was made to reproduce the effect of his hyper-phonetic spelling in my English translation, which would have been even more jarring and alienating, given that English spelling is far less phonetic than German. Panizza's punctuation within the play is marked by a plethora of extended ellipses (e.g., ...) and dashes that look like today's em-dashes (——). I have followed the convention of previous Panizza editors and shortened the ellipses to three or four dots at most. The dashes have been retained, generally with the spacing employed by Panizza in his handwritten manuscript, which is now readily available to a broad readership in my 2005 facsimile edition mentioned above. To avoid the accumulation of multiple single and double quotation marks, I have taken the liberty to consistently italicize the title of Panizza's play whenever it occurred within the title of another publication.

My research was supported by a sabbatical leave and by a Research and Creative Projects Award from SUNY New Paltz in 2007. My union, United University Professions, together with New York State, also helped fund my research through an Individual Development Award. The many wonderful people who helped make this book possible are far too numerous to mention, spanning a time period covering most of my adult life. The scores of directors, dramaturges and photographers who generously provided me with material for use in this publication were truly indispensable, and their individual contributions are credited separately. Wolfgang Rieger and Thomas Eden both maintain websites devoted to the lives and works of various authors, including Panizza. Over the years, we have reciprocally and collegially shared material with each other, for which I am indebted.

I am also particularly grateful to several descendants of Oskar Panizza's mother, Mathilde. Christine Harder of Fockbek very kindly gave me a copy of her great-grandmother's memoirs, as well as a copy of her portrait that is reproduced in this volume. Rainer Wirth of Bad Kissingen gave me access to his extensive collection of Panizza materials. Two fellow researchers on Panizza, Professors Rolf Düsterberg, Osnabrück, and Joachim Schultz, Bayreuth, have over the years shared their insights and advice with me. Jesusa Rodriguez of Mexico City kindly provided me with photos and information from her many productions of Panizza's play in Spanish. My friend and colleague François Deschamps generously provided of his time and expertise in helping to prepare many of the images included in this publication. The Berlin poet Klaus M. Rarisch, who organized the first public reading of *Das Liebeskonzil* in 1962, has graciously shared his personal experiences with me, as has Dietrich Kuhlbrodt, the former Hamburg district attorney, who co-wrote the screenplay for the *Liebeskonzil* film in 1981. I am also indebted to that film's producer, Hanns Eckelkamp. He not only shared his extensive film experiences and historical materials with me, but he also enabled me to obtain the five reels of Werner Schroeter's *Liebeskonzil* film, which I subsequently donated to the Museum of Modern Art in New York.

Richard Overstreet, Leonor Fini's close friend and the executor of her estate, has graciously allowed me to reproduce some of the artwork she created in connection with the 1969 production of *Le Concile d'amour*. Neil Zukerman of New York's CFM Gallery was also most helpful in providing me with some of Fini's etchings and drawings that appear in this book. The 1913 drawings by Alfred Kubin are reproduced here thanks to the generosity of Eberhard Spangenberg, whose reprint of *Das Liebeskonzil* was published by his press in 1991.

My colleague Yvonne Aspengren has been extremely helpful in reading over extensive portions of the manuscript, providing invaluable editorial suggestions and feedback along the way.

Lastly, I wish to thank my sister, Suzan Meves, my children, Stephanie Cullinane and Andrew Brown, as well as my partner, Carol Rietsma, for their unflagging encouragement, support and willingness to tolerate a sometimes obsessive literary preoccupation that has endured for decades. Since my parents, Vivian and Weir Brown, were the ones who first introduced me to Oskar Panizza's *The Love Council*, it is to their loving memory that this book is dedicated.

Abbreviations

Bauer = Michael Bauer. *Oskar Panizza. Ein literarisches Porträt*. Munich: Hanser, 1984.

ECHR *Judgment* = European Court of Human Rights, *Judgment*, Case of Otto-Preminger-Institut v. Austria. Application no. 13470/87. Strasbourg, 20 Sept. 1994.

Filmbuch = Oskar Panizza, Werner Schroeter, Antonio Salines. *Liebeskonzil Filmbuch*. Ed. Peter Berling. Munich: Schirmer/Mosel, 1982.

GmL = Gesellschaft für modernes Leben, Munich.

In memoriam = Friedrich Lippert and Horst Stobbe. *In memoriam Oskar Panizza*. Munich: Hort Stobbe, 1926.

KS = "Kritische Stimmen über *Das Liebeskonzil*." Appendix. Oskar Panizza. *Das Liebeskonzil*. 3rd ed. Zürich: Verlags-Magazin (J. Schabelitz), 1897.

LK 1997 = Oskar Panizza. *Das Liebeskonzil. Eine Himmelstragödie in fünf Aufzügen*. Ed. Michael Bauer. Munich: Luchterhand, 1997.

Memoiren = Mathilde Harder [Tilly, née Panizza]. *Die Memoiren der Mathilde Panizza*. Nieder-Olm: priv. printing [Antje and Hans-Wolfgang Redlich], 1996.

Müller = Jürgen Müller. *Der Pazjent als Psychiater. Oskar Panizzas Weg vom Irrenarzt zum Insassen*. Edition Das Narrenschiff. Bonn: Psychiatrie-Verlag, 1999.

OPI = Otto-Preminger-Institut für audiovisuelle Mediengestaltung, Cinematograph, Innsbruck.

öStGB = *österreichisches Strafgesetzbuch*, Austrian Penal Code, 1974ff.

Prescher = Oskar Panizza. *Das Liebeskonzil und andere Schriften*. Ed. Hans Prescher, Neuwied: Luchterhand, 1964.

TT = *Tiroler Tageszeitung*

Weinhöppel, *Visionen* = Weinhöppel, Richard. "Wer ist Oskar Panizza?" Foreword. Oskar Panizza. *Visionen der Dämmerung*. Introd. Hannes Ruch [Richard Weinhöppel]. Munich and Leipzig: Georg Müller, 1914. (2nd ed. 1923, 3rd ed. 1929.)

PART I: THE PLAY

Chapter 1

Oskar Panizza's Legacy

Who was Oskar Panizza? This question was succinctly answered by Walter Benjamin, one of the most influential German cultural critics of the twentieth century, who famously described Panizza as a "heretical painter of holy icons" (*Gesammelte Schriften*, II/2: 648). For Kurt Tucholsky, a leading journalist and outspoken left-wing satirist during the Weimar Republic, Panizza was simply "the freshest and bravest, the wittiest and most revolutionary prophet of his country" (*Freiheit* 11 July 1920: 2). Oskar Panizza, a physician turned author, was indeed part of the European cultural revolution of the 1890s, whose seismic shock waves continue to extend well into the twenty-first century. His scandal-ridden play, *Das Liebeskonzil* (*The Love Council*), deals with the origin of syphilis in 1495 at the court of Rodrigo Borgia, Pope Alexander VI. When it was originally published in Switzerland at the end of 1894, *The Love Council* was hailed by avant-garde intellectuals as a superb modern satire. One leading German critic, Michael Georg Conrad, called it "one of the most powerful and most significant works of art in modern dramatic literature, and, considering the difficulty of his topic, perhaps the very most significant work of the last years" (Panizza, *Meine Verteidigung* 32). For a brief period thereafter, Panizza's "heavenly tragedy," as he had aptly subtitled his play, occupied center stage during this cultural revolution, eliciting widespread acclaim from readers throughout Europe and from as far away as the United States.

Panizza, a native of Bad Kissingen, the once fashionable health resort in the Franconian region of northern Bavaria, had been a late bloomer, incapable of even completing his secondary schooling until the advanced age of twenty-three. However, his notoriety quickly soared to meteoric heights when, at the age of forty-one, he was charged by the Munich District Attorney in early 1895 with ninety-three counts of blasphemy contained in *The Love Council*. After a brief, one-day trial and conviction in April, intellectual heavyweights on the order of Theodor Fontane, Sigmund Freud and Thomas Mann weighed in with their strongly-held opinions about this blatant case of intimidation, human rights abuse and literary censorship. Panizza's punishment was a one-year prison sentence, certainly the harshest ever meted out against an artist during the Wilhelmine Empire, and it did succeed in its intended chilling effect. When the author emerged from Amberg prison in 1896, he was well on his way to becoming a broken man, and the furor surrounding his *magnum opus* had long since subsided.

Following his release from prison, an embittered Panizza emigrated from Germany to Zürich. There he republished several revised and expanded versions of *The Love Council*. He also continued to write both fiction and a raft of critical essays, which appeared under various pseudonyms in his own magazine, *Zürcher Diskussjonen* (*Zürich Discussions*). When the Swiss government expelled him in 1897, ostensibly for his involvement with a fifteen-year-old prostitute, but more likely for political reasons, he moved to Paris. There he remained until 1904, trying to keep his head above water by writing critical articles and poetry. His *Parisjana* (1899, *Parisiana*) contains some of the most vitriolic anti–German verse ever written and captured the renewed attention of legal authorities in the German Empire. By 1904, the author's mental health had deteriorated to the point where he voluntarily returned to Germany and was admitted to a psychiatric clinic. He spent the remainder of his life in a sanatorium in Bayreuth, where he died in 1921.

Even though Panizza continued to receive occasional notice from various iconic figures in German cultural history, ranging from Sigmund Freud, Alfred Kubin and George Grosz to Kurt Tucholsky and Walter Benjamin, *The Love Council* was all but forgotten for more than seventy years. The play's 1967 world premiere in Vienna went largely unnoticed. Two years later, Panizza finally reemerged on the international literary landscape with the spectacular 1969 Paris production by Jorge Lavelli and Leonor Fini of *Le Concile d'amour*. Since then, the play has been performed in some one hundred different productions throughout the German-speaking lands and around the world, including subsequent productions in Paris (2000 and 2001) and in a host of smaller French cities, as well as in England (London, 1970), the Netherlands (Rotterdam, 1976), Italy (Rome, 1981; Venice, 1995), the United States (Austin, 1983 and 1989; New York City 1987; Los Angeles, 1996), Mexico (Mexico City, 1987; Coyoacán, 1997), Canada (Sainte-Thérèse, 1972; Montreal, 1989 and 1999), Brazil (São Paulo, 1989; Rio de Janeiro, 1996; Porto Alegre, 2003), Spain (Grenada, 1988; Barcelona, 2000), Serbia (Belgrade, 2003) and Belgium (Ostend, 2006).

While syphilis has long been curable thanks to penicillin and other antibiotics, the scourge of AIDS has killed tens of millions and continues to spread throughout the world. This is the first edition of *The Love Council* to use the newly discovered manuscript of the play, written by Dr. Panizza in 1892–93. In the manuscript, the author refers four times specifically to a "virus" with which mankind will be devastated for its sexual excesses. Over a hundred years ago, Panizza not only posed but also answered the penetrating question: what kind of a God would visit such a horrendous disease upon his creation? The answer, it would seem, is that he is the same divinity whose wrath obliterated virtually all living beings in the Great Flood for their "wickedness."

Panizza's work entered another medium altogether, when the 1981 Roman production of *Il Concilio d'amore* was used as the basis for a feature film, *Liebeskonzil*, by the distinguished German director, Werner Schroeter. This film premiered at the Berlinale Film Festival in 1982, where it was greeted enthusiastically following its midnight screening. However, it enjoyed only a brief commercial run in a handful of German cinemas, where audiences, used to a diet of more hardcore action, violence and sex, shunned the film as too theatrical.

Some years later, the *Liebeskonzil* film touched off a lengthy series of legal battles in 1985, when Austrian authorities, at the behest of the local archdiocese, tried to stop its screening at an art cinema in Innsbruck. After the film was confiscated and banned throughout the entire country, the cinema owner sued the Republic of Austria for violating Article 10 of the European Human Rights Convention, which guarantees the right to freedom of expression. After almost a decade in litigation, this landmark case ended up before the European Court of Human Rights (ECHR) in Strasbourg, France. This is the highest court in Europe, from which no appeal is possible. In its 6–3 ruling, the ECHR ruled in 1994 that banning this art film, which contains no sex or violence of any kind, was fully justified "to protect the right of citizens not to be insulted in their religious feelings by the expression of views of other persons" (*Judgment*, section 48: 14). A subsequent article in an American law review assessed this case as having "ramifications possible throughout the world" (Walsh 78).

Through *The Love Council*, Panizza has left his mark on both high culture and pop culture in a variety of ways. The fact that an Internet search today elicits over a hundred thousand references to Panizza is certainly indicative of the breadth of his influence. Aside from the writings of numerous authors, including Thomas Mann and Sigmund Freud, there is the artwork by George Grosz, Alfred Kubin and Leonor Fini, or Franz Hummel's 1987 opera *Lucifer. A German Song in Memory of Oskar Panizza.* Another musical manifestation of an entirely different sort is Michael Bundt's "The Brain of Oskar Panizza," an almost ten-minute-long piece from his 1977 album *Just landed Cosmic Kid.* It continues to evolve through various mixed iterations following the original psychedelic rock version.

In an age when citizens in western democracies are amazed that publishing cartoons of religious figures in Europe can elicit violent rampages throughout the Middle East and beyond, the history of *The Love Council* challenges us to reassess the depth of our own commitment to artistic tolerance and freedom of expression. We should not be too quick to condemn intolerance in others before we have assured that freedom of

Oskar Panizza around 1890. Photograph by J. Reitmayer, Munich. Courtesy of Rainer Wirth, Bad Kissingen.

expression is indeed a value to which we ourselves are unalterably committed. For more than a century, Panizza's work has served, as few others have, both as a lightning rod for censorship and a litmus test of artistic freedom. Even in the Unites States, a relatively enlightened and advanced country, the attitude toward sexually transmitted disease among large sections of the population remains the same as it was five hundred years ago at the close of the Middle Ages in Europe. A Gallup survey near the end of the twentieth century showed that 43 percent of American voters continue to view AIDS as "God's punishment for immoral sexual behavior" (*Newsweek* Feb. 1, 1988: 7). As long as disease and death are seen as justified divine retributions for freedom of expression, sexual pleasure or humor, *The Love Council* will likely serve as a critical companion piece.

The Gay Nineties

The Gay Nineties, as the 1890s were termed a generation later, were years marked by a variety of sharp extremes and contradictions. On the one hand, this was a time of immense political, economic and military expansion. Germany's belated unification in 1871 and subsequent rapid industrialization led to the creation of an industrially-based upper class with enormous personal wealth. In the 1890s, the *Deutsches Reich* (German Empire) was ruled by Wilhelm II, the eldest grandson of British Queen Victoria. This often vain and reckless monarch, whom Oskar Panizza characterized not only as his own "personal adversary," but also as "the public enemy of mankind and its culture" (*In memoriam* 17), was to be the last King of Prussia and the last German Emperor.

At the beginning of the 1890s, Wilhelm dismissed his seasoned chancellor, Otto von Bismarck, and embarked upon his own much-heralded New Course. As Germany's industrial base expanded, Wilhelm's more activist policies sought to contain the rise of the new left-wing social democratic movement. At the same time, Wilhelm's foreign policies were inconsistent, blundering from one fiasco to the next, eventually pursuing a policy of massive naval expansion and in August 1914 leading Germany straight into the devastating First World War.

Simultaneously, the 1890s were marked as the decade of truly revolutionary cultural developments, most of which were quite at odds with the ongoing economic and military expansion. Some of these revolutionary intellectual developments had already found their most eloquent philosophical expression in the works of Friedrich Nietzsche. Writing in the 1880s, Nietzsche posited at the core of his philosophy the transvaluation of all values: vivisecting all collected wisdom and traditional values by radically challenging the foundations of theistic religion, nationalist patriotism, historical progress, government authority, artistic expression and philosophy itself. Panizza and his circle of self-proclaimed modernists also were enthralled by the writings of other anti-establishment thinkers, such as Max Stirner's *Der Einzige und sein Eigentum* (1844, *The Ego and His Own*) and Cesare Lombroso's *L'Uomo di Genio* (1889, *The Man of Genius*).

Another facet of the cultural revolution of the 1890s was a fascination with, and far greater openness toward, all manner of sexual phenomena. While the Austrian Sigmund Freud is today regarded as the foremost writer on sexual topics during the 1890s, there were others whose work was far more popular and influential in Germany during this decade. Foremost was Richard von Krafft-Ebing, a professor of psychiatry and neurology. His *Psychopathia sexualis* (1886) became the standard textbook in the newly established field of sexual pathology and was republished in expanded editions in later years. In his encyclopedic review of sexual "perversions," Krafft-Ebing first introduced the terms sadism and masochism. In addition, he argued for accepting homosexuality, which was generally considered immoral, dangerous and criminal, as an innate aberrancy that should not be criminalized.

In assessing the various homoerotic scenes in Panizza's *The Love Council*, it is helpful to appreciate the homophobia prevalent during the 1890s. Homosexual acts between men were a serious offense proscribed by §175 of the *Reichsstrafgesetzbuch*, the Imperial Penal Code. In contrast, lesbian acts were never criminalized, evidently because they were considered to be less threatening to lawmakers. Homophobia, while still a widespread attitude today, was just beginning to be openly challenged on a number of fronts during the last decade of the nineteenth century. Building on the work of Krafft-Ebing, in the late 1890s

Magnus Hirschfeld founded the Scientific-Humanitarian Committee in Berlin, perhaps the world's first organization to advocate decriminalizing same-sex acts between men. Hirschfeld went on to establish the Institut für Sexualwissenschaft, the world's first sexual research center.

In 1895, the same year that Oskar Panizza was sentenced to a year in prison for blasphemy, Oscar Wilde was convicted in London of "gross indecency" under Section 11 of the Criminal Law Amendment Act (1885) and sentenced to two years in prison. In a further parallel irony of fate, the two scandal-ridden, down-and-out ex-convicts both moved to Paris during the late 1890s, where they knew each other and even socialized on occasion.

The leading British sexual psychologist during the 1890s was Havelock Ellis. Together with John Addington Symonds, he authored the first English medical textbook on homosexuality, *Sexual Inversion* (1897). The book includes detailed descriptions of homosexual relations between men and boys, which the authors did not consider to be either immoral or criminal. Ellis is also credited with developing the concepts of autoerotism and narcissism, which Sigmund Freud elaborated on in later years.

Berlin Naturalists, Munich Moderns

During the Second Empire (1871–1918), the Prussian capital, Berlin, became the German capital and the cultural center of the new *Reich*. In the early 1890s, the revolutionary new trend in German theater was naturalism, ushered in by the premiere of Gerhart Hauptmann's *Vor Sonnenaufgang* (1889, *Before Sunrise*). In 1894, the year that *Das Liebeskonzil* was published in Zürich, Hauptmann's play *Die Weber* (1892, *The Weavers*), which portrays the Silesian weavers' insurrection of 1844, premiered at the Deutsches Theater in Berlin. It was only after years of litigation that it had finally been approved by the authorities. Though the play was enthusiastically received by audiences, particularly by social democratic sympathizers, Kaiser Wilhelm II angrily cancelled his Imperial loge in response to the production.

Gerhart Hauptmann, the leading proponent of German naturalism in the theater, sought a radical break with the classical, romantic, idealistic and heroic stage conventions of the earlier nineteenth century. Especially in his plays written during the early 1890s, there is an attempt to capture reality with a gritty, almost filmic precision. His plays, which are quintessential for Berlin naturalism, include minutely detailed scene descriptions and stage directions, while his characters, often uneducated peasants or laborers, speak in a strong vernacular dialect not always comprehensible even to Germans from other regions. Hauptmann's naturalistic works typically focus on the dark and seamy side of life, where we find depictions of extreme poverty, starvation, delirium, disease, suicide, alcoholism and incest.

There are a number of aspects of Panizza's *Love Council*, such as the minutely detailed scenic descriptions and stage directions, the hyper-realistic characterization of the leading figures, the sloppy language spiced with fashionable French expressions, the widespread use of ellipses and slang, the numerous hints of sexual "perversions" and the focus on a deadly venereal disease, all of which bear the hallmarks of naturalism.

It should be noted, however, that Panizza was living in Munich when he wrote *The Love Council*, and that his writing also reflects the influence of the authors with whom he was most closely associated in the Bavarian capital. Catholic Bavaria was far more conservative than predominantly Protestant Prussia to the north, yet the circle of "moderns" with whom Panizza associated had a decidedly Lutheran bent. The leading figure in this literary circle was Michael Georg Conrad, editor since 1885 of the influential journal *Die Gesellschaft* (*The Society*) and, like Panizza, a native of the Franconian region of northern Bavaria. Their close friendship lasted throughout the 1890s, during which time Panizza published over forty articles in *Die Gesellschaft*. These contributions ranged from book, art exhibit and theater reviews to articles on sexual topics, such as prostitution and homosexuality.

The Munich moderns were a loosely affiliated group of bohemians, authors and artists who socialized in various popular beer halls in the Bavarian capital. In December 1890, M.G. Conrad founded the Gesellschaft für modernes Leben (Society for Modern Life), whose original members included the sculptor Rudolf Maison, the authors Detlev von Liliencron, Otto Julius Bierbaum, Hanns von Gumppenberg, and the journalists Julius Schaumberger and Georg Schaumberg. Panizza joined soon thereafter, and was active on the executive committee for a year.

The GmL organized public readings and lectures, in addition to publishing periodicals and a yearbook, to which Panizza contributed a variety of short stories and poems. The organization walked a fine line between criticizing the political, social and cultural establishment, while trying not to run afoul of the ubiquitous censorship, which took a dim view of anything advocating atheism, left-wing social democracy or graphic eroticism. Police officers regularly monitored their public meetings, which were disbanded on occasion, and some of their publications were confiscated. The ensuing press notoriety helped to boost sales of their other work, which may not have been an entirely unintended consequence.

Among the Munich moderns, Panizza stood out as perhaps the most brazen, provocative, outspoken and fearless. He often pretended to be a kind of demonic Mephistopheles, who enjoyed playing the *enfant terrible* and cultivating his "bad boy" image. He even purported to be suffering from syphilis himself, a claim which was never medically substantiated. While most of his contemporaries have long since been forgotten, Panizza's work continues to be republished, translated and performed around the world. As Peter Jelavich observed, "Panizza was anomalous even within the context of the Munich naturalists, who lacked cohesion as a group. Aside from Panizza, none of them made any significant contributions to modernism" (*Theater* 135).

Panizza's Motivation

One of Panizza's closest acquaintances was Frank Wedekind, whose theatrical work has enjoyed great success since the nineteenth century. His pioneering play about puberty and teenage sexuality, *Frühlings Erwachen* (1891, *Spring Awakening*), contains scenes of teenagers involved in sadomasochism, homosexuality, masturbation and suicide. It has caused numerous scandals since its first performance in 1906. The New York production of 1917, sponsored by a medical journal in support of teaching sex education in the schools, was blocked by the New York City Commissioner of Licenses. Only after an injunction was issued by the State Supreme Court was a single matinee performance allowed to take place, which was strongly condemned by the critics as "prurient, disgusting, and offensive" (Tuck 1). Ninety years and three generations later, a musical version of the play became a smash hit on Broadway at the Eugene O'Neill Theatre.

There is some speculation that the forty-year-old Panizza, who was Wedekind's senior by ten years, may have been inspired by *Spring Awakening* to write a similarly provocative play in order to achieve the desired literary fame that had thus far eluded him. Some information covering the period when Panizza was writing *The Love Council* is contained in the autobiography of his friend, playwright Max Halbe. Halbe had also written a play dealing with sexual topics, *Freie Liebe* (1890, *Free Love*), and the two authors spent several summers together, working at the Tergernsee resort outside of Munich. Halbe writes:

> If the author smashed through the poetic barriers and rammed his lance against the religious feelings of a large group of believers, wounded them, wounded them fatally, and then succumbed to the counter-attack of superior enemy power: if the poet became a martyr to his convictions, would not the latter receive the crown of life, which was perhaps denied to the former? The poet as martyr. The martyr as poet. Was there a difference anymore? [*Jahrhundertwende* 76].

To suggest that, in writing *The Love Council*, Panizza set out to offend bourgeois sensibilities as part of some grand scheme to gain notoriety at any price, is to ignore his entire earlier literary development. Many of Panizza's previously published stories had been quite risqué and transgressive as far as social, sexual and religious sensibilities are concerned. Halbe admitted that in his discussion with Panizza he "represented a Catholicism which had been transmitted to me through blood and training." He also felt a sympathetic understanding for Rodrigo Borgia, one of the murderous villains in *The Love Council* (74f.).

At the time of his trial in 1895 and later, as well, Oskar Panizza publicly declared himself to be an atheist, but he was far from indifferent when it came to matters of religion. After his father died in 1855, when Oskar was only two years old, he grew up in a fiercely anti–Catholic household headed by his mother, Mathilde. She was a descendent of French Huguenots and had numerous run-ins with the Bavarian Catholic authorities in her quest to raise her children in the Protestant faith. In various essays and literary works, Oskar Panizza later lionized Martin Luther as the heroic warrior against what he considered a decadent, corrupt and oppressive Catholicism. Panizza's strident anti–Catholicism was strongly expressed in a satire published in 1893, *Die*

Title page for Oskar Panizza's manuscript of *Das Liebeskonzil*, 1893, with variant spelling. Photo by Bob Barrett. First published in Oskar Panizza, *Das Liebeskonzil. Eine Himmels-Tragödie in fünf Aufzügen*. Munich: Belleville, 2005. Copyright © 2005 Peter D.G. Brown.

unbefleckte Empfängis der Päpste (*The Immaculate Conception of the Popes*). Bierbaum hyperbolically characterized this work as "perhaps the most frightful and daring work ever written against Catholicism," praising it as a "perfect work of art" and "one of the most significant works of art that we possess" (*Die Gesellschaft* 9.8, 1893: 987).

Another overtly anti–Catholic work penned during the same time as *The Love Council* was the even more chauvinistic *Der teutsche Michel und der römische Papst* (1894, *The Teutonic Michel and the Roman Pope*). In this tendentious polemic, the author cites mountains of Church history, packaged in 666 theses and quotes, all part of an attempt to prove the incompatibility of allegedly corrupt Catholicism with supposedly healthy German nationalism. Even in this work, he reveals a strong interest in sexual matters, commenting: "Today we know from case histories in insane asylums and from the psycho-sexual investigations of Moll, Krafft-Ebing, Tarnowsky et al how fundamentally significant the structure of one's sexual drives is for the intellectual development of a human being. In this respect, the psychiatrist is a more important person for us today than the pope" (100). Not surprisingly, both *Die unbefleckte Empfängis der Päpste* and *Der teutsche Michel und der römische Papst* were banned throughout the German Empire.

Panizza's patriotic German sentiments were less in evidence after his release from prison in 1896. Gone also were his strong anti–Semitic feelings, which had been freely expressed in a number of previous essays and stories. In *The Love Council*, Panizza's anti-religious feelings are evident throughout the play. His visceral anti–Catholicism is most strongly reflected in his satirical presentation of the three "divinities." Both Jesus and the Devil are explicitly identified with stereotypical Jewish traits, the former reflecting perpetual weakness and the latter embodying both a superior intelligence and a strong streak of libertarian independence, with which the author himself readily identified.

During his trial in April 1895, Panizza was charged with "publicly blaspheming God with abusive statements, creating an offense, and insulting public institutions and customs of the Christian Church, especially the Catholic Church" (Panizza, *Meine Verteidigung* 36). The author explained his reasons for writing the play as follows: "I was not concerned with blasphemous things and obscenities, but rather with grasping the peculiar situation in which people found themselves at that time, a situation which naturally interested me, especially as a former physician" (6). After a vivid but accurate historical description of the licentious conditions prevalent at the fifteenth-century court of Alexander VI, Panizza told the jurors weighing his fate:

> Now transpose all this material into our present age, filled with skepticism and disbelief. Let this confluence of historical elements as an artistic conceit fall into the hands of someone who —perhaps to his own misfortune — is inclined toward satire, and then I ask you, gentlemen, how would *you* have portrayed the trinity, what kind of image would *you* have had of the divinities in Heaven, who under such circumstances sent the "lust scourge" [syphilis] down to mankind on earth? [7f].

Panizza never denied the devastating portrayal of historical corruption and farcical stereotypes in *The Love Council*, but he claimed that the truly divine was essentially untouchable:

> I *have* degraded the Christian gods and have done so intentionally, because I saw them in the mirror of the fifteenth century; because I observed them from Alexander the Sixth's point of view. Our conceptions of the divine, gentlemen, are contained in our *thinking*. You know as little as I do what really happens up there above us [...] If I attacked the divine, then I did not

attack that supernal spark that slumbers in the heart of every person, but rather I attacked the divine that had become a farce in the hands of *Alexander VI* [19f].

Literary Sources

The literary sources that Panizza drew on for his "Heavenly tragedy" are quite varied in nature; some are obvious, while others are quite obscure. Dialogues between the Judaeo-Christian God and the Devil are as old as the Bible itself, being most noteworthy in the Book of Job. Goethe's drama *Faust*, the most revered work in the entire German literary canon, begins with a Prologue in Heaven, a wager between God and the Devil that was inspired by a similar situation at the beginning of the Book of Job. In the second, revised edition of *Das Liebeskonzil* (1896), Panizza adds further elements from *Faust* in the form of a dedicatory poem ("Zueignung") and a Prelude that directly parody Goethe's masterpiece.

In his formal Defense Statement, included in Chapter 8 of this volume, Panizza launched into a capsule survey of world literature, arguing that the divine has always been a legitimate subject for literary satire. Quoting extensively from Parny's *La guerre des dieux anciens et modernes* (1799, *The War of Ancient and Modern Gods*) and Sailer's *Der Fall Luzifers* (1816, *Lucifer's Fall*), he painstakingly traces the millennia-long history of sacrilegious satire dating back to Aristophanes, all of which he had obviously carefully read.

In one of the many footnotes written into the original manuscript of *Das Liebeskonzil* by the author, he attributed the scenes at the court of Alexander VI to the pontiff's German master of ceremonies, Burchard. This papal official's published diaries describe frequent sexual entertainment performances at the Vatican court that were even more scandalous than those depicted by Panizza. In his defense plea, Panizza quotes Burchard's description of papal entertainment on the evening of 31 October 1501. On that occasion the Pope's son, Cesare, hosted a dinner in the papal palace, at which no less than fifty courtesans were present. After dinner they danced with the servants and others present, first in clothing and later naked. With Cesare, the Pope and his teenage daughter Lucrezia all watching, the naked girls dove and wrestled for chestnuts among the candelabra that had been placed on the floor. "Finally, prizes were distributed, silk robes, boots, capes, etc., to those who could have intercourse the most times with the aforementioned girls" (*Meine Verteidigung* 9). The playwright explains his decision to present a tamer version than the historical source for the following reasons:

> I toned down the scene, not out of consideration for the popes or the sensibility of Catholics, but for artistic reasons; because I always had the theater before my eyes, because I always thought about the possibility of a performance; and because the above scene could conceivably be performed, under certain conditions. The real scene, as it is documented in historical reports, would have been impossible, even in a book drama [7].

In Michael Bauer's detailed biography of Oskar Panizza, he conjectures that the play *Germania* (1800) was one of the main sources for *The Love Council* (157–162). Written by an unknown author using the pseudonym Pater Elias, *Germania* also takes place in heaven, where God, suffering from old-age and forgetfulness, calls in his circle of advisors to deliberate on how to aid Germania, the emissary of Germany. As in *The Love Council*, the play also attacks the power of the papacy, Mariolatry, corruption in the Church and the exploitation of the common people.

Plot Summary

The plot of *The Love Council* is quite simple. Act I takes place in heaven, where God learns from a messenger about the sexual excesses prevalent in 1495 at the Vatican court of Rodrigo Borgia, Pope Alexander VI. As retribution, he wants to obliterate mankind, but is reminded by Mary that it would be advisable to take a first-hand look, since his advanced age precludes him from any further creation. In Act II, a cannabis-induced vision enables God the Father, Mary and their son Christ to view the wild sexual excesses being practiced at the papal court on the eve of Easter. The actual "love council" takes place at the beginning of Act III, where the Devil is consulted and then charged with devising a severe punishment, one that will destroy the bodies of sinners, while still allowing their souls to be capable of redemption. The Devil returns to hell, where he decides that the punishment should take the form of a deadly virus that will initially be implanted in an irresistible Woman. He selects Salome to be the mother of this seductive creature, whom he introduces to an adoring Mary in Act IV. In the final brief act, the Woman arrives at the Vatican palace, where her appearance unleashes pandemonium and ultimately triggers the worldwide syphilis epidemic.

Stylistic Innovations

In his seminal work on politics, playwriting and performance during the 1890's, *Munich and Theatrical Modernism*, Peter Jelavich identifies the importance of Wedekind and Panizza for the development of modern theater:

> Because both Catholicism and official classicism evaluated the world in binary terms (good/evil, order/disorder, mind/body, sacred/profane), Panizza and Wedekind sought inspiration from traditions that denied such bifurcations: popular culture and "aesthetic paganism." Desiring to reverse accepted relationships and to unite what convention sundered, the two playwrights composed "carnevalesque" dramas in which traditional values were inverted, holy images were shown to be profane, and profanity was deemed a source of sanctity. In the process of seeking to destroy nineteenth-century values, Panizza and Wedekind contributed as well to the breakdown of traditional genres of nineteenth-century drama, and they opened the way for a modernist theater based upon unfettered play of fantasy and free play of theatrical forms. The composition of *The Council of Love* and *Spring Awakening* marked the birth of truly modernist drama in the Bavarian capital [53].

It should be evident to even the most casual reader that Panizza's "heavenly tragedy" is a satirical tragicomedy, employing a tradition-bending and tradition-breaking mixture of styles. In what is something of a modernized version of a medieval morality play, Biblical characters considered sacred are shown deliberating among themselves in solemn council, Church dignitaries engage in debauchery while a holy mass is being sung, wrestlers and courtesans entertain the Pope and his extended illegitimate family on the eve of a sacred holiday. All of this is somewhat reminiscent of a vaudeville or variety show. Indeed, this is exactly what the playwright's intention was, to forge a radically new form of entertainment that broke with all previous theatrical styles, including consistent naturalism.

The last article written by Panizza to appear in *Die Gesellschaft* was a seminal study on classicism and the rise of variety shows. Written during his final weeks in Munich, it represents one of the first incisive analyses of vaudeville's impact on modern German literature. Samuel Lublinksi acknowledged the author's achievement, remarking that "the 'artistic vaudeville' became the catchphrase to which a Bavarian, the fantastic Oskar Panizza, gave the signal" (135). In this article Panizza discusses the historical roots of vaudeville in great detail, citing the influences of Heinrich Heine, British comedians and especially African-American entertainers. "Naïve destruction is the essence of vaudeville," he notes, which was pushing neo-classical drama off the stage and simultaneously infusing literature with new life-blood ("Der Klassizismus" 1266). Without mentioning his own pioneering work, he hails *Spring Awakening* as "the classical vaudeville achievement of our time," a work from which "Germany will never...even in a hundred years, no matter how much it may mix with the Jews, be able to extract the sweet honey which is buried in the combs of this delightful book" (1270). Noteworthy here is also the welcome reversal of his previous anti–Semitic bias, likely the result of his prosecution and imprisonment by government authorities.

Panizza was profoundly committed to the avant-garde and to popular culture. There are times when he comes amazingly close to sounding like a cultural revolutionary of the late twentieth century: "We will take colors, blossoms, fruits, power and sensuality wherever we can find them. We want new life-juices, new nourishment for our nerves, new blossoms and forms, odors and intoxications, even at the risk of suffering pain and being poisoned. If there is nothing but hashish, then hashish. If there is nothing but vaudeville, then vaudeville" (1268).

Especially in Act II of *The Love Council*, we experience a variety of seemingly disconnected entertainments, including a pantomime in the tradition of the *commedia dell'arte*, twelve stripping and frolicking courtesans, one of whom is literally set ablaze briefly, a series of wrestling matches where the winner is awarded a courtesan of his choice, while murderous Vatican court intrigues unfold in the foreground and a Catholic high mass is performed in the background. Jelavich acknowledges that the jarring alienation produced by this stylistic mixture anticipates Brecht's anti-illusionist epic theater a generation later: "This juxtaposition of accepted genres destroyed the theatrical illusion of each, very much in the manner of what Brecht would later call 'Verfremdung' [alienation]" (*Munich* 72).

Characterization of Principal Figures

The characterization of the principal figures in *The Love Council* is what provides the basis both for the charge of blasphemy as well as for the satirical humor of the piece. The portrayal draws heavily on the style of naturalism, which avoids any romantic or idealized portrayal of reality, focusing instead on the seamy, diseased and decrepit side of life. It is a central Judaeo-Christian creationist belief that "God created man in his own image, in the image of God created he him" (Genesis 1, 27). Thus, God has traditionally been understood and portrayed, whether by Michelangelo or lesser artists, as a very old person. Panizza's naturalistic depiction of God is that of a pathetically senile man, demented, impotent, with failing eyesight, sore limbs and no prospect of ever being able to escape his painful predicament through death. If nothing else, Panizza's naturalistic depiction of God forces readers and viewers to question their own, probably anthropomorphic, conception of this divinity, to rethink the creation narrative, Biblical literalism and perhaps even their adherence to theism itself.

Once one gets beyond the shock of seeing the traditionally revered figures portrayed as exaggerated caricatures, it is worth noting that all three "divinities" in *The Love Council* are essentially tragic characters. All three are suffering from various physical ailments and remain more or less pained, lonely, sexually frustrated and unloved characters. Worst of all, they are condemned to remain so throughout the remainder of all eternity. Except for their immortality, they are all human, perhaps all-too-human. Here is a dysfunctional family consisting of a senile father, an oversexed, middle-aged "virgin" mother and their simpleminded, consumptive son. They are frozen in an inseparable bond of mutual contempt, resentment and mistrust, capable only of punishing and destroying.

The nearly cataclysmic scene in Act One, where God is on the verge of exercising his power of mass destruction, is cited by the father of psychoanalysis, Sigmund Freud, in his *Traumdeutung* (1899, *The Interpretation of Dreams*) as an illustration of the dream process. Referring to *The Love Council* as "a strongly revolutionary closet drama," Freud shows how the instantaneous fulfillment of God's destructive wishes parallels the immediate fulfillment of desires that occurs in our dreams (149n.) Panizza reminds us that God-the-Creator is also God-the-Obliterator. His desire for blind vengeance is only restrained by the more far-sighted Mary. She appears to be the only one who understands that humanity's perpetuation is essential to justify the continued existence of Heaven Inc. as an institution whose prime mission is to provide salvation for a "fallen" and sinful mankind in perpetual need of redemption.

It is remarkable that all three "divinities," as well as the Devil, bear some striking similarities to the playwright himself. Both God and the Devil have painful leg injuries which make them limp, as did Panizza, who had a gumma from a childhood fracture on his right shin. The God of *The Love Council* exhibits marked homoerotic tendencies, principally directed at the Cherub in Act I. While Panizza's sexual orientation remains obscure, there is certainly no evidence that he was ever in love with a woman.

None of the "divinities" appears capable of loving or being loved. They are emotionally, sexually and socially isolated, frustrated, crippled and capable only of distant voyeurism. Panizza's sexual confusion is reflected in a number of his earlier poems and stories, where the mere sight of a nude woman evokes revulsion. He often portrays himself as the other, the misfit, frequently using the term "dog" to describe himself. In 1892 he published the fictitious *From the Diary of a Dog*. This canine leads a chaste life and gets sick at the sight of his master and mistress having intercourse.

According to his friend Ernst Kreowski, Panizza was "almost always in the company of a little tousle-haired dog" (754), Puzzi. Panizza wrote Anna Croissant-Rust that after eight years, Puzzi had become "a human being" for him. When little Puzzi died, the author noted in his diary on 19 February 1897 that he had loved the dog as he had "hardly any other being in the world" (Bauer 198). For whatever reason, Panizza had from early childhood on and throughout his entire adult life always been a loner, plagued by frequent depression and other mental problems. He does not appear to have ever had a reciprocal, intimate relationship during his entire life.

Like Panizza, the Devil in *The Love Council* thinks like a scientist and pleads for the right to freely publish his books. Yet he, too, feels unfulfilled, lonely and isolated. At the beginning of his scene in hell in Act III, Panizza has the Devil wearing a coat of animal skins and feeling like a dog: "Here you are, you dog, all alone at home again; abandoned and ignored...without any relatives, respect or reputation..."

Superficially, Christ would seem to have little in common with the playwright. He appears somewhat dim-witted, in contrast to Panizza, who was known for his sparkling wit.

Yet the author's mental health grew increasingly fragile over the years, and even as a young child he was a very late bloomer and was called "dummy" by his siblings (*In Memoriam* 10).

Like the playwright himself, Mary in *The Love Council* appears to be cosmopolitan and almost obsessively fascinated with sexual matters. Panizza described his own mother as "hot-tempered, energetic, strong-willed, with an almost masculine intelligence" (*In memoriam* 9). Certainly Mary shares all of these traits with Mathilde Panizza. In addition to single-handedly running an upscale resort hotel in Bad Kissingen and raising five children as a widow, Mathilde was also an author in her own right, penning religious tales under the pseudonym of Siona. Like Mathilde, Mary seems to be the only "divinity" capable of keeping things running in heaven.

Certainly the dogs and bitches in heaven and hell reflect the tensions and tragedies of human individuals and their families, with some measure of exaggeration and distortion thrown in to make us laugh instead of cry. If these are Christian "divinities," they are also very Jewish. God the Father is the same vengeful Old Testament entity who did not hesitate to destroy virtually all living beings for the "wickedness" that he perceived in his creation gone awry (Genesis 6, 5–7). Mary has the stereotypical traits of a nouveau-riche, cosmopolitan, sensuous, pushy and overprotective Jewish mother. There is also no doubt that the figure of the irresistible Woman, the syphilitic daughter of the Devil and the Jewish princess Salome, epitomizes the stereotypical "beautiful Jewess." The highly attractive Jewish woman is a seductress well established in Western literature by the middle of the nineteenth century, whose roots extend back many centuries. Panizza describes the Woman as "a young, blooming creature dressed in all-white gown, with black hair and black, deep-set eyes that hide a consuming but still latent sexuality." She is the ultimate "other," whose dark allure is powerful enough to sweep even the Virgin Mary off her feet. She might well have had the same effect on Christ, had his frantic mother not effectively prevented the two from ever meeting.

Not to be outdone, Christ appears as a kind of heavenly sex idol, "the most beautiful, the most tender, the sweetest *Man*" (I, 5). His exotic beauty is almost intoxicating, with "dark hair, a little fluff of beard" and eyes "like a gazelle's." He confidently strides into the throne room in Act I "as King of the Jews." The Devil is explicitly characterized as having the stereotypical gestures of a Jewish merchant. He is certainly smarter, more independent and resourceful than the "divinities" in Heaven, yet resentful and filled with self-loathing, convinced that no matter what he does, he will never be fully accepted or appreciated. It is enough to make him physically sick, but his ultimate realization is that he can "only thrive in deprivation, in darkness, under torture."

Like the author himself, the playwright's characters in *The Love Council* exhibit a multitude of conflicting attitudes and intractable contradictions. Jelavich agrees that there may have even been an oedipal basis for the characters in Panizza's play:

> By assaulting the Holy Father in Rome, who had been championed by his own father, he vindicated his Protestant mother [...] Whether or not one sees such an oedipal underpinning in Panizza's project, it is undeniable that by creating an art that was both intensely aggressive and intensely personal, he attempted to conquer a social space for his private fantasies [*Munich* 71].

The supreme irony of *The Love Council*, of course, is that it is not at all about love, since nobody in heaven, hell or earth seems even remotely capable of such an emotion. All anyone is really able to do is punish, poison and destroy. For all its satirical and comical elements, *The Love Council* is another German tragedy of sex in the *Sturm und Drang* tradition of Goethe's *Faust*, where the middle-aged protagonist's uncontrollable lust for a teenaged girl ends up killing her, her mother, her brother and her baby. The ultimate tragedy of *The Love Council* is that these aged and destructive "divinities" will live on as a self-perpetuating penal institution, devoted to destroying people's lives for doing what comes naturally to them, so long as the "divinities" can ultimately "redeem" these sinful people's "souls."

Publication History

The first edition of *Das Liebeskonzil*, bearing the date 1895, was actually published in October 1894. This was a common practice for end-of-the-year publications, so that books would appear current for the following year's book fairs. The publication was based on Panizza's hand-written manuscript, which has recently been discovered and was subsequently published in a large-format facsimile with facing transcription in 2005. This original manuscript bears the date 1892/93 in Panizza's handwriting, which is presumably when most of the writing took place. This is the first and only manuscript version of the play, which the printer used to set the first edition. It includes many crossed out deletions, rewritten passages, insertions pasted in, as well as the typesetter's blue pencil markings indicating page separations.

The publisher was Johann Schabelitz in Zürich, Switzerland, who had previously published Panizza's 1893 spoof on the immaculate conception of the popes. Evidently, Panizza believed it was easier to evade German censorship laws by having his most controversial books published outside the German Reich, although this did not protect him from prosecution in the case of *The Love Council*. During his trial, he perhaps too honestly admitted that he had indeed intended for the book to be sold in Germany, which virtually guaranteed his conviction.

A second, expanded version of the play appeared with the same publisher in 1896. The principal additions are a dedicatory poem ("Zueignung") and a Prelude, both of which allude to similar introductory sections at the beginning of Goethe's *Faust* (1808). Panizza's dedicatory poem quotes and then attacks Goethe for being too old-fashioned, conservative and "soft." Panizza clearly preferred Friedrich Schiller, who was viewed by many nineteenth-century avant-garde writers as a more militant libertarian and a forerunner of their own anti-establishmentarian movement. At the end of this second edition, Panizza appended twenty-eight pages of "Critical Responses to *The Love Council*," culled from a variety of newspapers, magazines and personal correspondence.

Sales were evidently good enough so that a third edition of one thousand copies was published by Schabelitz in 1897. In addition to an expanded "Critical Responses" appendix that had swelled to thirty-five pages, the third edition contains four new pages preceding the reading of Boccaccio at the beginning of Act IV. The scene depicts Mary listening to her angels, all young pupils from Tyrol, reciting the Ave Maria in a heavily accented drawl. She finally blurts out: "God, I'm fed up to here with this Catholicism!"

This third edition also contains a preface written by the author on 4 September 1897 in Zürich. He frankly admits that "[t]he public may have already wondered about the fact that this book, though confiscated by the district attorney, continues to be published again and again. It probably has already assumed that the author is crazy. However, that is not the case." He concludes by suggesting that it would be advisable if the public and the var-

First scene of *Das Liebeskonzil* in Panizza's handwritten manuscript, 1893. Photo by Bob Barrett. First published in Oskar Panizza, *Das Liebeskonzil. Eine Himmels-Tragödie in fünf Aufzügen.* Munich: Belleville, 2005. Copyright © 2005 Peter D.G. Brown.

ious government authorities "accepted our writings for what they are, as something willed by God, and not waste time asking questions and carping." Beneath his name, he added the title: "Poet by Divine Right." While this playful title is an obvious spoof on the Kaiser, it is noteworthy that he feels the need to reassure his readership that he is not really crazy. This is the last publication of the play that was edited by the playwright himself. All material added in the second and third editions are included following the English translation in this volume, as are the extensive "Critical Responses," almost as voluminous as the play itself, which appear here in translation for the very first time.

The last edition of *Das Liebeskonzil* to appear during the author's lifetime, nine years after he had been institutionalized, was published by the Gesellschaft Münchner Bibliophilen (Society of Munich Bibliophiles) in 1913. Due to the strict censorship laws still in effect at the time, this was a private printing limited to only fifty copies, each of which bears the name of the individual subscriber who pre-purchased it. What makes this edition a favorite collector's item is the fact it contains nine somber pen and ink drawings by the noted Austrian expressionist artist Alfred Kubin. A founding member of the *Blaue Reiter* (Blue Rider) group of expressionists in Munich, Kubin's characteristically dark illustrations lend a sinister and foreboding interpretation to *The Love Council*.

Walter Mehring's *The Lost Library* (1951) was a critical link in introducing postwar readers to *The Love Council*. This work contains a penetrating analysis of the books collected by Mehring's father, the author and translator Sigmar Mehring, whose library was "lost" as he fled Nazi persecution. The book contains an entire chapter on *The Love Council*, which in his father's collection enjoyed special status "among the great contemporary dramatists [...]: Ibsen, Björnson, Strindberg, Rostand, Maeterlinck, Wilde, Shaw, Chekov. Though Panizza never had a play performed, my father put him in a place of honor" (67). Walter Mehring also compared *The Love Council* to the great works of Blake and Goethe, asserting that "its real subject was the contamination of all earthly authority" (69). He thought that "syphilis was the paradisiac original sin in materialist literature; it was the killer hidden in the marrow of sensual pleasure [...] Syphilis was the whiplash of the sexual enlightenment" (72). Mehring concluded his discussion of the play with some provocative and profound reflections on the persistence of evil:

> No social redeemer was hailed as was Dr. Paul Ehrlich for his discovery of the antiluetic drug salvarsan (Ehrlich-Hata "606"). He would now save mankind from the disease that was an allegory of the fall of man [...] A little bacteriology and Marxism would clean up the whole mess; the stupid devil would be cheated of his due. Where there was nothing left for him to work with, what could the devil do? [...] But was he really done for, really dead as a doornail? The trouble was, you never could be too sure, especially when you were an atheist, which meant a born doubter. And for that reason my father very often took *The Council of Love* off the shelves and read Panizza's slender volume again and again, with loving respect. You couldn't ever tell about Satan [72f].

The first time in the twentieth century that Panizza's infamous play became generally accessible to the public was when a French translation by Jean Bréjoux appeared in 1960. After reading about *The Love Council* in Mehring's account of his father's lost library, Bréjoux located a copy and read the play. It so impressed him that he translated and published it along with a preface by André Breton, the noted surrealist. "Even in our time," wrote an admiring Breton, "the audience's reaction would presumably force the curtain to be lowered before the end of the first scene" (*Le Concile d'amour*, 1960: 8). In less than a decade, however, the times had changed and *Le Concile d'amour* was enjoying a wildly successful

Poster by Leonor Fini for *Le Concile d'amour* at the Théâtre de Paris, 1969. Courtesy of Richard Overstreet, La Galerie Minsky, Paris, and Neil Zukerman, CFM Gallery, New York. Copyright © Leonor Fini Estate.

run with rave reviews and sold out performances in the French capital at the Théâtre de Paris.

The first publicly available German edition of *Das Liebeskonzil* in the twentieth century was a 1962 reprint of the first edition of 1894, published by the 26-year-old Peter Jes Petersen (1936–2006) in the tiny Baltic seaside town of Glückburg. Petersen was led to Panizza via George Grosz's seminal painting, "Dedication to Oskar Panizza" (1917–18), which he came across during a visit to the Staatsgalerie in Stuttgart. He then obtained permission from Panizza's niece to reprint four hundred copies of the play. After only a small number of copies were sold, in July 1962 the young publisher was arrested in a raid conducted by the Flensburg district attorney's office and charged with distributing obscene literature. As a result of the ensuing outcry in the German press, however, all charges were dropped several months later. Another eighty copies of the play were reprinted in 1964 after Petersen moved to West Berlin.

That same year, for the first time a major German press, Luchterhand, published *Das Liebeskonzil*, together with a "best of" collection of Panizza's fiction. Perceptively edited by Hans Prescher, this 1964 edition of *Das Liebeskonzil* and other works introduced a whole new generation of German readers to the scandal-ridden author from Bad Kissingen. Luchterhand has kept the play in print through a number of different editions published in the decades since then. A 1991 reprint of the 1913 limited edition of *Das Liebeskonzil*, which included the powerful sketches by Alfred Kubin, made these illustrations accessible to a wider readership. The complete list of German editions and foreign translations can be found in the Bibliography.

Translations

The current translation is the first ever to be based on the original handwritten manuscript of Oskar Panizza's, which was recently published in facsimile form in the original format, 23 × 36 cm (9 × 14½ inches), in 2005. However, obvious errors and inconsistencies that were removed in the first printed edition of 1894 were also deleted from the current translation. Every attempt has been made to retain the flavor and texture of the original as much as possible and not, as is too often the case, to smooth out the rough edges or attempt to "improve" on the original by making it sound more elegant, theatrical or literary. Where Panizza uses slang, obscure medical terminology, cosmopolitan French or common everyday vocabulary, every effort has been made to retain identical or similar vocabulary in the current English translation. Most of Panizza's extremely long sentences with many subordinate clauses, commas and semicolons have also been retained wherever possible. His original orthography, marked by a plethora of dashes, has been largely left untouched. The main exception is his use of lengthy ellipses, which sometimes run to more than ten dots in the handwritten manuscript, but were reduced to the customary three or four in the first printed edition.

It would seem that Panizza wrote quite fast, having little regard for consistency or much patience for proofreading. In the manuscript, there is an inconsistency in the spelling of individual words. Even in the first printed edition, the cover of the book bears the title *Das Liebeskoncil*, whereas the title page has the standard spelling normally associated with this play, *Das Liebeskonzil*. This inconsistency persists in the second and third revised editions, as well.

The first translation of the play to be published in English was by Oreste F. Pucciani in 1973. This edition, long since out of print, contains a number of excellent black and white photographs from the 1969 Paris production and drawings by Leonor Fini, in addition to translations of André Breton's introduction and Panizza's legal defense documents. A translation by Malcolm Greene of the third edition of *Das Liebeskonzil* appeared in 1992 in a limited edition of 300 copies. Based on the 1991 reprint of the 1913 private printing, it contains the nine pen and ink illustrations by Alfred Kubin.

In addition to French and English translations, *Das Liebeskonzil* has been translated, usually more than once, into Dutch, Italian, Japanese, Portuguese and Spanish.

Oskar Panizza's Legacy

Oskar Panizza's legacy consists of far more than just *The Love Council*. He is the author of several other plays, dozens of short stories, four volumes of poetry, books of dialogues, satire and polemics; scores of articles in a variety of journals, including some quite unique psychological, sociological and cultural studies; numerous theater, art exhibit and book reviews, as well as his medical dissertation on the composition of microorganisms in sputum.

The first critical biography of this seminal modernist appeared in 1983 (Brown, *Oskar Panizza: His Life and Works*). The following year, Michael Bauer's *Oskar Panizza. Ein literarisches Porträt* (1984, *Oskar Panizza: A Literary Portrait*), based on primary sources from some twenty German archives, added a wealth of information to round out the picture of this curious and complex author. The most recent biographical work is Jürgen Müller's psychiatric study, *Der Pazjent als Psychiater. Oskar Panizzas Weg vom Irrenarzt zum Insassen* (1999, *The Patient as Psychiatrist: Oskar Panizza's Journey from Doctor for the Insane to Inmate*), which mines a wealth of psychiatric evaluations written by various physicians who examined the "madman" from Bad Kissingen over a hundred years ago. The present volume contains a biographical portrait of Panizza that draws on these and other sources.

Panizza's legacy, in addition to his groundbreaking literature, also rests on his decision to stand trial and fight for unfettered freedom of expression. Even though his friends urged him to leave town and avoid prosecution, he chose to stay and have his day in court. Indeed, it was his trial that served to publicize his work and the cause to which he applied it. The present volume includes an entire chapter on the trials of Oskar Panizza, which extended over the course of an entire century, 1894–1994. More than seventy years after his death, lawyers and judges, clergymen and journalists continue to engage in the passionate debate unleashed by *The Love Council*.

The final chapter in this book focuses on Panizza's legacy on stages around the world, where international audiences have been able to view some one hundred different productions of *The Love Council* during the past five decades. Written four generations ago, at a time when the stage was dominated by such theatrical giants as Henrik Ibsen, August Strindberg, Gerhart Hauptmann, Anton Chekhov, Oscar Wilde and George Bernard Shaw, Panizza exploded the boundaries of conventional drama. In so doing, he broke with sacred traditions and offended many sensibilities. The fact that *The Love Council* was not premiered until three-quarters of a century after it was written attests to how far ahead of his time Panizza truly was. This final chapter will examine how Panizza's subversive legacy has inspired innovative theatrical productions on three continents, thereby re-infecting later generations with his audacious modernism.

Chapter 2

The Love Council: A Heavenly Tragedy in Five Acts, 1894

by OSKAR PANIZZA

To the memory of Hutten

"It hath pleased God, that in our time sicknesses shulde arise, whiche were to oure forefathers (as it may well be conjectured) unknown. But the divines did interpretate this to be the wrathe of God, and to be his punishment for oure evil livinge."

Ulrich von Hutten, a German knight
On the French Disease, 1519

„Dic Dea, quae o causae nobis post saecula tanta
Insolitam peperere luem?...."
[Tell me, goddess, what causes brought forth upon us an unaccustomed scourge after so many centuries?]

Fracastoro, *Syphilis or the French Disease*, 1539

Characters

GOD THE FATHER
CHRIST
MARY
THE DEVIL
THE WOMAN
A CHERUB
FIRST ANGEL
SECOND ANGEL
THIRD ANGEL

Figures from the Realm of the Dead
HELEN
PHRYNE
HÉLOISE
AGRIPPINA
SALOME
RODRIGO BORGIA, Alexander VI, Pope

The Pope's Children, Mother unknown
GIROLAMA BORGIA, married to Cesarini
ISABELLA BORGIA, married to Matuzzi

The Pope's Children by Vanozza
PIER LUIGI BORGIA, Duke of Gandia
DON GIOVANNI BORGIA, Count of Celano
CESARE BORGIA, Duke of Romagna
DON GIOFFRE BORGIA, Count of Cariati
DONNA LUCREZIA BORGIA, Dutchess of Bisceglie

The Pope's Children, still minors, by Julia Farnese
LAURA BORGIA
GIOVANNI BORGIA

The Pope's Mistresses
VANOZZA
JULIA FARNESE (married to Orsini)

ALESSANDRO FARNESE, her brother, Cardinal
DONNA SANCIA, the Pope's daughter-in-law, married to Don Joffre
ADRIANA MILA, the Pope's confidante, his children's governess

The Pope's Nephews
FRANCESCO BORGIA, Archbishop of Cosenza
LUIGI PIETRO BORGIA, Cardinal-Deacon
COLLERANDO BORGIA, Bishop of Monreale
RODRIGO BORGIA, Captain of the Papal Guard

The Pope's Confidants
GIOVANNI LOPEZ, Bishop of Perugia
PIETRO CARANZA, Privy Treasurer
JUAN MARADES, Bishop of Toul, Privy Intendant
GIOVANNI VERA ERCILLA, Member of the Sacred College
REMOLINA DE ILERDA, Member of the Sacred College
BURCARD, the Pope's Master of Ceremonies
A PRIEST
FIRST NOBLEMAN
SECOND NOBLEMAN
THIRD NOBLEMAN
PULCINELLO, ACTOR
COLOMBINA, ACTRESS
A COURTESAN

The Holy Ghost, archangels, older and younger angels, amoretti, Mary Magdalene, apostles, martyrs, Sisters of Mercy, a messenger; — Animals, buffoons, ghosts; — Church dignitaries, papal officials, emissaries, Roman ladies, courtiers, courtesans, actors, singers, wrestlers, soldiers, commoners. —

Time: spring 1495, date of the first historically documented outbreak of syphilis.

Act One

    Heaven; a throne room.

    THREE ANGELS *in swan-white, feathery-down outfits with tight, pageboy knee-breeches, short amoretti wings, hair cropped short and powdered white, white satin shoes; they are holding feather dusters in their hands.*

FIRST ANGEL: He's getting up late again today.

SECOND ANGEL: Be glad! This coughing, this watery-blue stare, this runny nose, cursing, spitting all day long — you never get a healthy moment.

THIRD ANGEL: Yes, it's weird up here!

FIRST ANGEL: By the way, is the throne tight?

SECOND ANGEL: Yes, for God's sake! Is the throne tight? It was wiggling yesterday.

THIRD ANGEL: Who was wiggling yesterday?

FIRST ANGEL: The throne, you silly little goose!

THIRD ANGEL (*surprised*): The throne? — Why is the throne wiggling?

FIRST ANGEL: Well, it just is.

THIRD ANGEL: What? Does anything at all wiggle up here?

FIRST AND SECOND ANGELS (*laughing loudly*): Ha, ha, ha, ha!

THIRD ANGEL (*growing more serious and surprised*): Yes, why is the holy throne wiggling?

FIRST ANGEL (*emphatically*): Silly little goose! Because everything up here is coming apart, gods and furniture, fringes and wallpaper.

THIRD ANGEL (*quivering inside*): God, if my mother knew that!

SECOND ANGEL (*frowning and mocking*): *Your* mother? — What's with your mother, funny face?

THIRD ANGEL: Oh, she just had the sixtieth requiem mass said for me today!

FIRST AND SECOND ANGELS (*with growing amazement*): For you?! — (*both burst out laughing*) So, how old are you?

THIRD ANGEL (*reflecting and then quoting with pathos*): "In the eyes of God a thousand years are but a single day, and a day like a thousand years!" —

FIRST AND SECOND ANGELS (*gesturing for her to stop and come to reason; drawling*): Yeah, yeah, yeah — it's alright; we already knew that! — But how old were you down there?

THIRD ANGEL (*childlike*): Barely fourteen!

FIRST ANGEL (*laughing*): Then why do you need any requiem masses?

THIRD ANGEL (*timidly*): Oh, you don't know; I died.

FIRST AND SECOND ANGELS (*laughing even louder*): Ha, ha, ha! He, he! — Well natch, otherwise you wouldn't be here! —

THIRD ANGEL (*with unshakable seriousness*): Oh, you don't know; I died in sin.

FIRST AND SECOND ANGELS (*burst out laughing again*): No kidding! — You poor sucker, what did you do, anyway?

Ink drawing by Alfred Kubin for private printing of *Das Liebeskonzil*, Munich, 1913. Courtesy of Eberhard Spangenberg. Copyright © Eberhard Spangenberg, Munich.

THIRD ANGEL (*hesitates, looks at her companions with eyes wide open and folds her hands*).

SECOND ANGEL (*mocking*): Didn't you do your homework?—Did you get ink spots on your notebook?

THIRD ANGEL (*still anxious and tense*): Oh, I'm so afraid.—You won't tell anyone else, will you?!—

FIRST AND SECOND ANGELS (*shaking with laughter*): What? Up here; and not tell anyone else?!

THIRD ANGEL (*surprised*): What? You already know?

FIRST ANGEL: No! But go ahead; we'll find out anyway!

SECOND ANGEL: Spit it out! What happened?

THIRD ANGEL: Oh, a great big man — crushed me!

FIRST ANGEL (*emphatically*): Crushed?

THIRD ANGEL: Or poisoned!

SECOND ANGEL (*equally emphatic*): Poisoned?

THIRD ANGEL (*naively*): I don't remember what my mother said.

FIRST ANGEL (*with growing astonishment*): Was your mother actually there?

THIRD ANGEL (*recounting with gleaming eyes*): She was in the next room; — But the door was half open; — then the big old man came in; — my mother had told me to just let everything happen; — the man was the school principal and was very strict; — and if I went along with everything; — I'd go to the top of my class; — and the big old man —

FIRST AND SECOND ANGELS (*coaxing*): Well, the big old man....?

THIRD ANGEL (*continuing*): ...was very strong.

FIRST AND SECOND ANGELS (*looking at each other and imitating the little one*): The big old man was very strong!

SECOND ANGEL: That sounds like *Dick and Jane.*

FIRST ANGEL (*shaking the little one*): Now, what did the old man do?

THIRD ANGEL (*bursting out*): He crushed me and poisoned me and spit on me with his hot breath and wanted to push into my body...

FIRST AND SECOND ANGELS (*clapping their hands in feigned amazement*): What? — And your mother didn't come to help you?

THIRD ANGEL: She stood by the crack of the door and kept saying: "Just be nice, Lilly. Just be nice, Lilly!"

SECOND ANGEL: Well, and then?

THIRD ANGEL: Then I lay sobbing on my bed.

FIRST ANGEL: And then?

THIRD ANGEL (*remembering*): ... — I heard my mother and the man talking...

SECOND ANGEL: What did they say?

THIRD ANGEL (*trying hard to remember*): ...I don't remember;... — they were already in the next room... I heard the number five hundred...

FIRST ANGEL: And then?

THIRD ANGEL (*remembering more slowly*): ...my mother came in...she said that we now had so much money that we could live happily ever after...(*the memory fades*)

FIRST ANGEL (*insistently*): And then? —

SECOND ANGEL (*likewise*): And then? And then? —

THIRD ANGEL (*almost transfigured*): Then I died.

> FIRST AND SECOND ANGELS (*rush apart, clapping their hands over their heads and emitting a long, shrill, girlish shriek, as if to release a pent-up emotion; they circle the*

room like two whistling tops in the largest possible radius; the THIRD ANGEL *retains her transfigured pose.)*

FIRST ANGEL (*breathless after running around so much*): And now your mother spends all that money on your requiem masses?!

THIRD ANGEL (*whining anxiously*): But I died in sin!

SECOND ANGEL (*even more insistently*): With the 500 marks or dollars or franks your mother now has masses said for you?!

THIRD ANGEL (*naïvely, uncomprehendingly*): ...with *part* of the money.

TWO OLDER ANGELS (*burst in, shouting*): HE's coming!— HE's coming!— Is everything ready?

(The three younger ANGELS *disperse and busily get to work.)*

FIRST ANGEL: For God's sake, go see if the throne is tight!

(One of the angels attends to the throne. Meanwhile, other angels enter, bringing blankets, cushions, pillows, etc.)

SECOND ANGEL (*hops on the throne and tests it in all directions*): Everything's tight!

FIRST ANGEL (*to the* THIRD ANGEL, *who is too shy to lend a hand and is watching all the activity in amazement*): Hey, you've got to tell me more about that later.— Now stand over here with us!

TWO OLDER ANGELS (*who have been standing guard by the door, now return hastily, as above, wildly waving their arms, shrieking*): HE's coming!— HE's coming!—(*a shuffling, dragging noise is heard approaching.*)

SCENE TWO

> *The previous characters.* GOD THE FATHER *shuffles onto the stage, an ancient geezer with silvery-white hair and beard, light blue, watery, gaping eyes over tear-filled bags; his head is bent over, his spine cyphotic; he is wearing a long, off-white robe, supported by a Cherub on either side, coughing and rasping, bent over and clumsily tapping his way forward; two angels stand by the throne, holding it on either side; the others fall to their knees, face downward and extend their arms; behind God the Father is an endless cortege of angels, seraphs, door keepers, attendants, all female, or sexless, some with expressions bored by routine, some look impertinent, some anxiously concerned; as well as some Sisters of Mercy dressed like nuns, carrying medicinal bottles, blankets, spittoons, etc.— Slowly and cautiously, they accompany God the Father to the throne, help him up the two steps by grasping under his legs and lifting him up, then turn him around at the top and slowly lower him onto the seat, fashioned in the oldest Byzantine style and elaborately decorated with mosaic, as two angels from the front, two from behind, and one on either side partly support and partly receive him; a final angel follows, carrying the crutches.*

GOD THE FATHER (*sinks into the throne, as he despairingly heaves a hoarse, weary sigh*): Aagh!— (*gapes fixedly into space, motionless but breathing heavily.*)

> *All the Angels, even those who have until now been kneeling, hastily run back and forth.*

CHERUB (*whispering in a tone of urgent command*): The footstool!

AN ANGEL (*hurriedly brings it*): The footstool.

CHERUB (*sliding the footstool under God's legs; as above*): The hot-water bottle!

AN ANGEL (*brings it*): The hot-water bottle.

CHERUB (*as above*): The foot-muff!

AN ANGEL (*hurrying*): The foot-muff.

CHERUB (*as above*): The quilt!

AN ANGEL (*brings it, hastily*): The quilt.

CHERUB (*as above*): The bolster!

AN ANGEL (*brings it*): The bolster.

CHERUB (*as above*): The back-warmer!

AN ANGEL (*brings a soft piece of flannel folded over six times*): The back-warmer.

CHERUB (*commanding ever more hurriedly*): The arm cushions!

AN ANGEL (*brings two cushions for the armrests*): The arm cushions.

CHERUB (*as above*): The foulard!

AN ANGEL (*brings a cherry-red silk scarf*): The foulard.

> *While the Cherub is tying the scarf around His neck, one hears*

GOD THE FATHER (*groaning and lamenting in a rough, inarticulate voice*): Aaeeh!— Aaeeh!— Aaeeh!— Aaeeh!—

VARIOUS ANGELS: What's the matter?— What's wrong?— Help! Help!— What's the matter?—

GOD THE FATHER (*continues to groan with his head bent forward*): Aaeeh!— Aaeeh!— Aaeeh!— Aaeeh!—

ALL THE ANGELS (*gather around the throne in great consternation; several kneel down and anxiously look at God the Father*): Help!— Help!— What's wrong?— What's the matter?— Divine majesty, what's wrong?— He's dying on us!— Get Mary!— Get the Man!— Help!— Help!—

GOD THE FATHER (*continues to groan; his face becomes engorged; large tears roll down his face from the strain*): Aaeeh!— Aaeeh!— Shooh!— Shpooh!— Shpooh!—

AN ANGEL (*jumps up, triumphantly, in a loud, clear voice*): The spittoon!!

ALL THE ANGELS (*jumping up, in one shrill chorus, relieved*): The spittoon!!

> *They rush to a table, where medicine bottles, wine decanters, cookie jars and such are kept, and bring back a pink crystal vase.*

GOD THE FATHER (*clearing his throat, rasping, with great effort finally relieves himself.*)

> *An angel removes the spittoon and ceremoniously carries it to the back; another angel wipes off God's beard with a silk cloth; then everyone expectantly crowds around him.— He first glowers around with a glassy stare, then suddenly his trembling hands seize the crutches lying in his lap and shakes them with an unexpected jab at the angels, along with a hoarse, menacing, feigned roar: Wooh!—Wooh!—*

> *The angels scatter shrieking and flee out the doors.— Only one Cherub remains behind, prostrating himself before God with his face buried in his hands.— Long pause.*

SCENE THREE

> GOD THE FATHER. A CHERUB. *The latter, a sexless angel, feathered, white, has a very pretty face, reminiscent of Antinous; kneels during the entire scene.*

GOD THE FATHER (*after looking down at him for a long time; very calmly; in a low-pitched baritone*): Is the earth still rolling in her spheres?—

CHERUB (*raising his eyes, solemnly*): The earth is still rolling in her spheres!—(*Pause*)

GOD THE FATHER (*as above*): Has the sun arisen?—

Cherub (*hesitating*): The sun *stands still*, most Holy Father!

GOD THE FATHER (*calm — unconcerned*): The sun *stands still?*— Ah so, I forgot.— I hardly ever see it anymore!—

CHERUB: How are your eyes, Venerable Father?—

GOD THE FATHER: Bad!— Bad!— God, have I grown old!—

CHERUB (*solemnly*): In your eyes a thousand years are but a day!—

GOD THE FATHER: Yes, yes; but they all pass just the same.

CHERUB: You will get better again, Divine Father!

GOD THE FATHER: No, I'll not get better again! (*bursting out*) God, it's awful to be old!— God, how awful it is to have to be this old and live eternally!— It's dreadful being a blind god!

CHERUB: You will recover your eyesight, Most Divine and Holy Father!—

GOD THE FATHER (*with certainty*): No, I'll never be able to see again!— I just keep getting older, more fragile and miserable! God, if only I could die!—

CHERUB (*tenderly*): You will *not* die!— You *can* not die!— You *should* not die!—

GOD THE FATHER (*moved, crying softly*): ....Ah, my limbs are twisted, swollen, edemic, contracted, withered.... (*rubs his knees*)

CHERUB (*slides very close to him, lays his head on the one knee and strokes the other one with his hand; whimpering softly, with deep compassion, childishly imitating God*): Your limbs are twisted,— are swollen,— are edemic — are contracted,— are withered,....Ah!— Ah!—

GOD THE FATHER (*crying more intensely*): My feet are all gnarled, cartilaged, burning with pain, twitching and torn....

CHERUB (*slides down to his feet, caresses them, cries and whimpers*): Your feet are all gnarled,— are cartilaged,— are burning with pain — twitching and are torn ....Ah!— Ah!—

GOD THE FATHER (*breaks out in violent, painful sobbing*): Ah!— Ah!—

CHERUB (*falls completely to the ground and embraces both feet, hiding his sobbing face in them*): Ah, my God! My God!—

GOD THE FATHER (*deeply moved, wants to bend forward, stretching both arms out toward the boy, whom he can't reach, while heavy tears drip down onto the Cherub's head*)

CHERUB (*realizing this, quickly gets up and embraces God's body, presenting himself in a half-kneeling position*)

GOD THE FATHER (*with violent passion seizes the boy's head with both hands, presses his wet and swollen face against the boy's cheeks and passionately kisses his forehead, eyes, hair, interrupted by sobbing. Dissolved in tears, the two remain in a wordless embrace, while God's passionate outburst begins to subside.—At this moment, there is a knock on the door)*

CHERUB (*jumps up*): Somebody's outside!

GOD THE FATHER (*tired*): Go see who it is!

CHERUB (*returns after a whispered inquiry at the door*): A winged messenger is outside; he wants to bring you news; he acts like he's in a great hurry.

GOD THE FATHER (*indifferent*): Let him in.—

SCENE FOUR

> *The previous characters; a more mature winged* MESSENGER, *who also has wings on his feet, enters with great agitation, accompanied by two angels.*

MESSENGER (*falls to the dust and kisses the ground; then rises to a kneeling position*): Lord, I have just come from Italy; from Naples; I have dreadful news to report to you; that cesspool of sin stinks up to here; all moral restraints have dissolved; the holy commandments, which you yourself gave on Mount Sinai, are being mocked; the city, under siege by the French king, is indulging in the most hideous abominations; lascivious women run through the streets boldly flaunting their exposed breasts; men blaze like billy goats; one vice follows the next; the sea has risen to street level and the sun has been darkened; yet they ignore both terrestrial and heavenly signs; social barriers have been lifted; the King breaks into the brothel; common porters visit the royal whores in the palace; dogs and game-cocks have periods of heat; but the Neapolitans are animals throughout the year; the whole city is one boiling cauldron of passion; Italy is the most love-crazed among the peoples of Europe; but Naples is to Italy what Italy is to the other countries; the siege has heightened the frenzy of the sexes to delirium; no age is spared, no mercy for youth; huge reproductive organs are pulled through the streets in festive processions, accompanied by droves of dancing girls and worshipped as omnipotent idols. And in your church I saw a priest before the altar with a harlot...

GOD THE FATHER (*having followed the account with growing astonishment, arises with the utmost exertion from his throne, in uncontrollable anger, and shakes his clenched fist*): I will *dash them to pieces!*—

> *All fall to the ground and hide their faces.*

CHERUB (*with an imploring gesture*): Don't do that, dear Holy Father.——Otherwise you won't have any people left!—

GOD THE FATHER (*gapes open-mouthed at the Cherub for a long time, then remembers and crumples*): That's right,——correct,—I forgot, (*sinks completely back onto the throne*) Creation is over;—I'm too old;—and my children can't do it.—

CHERUB (*naively*): Calm yourself, Divine Father!—You will show your threatening face from the clouds and give the Neapolitans an angry sermon; then they'll tremble.

GOD THE FATHER: They will *not* tremble!—They ridicule me!—They know that I can only *talk.* They know that they are left to themselves down there; they can court, love and hate, and don't need me anymore.——(*starting up*) But you (*to the Messenger*) call my daughter, the Ever-Blessed Virgin,—and you may also call my son,—and the cherubs and angels of death should stand by for my divine order;—and inform the Devil that he should make

his way up here: We wish to convene a council and deliberate what is to be done in this
dreadful matter!

> *Messenger noisily exists with all the
> other angels except the Cherub. —The
> Cherub busies himself with the
> exhausted old one, tucks him into the
> throne again, adjusting the footstool
> and hot-water bottle, tying his scarf,
> wiping off his face and beard, and
> finally snuggles up at his feet, while
> God seizes the Cherub's hand and lets
> it rest in his. —Silent scene.*

SCENE FIVE

> *The previous characters.* MARY *enters
> through the main door with a proud
> and haughty air, accompanied by a
> flock of angels dressed as amoretti,
> strewing petals as they scamper ahead
> of her; also accompanied and followed
> by adult male angels carrying lily
> stalks; wearing a little gold crown on
> her head and a blue, star-spangled
> dress, open at the front to reveal a
> white silk undergarment; she makes a
> stiff, courtly bow in front of God the
> Father, whose throne steps the Cherub
> has vacated, and then moves to a sec-
> ond throne, one with a high back in
> the style of the troubadour age, which
> busy-handed angels have placed along*

Tinted dry point etching by Leonor Fini for
Le Concile d'amour. Geneva: Grafik Europa
Anstalt, 1975. Courtesy of Richard Overstreet,
La Galerie Minsky, Paris, and Neil Zuker-
man, CFM Gallery, New York. Copyright ©
Leonor Fini Estate.

> *the wall a short distance from God the Father. She remains there throughout the fol-
> lowing scene, surrounded by her choir of angels, occupied solely with her make-up,
> using a little mirror, as well as sprinkling herself with sweet-smelling perfumes. —The
> soft whispering of roguish, flirting amoretti can be heard around her. —Meanwhile, on
> the opposite side of the room in the left foreground, the three angels from Scene One
> are conversing.*

FIRST ANGEL: The *Man* is coming.

SECOND ANGEL (*clapping her hands*): The *Man*, the *Man* is coming.

THIRD ANGEL (*pricking up her ears, seriously*): The *Man*? Who is the *Man*? —

SECOND ANGEL: Ah, the *Man* —you little monkey— he's the *Man*!

FIRST ANGEL (*didactically*): He's the most beautiful, the most tender, the sweetest *Man*; the
only *Man* in Heaven; that's who the *Man* is.

THIRD ANGEL (*curious*): Is he young?

FIRST ANGEL: Like a palm tree.

THIRD ANGEL (*after reflection*): Is he younger than the old man over there?

FIRST AND SECOND ANGELS (*almost together*): A hundred thousand times younger!

THIRD ANGEL (*upon further reflection*): Is he younger than the beautiful woman over there?

FIRST AND SECOND ANGELS (*as above*): A thousand times, a thousand times younger!

THIRD ANGEL (*reflecting again*): Is he younger than the nasty old man down on earth?

FIRST AND SECOND ANGELS (*as above*): Infinitely younger!

THIRD ANGEL (*aroused*): Is he beautiful?

SECOND ANGEL: White as ivory!

THIRD ANGEL: Is he slender?

FIRST ANGEL: Like a fir tree!

THIRD ANGEL: What kind of eyes does he have?

SECOND ANGEL: Like a gazelle's!

THIRD ANGEL: How does he talk?

FIRST ANGEL (*reflecting*): Like an Aeolian harp!— But sad, sad!

THIRD ANGEL (*compassionately*): Why is the *Man* sad?

SECOND ANGEL: Because he's wounded.

THIRD ANGEL (*silently inquisitive*)

FIRST ANGEL: Because they pierced his hands!

SECOND ANGEL: And his feet!

FIRST ANGEL: And into his side!

SECOND ANGEL: And there are drops of blood streaming down his forehead from his hair!

THIRD ANGEL (*who has been listening with growing amazement*): And he's still *alive*?

FIRST AND SECOND ANGELS: He's *alive*!

> *A procession can be heard approaching outside. A gaggle of young, girlish angels rushes in ahead of the others.*

FIRST AND SECOND ANGELS: The *Man* is coming!

THIRD ANGEL: The *Man* is coming! (*They step back a bit to make room*)

ADVANCE ANGELS (*scurrying ahead, twittering and giggling*): The *Man*! The *Man*!

> CHRIST *enters with arms crossed and pointing forward* (Ecce homo *pose*)*, as King of the Jews, wearing a purple cloak over a white robe, his head bent down with a deeply sad expression on his face, surrounded by mostly older angels bearing the cross and instruments of torture; his retinue includes apostles, martyrs, Mary Magdalene and mourning women. A tall, ethereal figure, he looks very youthful and pale with dark hair, a little fluff of beard; his entourage also has the character of deepest despondency and frailty. The younger angels shove their way toward him with fiery looks in their eyes, trying to touch the tip of his robe. Watched by God the Father with indifference and completely ignored by Mary, refusing in his own passivity to take notice of anyone*

himself, he strides toward a throne set up for him somewhat to the side of the other two, which is reminiscent of a Jewish teaching chair in its primitive form. There he apathetically sits down, still retaining his Ecce homo *pose, while his followers gather around him.*

After everyone has assembled, and the groups of angels have knelt down in front of the three thrones, where they take up the entire foreground:

GOD THE FATHER (*solemnly with deep pathos*): Are we all assembled?—

In the next moment, a fiery streak flashes straight across the very top of the stage, whistling like a rocket, fading with a clatter in the distance: the Holy Ghost.— Everyone solemnly looks up, the angels spread their arms: only Mary indifferently stares ahead, her head casually propped up on the left armrest of the throne; while Christ, his arms crossed over his chest, dips his head even lower and remains for a while in deep remorse.

GOD THE FATHER (*after a pause, during which all return to their previous positions*): We have summoned you here to seek your advice in a serious, dreadful matter.— Human beings, ignoring my commandments and behaving in an idolatrizing and self-destructive manner, have perpetrated the most hideous abominations, the most frightful atrocities. In a city — in Asia — in — in where was it again?....

CHERUB (*closest to God, with clasped hands*) in *Naples*, most Holy Father,—

GOD THE FATHER (*remembering*) In *Naples* they have fornicated like animals, completely removing their clothing, the guarantors of modesty, they have ruthlessly disregarded the limits and restrictions placed on carnal instincts, and have thus brought about divine wrath...

MARY (*interrupting, casually*): Ah yes, I heard about it.

GOD THE FATHER (*taking notice with surprise*): How? What's that?

MARY (*as above*): Yes, I know of the affair. The messenger came to me first... (*suddenly clamps her mouth shut, as if she wanted to take it back*)

GOD THE FATHER (*pale with rage, is about to lose his temper, tries to find the messenger in the crowd, then glares back at Mary and snorts*)

CHERUB (*silently implores God to control himself*)

GOD THE FATHER (*swallows his rage; bitterly*): Then I guess you're all filled in. (*struggles for a while to suppress his emotion*) — — We've decided upon the most terrible punishment...

MARY (*interrupting*): That riff-raff will never improve.

CHRIST (*looks up wearily and glassy-eyed, repeating in a consumptive babble*): No,— the — riff-raff— will never improve.

THE ANGELS (*nudging one another*) The *Man*! The *Man*!—

MARY MAGDALENE (*bitterly*): What did they do?

MARY (*curt*): I'll tell you later! The usual dirty stuff.

GOD THE FATHER (*angered*): We will *destroy* them!

CHORUS OF APOSTLES, MARTYRS, ANGELS (*lamenting*): Ah!—Ah!—

CHRIST (*confused*): Huh?

MARY (*brusque and bossy*): No, no! That won't do! We've got to have them.

CHRIST (*repeating*): Yes,— yes,— we've got to have them.

GOD THE FATHER (*feeling that he is in the minority, angrily*): Do we really have to keep them?— I want to wipe them out, these monsters.— Want — want to have a beautiful earth again with animals in the woods....

MARY (*mocking*): If we have animals, we've also got to have people.

MARY MAGDALENE (*empathetically*): Sin leads to purification.

GOD THE FATHER: They feed on sin like sweet cake, until they burst, until they rot.

MARY (*dryly*): We've got to allow them copulation.— You've got to grant them a little lust, otherwise they'd hang themselves from the nearest tree. (*God looks at her, fuming with growing anger*) At night! At night!— In springtime!— At certain times!— When the moon is shining!— With moderation and purpose!....

GOD THE FATHER (*growing angrier*): I will beat them to death like two lascivious dogs — at their moment of greatest pleasure!....(*Great commotion among those assembled. The younger angels look at each other in amazement.*)

MARY (*dryly*): Then who would make people?—

> *As the Apostles busily converse and a feeling of embarrassment spreads through the entire hall, God stares straight ahead with a flushed face, panting heavily; his face grows darker and darker, he rasps and wheezes; he appears close to suffocation; he flails his arms about; throws off blankets and crutches, groans and bellows; attendants run to his aid; they bring the spittoon and bottles with ethereal fluids; Mary is concerned and springs up; Christ, too weak to move, looks on with languishing, glassy eyes; great consternation. But God spurns all help and support, gesticulating wildly; he summons all his powers and bellows with excruciating exertion.*

GOD THE FATHER: I will smash them to pieces — trample them — in the mortar of my wrath — dash them to pieces (*is about to stand up and deal an almighty, irrevocable blow to coincide with the deed.*)

CHERUB (*rushes forward at this moment and throws himself at God's feet, imploring*): Most Holy and Heavenly Father, tomorrow is *Easter*!— They're eating the *Passover meal* down there!

CHORUS OF APOSTLES, MARTYRS, OLDER ANGELS (*chiming in*): They're eating the Passover meal.

GOD THE FATHER (*pausing*): What are they eating?—

CHERUB and the others: They're eating the Passover meal!

GOD THE FATHER (*looks around in astonishment*): They're eating the Passover meal?

CHORUS OF APOSTLES: They're eating the Easter lamb!

CHERUB: They're eating the Last Supper.

GOD THE FATHER (*reflecting*): The Last Supper?

CHERUB: They're eating the flesh and blood of Christ.

GOD THE FATHER (*thawing somewhat*): My son, they're eating *you*!

MARY (*with feigned tenderness*): My dear son, whom I bore in my body!

CHRIST (*childlike*): Whom you bore in your body.

GOD THE FATHER (*mechanically*): Whom she bore in her body.

THE YOUNGER ANGELS (*whispering among themselves*): The *Man!*— The *Man!*—

MARY (*as above*): They're eating you!

CHRIST (*as above*) They're eating me.

GOD THE FATHER (*as above*): They're eating him.

CHRIST (*erupting*): Yes, and yet We up here keep getting weaker and more miserable!— It's ghastly! (*coughs a bit*) Me they eat and get healthy again and free of sin. And We keep wasting away. First they eat themselves so full of sin down there till they burst, and then they eat me, and thrive, and become free of sin, and big and fat; and we get skinny and miserable. Ah! This cursed role! Someday I'd like to turn the tables on them and gorge *myself*, and let *them* starve! (*breaks into a consumptive coughing fit*)

MARY (*jumping up and rushing to him, concerned*): My God, my son, don't forget that you're invulnerable, divine, inedible, the same throughout eternity! (*lays his head on her breast and caresses him*)

CHRIST (*sobs violently at Mary's breast*)

THE YOUNGER ANGELS (*whispering among themselves*): The *Man!* The *Man!*—

GOD THE FATHER (*after a pause, to the Cherub, much calmer*): Who all is celebrating the Passover meal down there?—

CHERUB (*promptly*): The Christians, Holy Father; your faithful, Divine Master; your children, who place their hope in you; the devout, the Catholics, the only redeeming Church, your priests, the bishops, the Pope!—

GOD THE FATHER (*credulously, friendly*): Hmm!— Let's take a look at that!

MARY (*glad to have found a way out*): Yes, let's take a look at that! (*to Christ*) Come, my son, we'll take a look at that, it will amuse you!

> *Great relief among the entire assemblage; the compact groups dissolve; younger angels leave the hall; servant-spirits busy themselves with the throne, arranging everything back into splendid, ornate order; all medical equipment is removed; in its place, large, peculiar tripods are brought in during the following sequence; the groups of apostles, martyrs, angels and Sisters of Mercy file out in solemn procession; so that finally only the three divinities, the Cherub and a few older angels remain.*

GOD THE FATHER (*comfortably bedded down on his throne in a semi-reclining position, with a deep, sonorous, solemn voice*): Bring in the smoking racks and coal trays, and produce in Us omniscience and omnipresence!—

> *The tripods are placed in the middle of the hall, stoked with a brown drug mixed with sandalwood, and then lit; the doors are shut; the servant-angels remove themselves, the Cherub leaves last. The three divinities can be seen slowly sinking back and closing their eyes, as clouds of smoke spread out. As this happens, the curtain falls.*

Act Two[1]

> *A resplendent hall in the papal palace in Rome, which is bordered in the background by arcades set beneath a Romanesque gallery; the hall must be imagined as being adjacent to the Pope's private chapel, access to which can be provided by opening the wide*

*windows on the high gallery, so that the hall's gallery is roughly the same height as the chapel's choir.—The Pope and his family, together with the Vatican court and dinner guests, take up the entire stage left; ornate tables are set with costly silverware and bright, conspicuously high, three-armed candelabra. The entire center and stage-right, with the exception of a few groups of people talking at the extreme stage right, remain empty for the later evolutions and masquerades.—It is early evening on the first day of Easter 1495; food is being cleared off the tables. The Pope is dressed in the comfortable, inconspicuous garb of a house prelate (violet with velvet), with a small round velvet cap. Everyone else is dressed ornately.—Dazzling array of servants; continuous movement back and forth; animated conversation; repeated laughter; music in the background under the arcade; the gallery is filled with commoners; down in the hall, groups form, exchange news and disperse again.— In addition to The Pope, (*RODRIGO BORGIA, Alexander VI), a man in his sixties, his nine children GIROLAMA, ISABELLA, PIER LUIGI, DON GIOVANNI (Count of Celano), CESARE, DON GIOFFRE, LUCREZIA, fifteen years old, blonde, cheerful and childlike, LAURA and DON GIOVANNI BORGIA, a boy; his daughters- and sons-in law, including DONNA SANCIA, Don Gioffre's spouse; his nephews and other relatives, including COLLERANDO BORGIA, Almoner, Bishop of Coria and Monreale, FRANCESCO BORGIA, Archbishop of Cosenza, the Pope's Treasurer, LUIGI PIETRO BORGIA, Cadinal-Deacon of Santa Maria, RODRIGO BORGIA, Captain of the Vatican Guard; his confidants, including GIOVANNI LOPEZ, Bishop of Perugia, PIETRA CARANZA, Privy Treasurer, GIOVANNI VERA DA ECRILLA and REMOLINA DA ILERDA, members of the Sacred College, and JUAN MARADES, Bishop of Toul, the Pope's Privy Intendant; his two mistresses, the former one, VANOZZA, age 53, and the current one, JULIA FARNESE; the latter is with her husband, ORSINI, and her brother, Cardinal ALESSANDRO FARNESE; his confidante, ADRIANA MILA, his children's governess; BURCARD, the Pope's Master of Ceremonies; archbishops, bishops, cardinals, papal dignitaries, Roman ladies, soldiers and servants, commoners, later courtesans and actors.*

DON GIOFFRE: Didn't that Spaniard give another one of his boring sermons again today?

THE POPE: Awful, I couldn't listen to it.

DONNA SANCIA (*to Lucrezia*): I kept signaling you, but you weren't catching it.

LUCREZIA (*sleepily*): Pietro kept nudging me with his foot.

DON GIOFFRE: That Spaniard didn't understand his Holiness, either; he just wouldn't finish his sermon; and his Holiness was showing visible signs of displeasure.

THE POPE: He's from Valencia, where the men are stiff as rams; when one of them gets going, he never stops; every emotion becomes a rocket, he beats you over the head with every word. (*laughter*)

FRANCESCO BORGIA, the Bishop: But he honestly did try hard.

THE POPE: Honesty is always awkward.

DON GIOFFRE: And the people staring up with their ghostlike eyes, furious, possessed, lapping it up.

DON GIOVANNI: That's because Donna Sancia kept whispering and giggling.

DONNA SANCIA: No, it's because Lucrezia kept eating candy.

LUCREZIA: No, it's because Laura had fallen asleep and was snoring.

Drawing by Leonor Fini for *Le Concile d'amour* program, Paris, 1969. Courtesy of Richard Overstreet, La Galerie Minsky, Paris, and Neil Zukerman, CFM Gallery, New York. Copyright © Leonor Fini Estate.

DON GIOFFRE: I think he couldn't take his eyes off *Farnese's* beautiful pearls.

FRANCESCO BORGIA, the Bishop: Could the people see all that?

LUCREZIA: We were sitting up in the choir on both sides of the altar.

THE POPE: No, children, that's not it! You're allowed to laugh and joke, wear pearls and eat candy. But I saw some *Dominicans* sitting among them; they're Florentines from San Marco, followers of Savonarola, that troublemaker. They stir up the people, and they say all kinds of things, and look at you with ghostlike eyes....

DON GIOFFRE: Why don't we simply remove the bums?

FRANCESCO BORGIA: They're here on a mission, conferring with their general.

DON GIOVANNI: Oh-ho, have we too reached the point here where jewelry is torn off women's bodies, thrown on a pile and burned?

DON GIOFFRE: Will His Holiness continue to have laws dictated to him by this Florentine fool?

THE POPE (*winking*): We invited him.— He won't come.

DON GIOVANNI: What? He refuses to obey?

THE POPE: Medici is protecting him.— Lorenzo has turned penitent and daily asks *Savonarola* if he still has a chance to get to heaven.

LUCREZIA: Who is Savonarola, Santo Papa?

THE POPE: He doesn't allow you to eat candy and wear pearls. (*laughter*)

DON GIOFFRE: Isn't there a way...? Don't we have any church poison left?

CESARE (*darkly, dryly*): Later!—

   A group of Noblemen at the extreme stage-right

FIRST NOBLEMAN (*whispering*): Did you know that the Duke of Bisceglie was found in the Tiber River last night?

SECOND NOBLEMAN: Yes, he drowned.

THIRD NOBLEMAN: Yes, and with three severe wounds, as well!

FIRST NOBLEMAN: They say he was quite drunk when he left the Vatican last night....

THIRD NOBLEMAN Nowadays, it's always dangerous to leave the Vatican at night, regardless of what condition you're in....especially if you're married to the beautiful Lucrezia.

SECOND NOBLEMAN: You mean....?

THIRD NOBLEMAN: I mean the Duke of Bisceglie was strangled last night in the presence of his wife, Lucrezia, and her brother, Don Cesare.—(*First and Second Nobleman recoil*)

SECOND NOBLEMAN: And the deep wounds?

THIRD NOBLEMAN: They were inflicted four weeks ago during an attack in Saint Peter's Square, from which the Duke had the audacity to recover. (*Both are shocked anew.*)

FIRST NOBLEMAN: But look at Lucrezia; she's as cheerful as on her wedding day.

THIRD NOBLEMAN: She's a child! This morning his Holiness made her Princess of Nepi and sent her a large basket of candy.

SECOND NOBLEMAN: And does the Pope know anything about this matter?

THIRD NOBLEMAN: Alexander VI knows nothing; Rodrigo Borgia knows everything.

FIRST NOBLEMAN: And what will he do?

THIRD NOBLEMAN: He will have a requiem mass said for the Duke who fell into the Tiber and notify the Prince of *Ferrara* that Lucrezia is available.

> *Dance music can be heard coming from the background. The three noblemen disperse. Couples can be seen dancing in the background. Meanwhile, the table has been cleared and removed. The whole party is sitting or reclining on taborets or pillows. The space in the center has now become even larger. The groups do not remain static. People get up, walk over to others, chat, drink, nibble the array of sweets and return to their places. Meanwhile, some of the couples have stopped dancing. Some of the ladies come forward, hot and flushed. The Pope takes a basket of candy from one of the servants and throws some of it into the ladies' cleavages. Merry laughter below and from the gallery. The piece of music has concluded.*

THE POPE: What happened to our buffoni?—Let them in!—And We, We will make ourselves cozy here (*pointing to the left, where the seats are located; to Lucrezia*) Come over here,
my little child!

> *Pulcinello enters with Colombina and the rest of his troupe. They perform a pantomime.*
> *Pulcinello in a white pluder costume with a leather belt, neck ruffle, pointed hat and*
> *black half-mask, a slapstick in hand, first turns to the audience with low bows, gri-*
> *maces and contortions; while doing this, he suddenly pretends to strangle himself by*
> *holding his hands as if they belonged to someone else, gasping and moaning, close to*
> *death. Colombina approaches him from behind, pretends to be frightened, cannot bear*
> *to watch and covers her face with her hands. The Pope understands the allusion and*
> *raises his finger threateningly. They stop it and proceed with the pantomime proper, in*
> *which Colombina, the young wife of the old Pantalone, is abducted by Pulcinello and*
> *betrays her husband. Repeated laughter and lively conversation throughout the pan-*
> *tomime.*

THE POPE (*during the play to Lucrezia, who has sat down on a pillow at his feet, obsequiously*):
My sweetheart, today was actually a day of mourning for you; your handsome duke died
so suddenly.

LUCREZIA (*childlike*): Ah, yes, he fell into the Tiber.

THE POPE (*empathizing*): You probably liked him a lot?

LUCREZIA (*as above*): Oh, yes, I really did!

THE POPE: You'll be glad to know we already have another one for you!

LUCREZIA (*lively*): As handsome as my Duke?

THE POPE: Even better looking, kitten.

> *The Master of Ceremonies enters, as Colombina and Pulcinello are kissing loudly*
> *behind Pantalone, and the latter turns around to receive a salvo of white powder in*
> *his face, helplessly tumbling about, to the loud laughter of all present.*

BURCARD (*to the Pope*): Your Holiness, Vespers have begun in the chapel; the church is packed
with people awaiting your Easter blessing!

THE POPE: We want to watch the play down here; also, the sudden death of Our dear son-
in-law has shocked Us.—Get those windows (*pointing to the gallery*) opened up and tell the
people I'll be attending Vespers from the loggia up there. (*exit Master of Ceremonies*)

> *The windows between the arches on the gallery, where the people are standing, are*
> *promptly opened from the interior of the church in the background, exposing a view of*
> *the friezes, beams, statues and burning chandeliers.—Meanwhile, the pantomime con-*
> *tinues. Pulcinello chases after Pantalone, who has been running back and forth in*
> *confusion, and beats him with his slapstick; Colombina scampers behind Pulcinello,*
> *trying to stay hidden; suddenly one can hear, coming from the windows above the*
> *gallery, the strains of a painfully sad, polyphonic*

GRADUAL

CHOIR: De profundis clamavi ad te Domine; Domine exaudi vocem meam; Fiant aures tuae
intendentes in vocem deprecationis meae; Si iniquitates observaveris Domine, quis sustinebit?

Speravit anima mea in Domino; A custodia matudina usque ad noctem; quia apud Dominum misericordia at copiosa apud cum redemptio. Et ipse redimet nos ex omnibus iniquitatibus nostris.—[2]

> *At the very first notes of music, the people up on the gallery anxiously retreat from the windows and, crossing themselves, turn halfway toward the interior of the church. Down below in the hall, mainly toward the back, a number of faces can be seen with grim or embarrassed expressions. But the Pope and his family maintain their high spirits and the pantomime continues, if somewhat forced. Shortly after the gradual ends, the play ends, as well. The Pope gives his musicians a sign, and they begin a new piece, to which some couples begin dancing in the background. Pulcinello and his troupe take leave with deep and grotesque bows. Gold coins are thrown at them. The Pope waves Colombina over to him, strokes her cheeks and presses an extra gift of money into her hand, whereupon she throws him a kiss goodbye.—*

THE POPE (*after the music has ended, claps his hands*): Where are our beauties?

> *At this signal, a curtain at the back of the gallery opens and twelve courtesans of exquisite beauty, clothed in light, transparent gowns, enter the hall and line up at the front of the stage on the right; the Pope, along with the ladies and gentlemen of his entourage, walks up to them, looks them over and welcomes them with joking banter.*

THE POPE (*after he has inspected them, surprised*): Where is La Pignaccia?[3]

ONE OF THE GIRLS (*breaking the embarrassing silence*): She's gone to Charles[4] in Naples.

THE POPE: What? Are you too going over to Our enemies?

> *The Pope and his entourage return to the left, where they settle down on taborets and cushions, as before; Lucrezia sits on her father's lap, as he fawns over her; servants now move the large, bright, three-armed candelabras from the table onto the floor in the middle of the hall. Following a handclap, the girls throw off their clothes; papal servants, standing behind their masters, toss chestnuts from baskets over the heads of their masters into the center of the hall near the candelabra, where the girls dive and wrestle for them. Roaring laughter. A circle forms around the girls fighting on the floor. Laughter also resounds from the gallery, where the people have once more crowded together. As soon as one batch of chestnuts has been picked up by the courtesans and piled next to their clothes, new chestnuts are tossed out and the same fight erupts anew.— One of the girls with flowing hair gets too close to a candelabrum and her hair catches fire. The Pope leaps up — Lucrezia slides to the floor — and smothers the flames with his robes.*

THE POPE (*when it is clear that she is unharmed, slaps her*): You rascal, you almost took a trip to the beyond! (*laughter*)

THE COURTESAN: You wouldn't have let me burn in purgatory any longer than you did here, Santo Papa! (*renewed laughter, joined by the Pope*)

> *When the chestnuts have all been distributed and counted, prizes are presented to the girls according to the number collected.*

> *A new piece of music begins and the servants serve refreshments. Loud conversation throughout the hall, especially about the girls' attributes.*

> *When the music stops:*

THE POPE (*claps his hands again*): Now bring on our athletes!

From the other side of the gallery, two muscular naked men enter and are led to the girls, whom they ogle until sufficiently inflamed and then, on a further signal, begin their wrestling match.[5] Everyone crowds around the spectacle, cheering them on and applauding. Even the girls follow the match with interest. When the winner has thrown his opponent amid loud applause, he walks up to the courtesans, selects the prettiest one amid general joking by all present, and leaves the hall with her. The loser leaves alone. —Then a second pair enters the hall. —The spectators' excitement mounts from minute to minute. The cheering becomes more intense and impassioned. —Just after the fifth wrestler has thrown his opponent amid screams and applause and is about to make his choice, the deep, solemn, tragic strains of the Vesper's final chorus are heard coming from the interior of the church.

> **Veni sancte Spiritus[6]**
> Veni sancte Spiritus
> Et emitte coelitus
> Lucis tuae radium.
> Veni pater pauperum
> Veni dator munerum
> Veni lumen cordium.
> Sine tuo nomine
> Nihil est in homine,
> Nihil est innoxium,
> Lava quod est sordidum,
> Riga quod est aridum,
> Sana quod est saucium.
> O lux beatissima
> Reple cordis intima
> Tuorum fidelium.

An embarrassed silence follows the first chords. The outraged people on the gallery have again recoiled in order to clear the area in front of the windows. Some of those present leave the hall. —Meanwhile, the sixth fighter has already entered with his partner. The Pope signals to proceed with the match, which is eagerly watched by his family and confidants, though they are visibly annoyed by the disruption, and which contin-ues, accompanied by the chorus, until the seventh wrestler. —After the music concludes, the atmosphere warms up a bit and the interest rises. Once more, the circle around the fighters tightens. In the church one can see the chandeliers being extinguished and the windows closed from the inside. —The game continues.

During the ninth match, a messenger rushes into the hall and excitedly whispers to the people standing in the background. The commotion spreads to the front. One can hear shouting: What's happening? —What's going on? —

RODRIGO BORGIA (*Captain of the Vatican Guard*): Your Holiness, the French King has returned from Naples and is only a few miles away, marching on Rome.

THE POPE (*leaps up excitedly*): To hell with him! — Off to Orvieto! — Have the Spaniards and Catalans escort us! — Bring along our cashboxes and valuables! — The ladies should get ready;

forget about baggage and mules; we'll all go on horseback! Pallavicini will stay behind as governor of the city with part of the troops. Let him receive the King with all honors, but threaten to excommunicate him in Our name, as a disobedient son of the Church, if he remains on Our territory more than twenty-four hours.— Cesare will be in charge of providing cover for Us.— Don't forget the gold chalices! Let's go! (*Everyone leaves in a great fluster*)

THE GIRLS (*putting on their clothes, rejoicing*): Carlo's coming!— Carlo's coming!—

(*The curtain falls*)

Act Three

SCENE ONE

> *Heaven. An intimate council chamber in blue. Interim thrones, simple and comfortable.* GOD THE FATHER, MARY, CHRIST, *the* DEVIL; *the first three on their chairs; the latter in a black, tight-fitting costume, very slim, with a pointed face, clean-shaven, with weather-beaten, worn-out, yellowish-annoyed features, reminiscent in his gestures of a refined Jew, supporting himself on one foot and drawing up the other, standing upright in front of them.*

GOD THE FATHER (*serious and brief*): Friend, We have summoned you.— It's a special assignment that...(*falters*)...requires particular finesse;— — I know you think a lot —(*Devil takes a bow*)— couldn't you .... (*falters*) ..... it's a matter of, uh .... a being, uh....a thing, which....uh, an influence,— which would be capable of,— which — of leading this disgusting, completely degenerate mankind —(*Devil makes a comprehending, nobly sympathetic gesture*) ... uh, back onto the path of virtue .... uh, and true morality .... in the most sensitively punishing manner, ... uh, so that .... uh .... (*turning to Christ*) my dear son, you tell him;— I can't handle words properly;— I've always just acted,— not made many words.— —

CHRIST (*wearily sitting up after a moment's reflection, fluidly*): Sir!— — We wish to utilize your assistance — in a matter,— — which is designed to provide you as great a benefit as Us,— — I mean,— which shall in no way alienate mankind from you — in respect to its worldly sphere,— I say this explicitly in order to allay, from the very beginning, any suspicion you may be harboring in this regard —(*Devil makes a dismissive gesture, as if such a thing had never occurred to him*)— on the contrary, which — in a more comprehensive manner than ever before — will place this sphere — under your control:— We are referring to a compromise,— an agreement concerning a border adjustment — between our mutual, hitherto existing powers,— which should not infringe on either of the two opposing parties,— and for which We are counting on your proven skill, your cunning, your tact, your — conciliatory cooperation, your — education,— your — your — —(*begins to cough, suffers shortness of breath, moans and rasps, falls back into his seat gasping, his eyes bulge out, his forehead perspires, he suffers an asthmatic attack*)

MARY (*rushes to his aid, while the Devil nobly feigns reserved embarrassment*): Spare yourself, my son,— you should never talk,— you're getting worse,— you're suffering,—(*turning to the Devil, cordially*) my dear friend, we need your help,— nobody needs to know that *you* were involved in the matter (*the Devil makes a dismissive, calming gesture*)— please help us,— it will not be to your disadvantage (*winks at him*)— you understand (*winks to signal that God is deaf, old, feeble, and will place no obstacles in her path — the Devil bows—) —* let me be brief: prompted by some unfortunate whisperings (*points to God*), we just witnessed a scene at the papal palace in Rome, in the chambers of Pope .... whatsisname ....

DEVIL (*obligingly*): Ah, *Alexander*, the sixth of his name, Rodrigo Borgia — —

MARY: Quite right, this Borgia, — oh, it was scandalous, it was ghastly, — that was a Passover meal! ....

GOD THE FATHER (*suddenly bursting out, with utmost vulgarity*): Filthy *devil!* — Filthy *devil!* — Filthy *devil!* —

CHRIST (*joins in, recovered from his weak spell, almost inaudibly*): Yes, — filthy *devil!* — filthy *devil!* ....

DEVIL (*very confused, angry, insulted*): .... Please .... under these circumstances .... there is no point .... in my remaining here (*stepping back, about to leave*)

GOD THE FATHER (*to the Devil, conciliatory*): My God! — No! — Nobody was referring to you ....

DEVIL (*piqued*): Ah, but *still* ....

GOD THE FATHER: No, no! — And no again! — It wasn't so; .... it just slipped out of Us....the old habit —.... I forgot .....

DEVIL (*returns, gallantly conciliatory, smiling bitterly as he flicks a speck of dust off his sleeve*): Please, ... please ....

MARY: No, no, my friend, you belong to Us; no thought of any discord; We need your help too much; and (*very loud, over to God, suggestively*) We will in no way tolerate any insult to Our dear, dearest cousin, Our ally, Our dearly beloved brother (*Devil takes a very friendly bow*) — this is the situation in a nutshell: Disregarding, for higher reasons, the total extermination of mankind envisaged by the highest authority (*nods toward God*), We have decided to seek a sensitive vengeance of flood-like proportions and, therefore, need someone, a thing, an influence, a force, a person, a poison, a something to curb the lechery of mankind, especially of the Neapolitans and Romans, in a sexual relation — ah, fi donc! — (*pours some Eau de Cologne on a lace handkerchief and holds it up to her face, — seems to be sniffing quietly — leering over her handkerchief at the Devil*) — ah! I'm feeling better — (*continuing*) — which would *stem* the bestiality of men and women in those relations and apparently necessary contacts and comminglings intended exclusively for the purpose of procreation, and authorized only within these bounds — ah, c'est terrible! — (*sniffs Eau de Cologne again*) — enfin — you understand! —

DEVIL (*in a sonorous bass — somewhat theatrically*): — I understand! —

GOD THE FATHER (*cackling*): Yes, yes, — should *stem* it! —

CHRIST (*with a consumptive voice*): Yes, yes, — should *stem* it! —

DEVIL (*after some reflection*): Should it be very severe?

MARY (*pointing her handkerchief at the Devil, nodding forcefully, as if to include the others*): Indeed, it should be very severe.

GOD THE FATHER (*looks at them glassily; does not quite seem to have understood; finally croaks his assent in a thick, rasping voice*): Yes, yes! —

CHRIST (*still in attack, recovering slowly, whispering*): Yes, yes! —

DEVIL (*has been reflecting the whole time with his head lowered and two fingers on his lips*): Should this thing follow immediately afterwards?

MARY: Of course, of course it should!

GOD THE FATHER (*as above*):— Of course!— Of course!—

CHRIST (*wants to say his two "of courses" but is too late and collides with the following sentence by Mary, who nonetheless continues, trying to brush her son aside with a pacifying wave of her handkerchief; he follows her every move with a languishing look*)

MARY (*to the Devil*): You're on the right track, my friend, you can be certain of Our pleasure!

DEVIL (*casts a short, dry look in Mary's direction, then sinks back into his previous meditation;— after a long pause, during which one can only hear Christ's wheezing, he emphatically intones with a peculiar inflection*):— — then — one — would — have to — place — the thorn — the poison — uh — the something (*gesturing with a raised finger*)— into the thing itself,— into the — ahem! (*suggestively clearing his throat*)— into the act itself!—

MARY (*very worldly*): C'est charmant!— C'est charmant!—

GOD THE FATHER (*doesn't quite understand, looks at her with big, round, watery eyes, echoing more the inflection than the comprehension of Mary's words*): Yes,— yes, yes,—

CHRIST (*also wants to repeat it, but can't quite manage to bring it out and is startled by this, looking anxiously first to God the Father and then to Mary, finally produces a rhythmic, inarticulate*): Eh,— eh — eh!—

DEVIL (*having observed Christ's achievement with a detached expression, not wanting to interrupt his own train of thought, continuing*): One would have to poison the secretion during the sex act!—

MARY: Ah, what do you mean?— This is getting interesting! (*shifts position on her chair*)

GOD THE FATHER and CHRIST (*who seem to have caught at least something this time, staring goggle-eyed at the Devil*)

DEVIL (*repeating the newborn thought, as if to lay it all out again*): One would have to poison the secretion during the sex act!—

MARY: You mean the semen? (*dabs her mouth with her handkerchief, as if she were swallowing something unpleasant*)

DEVIL (*impatiently*): No, no!— Not the semen; not the egg; otherwise their offspring would suffer and, having wised up to the situation, would no longer be available.— They'll get their turn!— No, semen and egg should remain untouched, so that the propagation of mankind can continue.— But the culprit who indulges his instinct with carefree abandon shall be punished with a byproduct, a virus produced simultaneously with semen and egg and which, as with snakes, no longer affects the donor but does infect his counterpart, his vis-à-vis in sexual française — pardon!— if I may put it that way —(*Mary raises her eyebrows to signal agreement*);— so that the man can infect the woman, or the woman infect the man or, ideally, both get infected,— unsuspecting,— lost in their ecstasy — in the deception of their greatest joy —(*inquires with a hand gesture whether Mary has understood him, to which Mary gleefully and knowingly responds with her handkerchief*)— so that they will both stumble into the dreadful brew babbling like children!!!

MARY: C'est glorieux!— C'est charmant!— C'est diabolique!— Mais comment? ....

GOD THE FATHER and CHRIST (*just keep calmly staring*)

DEVIL: Ah, madam, let that be my problem!—

MARY: Good! But with *one* condition. Whatever you do with these people, they still must *need redemption!*—

DEVIL (*with extreme self-control*): They will still *need* redemption.

MARY: They must also remain *capable* of being redeemed.

DEVIL (*bouncing his hands back and forth at shoulder level like a salesman*): *Capable* of redemption,—after *I* poison them,—poison them on special request,—that's hardly possible.—

MARY (*leaps from her throne and rushes toward God and Christ*): Well, then the whole thing is in vain!—If we can't redeem people anymore, what's the purpose of this whole institution?!

GOD THE FATHER and CHRIST (*lift their hands in despair; Christ, having recuperated somewhat, begins to follow the conversation more actively*)

DEVIL (*twirls around on his right heel, smiling sardonically and shrugging his shoulders with the feigned regret of a Jewish merchant*)

> *Embarrassing moment. It looks as if there will be no deal.—Pause.*

MARY (*in order to distract everyone, walks slowly back to her seat and suddenly asks the Devil in a friendly voice*): A propos! How's your foot feeling?—

DEVIL (*accepting the diversion*): Oh,—so, so!—Not better,—but not exactly worse, either!—My God (*hitting his shorter leg*)—it won't ever change!—Lousy contraption!

MARY (*somewhat softer*): Is that from your fall?—

DEVIL (*understanding, nodding silently and seriously for a long time*)

MARY (*very friendly*): Well, and otherwise—how's your grandmother?

DEVIL (*likewise*): Lilith?—Oh, just fine—thanks!

MARY: And the little ones?

DEVIL: Thank you! Thank you!—Everyone's fine!—

> *New pause.—Mary, undecided, finally walks over to God the Father, with whom she quietly talks for a while.—Thereupon*

GOD THE FATHER (*ostentatiously*): Voyons! Voyons! My friend, you must be able to make something that will poison mankind, without completely wiping them out.—Then we'll redeem them again.—Won't we, my son?

CHRIST: We'll redeem them again!

MARY: We *have to* redeem them again!

DEVIL: Then the order is too complicated!—It's supposed to be nasty and lovable and poisonous all at the same time!—If I'm to strike them suddenly and violently in their secret amorous relations and poison them at the same time, *then the soul has got to go too!*—Because the soul is all part of it!—

GOD THE FATHER (*amazed*): The soul is all part of it?—

CHRIST (*likewise, but repeating more mechanically*): The soul is all part of it?—

MARY (*affirmative, half to herself, as if remembering*): The soul is all part of it!—

DEVIL (*after a pause to God, with a note of mockery*): My God, you're the Creator! Don't *you* know of something?—

GOD THE FATHER (*reluctantly*): We — uh — aren't creating anymore.—We're tired!—Besides, everything earthly and sensual belongs to your sphere.—So just figure out how you'll do it; tarnish their souls, but they must be capable of being restored again!

CHRIST (*still weak, wants to repeat the last phrase but only gets as far as*): Tarnish — their — souls ....

DEVIL (to *God the Father*): It should entice them to love, you say, and at the same time poison them?

GOD THE FATHER: Naturally, otherwise they won't bite!

CHRIST (*waking up*): In the throes of passion they are blind, I've heard.

MARY: You can't catch mice without some tasty bait!

GOD THE FATHER: Look around in your witch's cauldron! You've got all kinds of stuff in there; all sorts of things are stored in that hell of yours; you're a master of such concoctions!—Create, brew, produce, whip something up!—

MARY: But it's got to be something very seductive.—Preferably something feminine.

CHRIST: Yes, be very seductive.

DEVIL (*developing an idea*): Naughty and destructive at the same time, you say?—And still not definitively destroy the soul?

ALL THREE (*simultaneously to each other*): Naughty — destructive — seductive — poisonous — sensual — gruesome — scorching brains and veins!—

GOD THE FATHER: But not the soul!—Because of contrition!—Because of despair!—

DEVIL (*suddenly completing his train of thought*) Wait, I've got something!—I'll have a talk with *Herodias*!—(*softly, to himself*) both naughty and destructive!—(*out loud*) I'll bring something!—

MARY: Thank God!

DEVIL (*turning to leave*): I believe I have it!

GOD THE FATHER: Bravo! Bravo!

CHRIST: Bravo! Bravo!

ALL THREE (*joyfully stand up, to the extent they can; quietly applauding*): Bravo, Devil! Bravissimo!—

DEVIL (*taking leave, snaps his fingers as he goes*): I'll be back soon! (*Exits.—Outside, as he opens the door, he sees a few younger angels who have been eavesdropping. He grabs the closest one by the wings and gives him a good thrashing. The culprit runs away with the others, amid loud screaming.—The Devil opens a trapdoor outside, through which he descends and closes it behind him. The three divinities disappear during the following change of scene into the wings on the right.*)

SCENE TWO (CHANGE OF SCENERY)

The heavenly council chamber slowly rises upward; the scene darkens and gradually a gloomy, barrel-shaped tunnel emerges, lined with gray stones, which stretches out into infinity like the interior of a tower or a well; a rickety, barricaded, frequently-patched wooden staircase runs down the rear wall. The DEVIL *can be seen descending with some effort, groaning, firmly holding on to the railing, while the slowly rising scenery keeps him visible. Fantastic birds and monsters, some sitting on perches, others crouched in wall niches, greet him with hoarse cawing and hissing.—After a while, this passageway opens into a larger, gloomy, cellar-like room, illuminated by a greasy oil lamp and in which nothing can be seen initially except a crude bed of rushes and wickerwork in the right foreground. The Devil, who has arrived down below, tired and limping, takes a few sighing steps back and forth, then goes to the rear; a heavy chest can be heard opening up; he takes off his tight black outfit, which he carefully places in one of the boxes, and soon thereafter returns to the front of the stage wearing a warm coat patched together from animal skins. He takes a few groaning steps back and forth again, as if not knowing where to turn, and finally settles down across his bed, pulls up his feet and buries his hands deep in his wooly hair, covering his forehead and the upper part of his face in this way.*

DEVIL (*talking to himself*): Here you are, you dog, all alone at home again; abandoned and ignored; returned from the audience; without any relatives, respect or reputation; and once again you got to see the gold-filled chambers of the high and noble. And you still are, and will always remain, the bum, the scoundrel, the crooked rogue. And up there they can do whatever they please, and no matter how gross, low or mean, it's always noble and fancy, just because it happens in the halls of nobility. And whatever you do,—even if you used your head to dig all the way through to the other end of the earth,—you would still be lowly and common and vile.—(*Pause, reflecting*) If you were a count, then even your twisted leg would be noble. And even if you were only a doorkeeper up there, then your head and your ideas would be angelic, as would the robes you'd be wearing. But this way you're a dog and always will be!—Only when you're supposed to do something for them that they can't do themselves, or which is too dirty for them, then they smile at you and say, 'My friend! My friend!' But when the audience is over, then you've got to go back down to the dust and filth, and then they say 'Filthy devil! Filthy devil!'—And so your whole life long you're nothing but an earthborn, stooped over and disfigured fellow, hobbling along on your foot, consumed by anger and bitterness.—— And *yet*!—And *yet* you are more! More than those highfalutin folks with their grand fortune up in the clouds! You're stuck in the midst of the world; and your head contains the thoughts of the earth! And when you're here alone, alone with your earthy smell, and your head lights up, then there emerges in this bitter head, in the midst of despair, a spark, a poison, a force that ignites and flashes like lightning through the world, making those numbskulls up there tremble in their cloudy home.—And you don't need to wear any tiaras, drink ambrosia and champagne or look lavish and elegant in order to be happy. You're happy *as is*; happy as the others never *can* be! Happy in this hole in the ground, in this precious tunnel, with this whiff of earthiness and spice, this smell of the world, which strengthens and toughens you, and generates ideas and forces you to work!—And you don't need any ancestors and family tree; you're shiny and clean; you may begin anew; don't have to be doing nothing; your ancestors are your work! You produce your ancestors into the future!— Work!— Work!—(*leaps up*) Well, off to work now!

(*He walks back and forth for a while, stopping repeatedly to ponder.*)

So, it's supposed to be *seductive*, that thing.— Well, naturally, "otherwise they won't bite";— "something feminine," said Mary;— very well!— Women always know their own sex best.—

But it's also supposed to be *poisonous*; that's where the punishment comes in; and they're not supposed to notice the poison, just swallow it down like syrup;—very well!—That can be done.—But *body* and *soul* are to be poisoned; yet not definitively; only to the point of despair, to insanity;—so they can watch as mankind cringes and crumbles; as they empty out their souls like a stomach;—I understand;—but the soul must be reparable again, "redeemable," as they say;—well, I'll leave them *that* pleasure for the time being; them and them;—they didn't say that about the *body*; very well!—As if they could be separated!— Once I've contaminated the entire body to the gills and the whole fellow has gone to hell — oh, excuse me — gone to pieces, then they'd like to redeem the soul, after it's well on its way to me!—The mercy of it all!—Well, we'll see about that.—(*walks pensively back and forth again*) But what kind of poison should it be? One that ruins and yet doesn't ruin?—Organic or chemical poisons won't do!—Nor can I proceed *quantitatively*. They'd just keep on swallowing the stuff down—especially since it's so sweet—and then: zap, they'd be out on the floor. I can't calibrate the dosage. I can't just hang a yard-long prescription on their bedstead: such and such amount per dose!—It's got to be a subtle, new and very special poison!— One which won't immediately poison either the donor or the recipient!—It's got to be a subtle, stealthy, slow-acting virus, which quietly reproduces itself, and which can always be gotten fresh from living specimens!—Then—the poison should immediately follow upon man's greatest delight, his love-making, the most naïve and precious joy he has; so that it can assuredly spread to everyone!—Yes, that was actually *my idea*!—No denying intellectual property!—Oh, well!—How to proceed?—Where do you get the poison?—(*stands still while reflecting*) Well, *from yourself.*—(*coolly*) Is there anything more poisonous, more capable of penetrating through veins, than you yourself?—Very good!—And now?—How will you pull it off?—(*reflecting, very slowly, with an extended index finger, as if dictating*) *You first have to organically dilute the virus, which by itself is too strong and could be fatal, and then realize it in a living being!* (*smacks his hands together*) Hey, that's it!—One more time: *You first have to make the thing organically so mild, that initially their stomachs and livers can easily tolerate it, and at the same time embody it in a creature just like themselves!*—Damn!—And secondly, this creature must be a *woman*; and the poison must flow through the known channels!—And thirdly: this *woman* must be *beautiful*; and I her father!—Terrific! (*rubs his hands*) Now it's our turn to create!—(*walks excitedly back and forth*) .... Well, and if I pull off this work of art, what will I get for it?—Beware, my friend! You won't get another opportunity like this again! Now get out those wish lists that you're been saving for so long!— (*reflects*)——That staircase over there (*looks up*) He's got to get it repaired for me. The piece of junk. If I slip and break my foot, I'll be a *total* cripple.—Then, that trapdoor up there is beneath my dignity. I've been banging into it for a long time. It should be a nice new entrance, with a railing on it and a few rugs.—Then, I've also been fed up with this audience nonsense for a long time.—Once the entrance up there is open, I also must have free access! I have to be able to show up unannounced anytime.—He can always come down to me unannounced.—Then (*very emphatically*) He must allow my books to be freely printed and allow their widest possible circulation throughout Heaven and earth. That's a must. Without that I won't even begin to work. (*bursting out*) If someone is thinking and is no longer allowed to communicate his thoughts to others, that's the ghastliest torture of all.— This purest delight, this drop of pleasure, which makes barrels full of bitterness bearable, when others get to *follow* the thoughts that you have thought *before* them,—is that so hard to understand?!—So that's number one!—Then—the ventilation in here needs to be improved.—(*stares up at the ceiling for a long time*).... Actually, I could have the place here

Ink drawing by Alfred Kubin for private printing of *Das Liebeskonzil*, Munich, 1913. Courtesy of Eberhard Spangenberg. Copyright © Eberhard Spangenberg, Munich.

decorated with some gold molding.—Oh,—it wouldn't do any good.—.... How about if He made me a *count*?—Count Miraviglioso! Or completely Italian: Conte di Miraviglioso; Signor Conte di Miraviglioso.—Phooey, shame on you! Didn't you say you wanted to remain an honest fellow?—Well, then; I just briefly wanted to have the wild sensation of being something for no reason at all. Just for a week.—Then I can give it to my double.—.... They could also give me a few medals while they're at it!—It's not bright enough down here to see them, anyway. The lighting really needs to be fixed.—What else?—A better wardrobe! I've been wearing this Spanish costume now since Phillip II. It's outrageous. And only my extreme meticulousness allows me to appear up there at all.— Then, for God's sake, some furniture. I still ought to be worth a few pounds of horsehair. And a few warm blankets.— Keep going!— Some gold braiding on my clothes; at least the rank of lieutenant!— Then: membership in at least the lowest court rank; my God, I do help the folks in a most extraordinary fashion.— Furthermore: a little "von" in front of my last name, and the possibility of a liaison with an angel of corresponding social rank; God, it would be delightful to have one of those little creatures by my side; however skinny and young she might be, I'd fix her up for me!— What else?— A gold sword buckle, the title of chamberlain, a little crown, a ducal collar or.... (*suddenly stops, clenches his forehead with both hands and screams out like an animal*) Agh!— Agh!— Stay away! (*he stretches out both hands as if to ward off something attacking him, stepping back*) Agh!— It's coming!— It's got me!— You dog, didn't I tell you it would get you, if you stepped over the line!— Filthy devil! (*spits out, as if to rid himself of something from his insides*) Filthy devil!— It's coming!— The *nausea*.— It's got me!— Ugh!— Ugh!— Oh, it's too late!—*Nausea! Nausea!* Damned gravy!—— Devil, don't you remember?— Don't you know that you only thrive in deprivation, in darkness, under torture?— And then the guy wants to be proud!— Ah,— ah,—(*Retches as he drags himself back to his bed, throws himself down on his stomach, convulsed in cramps, pulls straw out of his mattress, makes a gag and stuffs it into his mouth with furious relish;— then gradually calms down, lies motionless and appears to sleep.— Long pause.*)

> *Meanwhile, the scene in the background at the rear wall of the vault has become lighter; the backdrop gets brighter and brighter; finally transparent; a new, seemingly endless vista opens up; gradually, even the last hazy veil disappears, and one sees an immense field of the dead, where a sheer unfathomable number of what appear to be only women are lying as if asleep, wearing pale robes, some crouching, others stretched out, some leaning on their arms, some with a face buried in the crook of an arm; the entire scene bathed in a cold, shimmering glow resembling moonlight.— Deep silence.—*

DEVIL (*slowly awakens, wearily props himself up with both hands; as he turns and notices the scene, he suddenly sits up and pulls the gag out of his mouth*) Ah!— My thoughts have rushed ahead of me! (*regards the scene for a long while with delight*) My good thoughts have realized themselves!— And the bad ones went to my stomach and made me sick;— that's alright!—— You've done your penance,— and now you're an honest guy again!—(*still somewhat exhausted, he sinks back into his reclining position, in such a way as to keep the scene in view—slowly and wearily*) Now, which one of these should I pick to be the mother of my glorious creature?—....Beautiful!— Seductive!— Sensual!— Poisonous!— Scorching brains and veins!— Unsuspecting!— Clumsy!— Cruel!— Unaware!— Rotten to the core!— Naïve!— (*Long pause.——He sits up and gently calls out in a low but clear and gentle voice*) Helen,— of Sparta,— Priam's lover,— Trojan queen!——

> *From the rows of sleepers in the background, a figure slowly arises, trailing a long robe, which is tied at the waist with a cord of the same color; she slowly comes forward, as if somnolent, with eyes closed, accompanied by the shimmer of light from the Realm of the Dead, and stops in front of the Devil.*

DEVIL: You made off with that young lout, the Trojan prince, and abandoned your husband, the king; purely out of love?—(*Helen denies this by shaking her head sluggishly*)— What? You weren't even in love?— Out of curiosity?—(*She seems to be thinking; then nods sleepily*)— Just because you felt like it?—(*Helen nods*)— Without giving it any thought?—(*nods*)— Really?

(hesitates, and then nods) — And then when the war broke out, did you think anything? — *(nods mechanically, then reconsiders and shakes her head)* — Did you think: oh, that's just the way it is! *(nods emphatically)* — Go on back to sleep again, — you poor, dumb thing! —

> *She waits a moment, then slowly turns around and goes back to her place the way she came.*

DEVIL *(after a pause, with the same bright, gentle voice)*: *Phryne* — of Athens — smoothest of all hetaerae — come! *(A woman from another row, dressed in the same attire as the first one, arises from the field of the dead and steps forward)* Palest of all enchantresses, you lured thousands of men into your net, rendered them poor and miserable, robbed them of their money and their thoughts, — ensnared philosophers, — bribed judges, — overturned state laws, — started wars, — amassed fortunes, — carried on like a goddess, — had yourself worshipped, — wanted to put your name up like a dirty poster on all the walls in Thebes, — and paid for it, — appeared nude in front of all the people, — had temples and statues built for you in Corinth, — kept whoring along until your hair turned white — and were finally slaughtered, like an unclean animal, in the temple to which you had fled? — *(repeatedly nods affirmatively to all questions)* — Why? — Out of love? *(shakes her head)* — Out of passion? *(shakes her head)* — On a whim? *(nods)* — Because you were prettier and paler than all the others? *(nods)* — Didn't think anything of it? — *(shakes her head)* — Just let things run their course? — *(nods)* — Go, you harmless child, you're innocent! — *(She slowly and silently leaves, as the first woman had)*. —

DEVIL *(after a pause, as above)*: *Heloise*, — Abbess of Paraclet — twelfth-century Latinist! — *(a third figure arises from the field of the dead and approaches, wearing the same attire as the previous ones)* You studied, — and loved, — and had children, — and seduced your teacher, *Abelard*, the shining light of his century, — and plunged your family into shame and ridicule, — until they made a capon out of your lover, — and a nun out of you, — and you continued to love your castrated *Abelard*, — and wrote him passionate love letters — until they made you an abbess; — and as abbess you continued to study, and continued to love him, and continued — at least in your imagination — to have children; and with your boyfriend, whose flame had long since been extinguished, you continued to indulge in imaginative perversions, the likes of which shouldn't even be mentioned in Hell, — and you wrote him that you'd rather be *Abelard's* whore than the Emperor's legal wife; — and when he died you had his body sent to you, and you still loved him and buried him with your own hands; — and then you continued to love him for another twenty years at the expense of your imagination, — until you yourself died? — *(she has silently nodded to all questions)* — Why? — Out of love? — *(nods emphatically)* — Out of pure love? — *(nods decisively)* — Child, you're almost ripe for Heaven! — Stand by, when the trumpet sounds, you'll be first. — In the meantime, go back to sleep! — *(Figure exits)*

DEVIL *(to himself)*: I've actually got damned little here in Hell to brag about; I need to find me a real bitch! — *(reflects some more; then, after a pause)* *Agrippina*, — mother, wife and murderess of emperors, — and murdered by an emperor, — come! — *(a figure arises from another area)* — You've got quite a bit on your conscience, my friend; — at the age of 14 you married your husband, and after nine years you saw fit to give birth to one of the greatest monsters, to *Nero*? — You can't help that! — Don't worry, we now have a school of thought that proves you're not responsible for the other things, either; except that this theory hasn't made it up to Heaven yet. — So, you neglect your husband and give yourself to *Lepidus*; — that was the custom then! — Then you plot with your suitor to murder your brother, the Emperor

Caligula;—it doesn't succeed!—You can't help that, either.—That is, you weren't clever enough!—Finally, *Caligula* does get murdered,—as was the custom then—and you can be seen at court again;—Then you try unsuccessfully to bag a few high ranking Romans, until finally the wealthy lawyer *Passimus* agrees to enter into a second marriage with you—I really thought he had more sense than that—; you then poison him and inherit everything!—But others have already done that before you; that was the custom then!—Your subsequent little game, on the other hand, was far more original: you play your backstage role so well—from your villa—that you have the Empress *Messalina* slaughtered by her husband, the Emperor *Claudius*, then proceed to marry *Claudius* yourself and become Empress!—What then followed, the suicide of *Lucius Silanus*, which you staged, the banishment of his sister, *Junia*, and the banishment of *Lollia Paulina*, whose head you later had brought back to you from exile, those were mere sideshows; you were just following the customs of your time.—Then you acquire the epithet 'Augusta,' the holy one; you have your son, *Nero*, adopted by your husband, Emperor *Claudius*, get him married to *Octavia*, the daughter of this Emperor *Claudius*, then poison this Emperor, your husband, and proclaim your son, *Nero*, to be the new Emperor.—Now that was something totally new!—You then poison a few more consuls, proconsuls and rivals, and are finally murdered by your own son, *Nero*!—(*the figure has nodded affirmatively to all points*)—Listen, Agrippina, you're quite a charming person, but in your entire behavior I miss the basic artistic impulse—the naïveté;—everything depends on your inordinate ambition!—That's sick!—In the long run it gets boring!—We take a different view of things now!—Not one pretty murder in your entire story!—I really can't use you!—Just go back to sleep again!—Sleep soundly! (*figure exits*)

DEVIL (*ponders a while, then to himself*): I've got one more number left, *Herodias*;—but wait, I'd rather have the daughter than the mother!—(*calls out*) Salome,—a beautiful young dancer—come to me!—(*far to the back, a slender young figure arises and comes forward with a friendly, cheerful memory on her face*)—Tell me, my pretty child, you were present at *Herod's* banquet back then?—(*affirms*)—And you danced there?—(*affirms*)—Why did you dance?—(*she doesn't know*)—Well, you simply danced because pretty girls like to dance,—and because you were taking dancing lessons?—(*affirms*)—And you received applause?—(*nods*)—and Herod said you could have a present?—(*nods*)—And you had him give you a head?—(*nods*)—A human head? (*affirms*)—The head of a living person?—(*affirms*)—Why?—(*she doesn't know*)—To play with?—(*she hesitates and finally affirms*)—And *Herod* sends you to the prison with the executioner, and he cuts off a head for you there?—(*nods*)—that was the head of *John*?—(*affirms indifferently*)—It was put on a platter for you, and then you came back into the banquet hall with it?—(*nods*)—The blood probably oozed out into the platter,—and finally filled it?—(*nods*)—It wetted your fingers?—(*affirms vigorously*)—Did you find that agreeable or disagreeable?—(*affirms*)—Yes, what?—Agreeable or disagreeable?—(*she rubs her hands together*)—It tickled you?—(*affirms very distinctly*)—You probably have very delicate fingers?—(*no answer*)—And then,—you gave the head to your mother?—(*affirms*)—Why?—(*shrugs her shoulders*)—Because it was already dead?—(*nods sadly*)—And you wanted a live one?—(*affirms*)—Yes, freshly cut human heads don't keep very long!——Tell me, did you ever like or, as they say, love any one of these people?—(*doesn't know what to say, finally shakes her head*)—Herod?—(*shakes her head*)—John?—(*shakes her head*)—Your *mother*?—(*shrugs her shoulders, then shakes her head*)—But your head, you liked that?—(*affirms emphatically*)—

DEVIL (*suddenly leaps up*): Child, you're just what I need!—(*walks toward her*) You've got

the makings of something great!—(*comes up from behind and wraps her lightly in his arms*)
Today you'll follow me into my bed chamber!—

THE FIGURE (*can be heard moaning deeply and audibly*)

> *During the following, transparent black gauze screens and shadows descend over the*
> *field of the dead, as well as over the foreground, gradually obscuring the entire scene.*

DEVIL (*gently leading the figure off to the right with him*): We have great things in store for
you!— You'll be the mother of a fabulous line, with which no aristocrat will be able to compete!— Your descendants will have neither blue nor red blood in their veins, but something
much more extraordinary.— And you'll be their mother.— Your qualities are unique in my
grand, enormous realm!— Even up there at court, our liaison is regarded with benign favor!—
(*He disappears with her, his voice trailing off in the distance.*) You can return to your sisters
tomorrow!— Our fiery temperament permits procreation and gestation to be completed in
an incredibly short time!— Our powers move conception and childbirth to within a few hours
of each other.— Come, my child, come!—

> *The field of the dead has now disappeared. The gauze screens fall ever more densely*
> *over the foreground, as well, so that the entire scene is soon completely darkened.— In*
> *the distance one hears a piercing, female scream!—Then it is black night and the curtain*
> *falls.*

Act Four

> *In Heaven. A sumptuously decorated room in pink.* MARY *is sitting on her throne,*
> *elegantly outfitted, surrounded by predominantly younger angels in light, colorful cos-*
> *tumes, who are either sitting on the steps of the throne or reclining in artistic poses.*
> *One of them is holding a book and reading aloud from Boccaccio with the monoto-*
> *nous, flat voice of a schoolgirl.*

ANGEL (*reading*): "....Agiluffo, King of Lombardie, according as his Predecessours had done
before him, made the principall seate of his Kingdome, in the Citie of Pavia, having
embraced in marriage Teudelinga, the late widow of Vetario, who likewise had beene King
of the Lombards; a most beautiful wife and vertuous Lady, but made unfortunate by a mis-
chance. The occurances and estate of the whole Realme, being in an honorable, quiet and
well settled condition, by the discreete care and providence of the King; a Groom apper-
taining to the Queene's Stable of Horse, being a man of meane and low quality, though
comely of person, and of equall stature to the King; became immeasurably amorous of the
Queene. And because his base and servile condition had embued him with so much understanding, so as to know infallibly, that his affection was mounted beyond the compasse of
conveniencie: wisely hee concealed it to himselfe, not acquainting any one therewith, or
daring so much, as to discover it either by lookes, or any other affectionate behaviour. And
although hee lived utterly hopelesse, of ever attaining his hearts desires; yet notwithstand-
ing, hee proudly gloried, that his love had soared so high a pitch, as to be enamoured of a
Queene. And dayly, as the fury of his flame increased; so his carriage was farre above his
fellowes and companions, in the performing of all such serviceable duties, as any way hee
imagined might content the Queene. Whereon ensued, that whensoever shee roade abroad
to take the ayre, shee used oftner to mount on the Horse, which this Groom brought when

shee made her choise, than any of the others that were led by his fellows. And this did esteeeme as no meane happinesse to him, to order the Stirrope for her mounting, and therefore gave dayly his due attendance: so that, to touch the Stirrope, but (much more) to put her foote into it, or touch any part of her garments, he thought it the onely heaven on earth.—But, as we see it oftentimes come to passe, that by how much lower hope declineth, so much higher love ascendeth...."

MARY (*interrupting*): Aren't these two ever going to get together?

READING ANGEL (*stops reading*):——I don't know, Everlasting Virgin.

MARY: Take a look: how many more pages are there in the story?

READING ANGEL (*counting carefully*): Twenty more, Most Blessed Mother of God.

MARY: That's awfully long; can't we skip over some of it? (*is handed the book*)—Well, I think it gets a bit livelier here. Start reading! (*gives the book back*)

READING ANGEL (*as above*): "....so much the higher love ascendeth; even so fell it out with this poore Groom; for, most irksome was it to him, to endure the heavy waight of his continuall oppressions, not having any hope at all of the very least mitigation. And being utterly unable to relinquish his love divers times he resolved on some desperate conclusion to *die*...."

> At this moment THE WOMAN, *a young, blooming creature dressed in an all-white gown, with black hair and black, deep-set eyes that hide a consuming but still latent sexuality, steps timidly over the threshold; everyone is aghast and leaps up, as if blinded by the newcomer; the angels remain motionless and fix their gaze on the Woman, unsure of what to do.*

MARY (*has stood up, imperiously*): Who is this person?—(*when no answer is forthcoming*) Who let you in?—Where are you from?—Are you from down there?—Are you dead?—Or something better?—A saint?—What do you want here?—Trying to upstage me?—Who gave you the right ....? (*begins to tremble*)

> At this moment the DEVIL *enters behind the Woman, out of breath as if late, and makes a deep reverence before Mary.*

DEVIL: Madam,—(*introducing the Woman*) may I introduce *my daughter*?

> The angels run off screeching to the left.

MARY (*descending the steps of her throne, with an expression of greatest amazement*): Ah!—

DEVIL (*waiting to see what her reaction will be; then after a pause*): Do you like her, I hope?

MARY (*hesitating, collecting her impressions*): Like?—No, she's too beautiful for that. This beast trumps everything in Heaven and on earth.—I was expecting a monster.

DEVIL: Madam, in order to...

MARY (*angrily interrupting*): 'Madam!—Madam!'—I am the Everlasting Virgin and Most Blessed Mother of God!—Don't you forget that!—(*casting a glance at the Woman*)

DEVIL (*very submissively, subdued*): *She* can't grasp such fine distinctions yet.—She's like a child.

MARY: What, can't she speak?

DEVIL: God forbid!

MARY: She doesn't speak any language?

DEVIL: She speaks the language that all women speak, the language of passionate seduction.

MARY: I think you went beyond what was in our program. — What is this exquisite person supposed to...?

DEVIL: Somehow, I had to make her...

MARY (*interrupting*): If that's what I had wanted, I could have taken one of my angels, I myself could have...

DEVIL: Oh, lovely lady, nevermore; you have forgotten...

MARY: Yes, yes! — Quite right! — Of course! — But why so dazzling? — A sheer delight! — (*turning to the Devil, softly*) Do you suppose I could sneak a little taste now?

DEVIL: Go ahead and admire her; she doesn't know anything yet.

MARY (*devours* THE WOMAN *with hungry eyes; then goes and kisses her in a sudden burst of passion*)

THE WOMAN (*recoils in fright*)

MARY (*overwhelmed*): Sheer enchantment! — Like a child! —

DEVIL (*with comic pathos*): "...emerging fresh and pure from the hand of the Creator!"

Tinted dry point etching by Leonor Fini for *Le Concile d'amour*. Geneva: Grafik Europa Anstalt, 1975. Courtesy of Richard Overstreet, La Galerie Minsky, Paris, and Neil Zukerman, CFM Gallery, New York. Copyright © Leonor Fini Estate.

MARY (*getting the gibe*): Oh — buffoon! — — Where did you get her?

DEVIL (*very affected*): Certain manufacturing secrets can't be revealed; — however — I can tell you who the mother is.

MARY: Ah!

DEVIL: A certain *Salome*, — the lovely beheader — who got herself a warm human head with one twirl of her dancing leg.

MARY (*trying to remember*): Don't *We* have her up here?

DEVIL (*dryly*): No, no! — You don't have people like that up here.

MARY (*mesmerized*): "....you don't have people like that up here! ...." And so dazzling! —

DEVIL: What you are seeing, she has from her mother.

MARY: From her.

DEVIL (*sarcastically*): And some other things you can't see!

MARY (*glancing at him, knowingly*): Of course! — What else? —

DEVIL: Her father's traits won't show up until later on; — — after she's had some practice....

MARY: I can believe that!

DEVIL: I was in one of my glorious moods!

MARY (*who can't take her eyes off the figure*): And this chaste rapture, these incomparable eyes, this breath of heavenly pleasure, this ideal of superhuman goodness and mercy, you say, shall poison and ruin mankind? ....

DEVIL: That it *shall.*

MARY: *Should it?*—Can it?—

DEVIL (*scornfully*): *Can* it?—Let me tell you how strong the poison inside of her is: after two weeks, whoever touches her will be staring out at the world with eyes like glass marbles; his thoughts will congeal and he'll be gasping for a whiff of hope like a fish out of water; after six weeks, he'll look at his body and ask: Is that me?; his hair falls out, his eyelashes fall out, his teeth fall out; jaws and joints become shaky; after three months, his entire skin is perforated like a sieve, and he stands in front of shop widows, wondering if he can buy a new suit of skin; despair not only constricts his heart but also drips out of his stinking nose; friends observe one another, and those in the first stage of the infection poke fun at those in the third or fourth; after one year, his nose drops into his soup bowl, and he goes out to try and buy a rubber one; then he withdraws, moves to another city, changes his job, becomes pitying and sentimental, won't hurt a flea, develops moral principles, plays with little insects in the sun and envies the young trees in springtime; he becomes Catholic—if he was Protestant; and Protestant—if he was Catholic; after two, three years, his liver and other large organs are like rocks in his body, and his mind turns to lighter foods; then an eye begins acting up, in another three months it's closed shut; after five, six years, convulsions shoot through his body like fireworks; he still takes walks and frequently checks to see if he has any feet attached to his body; a little later, he prefers to stay in bed; he loves the warmth; one day, after about eight years, he picks up a bone from his own edifice, sniffs it, and tosses it aside in horror; then he starts getting religious, more religious, most religious; he loves those leather-bound, gilt-edged books with a cross on them; and after ten years, his emaciated body will be lying there, a withered skeleton, his mouth pried open in a yawn toward the ceiling, asking "Why," and dies.—The soul will then belong to you!—

MARY (*turning away in disgust*) Ugh!

DEVIL (*surprised*): What?—Didn't I do my job well?—Wasn't this what you ordered?—

MARY (*burying her face in her hands, sobbing*): Oh, those poor people!

DEVIL (*interrupting*): ...will remain both *in need of redemption* and *capable of redemption!*—

MARY (*turns around again and stares at the Woman in utter fascination. The Woman maintains her original naïve pose, beautiful and unaware*)

    Sounds of people approaching can be heard offstage.

MARY (*coming to her senses and rushing to the door*): No, no one should come in here!—(*after going to the door to see who is approaching*) No, my son should not come in; can't come in; may not come in!—(*returning, wildly*) Get that woman out of my house!—Do whatever you want with her; but go, go!—This instant!—

DEVIL (*pleading*): Dear Mary, Everlasting Virgin, Most Blessed Mother of God, I have a few requests, I think I deserve,.... You know....

MARY (*hastily*): Yes, yes!—You'll get your *staircase,*—but just get out, go!—

DEVIL (*whining*): And *freedom of thought!*—

Ink drawing by Alfred Kubin for private printing of *Das Liebeskonzil*, Munich, 1913. Courtesy of Eberhard Spangenberg. Copyright © Eberhard Spangenberg, Munich.

MARY: My friend, you already think much too much!—I'll see about what I can recommend;—but now go!

DEVIL (*sighing heavily, bows deeply before Mary, then escorts the Woman to the door with great dignity, allowing her to exit first*)

MARY (*stares open-mouthed at the departing couple*)

    The curtain falls.

Act Five

SCENE ONE

> *Rome. A hall in the papal palace; along the wall on the stage-right, a temporary altar has been erected, at which a priest is officiating; on the left are armchairs extending toward the center of the stage, some with prayer stools attached to them, on which are seated the Pope and his family, including Cesare and Lucrezia Borgia, Vanozza and Julia Farnese, with members of the Sacred College, bishops and archbishops, almoners, Burcard, the Master of Ceremonies, the Captain of the Vatican Guard and others belonging to the Pope's immediate retinue; at the extreme left, standing tightly packed behind the chairs and completely obscuring the end of the hall on this side, are clergy and lower Vatican officials, and way in the back are some servants, who are all following the holy service with greater or lesser attention. The entire hall is illuminated solely by the four large candles at the altar, so that the more distant parts of the room are cloaked in semi-darkness. In the background is a single large portal, which stands open.*

PRIEST at the altar (*who has been going about his tasks and whispering for a while, after a short organ prelude has concluded*) Hoc est enim Corpus meum.[7] *(the bustling and whispering continues)*— — Hic est enim Calix Sanguinis mei, novi et aeterni testamenti; mysterium fidei; qui pro vobis et pro multis effundetur in remissionem peccatorum.[8]

> *While the Pope is apparently sitting indifferently in the midst of his kneeling and standing guests, with legs crossed and hands folded in his lap, loud, gossipy chatter, especially from the female members, can be heard all around, which is repeatedly interrupted by a discreet "Pst!" of those standing behind them.*

PRIEST (*at the altar*): ....Hostiam puram, hostiam sanctam, hostiam immaculatum, ...[9]

> *Lucrezia passes a bag of candy around to her younger siblings.*

PRIEST (*at the altar*): ....Panem sanctum vitae aeternae, et Calicem salutis perpetuae....[10]

> *The younger children seem to be quarreling over the candy; some of it falls to the ground; they scamper to pick it up; scuffling and curses can be heard; chairs are shoved aside; the ladies try to control the little ones; the gentlemen admonish them to be quiet; the Pope looks over and smiles; repeated sounds of "Pst!— Pst!" from the back.*

PRIEST (*at the altar, in a loud voice*): ....Per omnia saecula saeculorum.[11]

All present (*mumble mechanically*): Amen.

> *Cesare has gotten up from his chair and walks over to his father, the Pope, with whom he quietly talks for a while, leaning over the back of his father's armchair; the ladies also begin subdued conversation among themselves; the children have calmed down and are munching their candy.*

PRIEST (*at the altar, in a low voice*): Agnus Dei, qui tollis peccata mundi....[12]

> *At these words, the Woman has suddenly stepped onto the threshold of the rear portal. A black figure can be seen disappearing behind her. She has the same naïvely enchanting bearing as up in Heaven, and is wearing the same youthfully modest white gown*

as before, from which there seems to emanate a brightness that is independent of the candlelight.

PRIEST (*concluding*) ....miserere nobis![13]

Intense excitement and a general unrest immediately seize all present, whose eyes remain fixed on the door; there quickly develops an inextricable mixture of admiring exclamations on the part of the men, juxtaposed with cursing on the part of the women.

PRIEST (*at the altar, as above*): Agnus Dei, qui tollis peccata mundi, Miserere nobis!.....

The unrest continues to grow; the Captain of the Guard has taken a few steps toward the portal; the servants press more forcefully from the side toward the center of the hall.

PRIEST (*at the altar*): Agnus Dei, qui tollis peccata mundi, Donna nobis pacem.[14]

Now the Pope has also stood up and stares fixedly at the door, where the Woman remains in her static pose; groups form and excitedly exchange opinions. Burcard, the Master of Ceremonies, has come forward to consult with the Pope, who simply ignores him. Little children can be heard screaming.

PRIEST (*concludes and says his*): Dominus vobiscum![15] (*its response:* "Et cum spiritu tuo,"[16] *is no longer audible*)

Now one hears shouts from the crowd, such as: "Who is she?"— "Where's she from?"— "A Neopolitan!"— "Get her out of here!"— "Stop! Stop!"—*The Pope's voice can be heard:* "Careful! Careful!"—

PRIEST (*at the altar, turns around and is shocked to see the confusion, but says his*): Ite missa est[17]—(*and thereupon gives his benediction, ignored by all*)

Now all leave their seats and press toward the door; the men push their way forward, shoving the women to the rear; the Pope, surrounded by his son, Cesare, the Master of Ceremonies and the Captain of the Guard, formally welcomes the Woman by escorting her to the center of the hall, amid a tumultuous surging on the part of the men and shouts and curses from the others.—The Priest has meanwhile made his reverence before the altar and exited to the right; a sacristan has entered and extinguishes the large candles in the prescribed manner.— In the semi-darkness thus created, where the Woman radiates as if magically illuminated, one can still see how the men wildly lunge toward the bright figure, whom the Pope has now firmly taken under his arm, while the Captain of the Guard draws his sword, Burcard raises his long, mighty arms in an attempt to restore calm, and Cesare repulses the attackers with his furious blows. The prayer stools are knocked over; here and there, daggers can be seen flashing through the air; from the rear come muffled screams of women, "Hey, help!"— "It's not me!"— "I'm not the one!"— "To arms!"— "Soldiers!"— *Lucrezia can be heard screaming:* "Cesare!— Cesare!— Mio papa.— Help!"—*Finally, the group around the Woman forces its way out the door; everyone frantically chases after them; the women rush off screaming to both sides;— and the curtain falls.—*

Final Scene

A street in Rome in front of the papal palace. Cold, wet, bleak dawn; on the corner, a flickering oil lamp has almost burned itself out.—Dead silence.—

A door to the papal palace quietly opens and out steps THE WOMAN, *her skirts loosely gathered, protecting her partially exposed breasts from the cold, with disheveled hair and hollow eyes, exhausted and battered; she quietly closes the door behind her; shuffles a few steps forward; she is wearing two different slippers, both too large; diamond jewelry in her ears and around her neck; she looks around timidly and cautiously; then the*

Ink drawing by Alfred Kubin for private printing of *Das Liebeskonzil*, Munich, 1913. Courtesy of Eberhard Spangenberg. Copyright © Eberhard Spangenberg, Munich.

DEVIL (*who has been standing unseen in the shadow of the eaves, hastily leaps out at her, imperiously*): Now on to the cardinals! Then to the archbishops! Then to the ambassadors! First to the ambassadors of the Italian states; then to the foreign ambassadors! Then to the camerlingo! Then to the Pope's nephews! Then to the bishops! Then through all the monasteries! Then to the rest of the human pack!—Hustle along now, and stick to the rank order!—(*The Woman slowly exits.*)

(*The curtain falls*)

(*The End*)

Panizza's Notes

1. Burcardi (Alexander VI's Master of Ceremonies), *Diarium.* Nouvelle édition par Thuasne. 3 vols. Paris, 1885.
2. Out of the depths have I cried unto Thee, O Lord; Lord, hear my voice; Let Thine ears be attentive to the voice of my supplication; If Thou, Lord, shouldst count our sins, who shall stand? My soul hopeth in the Lord; From the morning watch even until night; For with the Lord there is mercy; and with Him is plentiful redemption; and He shall redeem us from all our sins.
3. A famous hetaera of her time, who was later executed.
4. Charles VIII of France, who had just captured Naples.
5. These spectacles at the court of Alexander VI were known as battaglie d'amore, love fights.
6. Come, Holy Spirit, and send a ray of your light from heaven. Come, father of the poor. Come, giver of goods. Come, light of our hearts. Without your name, nothing is in man. Nothing is free of harm. Wash away what is sinful, refresh what is dried up; heal what is wounded. O divine light, fill the hearts of your faithful.
7. For this is my body.
8. For this is the chalice of my blood of the New and eternal Testament; the mystery of faith; which shall be shed for you and for many unto the remission of sins.
9. A pure Host, a holy Host, an immaculate Host.
10. The holy bread of eternal life, and the chalice of everlasting salvation.
11. From eternity to eternity.
12. Lamb of God, which taketh away the sin of the world...
13. Have mercy on us!
14. Lamb of God, which taketh away the sin of the world, grant us peace.
15. The Lord be with you.
16. And with thy spirit.
17. Roughly: The service is completed.-

Chapter 3

Additions to the Second and Third Editions, 1896–1897

The Second Edition of *The Love Council*, 1896

The second edition of *The Love Council*, "augmented by a Dedication and a Prelude," appeared in 1896 and was also published by Verlags-Magazin Johann Schabelitz in Zürich. In addition to the aforementioned material, there are some relatively unimportant changes at the end of the second scene of the third act set in hell.

The Dedication and the Prelude that follows it are clear allusions to Goethe's *Faust*. In the first three stanzas of the Dedication, Panizza quotes the corresponding lines verbatim from Goethe's Dedication and rejects them as being too conservative and elegiac. For Panizza, the modernist, the Weimar classicist was much too old-fashioned, too reactionary and "too softish." Contrasting with the lofty language of the Goethe, the Privy Councilor, Panizza championed another mode of speech, that of naturalism: "today the people speak out."

Panizza, who had belonged to Munich's Modern Life Society since 1890, viewed himself as a modernist revolutionary: instead of beautiful forms draped in "folds of antiquity," in his verse "gangly skeletons" can be seen to "jump out of bed stark naked." He preferred Schiller and wished to have nothing to do with Goethe's backward-looking "sentimentalities." Art was to be provocation, parody and protest.

Panizza not only attacked the literary canon, he also increasingly challenged civil authority. His model was always Martin Luther, who lambasted entrenched authority in his crude vernacular.

Unlike the Dedication, the subsequent Prelude does not represent an aggressive contrast to Goethe's original Prelude in *Faust*. Whereas in the Dedication Panizza praised "the people" as pointing the way to the future, in the Prelude he warns us to beware of "the masses, always allied with evil." This rather contradictory attitude toward "the masses," which is already apparent among early "revolutionary" 19th-century authors such as Georg Büchner, reflects the distance between the Modern Life Society and social democracy. Compared to their contemporary literary colleagues in Berlin, the politics of the Munich modernists usually had a more conservative and nationalist orientation.

One important issue shared by the Munich modernists is expressed in the Prelude, which relates to art, politics, sex and religion. At the end of this scene, the producer mentions that he first has to submit the play to the state censorship authorities, "otherwise they'll delete the best passages." More than any of his contemporaries, Panizza suffered under the repressive censorship of the Wilhelmine Empire. For the past half-decade, he had been prosecuted under Paragraph 184, forbidding distribution of obscene publications, and especially Paragraph 166, dealing with offenses against religion. It goes without saying that the clumsy efforts at censorship usually backfired, in that the ensuing free publicity enabled the often marginal artists to reach a larger audience.

Dedication

"You approach again, wavering figures,
Who long ago appeared before my dimming eyes?"—
That's right!— Yet these are other forces,
Another tune, which their soul is fiddling.
We don't wrap ourselves in folds of antiquity,
Revealing the curve of a beautiful leg.
Today we jump out of bed stark naked
And present ourselves as gangly skeletons.
"Are you bringing back the images of happy days?"—
Oh, no! Instead we look to the *future*.
What is *coming*— that's our prime question today;
Don't bother us with pretty elegies.
What's the point of mourning the past
And similar sighs and murmurs?
Sentimentalities don't do any good today!
What's dead is dead!— What's alive should speak!
"They don't hear the following songs,
Those souls, to whom I sang the first ones?"—
No, no! There has since been a massive crush
That devoured the strains of harps and lyres.
In the terribly bloody stampede
Whoever could not stay on top fell down.
Poets died, and books in the heat of battle;
Even publishers like Cotta were ruined!
— What? You no longer speak the language of Goethe?—
No! Another language has emerged.
Goethe is too hoity-toity for us today,
The sound of his Aeolian harp too softish.
Not cabinet ministers — today the people speak out,
A signal flame has risen in the sky:
We want to scream, shout, lament,
Give voice to our soul's deepest misery!

Prelude

PRODUCER
ACTOR
DIRECTOR
PLAYWRIGHT

————

PRODUCER
The theaters are empty and so are our cash registers,
The public avoids us like a box of poison.
We have loads of plays,
But folks don't like these plays.
Nothing but crash-bang-wallop, mayhem, shooting,
— Then the police usually aren't far behind —
And people shouting, dubious jokes, catch-words:
In the audience they're holding their noses...

DIRECTOR
You just have to connect it to an *idea*.

ACTOR
Nope, nope!—*Bias!*—For God's sake don't!

PRODUCER
What do you mean "bias"?!—Let me find something beautiful!

ACTOR
Beauty slaps truth in the face.
The playwright should stick to the *plot*,
And show himself to be *objective*. No other way!

PRODUCER (*pointing to the* ACTOR)
Are you "objective"—with your legs,
Wigs, stilts, humps and pomades?!—

ACTOR
That's something else!—That's just hollow pretense,
And it has to be; for that the stage...

PRODUCER (*indignantly*)
Leave me alone with your jargon!—
If I dare to produce tragedy
Then it has to be written accordingly;
And I want tears, misery, guilt and punishment:
They should be sobbing again in their orchestra seats,
Before they gratefully return home.

ACTOR
You are totally breaking the rule.

PRODUCER
I've never stuck to rules!

ACTOR
You are bringing up the same old stuff.

PRODUCER
An artist is someone who can draw a full house!

ACTOR
And then the theater becomes a shabab,
Where everyone is just striving for pathos
And somersaults, pirouettes, warbling
With power cheering à la *Schubart, Schiller.*

DIRECTOR
Gentlemen, it seems the argument has gone on too long.
The important thing is *what* is being acted.
Some people wear their clothes tight, others loose,
Since each is just concerned with *his* measurements.
Let each wear what suits him best —
And study your lines well! —
Look, the man over there in the long robe,
Ask him, and his let genius reign!

(They have all noticed the dramatist, lost in deep thought, who is about to walk past them in the background.)

PRODUCER
Hey, friend, are you just coming from Parnassus?
I can tell from the way you walk and your expression;
Surely you were talking to *Clio, Euphrosne*—
And here the style, the role — joking aside,
You do still write for the German stage —
May I ask, what in your breast
Awakens the diverse, chaste muses? —

DRAMATIST (*dryly*)
I'm just heading back from the brewery — Pardon, gentlemen!
It's not normally my favorite place;
I'd much prefer to dwell in solitude,
Where my intellect would have been richly fertilized —
Just to find some material there, as fashion dictates,
I was engaged in drinking games —
But from the midst of that steamy place
I was driven in my mind to heaven, hell...
What happened around me, my ear did not perceive,
Transported as I was to distant horizons,
Only faintly did I perceive the drunken choir
As I knelt before the Trinity...

ALL THREE (*rush toward him*)
You wrote a play!

ACTOR
Hell appears in it!?

PRODUCER
I see it opening up fantastically!

DIRECTOR
Did you use meditation, flying machines?

ACTOR
Can I have the role of the devil?

DRAMATIST (*steps back, seriously*)
I warn you!...

PRODUCER (*seizes the script from him*)
Let's have it!— You never know
When you succeed in getting a smash hit;
You write all night and into the morning,
You've wrestled with devils and with God,
And then, when it's finally ready for the stage — look,
You're almost overcome with melancholia.

DIRECTOR (*to the* DRAMATIST)
Let me see it!

PRODUCER (*extending his hand to settle things*)
I'll take it! I'll take it blindly!
And later we'll discuss royalties.

DRAMATIST (*more seriously*)
I'm warning you about the play!...

PRODUCER (*soothingly*)
What can it be?—

DRAMATIST
Must, what the dramatist has envisioned in a serious hour,
When he was upset, feverish and alone,
Be brought right onto the stage, be discussed everywhere
And shouted about in the market place?
The masses, always allied with evil,
Immediately blow up every spark into a blaze.....

PRODUCER
The guy has a hit!— Move him along!
I'll go right away to the costumer and the tailor.

DIRECTOR
(*pushing the resisting* DRAMATIST *away with the help of the* ACTOR)
Let's read it!—

PRODUCER (*to the reluctantly yielding* DRAMATIST)
Just go along with the two of them!
Then come to the rehearsal, if more script is required!
(*Leafing through the manuscript while the others exit*)

I'll also have to submit it to the censor,
Otherwise they'll delete the best passages.
The police station is not exactly the best place
To distinguish between "fallen regimes" and "fallen angels."
(*He closes the script and holds it up with his left hand.*)
But if I make it through all the winding challenges,
I'll once again see packed houses. (*Exit.*)

The Third Edition of *The Love Council*, 1897

The following Foreword, the three pages in Tyrolean dialect at the beginning of Act IV and the thirty-five pages of "Critical Responses" were added to the third edition of 1897, also published by Schabelitz in Zürich. The Foreword, in which Panizza vigorously denies "that the author is crazy," does reveal something about the author's unstable mental health at the time of its writing. He sarcastically refers to his own work, which had been outlawed as blasphemy, as "something willed by God," and to himself majestically as an "author by the grace of God." The blasphemer as a moral crusader? If we knew nothing about this man's mental history, we might just take this text to be a sarcastic parody.

Surely it is absurd for an atheist such as Panizza to seriously praise the "divine right of authors." He publicly identified himself as an atheist during his 1895 trial. He later expressed his religious convictions, or lack thereof, even more clearly in his private diary entries, for example: "I believe in no God of any kind, nor in any personal intelligences which, without being humans of flesh and blood, would be capable of having an effect at any time or any place on our physical existence" (Diary 61, 21 November 1895 to 31 May 1896, cited in Müller, *Der Pazjent* 88).

The warning at the end of the Foreword for "the public, the parliament, the ministers, the princes, the Kaiser" to simply accept his writings for "what they are," clearly points in the direction of his future delusions. However, Panizza does not yet view Emperor Wilhelm II as his "personal adversary" and the "public enemy of mankind and its culture (*In memoriam* 17), as he would several years later.

The children mindlessly repeating their prayers at the beginning of the fourth act clearly reflect Panizza's full-blown, unmitigated anti–Catholicism. In this expanded scene, even Mary expresses her disgust with this so-called Mariolatry when she screams: "God, I have it up to here with this Catholicism!" The previous year, the author had shown a similarly visceral antipathy in his bid farewell to the city of Munich, when he referred to Bavarian Catholicism as a "religion of bones, flesh, milk, hair and reproductive organs" (*Abschied* 14). It should also be pointed out that it is, of course, quite impossible to adequately reproduce the children's broad Tyrolean dialect in English.

Although this third edition of *The Love Council* apparently did not sell as well as the first two, it is the final one edited by Panizza and thus might be considered in some sense to be "definitive." The thirty-five pages of appended "Critical Responses" were collected by Panizza from letters, personal statements, newspaper articles and other sources. They appear separately in Chapter 11 of the present volume.

Foreword to the Third Edition

The author owes a few words of explanation in regard to this third edition. The public may have already wondered about the fact that this book, though confiscated by the district attorney, continues to be published again and again. It probably has already assumed that the author is crazy. However, that is not the case. The public simply has no idea of the circumstances under which an author produces and publishes the contents of his inspiration. It simply does not know that the jewel which he alone possesses, and which enables him, independently of all other factors that might come into consideration, to follow only his inspiration and bring it to full expression: *the divine right of authors.* The divine right with its weighty obligations, its never-ending, continuous efforts and labors, with its terrible responsibility to God alone, from which no human being, no district attorney, no parliament, no people [Volk] can absolve him. This is the jewel, which certainly was more or less known before, but which has only recently been comprehended in utter clarity by authors and also made clear to the people [Volk]. It would, therefore, be good if the public, the parliament, the ministers, the princes, the Kaiser and the district attorney accepted our writings for what they are, as something willed by God, and not waste time asking questions or carping.

Zürich, 4 September 1897
Respectfully,

Oskar Panizza
Author by Divine Right

Act Four

In Heaven. A sumptuously decorated room in pink. MARY *is sitting on her throne, elegantly outfitted, surrounded by predominantly* YOUNGER ANGELS *in light, colorful costumes, with books, school notebooks, writing slates in their hand; they are either sitting or kneeling on the steps of the throne or reclining in artistic poses. It is school-time. To the right, halfway in the coulisse, stands the* SCHOOLTEACHER, *a tall, unspeakably skinny man in a long black suit, with an embittered, clean shaven face and a combed-over bald head.*

MARY (*playing with a peacock feather*): Recite your prayer!

CHILDREN (*in unison, in a broad, screechy tone, with false intonation and a rhythm dictated by the principle of least sound resistance*): Hael Maery, full of graece, the Loward is with thee; blessed aert thou among women, blessed is the fruit of thy womb, Jeasus Christ — Hael Mary, Mother of Goad, praey for us poor sinners, naow and at the houar of our death...

MARY (*appalled*): Oh, for God's sake, where did you learn that?

CHILDREN (*jumbled, gurgling*): In Tyroll — in Tyroll — in the beautiful land of Tyroll!

MARY (*appalled*): God, what a messed-up bunch!—(*Looks around to the* TEACHER, *who stands emaciated at the right of the stage.*) Can't you teach the children to at least pray meaningfully, instead of just rushing to finish as quickly as possible?

TEACHER (*miserably, with a throaty voice*): That's no longer possible, most blessed Mother of God, their throats are completely deformed in one direction — the result of a thousand-year practice.

MARY: Why are you making such a miserable face?

TEACHER: I don't feel well — I always feel so bad...

MARY (*to herself*): God, the man is hungry and too decent to say anything — (*aloud*) Are you still paid so miserably?... Now come into heaven and bring along your insatiable hunger from earth — unfortunately, I can't offer you anything — the only things eaten up here are hosts — I can't even offer you a sip of wine — we don't tolerate any Utraquists up here — you should have a filling meal shortly before your death — go collect something from your neighbors — a few pennies worth of beer from the men — and perhaps some lard from *among the women*...

CHILDREN (*responding to the cue*): ... and blessed is the fruit of thy womb, Jeasus Christ, Amen! — Holy Mary, Mother of Goad...

MARY (*appalled*): For God's sake, were you wound up? — I didn't push the button! — They're just like machines...(*to the* TEACHER). You have to teach the children — in spite of their hunger — to pray with *meaning* — even after 2000 years — so that when I mention the word *lard*, they don't bring up *the fruit of my womb*!...

CHILDREN (*correcting, in unison*): "...fruit of *thy* womb!..."

LITTLE CHILD'S VOICE (*solitary, naïve*): ....hour of our death, Amen...

MARY (*overcome*): — Oh, how sweet! — — What's your name, honey?

LITTLE CHILD'S VOICE (*as above*): ... Maria Ebner — master chimney sweep's daughter from Kleinhüttenbach — they throwed me in the water cause they was six of us — and my papa didn't make any more — and ma said I'd be an angel right away...

TEACHER (*wiping away a tear*): Yep — that's the way they are down there — in that region — between Brixen and Kufstein...

CHILDREN (*in unison*): In Tyroll — in Tyroll — in the beautiful land of Tyroll!

MARY (*with a grimace*): God, I have it up to here with this Catholicism! (*makes an expression of disgust*) — — (*resolutely*) Let's talk about something else! — — Take your books out! — — (*to the* TEACHER) You can go and rest up a bit — (*to the* CHILDREN) Where were we? — Now read nicely in High German! — In Prussian!...

LARGER ANGEL (*reads, while all the others open their books, from one of Boccaccio's novellas, with a broad, scratchy voice lacking in intonation*): "....Agiluffo, King of Lombardie, [...]"

Chapter 4

The Early Decades, 1853–1894

The available Panizza family history, though certainly extensive compared to most families, is often of a superficial or personally biased nature. Oskar Panizza's mother, Mathilde (1821–1915), herself a prolific writer and a key figure in her son's life, writes that she was descended from an aristocratic French Huguenot family by the name of de Messlère. Much of her family history is contained in Mathilde Panizza's 700-page memoirs. Part I, completed in 1888 at the age of sixty-seven, includes addenda extending to 1895. Part II covers the period from 1895 to 1911. In 1981, a typescript of these handwritten reminiscences was prepared by her granddaughter, also named Mathilde (Tilly) Panizza Harder (1899–1935), then in her eighties. A dozen copies of the complete memoirs, *Die Memoiren der Mathilde Panizza*, were privately printed in 1996 by the elder Mathilde Panizza's great-great-great-granddaughter, Antje Redlich, née Wirth (b. 1941). Further biographical material on Oskar Panizza comes to us from the deacon who eventually became his legal guardian. Friedrich Lippert's *In memoriam Oskar Panizza* was published in 1926, five years after his ward's death. The most complete and authoritative information about the physician-turned-author is to be found in the more recent biographies by Michael Bauer and Jürgen Müller.

One branch of the Huguenot de Messlère family escaped persecution by emigrating from France to a safely Protestant German region in 1685, settling in Sonnenberg, Saxony, and changing their name to Mechthold. Oskar's maternal grandmother, a descendant of these Mechtholds, married a merchant by the name of Speeth. Although she had secured a written agreement to raise their children in the Protestant faith, Speeth, after moving to Catholic Würzburg, decided to break this contract. Thus Panizza's mother, Mathilde (b. 8 November 1821), was baptized a Catholic. But in 1833, two months before her first communion, her father died, and this enabled the girl to return to the Protestant fold.

Oskar's paternal grandfather, Leopold Panizza, came from a family of fishermen in Bellagio on Lake Como. He had been a traveling salesman who settled down in 1794 and established his own business in Würzburg. Leopold married a local girl who bore him fourteen children, of whom the youngest, Karl (b. 30 September 1808), was Oskar's father. Karl is depicted as a ne'er-do-well, a man of limited talents and ambitions, who nonetheless learned enough about the hotel trade to manage several such establishments himself. Oskar describes him as "passionate, eccentric, irate, and a clever man of the world; a poor manager of household affairs" (*In memoriam* 9). A bigoted Catholic tyrant not unlike his father-in-law, Karl was an unstable character who inclined towards gambling, an undistinguished husband and a worse father.

Oskar Panizza's parents, Karl and Mathilde, met at a concert in Würzburg on 6 January 1844, when he was thirty-five and she had just turned twenty-three. For Mathilde, it was hardly love at first sight, since Karl initially caught her attention only by his large size. She thought he might be a singer named Breiding, about whom she merely "knew that he was supposed to be extraordinarily fat" (*Memoiren* I, 42). Five days after their first encounter at the concert, Karl gained Mathilde's reluctant consent to marry him through his persistence, impetuosity and repeated declarations of love. They were married three months later on 17 April after a brief and turbulent engagement, which more than once came close to being called off. Financial and religious disputes began almost immediately, with Karl insisting that all their children would have to be raised Catholic, otherwise his family would disown him. The two families finally arranged a compromise, whereby all offspring were to become Catholic or Protestant depending on whether their first child was a boy or a girl. Shortly before their wedding day, however, Karl led his unsuspecting fiancée out for an afternoon stroll which ended in the Catholic parish house, where the 23-year-old girl was confronted with prepared documents authorizing a Catholic education for all her children. If she refused to sign, then the marriage was off. She reluctantly consented and, although her first baby was a girl, all seven Panizza children were baptized in the Catholic faith — initially.

Oskar's elder sister, Maria, born in 1846, outlived all the other children, married a hotel proprietor in Bad Kissingen, Gustav Collard, and died in 1925. The second child, Felix, born in 1848, became a hotel proprietor in Hong Kong and died in 1908. In 1850, Karl and Mathilde Panizza purchased the Hotel Russischer Hof, a large resort hotel on the main promenade, right across from the central mineral bath house in Bad Kissingen. This establishment, which remained in the Panizza family until 1897, proved to be quite a success, even attracting such aristocratic visitors as Russian Czar Nicholas II and his family. A detailed, illustrated history of this landmark establishment, currently operated as a rehabilitation clinic by the state of Baden-Württemberg, was published in 2004 by Hanns Klüber.

Oskar Panizza's mother, Mathilde, née Speeth, around 1870. Photographer unknown. Copyright © 1996 Christine Harder.

Karl and Mathilde Panizza's next two children died very young. A boy, baptized Karl, was born two months premature in April 1849 and died the same day. The next child, Ida, was born a year later and died of dysentery before the age of two in 1852. Mathilde's fifth pregnancy produced a third son, again named Karl (b. 1852), who became a legal official (*Amtsgerichtsrat*) in Kiel and died in 1916. Leopold Hermann Oskar was born in his parents' hotel on 12 November 1853. Today, after years of considerable public controversy, an official historic plaque hangs on this grand building, reminding passers-by of Bad Kissingen's most prominent literary figure. The seventh and last child of this union, again named Ida, was two years Oskar's junior. She became blind at the age of twenty while pursuing her studies as a singer. Like the youngest of her brothers, she had a very difficult life and died in 1922, one year after Oskar's death.

Family history repeated itself when Karl Panizza died of typhus in November 1855, an event that Mathilde was able to write about in vivid detail thirty years later (*Memoiren* I, 98–113). On his deathbed, Karl Panizza blessed his five children and signed a document granting their mother permission to raise them in her own Protestant faith. In spite of this, Mathilde Panizza, whom son Oskar later described as being "energetic, strong-willed, with an almost masculine intelligence" (*In memoriam* 9) was forced to go to extraordinary lengths to secure a Protestant education for her children. His Catholic priest, Anton Gutbrod, challenged the validity of the document that Karl had signed on his deathbed. The Catholic diocese maintained it had a legal basis, in the form of the authorizations that Mathilde had signed eleven years previously, for demanding the children be brought up Catholic. Thus, she saw no alternative but to secretly leave Bad Kissingen with the children and bring them to a family in Prussia, where they were well hidden from Catholic investigators. Frau Panizza offered to renounce her Bavarian citizenship in order to live in Bad Kissingen as an alien, outside any official Catholic jurisdiction. When her efforts met with continued hostile resistance, she journeyed to Munich with the intention of pleading with King Maximilian II for special dispensation. However, the King refused to receive her, and when the authorities threatened to send her to prison, she was spared only due to her poor health. It was after years of toil and several lost trials that King Maximilian finally granted this persistent woman the permission to educate her children in the Protestant faith.

During the years that followed, Oskar's mother continued to be at odds with the law. For her charitable practice of feeding the poor, for instance, she was charged with "fostering mendicancy" and sentenced to three days in jail. This sentence was later commuted to house arrest, with Frau Panizza still maintaining that it was her prerogative to serve "people in silk clothes and those without, with shoes and without" (*Memoiren* I, 177). Throughout his life, Oskar was to continue these religious and legal battles, launching bitter and often savage attacks against the authoritarian dogma of the Roman Catholic Church. To some extent, his later literary activity served to avenge the sufferings and humiliations his beloved mother had been forced to endure.

One rather important aspect of the Panizza family history needs to be mentioned before proceeding with a discussion of its most infamous member. As a mature man, Dr. Panizza considered the incidence of mental disease and instability on his mother's side of the family to be a decisive influence on the formation of his own character. The Autobiographical Sketch he wrote in 1904, which appears in English for the first time in this book (Chapter 6), begins with the sentence: "Oskar Panizza [...] comes from a troubled family." One of his mother's brothers suffered from "religious madness" and died after a fifteen year sojourn in a Würzburg insane asylum. Another uncle committed suicide at a young age. An aunt is described as having been "psychologically abnormal and somewhat retarded." Oskar's younger sister, Ida, suffered from fits of depression at an early age and had a hysterical condition which twice led her to attempt suicide. He sums up his early home environment in the following words: "In the entire family there exists a prevalence of mental activity with an inclination toward discussing religious questions." It is also significant that his mother's books, published under the pseudonym Siona, deal almost exclusively with religious issues and themes.

Postcard of the Panizza family's Hotel Russischer Hof in Bad Kissingen, after 1876. Lithograph from *Souvenir de Bad Kissingen*. Bad Kissingen: Friedrich Weinberger, ca. 1900.

From the moment of Oskar's birth, there existed a very special relationship between him and his mother. She fell deathly ill right after giving birth, and her family expected the illness to be fatal. But this mystically inclined woman had a dream in which she was told she would indeed survive, a vision that kept her from despair and helped her pull through this difficult period. After her recovery, Oskar's baptism was celebrated with unequalled pomp and festivity; three clergymen were in attendance, two Catholic and one Protestant. Little Oskar did not remain the apple of his mother's eye for long, however. As a youth he was to cause her much aggravation, and by the time he was a middle-aged man it had reached the point where she feared the mere sight of him might be enough to kill her.

Karl Panizza died when Oskar was only two years of age, leaving the boy without a paternal role model whose example and authority he could emulate and respect. He developed slowly, had great difficulties learning to read and was often called "dummy" by his siblings. A quiet, introverted child, Oskar was a dreamer with a vivid imagination that he found difficult to harness. He came down with all the usual childhood diseases, but at the age of twelve, when he was sick with the measles, he experienced an extraordinary state of somnambulism: in broad daylight he left his bed in a deep trance, walked around his room and remained unconscious until someone found him as he knelt praying before his bed. This experience had prophetic significance for him; indeed, it is the only childhood incident which he bothered recounting in the seventeen-page autobiographical sketch he wrote as a fifty-year-old man in 1904.

Late Bloomer

In 1863, Oskar followed his two older brothers and was sent to Kornthal, Württemberg, to attend a Pietist school. He had great difficulties as a student and received low grades, still being very much the dreamer who saw no purpose in applying himself to subjects he found boring and irrelevant. He was confirmed there in 1868 and discussed the typically pietistic verse from II Corinthians 12, 9: "My strength is made perfect in weakness." According to his mother, Oskar once told her that "in his youth he had never had a friend" (*Memoiren* II, 205). The following autumn, he transferred to the humanistic *Gymnasium* in Schweinfurt, where he was forced to major in Latin, despite the fact that his Greek was decidedly better. During this period he lived at the home of a book dealer named Giegler, who conscientiously supervised the lad's academic work as well as his piano practicing. Within two years Oskar had successfully completed the *tertia* class and now expressed a strong desire to continue his *Gymnasium* studies in the far more exciting city of Munich.

Mathilde Panizza reluctantly submitted and allowed her seventeen-year-old boy to pursue his education in the Bavarian capital. She believed he would be kept under strict supervision in the parish house of her brother-in-law, Franz, and her childless sister, Maria. But the colorful metropolis proved too great a distraction for the excitable and hedonistic teenager, who discovered a host of activities far more interesting than anything to be found in his school books. His first year in Munich proved to be an academic disaster and he failed the *secunda* class. He pleaded with his mother that he was wholly unfit to realize her long-held wish that he become a clergyman; instead, he wished to be a singer or at least a businessman. But Frau Panizza, whose stubbornness had won out on many a previous occasion, firmly insisted that Oskar repeat the class while continuing his music studies. After this second year in Munich, he wanted more than ever to devote himself exclusively to a musical career, telling his mother that "at nineteen, one really ought to know what profession one wants to pursue" (*Memoiren* I, 241). Frau Panizza saw little point in forcing her openly rebellious son to remain at the *Gymnasium*. She did, however, extract the concession from him that he spend at least part of his time getting some 'practical' instruction while continuing his studies in singing at the Music Conservatory. Since he was too proud to attend the local trade school together with much younger boys, his mother had to pay for private tutoring in French, stenography and business mathematics. Despite his lackluster academic record, this nineteen-year-old dropout had a firm premonition that he was destined for greatness. In a letter to a former classmate at the Kornthal school, he describes how in October 1872 he "was suddenly overcome by inexpressible feelings that I had never previously felt [...]; all of a sudden I became absolutely convinced *that I was created to be a great man*" (Bauer 90).

By the spring of 1873 it had become quite obvious to Frau Panizza that her youngest son was not destined to be a success either as a singer or as a businessman. She could no longer bear to see him frivolously wasting his time and her money on these futile pursuits; it was high time the boy stopped deceiving himself. She therefore went to Munich and resolutely brought her nearly twenty-year-old son back to Kissingen with her. But there was really nothing for him to do at home except help out in the Hotel Russischer Hof, which Mathilde was operating with far greater success than her late husband. The hotel business, however, was not at all where Oskar's ambitions lay, and he let it be known that he hated his mother for what she was doing to him; he spent most of this period loafing and generally irritating his mother with this recalcitrant behavior. She wrote that "Oskar's behavior got more intolerable by the day: he had no real occupation and was at odds with himself. He never went to church, and when I returned home one Sunday, he stood by the front door in such a dilapidated suit that he resembled a degenerate waiter [...] like an artist, oblivious to external appearances" (*Memoiren* I, 244). Oskar told his sister Ida that their mother was the cause of his strange behavior: "Yes, I hate our mother, she disgusts me." When this got back to Mathilde, she instantly realized, "as if I had been informed of a child's death," that she could not keep Oskar at home any longer.

Frau Panizza decided to send her son to Nuremberg to work with his brother Karl in the Bloch banking firm. This proved to be yet another disaster, since Oskar Panizza displayed about as much talent and enthusiasm for banking as Heinrich Heine had a half-century previously. He also continued to behave inappropriately for a young intern, "he entered the office with a cap on his head and often a cigar in his mouth, without even saying hello, so that the young people were distraught about this and Herr Bloch had to forbid this behavior. He was, as far as I can recall, there for only a short time: numbers and nothing but numbers got him upset — he also let himself go as far as his clothing was concerned" (*Memoiren* I, 245). He defiantly misbehaved until his exasperated mother allowed him to resume his studies at the Music Conservatory in Munich.

Hardly had he resettled in Munich when he was called to military service. Life in the 7th Company of the 2nd Bavarian Infantry Regiment was considerably rougher than anything he had experienced to date, and he would have followed his natural inclinations and deserted, had not his mother pointed out to him the severe consequences of such an action. He utilized frequent disciplinary detentions to pursue his nascent literary interests. His captain once remarked: "I can't figure you out, I never know where I'm at with you" (*Memoiren* I, 249). The first of his numerous notebooks, begun in October 1873, shows the twenty-year-old eagerly sketching and composing music. It also reflects his development as a voracious reader on a variety of historical subjects from antiquity to the French Revolution, while exploring the literature of such disparate authors as Shakespeare, David Friedrich Strauss and Charles Darwin. Military service seems to have had something of a sobering effect on young Panizza. After a grave bout of cholera in the fall of 1874, he had become decidedly more serious about life, even showing signs of remorse over how he had been treating his mother.

Following his discharge, he returned to Munich and picked up his singing career where he had left off. Although he was receiving very good grades in music, his intellectual horizons were now broadening and he began to audit lectures in philosophy at the Ludwig Maximilian University in Munich. It became clearer than ever to him that his unfinished *Gymnasium* training would be an obstacle to almost any desirable profession, and he therefore resolved to complete his secondary education at all costs. With the help of private tutors, he painstakingly reviewed his academic subjects and was readmitted to his old *Gymnasium* in Schweinfurt where, at the advanced age of twenty-three, he completed the remaining class and finally received his *Abitur* degree. This was the first major achievement in the life of Oskar Panizza; it was a turning point inasmuch as it stabilized him, creating the necessary self-confidence and discipline to undertake more ambitious ventures.

He wasted no time in putting his newly earned degree to use. In 1876, when he returned to his favorite city, he enrolled not in the music conservatory but in the medical faculty of Munich's Ludwig Maximilian University. His mother seems to have been decisive in his choice of studies:

Oskar had not yet decided which subject to study: law or medicine. He asked me and also wrote to [uncle] Feez. "My plan," I told him, "when I supported your studies, was that you should become a clergyman — I would have been delighted if one of my sons had pursued this splendid profession with heart and soul; but since you now reject this preference, I would recommend doctor over lawyer. This is my opinion, since you ask." Feez also preferred that he become a doctor. Now he was resolved to study medicine [*Memoiren* I, 266].

It appears to have been one of the happier periods in his otherwise troubled life. He was almost totally absorbed by his medical studies and research, which he admits to having pursued "with great love and zeal" (*In memoriam* 10). His often critical mother recounts how "he was extraordinarily hard-working and punctual in attending his classes. He acquired a skeleton in order to pursue his studies more thoroughly, and often brought human body parts home in order to study them" (*Memoiren* I, 267). Professor Hugo von Ziemssen made Panizza one of his assistants and supervised his fledgling's work at the Clinical Institute. Writing in April 1879 to his friend and composer, Engelbert Humperdinck (1854–1921), Panizza refers to pursuing his political reading in the bathroom, thus making optimal use of his limited time (Bauer 96).

In the spring on 1878 he took a trip to Italy where, by his own account, he supposedly contracted syphilis. Although Panizza's own assertions were later repeated by his early biographers, no real evidence has emerged that the author actually contracted syphilis while a student or at any other period during his lifetime. He did indeed have a pronounced limp that likely resulted from a childhood injury, when, after a fall off a high monocycle, he suffered a fractured right shin that was not properly splinted. This curvature of his right tibia may have resulted in a chronic inflammation, which required him to wear an orthopedic device throughout his later life. Complementing his awkward limp, he cultivated a decidedly Mephistophelean outlook, dress and manner, which early in life earned him the moniker "Mephisto."

In 1880, after slightly less than four years of intensive work, Oskar became Dr. med. Panizza with his medical dissertation *On Myelin, Pigment, Epithelia and Micrococci in Sputum*. This study, by the young man who only a few years previously had been single-mindedly bent on pursuing a singing career, was so well received by his professors that they enthusiastically endorsed it with the distinction of *summa cum laude*. After a few months of working in a field hospital to complete his military obligation, he was promoted to *Assistenzarzt II. Klasse* in the army reserves. The successive years of rather restricting discipline first in the army, then at *Gymnasium*, medical school, and again in the army, had their cumulative effect on young Dr. Panizza. He had become so restless that he felt he could no longer remain in Munich. Thus, armed with numerous letters of introduction which von Ziemssen had written, he set off for Paris in 1881 to see what he could learn about French medical advances. Once in Paris, though, he hardly visited any hospitals; instead, he became absorbed in the study of French literature, especially drama, a genre in which he was later to attain his greatest distinction and notoriety.

Writing as Therapy

After half a year of somewhat surreptitiously following his literary inclinations in Paris, he returned to Munich in 1882 to assume the position of *IV. Assistenzarzt* at the Oberbayrische Kreis-Irrenanstalt, the district insane asylum in Munich. Another young colleague at this hospital was Emil Kraepelin, a brilliant physician who would go on to become one of the most influential psychiatrists of his time. It did not take long, though, before Panizza's former inability to hold down a permanent job began to manifest itself again. A combination of poor mental health, the desire to spend more time on literary pursuits and strained relations with his superior, the renowned psychiatrist and neuroanatomist, Dr. Bernhard von Gudden, forced him to leave after only two years. The sustained exposure to psychotic patients, as well as the frustrations and confusions besetting his own life, brought upon a deep state of depression which lasted almost an entire year. But Dr. Panizza, who had never lost sight of literature since his visit to Paris, managed to pull himself out of this state by a therapeutic activity which was wholly new to him: writing poetry. This was perhaps the most critical discovery in his life, for he came to believe that the only way he could maintain his psychological equilibrium was by constantly writing. With the exception of a few minor and temporary activities as a general physician, Dr. Panizza permanently abandoned the practice of medicine and "turned definitively to literature" (*In memoriam* 11).

This process of turning to literature involved several aspects. It meant that henceforth all activity was to be geared toward producing literary works, even if this involved sacrificing personal comfort and security. Aside from his own creative efforts, the books of other men began to occupy more and more of his time, as Panizza quickly evolved into a voracious, yet highly eclectic, reader. He went from the standard *Gymnasium* curriculum, opera libretti, and psychology textbooks, to French drama, Russian novels, German philosophy, English ballads and American short stories. His knowledge and appreciation of German literature ranged from the works of Luther and other Reformation polemicists to those of Schiller, the Romantics, Young Germany and his own contemporaries. Nobody who ever talked at length to Panizza failed to be impressed by his immense encyclopedic knowledge.

A final consequence of dedicating his life to literature was financial. In 1880, when Mathilde was ready to retire, Oskar's brother, Karl, took charge of managing the family hotel together with his brother-in-law, Gustav Collard. Oskar's brother Felix took over from Karl the following year. In 1883, following a bitter family feud, Collard was bought out and established his own hotel nearby. Eventually, Felix remained in charge, and in 1884, thanks to their mother, Oskar began receiving his financial interest in the estate in the form of 6,000 RM annually. Surveying Panizza's not exactly short life-span of sixty-eight years, we see that during only two of these, as Professor Gudden's psychiatric assistant from 1882 to 1884, was he entirely self-supporting. There were few other German modernist writers who were financially this well off, and this was due not to his own literary success, but rather to his mother's achievements as a hotel proprietress.

It is hardly surprising that Panizza's first literary effort was a poem he wrote for his mother back in 1871, occasioned by her fiftieth birthday. This poem is filled with love and gratitude, celebrating his mother's indomitable spirit and victorious struggles against overwhelming odds. His poetic output over the next one-and-a-half decades was rather modest, but after his major depression of 1884 and his discovery of writing as 'therapy,' he came to view poetic creativity as the highest form of human activity. The desire for fame and glory certainly cannot be discounted as a major factor in his decision to devote himself to literature. Writing twenty years later as a failed and forgotten poet, he curses the muse who seduced him away from the straight path with promises that remained unfulfilled:

> Damn you, he shouts, you who led my soul
> Down false paths, an errant will-o'-the-wisp, —

Who seduced me with deceptive fantasies,
And once so sweetly beguiled my foolish heart;—
You sang me songs with false allures,
To the lad of yore you spoke of fame and glory... [*In memoriam* 53].

The fruits of more than a year's sustained poetic productivity were collected in a 124-page book whose title, *Düstre Lieder* (1885, *Gloomy Songs*), reflects the somber mood of its contents. For the most part, the poems are rather crude constructions in jagged tetrameter, consciously inspired by the much-admired verse of Heinrich Heine. Though the collection failed to sell or arouse even a ripple of critical acclaim, Panizza says he felt "substantially elevated and refreshed as a result of this literary release" (*In memoriam* 11).

While working on his first collection of poems, he was also busy studying English language and literature with a Mrs. Callway in Munich. After submitting the manuscript to publisher Albert Unflad at the end of 1885, he left for England, where he remained for an entire year. Most of this time was spent in London studying old English songs and ballads in the British Museum, while still continuing his own poetic pursuits. When he returned to Munich in the fall of 1886, after a brief stay in Berlin, he compiled his second collection of poetry, which appeared the following year under the title *Londoner Lieder* (*London Songs*). This proved to be no more successful than his first poetry collection, and dismay at the lack of any public response to his poetic outpourings may have contributed to the slackening of his output. His third volume of poetry, compiled in 1888 and published in 1889 under the romantic title *Legendäres und Fabelhaftes* (*Legends and Marvels*), marked the beginning of a ten-year hiatus in poetic production. Panizza gradually lost interest in the smaller literary forms; what he had to say now would require prose, could no longer be confined to four-beat lines. One thing remained very certain in his mind, the realization that "intensive involvement with foreign languages and literary production proved to be the best antidotes for all kinds of psychopathic fits" (*In memoriam* 12). Towards the end of the 1880's Panizza experienced a renewed interest in the land of his forefathers. He studied Italian language and literature with a Signora Luccioli and made several more trips to Italy.

Early Prose

A gradual diminishing of Panizza's poetic output has already been noted, but this does not mean that he was doing any less writing. What occurred during the late eighties was a decided shift from poetry to prose, the latter not only more likely to appeal to a larger audience, but also more consonant with the general tenor of naturalism. His first book of prose fiction, *Dämmrungsstücke* (*Twilight Pieces*), appeared early in 1890 and is "dedicated to the memory of Edgar Poe." It is a collection of four stories, all fairly short except for the last one, which is 180 pages in length and represents the longest work of prose fiction written by Panizza. As the book's title implies, these stories are located in the twilight zone between day and night, reality and fantasy, sanity and insanity, reverence and blasphemy. Yet Panizza transcends his obvious literary ancestors, Edgar Allan Poe and E.T.A. Hoffmann, by his striking and consistent use of what can only be called the grotesque: a ludicrously realistic presentation of Christ's Passion by some wax puppets at a fair; the mass production of "perfect" human beings in a Meissen factory; a visit to the moon, whose lower-class inhabitants dwell in a ramshackle hut and subsist on monthly supplies of Dutch cheese. Panizza revels in grotesque fantasies, but the language with which he recounts these absurdities is essentially naturalistic, casual to the point of being flippant and meticulously accurate in detail, as one might expect from a clinician. At its best, Panizza's prose anticipates the far more popular grotesque writings of such twentieth-century authors as Franz Kafka, Samuel Beckett, Günter Grass and Friedrich Dürrenmatt.

Dämmrungsstücke received a modest amount of critical acclaim in the press and brought the author to the attention of Germany's leading literary figures. The most significant of these men in regard to Panizza's literary career was Michael Georg Conrad, who was also living in Munich at the time and had been editor of the influential journal *Die Gesellschaft* (Society) since 1885. The two Franconians became close friends. Between 1890 and 1896 Panizza published over forty articles in *Die Gesellschaft* on disparate topics, ranging from theater reviews to theoretical considerations of prostitution. Their friendship, cooperation and mutual esteem lasted through the middle of the 1890s, after which they became embittered enemies and wanted nothing to do with each other.

Panizza first met Conrad in the summer of 1890. As editor of one of Germany's leading avant-garde journals, Conrad's wide circle of literary friends included most of the writers who were active in Munich at the time: Frank Wedekind, Otto Julius Bierbaum, Max Halbe, Hanns von Gumppenberg, Anna Croissant-Rust, Georg Schaumberg, Julius Schaumberger, Wilhelm Weigand, and Ludwig Scharf. Berlin-based writers such as Ernst von Wolzogen and Maximilian Harden made frequent trips south to Munich and were introduced to Panizza. By the end of 1890, the obscure psychiatrist had not only gotten to know most of the Munich "moderns," as the young naturalists called themselves, but had begun to make quite an impression on them. Hanns von Gumppenberg writes that of the entire Munich literary circle, "probably the strangest character [was] the former psychiatrist and fledgling poet Oskar Panizza, a curious mixture of Old Franconian loyalty, theological, philological, medical, and scientific erudition, whimsical poetic fantasy, biting satire and daring exuberance" (*Lebenserinnerungen* 135).

Richard Weinhöppel, another member of Conrad's circle, was equally overwhelmed by Panizza's "eminent erudition and general wealth of knowledge" (Weinhöppel, *Visionen* viii). It almost seems as if his friends considered Panizza to be a walking encyclopedia:

> His stupendous erudition and his unusual memory had an amazing effect. He was one great reference book, which one never consulted in vain. He spiced his conversations with innumerable examples from the literatures of all countries and epochs [...] Panizza's ability to quote everything in its original language, and then to immediately render a perfect translation or comment extemporaneously, elicited astonishment and admiration from everyone. I was soon completely under the spell of this wondrous person and sought his company wherever I could; at that time my productivity, which had begun with such vehemence and self-satisfaction, stagnated completely: I felt so retarded compared to this omniscient man [Weinhöppel, *Visionen* ix].

Although his friends were impressed by his staggering erudition, no one describes Panizza as having been an overly serious or even bookish individual. Weinhöppel recounts how Oskar's "light blue eyes would flash with a devilish slyness, and the almost uninterrupted, Jesuit smile of his mouth stood in curious contrast to the incredible crude or frank statements he would make whenever we were discussing anything" (viii). This same impression was also mentioned by Ernst von Wolzogen, who wrote that Panizza came "from an arch–Protestant Franconian family and yet looked like an arch–Jesuit" (175). Writing some thirty years after their first encounter, von Wolzogen echoes his contemporaries when he maintains that "Oskar Panizza was probably the strangest character" among his Munich cir-

Members of the Gesellschaft für modernes Leben in Munich around 1893. From left: Otto Julius Bierbaum, Georg Schaumberg, Oskar Panizza, Michael Georg Conrad, Hanns von Gumppenberg and Julius Schaumberger. Photographer unknown.

cle of friends. He readily admits that "Panizza exerted a strong influence on me and belongs to the forerunners of my later conversion to anti–Christianity" (174).

Modern Life Society

In December 1890, M.G. Conrad founded the *Gesellschaft für modernes Leben* (GmL, Modern Life Society) in Munich. The original members included the sculptor Rudolf Maison, in addition to the authors Detlev von Liliencron, Otto Julius Bierbaum, Julius Schaumberger, Hanns von Gumppenberg and Georg Schaumberg. The GmL was the southern counterpart of the *Freie Bühne* (Free Stage), which had been established the preceding year in Berlin. The moderns in Munich were far less revolutionary in their demands for social reforms, and they were less consistent in their attempt to create a radical style of naturalism in literature. They were, however, angry young men determined to "naturalize" German society and rid German culture of what they felt to be the oppressive yoke of popular epigonic literature, epitomized by the writings of Paul Heyse. Except for Panizza, the only one to have made any significant contributions to modernism, the entire GmL group is largely forgotten today.

The GmL met periodically in the large assembly hall of the Isarlust inn, where individual members presented lectures or readings from their works, followed by a discussion with what was usually a fairly sizeable audience. What made these GmL meetings such a daring and exciting venture for their sponsors was the fact that there was a stringent censorship of the press in Wilhelmine Germany in general and Bavaria in particular. Thus, police officials could be expected to be present at every public meeting, and it was not unusual for GmL assemblies to be disbanded or their publications confiscated by the authorities. It is obvious why the Bavarian establishment should feel threatened by what was basically a staunchly Protestant libertarian movement. Aside from such foreigners as Zola, Ibsen and Strindberg, the intellectual roots of the GmL go back to Luther, Wagner, Nietzsche and Bismarck. The latter's abortive *Kulturkampf* had merely strengthened the Catholic political forces in Germany, and they were not about to see their entire culture subverted by a group of "bohemian" immigrants.

One of Panizza's presentations was a lecture on "Genius and Madness," which he delivered under the auspices of the GmL on March 20, 1891. It is a loosely structured, historical rambling through the topics of genius, talent, and madness as they relate to art and artists. His central thesis is Lombroso's idea that genius is precariously akin to insanity; genius is frequently lonely, miserable and sick, but sustained creative productivity can restore the artist to a healthful state. Although this concept could hardly be termed Panizza's intellectual property, he had indeed already applied this insight to his own creative development and achieved moderate results. Perhaps of greater psychological interest today are his discussions of hallucinations and model psychosis, hashish and the hallucinatory basis of religions. His encyclopedic literary survey ranging from Alfieri to Wagner is quite superficial, yet revealing as far as the author himself is concerned. His decided preference for Schiller over Goethe, for instance, was certainly not unique for his time, but his individual value judgments do seem quite extreme. Thus, he states of Schiller's play *Die Räuber* (1781, *The Robbers*): "Perhaps no literature of the world contains a bolder work" (11). Panizza ended his lecture with a glorification of Martin Luther, his revolutionary hero par excellence.

A great deal of prophetic significance has been ascribed to this lecture on genius and madness. Lippert concludes his monograph with the hope that "a small stone monument will be erected to him, to 'Genius and Madnes,'" (*In memoriam* 50). Weinhöppel flatly states that "it was his own diagnosis" (xv), a conviction echoed by Prescher half a century later, when he wrote that Panizza "anticipated his own fate" (Prescher 251). An indication that the author was indeed thinking about the possibility of becoming insane can be found in the memoirs of Max Halbe, who spent much time together with Panizza in Egern during the summers of 1892 and 1893:

> This proud, secluded heart thirsted for praise, for applause and fame as one who longs for a redeeming drink [...] The 40-year-old man saw his life's goal, which he was pursuing with a passionate determination, fade further and further into the distance. He had to pursue it, whether it was on a literary path or on that of an activist or a protestor against the hostile forces of his time. He had to seize it, whatever the cost; even if he had to pay with his life or his sanity. Already at that time he admitted to me in moments of confidence that things were not quite alright with him up there and would not come to a good end [*Jahrhundertwende* 72].

Against Prudery and Lies

"Die Unsittlichkeits-Entrüstung der Pietisten und die freie Literatur" (The Pietists' Moral Outrage and Free Literature) is the title of another lecture Panizza delivered under the auspices of the GmL at their seventh public meeting on 2 December 1891. It was published in a collection entitled *Gegen Prüderie und Lüge* (*Against Prudery and Lies*), which includes another lecture by Julius Schaumberger, as well as poems by Maurice von Stern and O.J. Bierbaum. The collection is part of a two-pronged protest against an increasingly prudish censorship and the appearance of Paul Heyse's play *Wahrheit?* (1892, *Truth?*) on the Munich stage. Panizza's lecture deals with the topic of prudery. In his usual manner, which includes a sweeping survey of past German writings, he refutes the assertion that moral standards are degenerating in modern literature. Beginning with Hrosvit von Gandersheim, he briefly discusses all the great writers from the Middle Ages through the nineteenth century who unabashedly wrote about the tempests of physical love. The point he was trying to make was simple, indeed: "Yes, ladies and gentlemen, all of German literature, which we have just surveyed, is one single chain of sensuality" (*Gegen Prüderie* 22). Not only would it be a departure from the "good old times" to censor the treatment of sex in literature, but a sheer impossibility: "We cannot command love. Love commands us. It is the 'summa lex' and the 'suprema voluntas!'—German love cannot be decreed in Potsdam!" (24). In keeping with his previous talk before the same forum, he ends with an admonishment for clerical prudes to bear in mind the dictum of their spiritual progenitor, Martin Luther: "Thu's Maul auf!—Hau fest d'rauf!—Hör' bald auf!" (25; "Open your mouth!—Hit 'em hard!—Keep it short!"). Four years later, Oskar Panizza was to present a similar survey of German literature in an attempt to prove himself innocent of charges brought against him for his infamous play, *The Love Council*.

Although none of this sounds very daring today, it must be borne in mind that Panizza was writing at the very beginning of what turned out to be a general sexual liberation movement that began in the 1890s with Richard Krafft-Ebing, Magnus Hirschfeld, Havelock Ellis and others. A decade before the publication of Sigmund Freud's *Interpretation of Dreams*, there were very few writers in Germany or anywhere else, for that matter, who could freely write about such topics as homosexuality, masturbation, venereal disease and hermaphrodism. Panizza's frank discussion of sexual topics continually annoyed the guardians of public morals, yet deeply impressed the young modernists, who compared him to the classics of erotic literature: "This brilliant individual with the piercing look of intellectual superiority and great worldly experience, with his vital brain, with his refined taste of a decadent *Weltanschaung* and his blasphemous audacity, had an appeal for us similar to the forbidden reading of a Boccaccio or Casanova when we were still in school" (Weinhöppel, *Visionen* ix). Naturalism helped pave the way for the acceptance of sex as a topic for discussion, literary presentation and scientific investigation. Perhaps due to his own personal situation, Oskar Panizza appears to have been at least as concerned with sexual topics as were his better-known writer-colleagues Max Halbe (*Freie Liebe*, 1890, *Free Love*), Gerhart Hauptmann (*Einsame Menschen*, 1891, *Lonely People*) or Frank Wedekind (*Frühlings Erwachen*, 1891, *Spring Awakening*). Throughout his literary career, he emerges as a pioneer in the struggle for literary freedom, a man who paid a dear price for asserting his right to uncensored publication.

The first work to bring Panizza into direct conflict with the law was a little story called "Das Verbrechen in Tavistock-Square" (The Crime in Tavistock Square), which appeared in a GmL anthology toward the end of 1891. His bizarre tale climaxing in plant masturbation was found offensive to public standards of decency. All copies of this anthology were confiscated by the police, and Panizza, along with Bierbaum, Conrad, Brand, Scharf and Schaumberger, was charged with violating paragraphs 166 and 184 of the *Reichsstrafgesetzbuch* (Imperial Penal Code). Although the Munich district attorney eventually dropped the charges, the adverse publicity certainly had its effect. Dr. Panizza, who had gradually risen to the rank of *Assistenzarzt I. Klasse* (Asst. Physician First Class) in the reserves, was formally admonished by the commander of his militia unit and ordered to withdraw from the GmL. When he refused, the military maintained its purity by brusquely discharging the physician who had written about roses and magnolias masturbating in a London square.

Working steadily through 1891, Panizza also developed his particular talent for penning critical and polemic magazine articles. Prior to this he had only written one article, but in 1891 he suddenly published over one dozen. Three of these were theater reviews which appeared in *Die Gesellschaft*; the others helped fill the pages of the GmL's journal, *Moderne Blätter*. Characteristically, we find the author writing on numerous different topics ranging from Wagner and literary criticism to suicide, sacrilege and capital punishment. Although he could write reasonably well on a wide variety of literary and social topics, Panizza did not require many years to develop a distinct preference for the religious polemic. By 1893, he had developed his expository style to the point where he was writing both articles and books on one of his very favorite topics, the Roman Catholic Church.

Whores and Dogs

Only one article for the entire year of 1892 can be found, a highly progressive study of prostitution which appeared in *Die Gesellschaft*. Not unexpectedly, the author begins with a fairly well-documented historical survey of his subject, including the usual references to Martin Luther. Far more indicative, however, of the tremendous influence this Protestant reformer had on Panizza is the zealous tone with which he vehemently condemns the hypocrisy of German morality. Although he views "woman" as the great seducer and temptress, he claims that prostitution "is as natural and necessary as marriage, and certainly older" (1180). Panizza appears to have had a special fondness for prostitutes, who may well have been his only sexual partners. Nonetheless, few authorities on the subject today would disagree with most of his conclusions: men, not women, are the prime cause of prostitution; prostitutes are human beings and should be treated humanely; the differences between wife and prostitute have often been exaggerated; men have no right to disparage prostitutes whom they have enjoyed; women who take care of men's intellectual and physical needs should be freely permitted to do so, even if they are working for money; existing laws governing prostitution are unjust, ineffectual, and unenforceable. Panizza's progressivism is apparent even down to his spelling, which here for the first time begins to deviate from traditional German orthography. Although only one word has been "liberated" from the conventional spelling in this article, it certainly was a fateful one in the life of Oskar Panizza: Sifilis (1162).

Most of the year 1892 was spent writing fiction. Besides preparing the stories which appeared the following year in the collection *Visionen* (*Visions*), he produced the delightful little Hoffmannesque animal diary, *Aus dem Tagebuch eines Hundes* (*From the Diary of a Dog*).

What begins as the harmless chronicle of a country dachshund, adjusting to a new master and the often absurd complexities of modern urban living, ends with a howl of profound existential despair. The book achieves its unsettling effect not just by criticizing human foibles and ridiculing grotesque philistines, but through the gradual shift of focus from man to dog, i.e., from other to self, Panizza is able to present an uncomfortably penetrating look at man — and himself.

It is hardly a coincidence that the closest Panizza ever came to writing a novel was from the point of view of a dog. He often described himself as feeling like a dog, and his poetry, prose fiction and drama offer numerous examples of this. Not only did he feel like a dog in the metaphorical sense, but he also felt an intimate kinship with an actual canine. When Panizza was living in his Munich apartment on Nussbaumstraße 5, his only steady companion was his pet terrier, Puzzi. Panizza's friend Max

Oskar Panizza with his dog, Puzzi, around 1895. Photograph by J. Reitmayer, Munich. Courtesy of Rainer Wirth, Bad Kissingen.

Halbe, in a letter written to his wife early in 1894, commented: "Panizza has not changed a bit! He is still living in his bachelor's quarters, and Puzzi keeps him company" (*100. Geburtstag* 52). Indeed, for eight years Panizza was rarely ever seen outside the company of his dog, to whom he would not merely speak but also read. There exists at least one formal portrait of master and dog, as well as a woodcut depicting Panizza and Puzzi in an affectionate embrace. When the dog died in February 1897, Panizza admitted to having loved Puzzi more than virtually "any other being in the world" (Bauer 198).

Despite his fondness for Puzzi, Panizza did spend a lot of his time with his human friends. According to Gumppenberg, their three favorite cafes were Stadt London on Frauenplatz, Parsival on Herrenstraße and the Arabisches Cafe on Müllerstraße, where the moderns would regularly meet and spend their afternoons. Theodor Lessing, writing his autobiography forty years later, remembers Panizza's apartment as a rather wild place. "Every young girl without a home or a place to stay was invited in by Panizza; and every young writer without discipline or future could dump his emotional baggage there" (*Lebenserinnerungen* 235). Panizza was far better off financially than even the more successful writers of his time, and he distinguished himself by his repeated generosity toward his less fortunate colleagues. Among his many beneficiaries was Ludwig Scharf, who was able to publish his first volume of poetry thanks to a sizeable contribution from Panizza.

Luther and Anti-Semitism

The figure of Martin Luther emerges again and again in the writings of Oskar Panizza, and one can scarcely escape the conclusion that this German reformer represented something of a heroic father-figure, a towering symbol of Teutonic bravery, intelligence and virility. He seems to have been the only man whom Panizza could ever view uncritically. Luther embodied all virtues and evolved a profound personal happiness despite, or perhaps because of, his courageous opposition to established social and cultural values. Luther was not only a personal model for manly conduct, he was also a glorious German hero to be championed in public. Thus, when a passing remark in his previously discussed essay ("Prostitution") about Luther's premarital sexual activity was denounced as wholly unfounded in an official Protestant publication, Panizza vigorously defended his initial assertion with an eight-page rebuttal in *Die Gesellschaft,* titled "Luther and Marriage. A Defense Against Defamation" (1893, 355–363). Calling him "our greatest German intellectual hero," Panizza cites a mass of inferential material in a somewhat frenetic attempt to prove that Luther was not a celibate during bachelorhood. He lambastes the Protestant clergy for its prudery and contrasts this attitude with the robust virility of Luther, "the Rousseau of religion" (361). One gets the distinct impression that the "Rousseau" in Luther had a far greater impact on Panizza than did his religion.

This view is further corroborated by the atheistic hedonism expressed in an article on eugenics, which had appeared somewhat earlier in 1893, "Prolegomena zum Preisausschreiben: Verbesserung unserer Rasse" (*Die Gesellschaft* 275–289; Introductory Remarks Concerning the Contest: Improving Our Race) Although Panizza continually championed the anti–Catholic cause and its early leaders, particularly Martin Luther and Ulrich von Hutten, he appears to have been motivated by anything but theological considerations:

> Sun, air, wind, forest and sea, these are what we should be concerned with. Our own joy. No transcendental god should keep us from our [...] daily joys. If he is omnipotent, why did he create us so critical and contemptuous of HIM?!— No! To be born, struggle, enjoy and then die, that is what we should care about, and how best to do it. The rest does not concern us [289].

Unless one accepts Panizza's glorification of Luther as being primarily motivated by extra-religious considerations, it would be impossible to reconcile his fervent anti–Catholicism with his equally consistent anti-religious hedonism.

Panizza's ideas on racial questions are both interesting *per se* and quite typical of German intellectuals at the end of the nineteenth century. He speaks out very forcefully against the notion of eugenics as a means of "purifying" the race, and yet the worshiper of Luther and Wagner eagerly embraces his masters' racial prejudices. His bias is especially evident when discussing the Jewish "race": "With their decided ugliness and their decrepitude, they are undoubtedly inferior [...] to the Teutonic race. But their mind is so much better developed, especially in one direction, the mercenary one" (277). At this period in his life, Panizza was an outspoken anti–Semite, a circumstance which accounts in large part for the few futile attempts to revive him as a cultural hero during the Third Reich.

His anti–Semitic prejudices did not leave his fiction entirely unaffected; the clearest example of his bias can be found in the story "Der operirte Jud" ("The Operated Jew"), one of ten novellas included in the collection entitled *Visionen.* There is much hatred and little humor in his tale of the Jew who goes to ridiculous lengths to rid himself of all "Semitic" physical and mental characteristics, only to have the deception uncovered on his wedding night with a Protestant bride. Although it is not possible to disregard his blatantly derogatory remarks about Jews, the story must also be seen as a satire on self-negation. The affirmation of self, so forcefully enunciated in the writings of Nietzsche, was a concept which Panizza wholeheartedly embraced and with which he concluded his article on eugenics: "We cannot be anything other than what we are. And as we are, so we want to be" (289). To his credit, Panizza's anti–Semitic attitude did change in the mid–1890s. After his release from prison in 1896, he had become an outspoken opponent of anti–Semitism.

There are other instances of eclectic sensationalism in *Visionen*, "dedicated to the memory of Ernst Theodor Amadeus Hoffmann." Aside from the obvious hallucinatory nature of these stories implied in the title, there is the element of the grotesque and fantastic which stamps them as the products of Oskar Panizza's imagination. Hermaphrodism, genocide, prostitution, cannibalism, lesbianism, church desecration and insanity are but a few of the more sensational topics which the author chose to explore in his novellas. This tendency of Panizza's runs counter to the dominant trend of naturalism, which was to dwell on the everyday and ordinary things of life. Sexual ambivalence, religious hatred and psychological disintegration were, however, of great personal importance to Oskar Panizza, and he exploited them with a frequency that anticipates the numerous subsequent authors who focused on similar literary themes.

Anti-Catholicism

With the publication in 1893 of *Die unbefleckte Empfängnis der Päpste* (*The Immaculate Conception of the Popes*), Panizza embarked on a path of militant anti–Catholicism that put him behind bars within two years. In his own confused words, the book represented "an attempt, in what appeared to be the most serious style, to extend the dogma of the Immaculate Conception of the Virgin, proclaimed by Pius IX in the year 1894 [1854], to the popes, with all embryological, anthropological and theological consequences" (*In memoriam* 13). According to the title page, which bears the papal coat of arms, the Vatican imprimatur and a dedication to the fiftieth bishop's anniversary of Leo XIII, the book was authored by a Spanish Friar Martin O.S.B. and translated into German by Oskar Panizza. Although a number of credulous readers naively took it to be the work of a Jesuit priest, it was clearly the type of monumental spoof of which Panizza was so fond. Summoning an immense wealth of scholarly minutiae from church history to support his imaginative thesis, the author cites 101 proofs in 108 pages to demonstrate the immaculate conception of the popes. His irreverence is not confined solely to the popes, but is also aimed at the Virgin Mary and even the Trinity.

As was to be expected, there were few Catholic authorities who considered the book to be very funny. A stern memorandum was circulated through the Catholic press of Germany, Austria, and Switzerland, warning that "from beginning to end, this brochure is a blasphemy surpassing any and all bounds. A Christian cannot possibly have written it" (Panizza reprinted excerpts of this review and others, which he appended to the third edition of *Das Liebeskonzil*, 1897, 36). The Protestant press, as well, was equally quick to condemn the booklet as the outpouring of a madman, although there were some independent thinkers who were able to appreciate Panizza's brand of biting satire. Irma von Troll-Borostyani, writing in the *Milwaukee Freidenker*, stated that "the work is a satire, one of the bloodiest and wittiest that has ever been written" (36). Bierbaum characterized it as "perhaps the most frightful and daring work ever written against Catholicism" and went on to praise it as a "perfect work of art" and "one of the most significant works of art that we possess" (*Die Gesellschaft* 1893, 987). The criminal court in Stuttgart considered the book significant enough to order all unsold copies confiscated and permanently banned from the entire German Empire.

Throughout 1893, Panizza was busy combing through mountains of church lore and penning his most tendentious book to date, *Der teutsche Michel und der römische Papst* (1894, *The German Michel and the Roman Pope*), in which the differences between Germany and the Vatican are seen as irreconcilable. Reading through this weighty volume, with its hundreds of scholarly references, one gets the impression that Panizza wanted to "replay" the Reformation, so that he might assume the leading role of a modern-day Martin Luther. The only problem is that, unlike the sixteenth-century reformer, the twentieth-century psychiatrist is not the slightest bit concerned with God. Nationalism and a fierce desire for independence are what motivate this broadside against Vatican dogma, history and politics. There is also more than a trace of megalomania in his casual observation that religion has taken a back-seat to psychology in our age: "Today we know from case histories in insane asylums and from the psychosexual investigations of Moll, Krafft-Ebing, Tarnowsky, et al. how fundamentally significant the structure of one's sexual drives is for the intellectual development of a human being. In this respect, the psychiatrist is a more important person for us today than the pope" (100). This book, despite its respectable scholarly apparatus, met the same fate as the author's previous book on the subject; it was confiscated and banned throughout Germany. A half-century later it earned the dubious distinction of being Panizza's only book to be republished during the Third Reich, though in abbreviated form and missing both his copious notes and the original phonetic spelling.

Dramatic Stirrings

Oskar Panizza's literary career reached its peak in 1894. By this time he had already published three volumes of poetry, the "tragic-comical" (*In memoriam* 13) diary of a dog, two collections of stories totaling six hundred pages, and two substantial polemics against the Roman Catholic Church. He had gained a reputation in Germany as one of the most radical of the Munich modernists, an avant-garde writer who had gone from poetry to prose to polemic in what some saw as an attempt to win literary notoriety. In early 1893, he had taken the decisive step that anyone would take who wanted to join the really greats — Sophocles, Shakespeare, Molière, Schiller — he turned to the theater. Not that the stage represented a wholly alien world to him, for he had been an avid theatergoer since the days he dreamed of being an opera star. But writing for the theater was a different matter, something Panizza had shied away from in his eight years as a full-time author. Perhaps the fact that the main emphasis of German naturalism was on dramatic works prompted Panizza to try his hand at this genre. His close friend Max Halbe, twelve years Panizza's junior, literally reached the pinnacle of his fame overnight with the first public performance of *Jugend* in 1894; Frank Wedekind, another friend who was also more than a decade younger than Oskar, had created a minor storm with the publication of his *Frühlings Erwachen* in 1891 and was busy completing work on *Erdgeist*. What is surprising is not that Panizza turned to the theater, but that he did not do so sooner.

The forty-year-old author's first attempt at dramatic writing was a less than mediocre

Oskar Panizza and his brother Felix, left, around 1890. Photograph by J. Reitmayer, Munich. Courtesy of Rainer Wirth, Bad Kissingen.

little piece called *Der heilige Staatsanwalt* (1894, *The Holy District Attorney*). Panizza's two main fields of interest, sex and religion, are fused together in this morality play dealing with the trial of a prostitute. Eternal Goodness, Truth, Beauty, and even Morality herself come forth to testify against the accused prostitute, Lust. The only real action occurs in the last scene, where the trial is decided by the miraculous appearance of Martin Luther. He gives a hearty sermon in defense of Lust and then leaves the courtroom with her amid cheers from the public. The play has, quite deservedly, hardly ever been performed, its chief merit being that it provided the author with a modicum of experience in dramatic writing and in many ways anticipated his most important work, *The Love Council*.

Chapter 5

Downward Spiral, 1895–1921

Das Liebeskonzil was published on 10 October 1894 in Zürich by Verlagsmagazin J. Schabelitz, the same firm that had previously published Panizza's spoof on the immaculate conception of the popes. Subtitled "A Heavenly Tragedy in Five Acts," the play depicts the origin of syphilis as God's vengeance on his sexually overactive human creatures. One can only agree with Prescher that "this book certainly contains the wildest rebellion against God that exists in our recent literature, and the strongest satire on those figures worshiped by Christians" (Prescher 252).

Even before the book went on sale in Germany, the author had become a literary *cause célèbre* by sending copies to friends and reviewers. For the first and last time in his life, Panizza reaped the outspokenly enthusiastic praise from many of his fellow German writers. Detlev von Liliencron, one of the most respected and widely-read authors of his time, wrote Panizza that "the second act and Satan's choice of women are absolutely colossal!! The 'de profondis' etc. smack into the orgy! Again: absolutely colossal!" (KS 2). Otto Julius Bierbaum maintained that "*The Love Council* is your most mature, artistically best balanced work. If you can keep it up (as far as this side of your talent is concerned) [...] then we may hope to view in you our Aristophanes. But you must leave the country, for now they will lock you up" (KS 2). Although Bierbaum's prophecy came to pass within a few months, Anna Croissant-Rust's vision of an actual stage production was not to be realized for another seventy-five years: "You should know: your *Love Council* is the most significant work you have written so far. A work of *one* pitch, of such power and artistic unity, strutting with marvelous images and obscene audacity [...] If only one could see it! Truly, I would give much for it; to have money, actors, sets!" (KS 3). Maurice von Stern called it "the most cynical book I have ever read!" (KS 2). Panizza's shock waves even spread to the German community living in the United States. Writing in the *Milwaukee Freidenker*, Irma von Troll-Borostyani concluded that "as far as wit and sheer force is concerned, Panizza's sarcasm has not been surpassed, indeed has not even been equaled, by the most famous satirists in world literature..." (KS 1). *The Love Council* obviously made a great impression on Sigmund Freud, the father of psychoanalysis, who mentioned the "strongly revolutionary closet drama" several years later in his 1899 landmark study, *The Interpretation of Dreams* (149 n.). Theodor Fontane, the grey eminence of German letters, discussed the play in three separate notes to the author Maximilian Harden. He urged his younger colleague to "read it and write about it, if you can; it is very difficult (legally) but very rewarding. It is an extremely significant book [...] They ought to erect either a stake for him or a monument. Our public should finally learn that atheism also has its heroes and martyrs" (*Merkur* X: 1094f.).

On 12 January 1895, only a few weeks after the play had been on public sale, the *All-*

94

gemeine Zeitung in Munich reported that the book had been confiscated by the Public Prosecutor. This touched off a new round in the stormy controversy, for while most writers,
even if they disliked the play, strongly decried the official move to suppress literary freedom, the press was sharply divided in their response along partisan and ideological grounds.
The better-known publications that came out strongly in support of Panizza included the
Berliner Börsen-Courier, Berliner Zeitung, Deutsche Zeitung, Badischer Landesbote (Karlsruhe), *Fränkischer Kurier* (Nuremberg), *Kölnische Zeitung, Neue deutsche Rundschau, Vossische Zeitung,* and *Vorwärts.* Typical of the numerous newspapers which vehemently
denounced the play, usually without having any first-hand knowledge of the book, is the
following comment which appeared in the *Neue bayerische Landeszeitung* (Würzburg) of 17
January 1895: "His canvas is only painted with dung, spinach, and 'rhinoceros oil' [laxative]. It is no pity if such books are confiscated and burned" (KS 1).

Similarly biased evaluations can be found in most of the standard German literary histories, some of them written well into the twentieth century. Thus, Josef Nadler claims that
Panizza represents the transitional link from "good to evil, from the wrath of love to the
contempt of hate, from elixir to poison, and from Munich of 1870 to the city of 1918"
(691f.). Otto von Leixner went so far as to say that "the way he presented God, Christ, and
Mary, besmirching them with filth, was irresponsible. One might perceive wit here and there,
but the whole thing elicits revulsion, even from those persons who no longer possess any
religious feelings at all" (992). Eduard Engel simply dismissed the entire play as "wild and
repulsive [...] certainly the outgrowth of insanity" (341).

Preparing the case against Dr. Panizza was not as simple as the Public Prosecutor's office
in Munich under Baron von Sartor had first believed. A mere fifteen copies of the play had
been sold in Munich in the weeks prior to confiscation, and none of these readers had been
sufficiently outraged to file a complaint against the author. The dilemma was finally solved
after von Sartor sent a request for assistance to officials in Saxony, marked "very urgent!"
(Bauer 154). As a result of this request, a police sergeant purchased a copy of the play from
a Leipzig book dealer, read it with outrage and proceeded to show it to a higher police
official; the latter was equally offended and decided to file a complaint. Panizza was subsequently charged with 93 counts of sacrilege in violation of paragraph 166 of the *Reichsstrafgesetzbuch,* the Imperial penal code. A post-card written to Max Halbe on February 15 clearly
reveals that Panizza was well aware how slim his chances for acquittal were:

> My case looks pretty hopeless [...] the district attorney will ask for one year imprisonment and
> immediate arrest — unless he is foiled by the fact that the book was published abroad. Legal
> opinion stands against legal opinion. My friends and certain lawyers have advised me to leave.
> But they don't know a German writer of today, they think he would miss the opportunity for
> a — speech to the jury. I will defend myself like a hyena [Prescher 138].

Illusionism

There is a crucial question arising at this point: Why did Panizza not follow the advice
of his friends and legal advisors to leave the country? Why did he decide to remain and
stand trial, a trial he knew he could not possibly win? Was it simply that he did not want
to "miss the opportunity for a speech to the jury"? Perhaps the answer can best be found
by taking a brief look at Dr. Panizza's philosophy as contained in a book written during
the pre-trial months, *Der Illusionismus und die Rettung der Persönlichkeit: Skizze einer Weltan-*

schauung (1895, *Illusionism and Saving One's Personality: Outline of a Worldview*). Dedicated "to the memory of Max Stirner," it is Panizza's only attempt at writing philosophy and, as such, quite revealing. What he tries to do is find a rationalization for Stirner's solipsism that will integrate the scientific and psychological data collected during the second half of the nineteenth century.

Without tracing the labyrinthine course of Panizza's often grotesquely twisted logic, his conclusions can be summarized as follows: citing Descartes, he postulates thought as his ontological and epistemological point of departure (14). Thoughts can only be examined by thinking. Thoughts come to us through inspiration (15); the source of a person's inspiration is his *daimon*, his *brahma*, the mysterious and unknowable spring of hallucinations and creative insights (25). He strongly rejects the pre–Freudian notion of a sub- or unconscious, stating that "only in the character of consciousness do we know mental activity" (17).

Dr. Panizza was well acquainted with the clinical findings of neurosurgery that cortical stimulation could elicit hallucinations in the form of sensory perception, memories, etc. But the conclusions he draws from these data are rather startling. Since there is no way for an individual to distinguish between "true perception" of the external world and his own hallucinations, there is no valid reason for separating the two, "thus the world is a hallucination" (20), "the entire external world is contained within me" (28). This certainly is not an original idea of Panizza's, and he is careful to credit his predecessors Berkeley, Kant, Fichte and Schopenhauer. However, the lengthy discussions of hashish (40ff.) and of his personal experience with hallucinations (29) often appear to be part of an attempt to come to terms with what he elsewhere referred to as his "psychopathic fits" (*In memoriam* 12). It is almost as if he felt compelled to create an entire philosophy of life wherein his own psychological pathologies would appear to be perfectly normal. "What is the purpose of your life? To dissolve the phantom of the world. To devour it in thought. To know that you are hallucinating. And with that to

First edition cover of *Das Liebeskonzil*, Zürich: Verlags-Magazin (J. Schabelitz), 1894, with variant spelling of title, subtitle and author's name. Cover art by Max Hagen.

return to yourself. You don't have to escape into the woods. You may seize the world. Simply because you cannot do otherwise. Simply because your *daimon* forces you to phantasmagorize" (*Illusionismus* 52).

The author's obvious fear of insanity grows in frightening proportions from page to page, and what had been set forth in the book's title as an attempt to save the personality ends with its virtual destruction:

> As soon as we pull the switch and the brain begins to work, illusion is created. And the most fundamental, gruesome and elemental illusion emerges, when the brain — for my illusion — consumes itself, melts: the softening of the brain (paralysis of the brain); where within a few months the organ loses hundreds of grams of matter precisely in those parts, which — according to our empirical conception — are the seat of (illusionistic) thought and, while suspending all dimensions of time and space, simultaneously produces the most colossal megalomania, a hashish-like, illusionistic fireworks (sparkling during destruction). — However, there is only a gradual distinction between this combustion of brain matter — i.e., piles of illusion production — and our lucid thought [54].

The ethical system at which Panizza arrived is heavily derivative of both Socrates and Nietzsche: know yourself, find your *daimon*, "if there is any truth it is undoubtedly [...] your psyche" (58). The conclusion he derives from this, however, was one which Nietzsche had rejected: "Whoever gives his life for his idea is always a saint" (60) He lists numerous such martyrs, among them Savonarola, Pope Alexander VI's great antagonist, who "expected nothing in his life but the bloody halo which surrounds the martyr's head" (59). Writing in his prison diary a year later, Panizza wondered "why Goethe, for all his genius, remains in our memory enveloped by the flabby vapor of stale tea and lacks the bloody halo which shines on Schiller's temples?" The answer, "because he never dared, never risked his life" (Prescher 186) is also the answer to our original question of why Oskar Panizza chose to appear before a trial he could not possibly win.

He had been a fearless artist with the creativity and the courage to write about things never before even mentioned in literature. Was he now going to run away just because things were getting rough? Savonarola was beheaded, Giordano Bruno was burned at the stake, Charlotte Corday was guillotined, Martin Luther risked the flames of eternal hell fire — how could he shrink from what would probably be no more than a year in prison? And who could overlook all the publicity that such a trial was bound to stir up? Couldn't this be the way to earn his "bloody halo"? Panizza had always been an intellectual warrior, and he was not about to change. His decision to face a hopeless trial merely confirms what he had bravely written a few months previously:

> And only then may you see your mission fulfilled at the end of your life, when you can say to yourself that you have expressed your *daimon* in the world. That is your categorical imperative. Act according to the dictates of your *daimon*. If you shrink back before the consequences in the world, then it is stronger than you. If you prevail, then you will be the victor. Perhaps you will perish. But to perish in the world of appearances is the lot of us all [*Illusionismus* 62].

The Fateful Trial

One of the principal reasons why Panizza had to defend himself was because he could not find anyone else to do it. On the day before the trial, the *Neues Münchener Tagblatt* reported on 29 April 1895 that "Dr. Panizza has not yet been able to find an attorney who will handle his defense." At the last minute, Georg Kugelmann agreed to take care of the legal technicalities; but the author had already carefully researched and drafted his own defense plea, most of which he delivered himself at the trial. This speech, together with other trial documents, was published later by his Swiss publisher, Johann Schabelitz.

On the eve of his fateful trial, Panizza participated in a bit of theater history by taking part in the first of the two private performances produced by Max Halbe's *Intimes Theater*. This intimate theater was a short-lived experiment by the Munich modernists designed to free dramatic productions of all commercial and political pressures. The performance on 29 April 1895 at the apartment of writer Juliane Déry was of Strindberg's *Creditors*. Max Halbe remembers Panizza as:

> [...] the helpfully concealed spirit behind the carpet who provided the necessary cues. It was Oskar Panizza who was the prompter on this memorable evening. Panizza's trial [...] began at eight o'clock the next morning. Almost straight from the theater performance — we hardly made it home that night — we went to the courtroom, which looked to all of us like a roomy but no less terrifying mortar. And high up on the ceiling was the pestle of the law, a powerful colossus which descended hour by hour, lower and lower onto all of us. And when the evening shadows appeared, one of us lay crushed under the pestle [*Jahrhundertwende* 148].

The trial, which is described here in greater detail in Chapter 7, contained no surprises. Freiherr von Sartor, the prosecutor, charged the author with having committed sacrilege "by publicly blaspheming God with abusive statements, creating an offense and insulting public institutions and customs of the Christian Church, especially the Catholic Church" (Panizza, *Meine Verteidigung* 36). He demanded that the jury find the defendant guilty and that the culprit be sentenced to a year-and-a-half in prison.

Panizza began his defense by summoning an "expert," none other than M. G. Conrad, and asking him to evaluate whether or not *The Love Council* was a work of art. After a lengthy, pompous, and often patronizing testimonial, Conrad not unexpectedly arrived at the conclusion that the play was indeed "a genuine, German, modern work of art, despite individual aesthetic flaws" (*Meine Verteidigung* 34). Panizza's own defense plea was more finely tailored to the rather limited cultural background of his jurors. He described the sudden emergence of the first syphilis epidemic at the end of the fifteenth century and how it was viewed as God's punishment for man's sexual excesses: "I was not concerned with blasphemous things and obscenities, but rather with grasping the peculiar situation in which the people found themselves at that time, a situation which especially interested me as a former physician" (6). After a vivid but accurate historical description of the licentious conditions prevalent at the court of Alexander VI, he suggested for his listeners to:

> [...] move this entire topic into our present age filled with skepticism and disbelief. Let this configuration of historical forces as an artistic subject fall into the hands of a modern person who — perhaps to his misfortune — is inclined toward satire, and then I ask you, gentlemen, how would you have depicted the Trinity, and what kind of conception of the divinities in heaven would you have presented, who under such circumstances sent venereal disease as a punishment for mankind on earth? [8].

Without waiting for an answer to his rhetorical questions, Panizza plunged into the most famous of his capsule surveys of world literature, in an attempt to illustrate that the divine has always been a legitimate subject for literary satire. Quoting extensively from Parny's "La guerre des dieux" (1799, "The War of the Gods") and Sebastian Sailer's humoristic drama *Der Fall Luzifers* (1850, *Lucifer's Fall*), he tendentiously traced the development of sacrilegious writings from Aristophanes to Oskar Panizza. At no point does he ever deny the devastating portrait of the divine in his play, but the reasons for his choice of such a presentation are deceptively superficial:

> I *have* degraded the Christian gods and have done so intentionally, because I saw them in the mirror of the fifteenth century; because I observed them from Alexander VI's point of view. Our concepts of the divine, gentlemen, are contained in our thinking. You know as little as I do what happens in reality up there above us [...] If I attacked the divine, then I did not attack that divine spark that slumbers in the heart of every person, but rather I attacked the divine which had become a farce in the hands of Alexander VI [19f.].

What the author failed to mention, however, is that the "mirror of the fifteenth century" provided a convenient foil on which to project his own religious or irreligious attitudes. The jury, too, considered the caricatures of the divinities a reflection of the author's own views. After his swift conviction, the author was immediately arrested and held on 80,000 RM bail to prevent him from becoming a fugitive.

Literary Responses

After Panizza's conviction and the harshest prison sentence ever meted out to any artist during the 47-year Wilhelmine Empire, German intellectuals were generally outraged. Theodor Fontane concluded that "whoever expects me to believe the story of Christ's conception, whoever demands that I furnish my heaven in accordance with the pre–Raphaelite painters: God in the middle, Mary on the left, Christ on the right, Holy Ghost in the background as a radiant sun [...] forces me over to Panizza's side" (*Merkur* X: 1095).

Contrasting sharply with the enlightened skepticism of the 76-year-old Fontane is the attitude expressed by a youthful reviewer in *Das zwanzigste Jahrhundert. Blätter für deutsche Art und Wohlfahrt* (*The Twentieth-Century: Journal for the German Way and Welfare*). This was a pseudo-progressive, right-wing journal edited by Heinrich Mann, and the outraged reviewer was none other than his brother Thomas, a 20-year-old clerk working for a fire insurance company in Munich. Thomas Mann contributed eight reviews to this outspokenly anti–Semitic publication. Curiously enough, it was Oskar Panizza's *cause célèbre* that launched Thomas Mann's distinguished career as a critic: his review of *The Love Council* stands at the beginning of six prolific decades and is Mann's very first work of non-fiction to appear in print. Since he knew Panizza personally, it is probable that Mann actually obtained and read a copy of the controversial play, a practice not always followed by other critics. In line with his then reactionary sympathies, he severely denounced the "heavenly tragedy" and even went so far as to applaud the playwright's stiff prison sentence, stating that blasphemy was to be condemned as "tastelessness." It should not be overlooked, however, that Panizza's dual themes of syphilis and the Devil as the source of creativity reappear, more than half a century later, in Mann's own novel, *Doktor Faustus* (1947).

Dr. Laubmann, director of the Munich *Staatsbibliothek* (State Library), observed that "in 300 years it will be as difficult to comprehend that someone was imprisoned for a book in our time, as it is for us today to comprehend that 300 years ago someone was burned for a book" (KS 6). Enlightened public opinion felt that the punishment was far out of proportion to any possible crime, while the most parochial law-and-order advocates felt that the author had received what he deserved. As one of the jurors remarked to a Munich journalist, "If the dog had been tried in Lower Bavaria, he wouldn't have gotten out alive" (KS 6).

One of the persons deeply incensed by Panizza's sentence was the philosopher Theodor Lessing (1872–1933), at that time a young medical student in Munich. As a matter of fact, Lessing launched his literary career by writing the pamphlet titled *Der Fall Panizza. Eine kritische Betrachtung über 'Gotteslästerung' und künstlerische Dinge vor Schwurgerichten* (1895, *The Case of Panizza: A Critical Look at 'Blasphemy' and Artistic Issues Before Jury Courts*). The very same night he learned of Panizza's fate, he:

> [...] sat down, drunk with wine, ambition and anger, and in one wild fury wrote a defense, without even having read the condemned play. (To this day [1935], I have not seen it.) I delivered a very general and arrogant "appeal to mankind." The concept of blasphemy was senseless; certainly inapplicable to works of art, for wit, satire and irony had to be as free as the imagination. Literary questions did not belong in civil courts.—A young book dealer, Max Wohlfahrt, published the sermon; in a few days it was already out of print. The insulted district attorney had old lady Rauh's house searched; the police confiscated my poems [...] and I was placed under surveillance for being suspected of atheism, communism, or some other -ism. But thanks to this event, there now came offers and queries, and without having wanted or considered it, I was suddenly swimming in the fresh water of literature. Farewell, studies and medicine [234–235].

While Lessing's pamphlet was of no benefit to Panizza, it does convey a sense of how forcefully his fate affected the other writers of his time. "The public [...] should finally learn from such trials," wrote young Lessing, "that literary and artistic charges and violations ought to be outside the state's jurisdiction — artistic products should be measured by artistic standards, not by legal, medical, philological or any other criteria — in extreme cases they should be censored by an intellectual elite — not by a jury" (35).

Imprisonment

On 1 July 1895 the lower court's decision was upheld by the Imperial Court in Leipzig (text of Judgment in Chapter 11). Because his deformed right leg rendered him unfit to stay in the main penitentiary in Nuremberg, Panizza began serving his twelve-month sentence on August 8 in the prison of Amberg. His family made one last attempt to free its black sheep with a plea for clemency on the grounds of insanity. This incident was described in the autobiographical sketch of 1904: "[...] in response to a subsequent claim of insanity submitted by the attorney (without consulting the prisoner), there followed an investigation *quoad psychen intactam*—'Are you insane?'—'No'—, which led to a negative conclusion" (*In memoriam* 14–15).

The expert testimonials offered by the consulting physicians tell a different story. Dr. Paul Ostermaier, who had known the prisoner for many years, wrote that he "is pathologically predisposed to a high degree and cannot be held responsible for all his words and deeds" (*In memoriam* 26). *Hofstabsarzt* Dr. Nobiling, a Court Staff Physician, was also of the opinion that Panizza was "genetically tainted to a high degree and has not been psychologically free for many years now." The prison physician at Amberg, Dr. Schmelcher, however, did not agree, and Panizza was forced to serve out his entire sentence. The similarity and studied vagueness of Ostermaier's and Nobiling's evaluations suggest that they were written under personal or financial pressure from the Panizza family. A family history of mental pathology and the denial of free will do not constitute a diagnosis of mental disease, nor does a long personal acquaintance guarantee legal objectivity when a man's whole future well-being is at stake. Panizza did not consider himself to be insane when he entered Amberg, and there is really no evidence to contradict this.

The long year of incarceration at Amberg, however, gradually destroyed the author's psychological equilibrium. His physical environment was oppressive, to say the least. So repulsive to him were his fellow inmates — uneducated peasants whom he referred to as "gorillas" (Prescher 180) — that the many hours spent in his solitary cell were preferable to those spent exercising or eating with the fifty other prisoners. He was a refined man of letters and science living in a colony of thugs. "A man like me is considered a head-hunter here, someone who is off his rocker, a 'professor.' The guards can't find the right tone to talk to me. And I am even uncomfortable for the officials, since they have to invent a new means of communication" (Prescher 183). The ingestion of food, formerly a delight to the hotel proprietor's son, now became a daily torture: "Most of the soups taste like book-binder's paste. And there is nothing but soup. The torture involved in swallowing it is unspeakable."

Fortunately for Panizza, the prison director realized that he had a rather unusual inmate on his hands and allowed him to pursue his literary activities with a minimum of restrictions. During this year in Amberg, he wrote the *Dialoge im Geiste Huttens* (1897, *Dialogues in Hutten's Spirit*) and kept a diary that was later to have been published by Schabelitz under the title *Ein Jahr Gefängnis* (*A Year of Prison*). According to Deacon Lippert, the clergyman who conducted Protestant worship in the prison, Panizza could "occupy himself with his books however he wanted" (*In memoriam* 44–45). Lippert did note, however, that Panizza "turned down the beer, which he could have had. He only missed his walks through the countryside, but endured patiently like a martyr to his cause, and his behavior was impeccable."

On the positive side of things, Panizza's political awareness sharply increased as a result of living with "a conspiratorial society that does not reckon and speculate according to politics, flags or language, but rather from jail to jail, from prison to prison, from penitentiary to penitentiary" (Prescher 181). He recognized the essentially conservative nature of the working proletariat, as opposed to the criminal, anarchic prison population, whom he viewed as society's true revolutionaries:

Here, here in Amberg and the other penal institutions, this is where your social democrats live the way you imagine them, these are the revolutionaries, these are the enemies of law and order whom you are continually talking about, the irreconcilable enemies of any culture. If, on the other hand, I look at members of the Social Democratic Party, the politically organized workers as we see them at their public meetings, then I inevitably reach the conclusion that [...] they are the conservatives, and that the people I see around me here are the uneducated, uneducable revolutionaries [Prescher 181].

Deacon Lippert proudly reports that Panizza "attended every religious service and even went to confession and communion — what was he seeking there? The peace 'which the world cannot give'?" (*In memoriam* 46). The author's own explanation of these events differs markedly from Lippert's:

Today I went to communion. Well, I must say, I too believe now that man consists of two-thirds stomach, one-third imagination, and one-sixteenth intellect. Although I am not an indifferent person, but rather an outspoken enemy of Christianity, I was powerfully shaken by the event [...] They knelt there on their communion stools like tamed Hectors, these propagandists of action [...] Isn't that a fitting ceremony for henchmen and highway robbers? Take! Take! Take and eat! Take and drink! [...] A splendid symbolism, which these people understand very well.

It made a powerful impression on me [...] I went primarily to please the minister, who treats me with so much kindness; secondly, because I wanted to please myself, because I wanted to enjoy the sensation. I did not regret it. It was tremendous. And the wine was good. A swig of wine in this desert of semolina soup, oat groats and meal-pap! [Prescher 174–75].

Panizza's vehement rejection of Christian ritual is expressed even stronger in another diary entry. He had just witnessed a service attended by a dozen Protestant worshippers. A famous sixteenth-century hymn they sung, which began with the words, "Oh, innocent lamb of God, slaughtered on the trunk of the cross," prompted the following outburst:

Who introduced this butcherous, bloody conception of the supernatural into the emotional realm of mankind? Who conjured up this slaughter-house odor and animal carnage as symbols for mercy and pity?! Slaughtered lambs! For whom? For me? For my sins? I will settle my sins with myself and stand accountable to society. And these hangman songs, this complacent slaughter of lambs and men spiced with incense and rosemary, can they really be expected not to have a brutalizing effect on your feelings? Society for the Prevention of Cruelty to Animals, I call on you to help stop this glorification of the slaughtering of poor animals! Are you therefore so cruel to poor people, the poor mammals called workers? Because you have drunk so much blood for 2000 years? Lord God in heaven! Never, never has Christianity appeared to me to be so wretched, so helpless, so miserable as this morning, when I heard the poor prisoners singing these verses with dried pathos [Prescher 176].

These are hardly the words of a man who found his spiritual peace in Christianity, and one can only conclude that Deacon Lippert, kindly gentleman though he was, may not have really known Oskar Panizza as well as he thought he did.

In numerous diary entries, the author delivers a devastating critique of the penal system as one of the cruelest perpetrators of injustice. Much of what he had to say about these anachronistic institutions remains valid for many of today's prisons. Dr. Panizza was especially concerned with the effects of incarceration on the human mind, and his conclusions are based on observation of others as well as his own personal experience:

I can sit here for hours or days over my books and thoughts, don't miss a thing, am as happy in my solitude as I am outside. But then comes a moment when I have worked myself tired, where I want to breathe, take a spiritual deep breath, want to see horizons and then — I suffocate. And this moment is ghastly. Then the dusty cell walls collapse over my soul and crush it. A little piece in the brain, if I may put it this way, melts, and the function is extinguished. The next time this burning thirst emerges less intense, it only becomes a moderate itching. And this is the moment of imbecility [Prescher 185–86].

There are indications that Panizza's later psychological disintegration first became manifest in Amberg. Without citing any concrete examples of paranoid thought, Lippert maintains that "the sentence of one year in prison for *The Love Council* appeared exorbitantly high to the 'atheist' Panizza, who obviously had no feeling for how much he had offended the religious and moral feelings of others; and he saw this punishment as the result of a persecutory system directed against him" (*In memoriam* 28). Since there are no signs of a conceptualized "persecutory system" in any of his writings at this time, perhaps Lippert, writing thirty years after the Amberg episode, extended Panizza's later attitudes to this earlier period of their friendship. But while there do not seem to have been any systematic delusions of persecution in 1895–1896, one does come across occasional flashes of acute anxiety and despair. Passages such as the following are characterized by their brevity, humor, scholarly allusions and terror:

God! What's that? What kind of shadow is that over there with the crooked legs? This twisted silhouette? God, that's you! You, too, are a gorilla. In linen overalls. And just look, the others are grinning at you. They recognized you a long time ago! For God's sake, be quiet! Quiet! We are in the zoological ward here. It's a kind of primordial state of mankind. And what about him over there with the polished boots and the close-fitting slacks and the uniform jacket? Quiet! Quiet! That's Adam. We are in Paradise here. He is just counting the animals and giving them names. We are after The Fall [Prescher 181].

It is obvious that Panizza's confinement drastically upset his already fragile psychological balance. He became permanently estranged from the entire circle of his Munich literary friends, including the man who had done so much to help him, M.G. Conrad. Lippert relates that "when Conrad sent him his *In purpurner Finsternis* [1895, *In Purple Darkness*], a satire on the equality of people 'under ground,' he rejected the book as incomprehensible and smugly let himself be called an 'ass'" (*In memoriam* 46). Lippert also noted that Panizza "could be extremely rude in letters to people who had done nothing but good things for him." The following excerpt from a letter to Max Halbe, written three weeks before the author's release from prison, clearly indicates an excessive preoccupation with his "image" and an inability to relate to his former friends:

As a quiet criminal I will have to slink along the houses to Munich. Instead of with cannon fire, torch lights and a military honor guard, as I would have liked to have done. This thought is terribly painful for me. You must know there are — not among us —, but in general, in the shops, stores, coffee houses, among distant bygone acquaintances many, many who do not know how they should treat me, avoid me — out of consideration for me!! — or, if not avoid, then don't find the proper tone and "gently" walk away. This kind of thing is ghastly! For me, who always led his life in the form of "check mate!," unbearable and disastrous. I would prefer that one half shouted: Look, there's the criminal! And that the other little group would call out: He belongs to us! — Oh, if only I could be a Social Democrat and know to which group I belonged! — The distress about this situation is primarily what is driving me away, to Switzerland or Berlin [Prescher 166–67].

Dr. Panizza was released from prison on 8 August 1896. After a brief excursion with Lippert to view a 1525 portrait of Luther by Lucas Cranach, he returned to Munich for a few months. Contrary to the fears expressed in his letter to Halbe, his Munich friends did not avoid him and actually threw a lavish party to celebrate his release. But Panizza was no longer the man they had once known. The transformation was readily apparent to his shocked friend Richard Weinhöppel:

He had become somewhat pale and gaunt, yet he seemed to be cheerful and of good spirits. But talking to him alone I soon noticed the drastic change which the grey hours in the prison cell had produced. Out of the thinker had become a brooder, out of the knower a doubter, out of the laugher a grinner. His subdued voice and his tearful eyes stood in shocking contrast to the intoxicating atmosphere and noisy gaiety of these hours in the Munich Ratskeller [Weinhöppel, *Visionen* xi].

Vaudeville in Bavaria

The last article by Panizza to appear in *Die Gesellschaft* is a pioneering study of "Der Klassizismus und das Eindringen des Variété. Eine Studie über zeitgenössischen Geschmack" (1896, "Classicism and the Infusion of Vaudeville: A Study of Contemporary Taste"). Jelavich considers this seminal essay to be "the first German analysis of the implications of popular

Amberg correctional facility, where Oskar Panizza served his twelve-month sentence beginning 8 August 1895. Copyright © 2010 by the photographer, Peter D.G. Brown.

theater for traditional elite culture" (*Munich* 162). Panizza dismissed classical culture as the "renunciation of all joviality, all secretiveness, all sensuality, and everything pleasing and graceful, a renunciation of color, aroma and fragrance" (Panizza, "Der Klassizismus" 1252). In his opinion, vaudeville, with its "absolute naiveté in the use of artistic media," its "sparkling joy, childish enthusiasm and purest delight in the result, whatever its origin," represents the most radical, hence "the absolute contradiction" to classicism (1252–53). Traces of his new sociopolitical awareness, previously noted in his Amberg diary entries, are also in evidence here, as when he points to "the great question which will move the rest of our century, the status of the worker, the fervent struggle for the liberation of the individual, the destruction of old hierarchic, dogmatic and monarchic formulas."

One of Panizza's last literary projects before leaving Munich was to revise and expand to book-length his previously published essay on "Die Haberfeldtreiben im bayrischen Gebirge" (1894, "Charivaris in the Bavarian Mountains"). The author had been fortunate to interest the prestigious publisher Samuel Fischer in his study of the curious custom of *Haberfeldtreiben*, a secret peasant tribunal dating back to the days of Charlemagne. Panizza presents a scholarly-detailed, comprehensive historical examination of these strange rites. The last quarter of the book consists of textual samples from *Haberer* protocols, all in thick Bavarian dialect and employing Panizza's characteristic phonetic spelling. Since the *Haberer* primarily tried sexual offenders, the text is replete with typical peasant vulgarisms and obscenities. At the last moment, as the page proofs were about to be returned to the printer, "one of the most distinguished legal advisors in Germany" informed the publisher "that according to the latest legal decisions, the question of what is immoral or damaging to the public interest can no longer be answered with certainty" (*Haberfeldtreiben* 1897, 104). Consequently, the publisher felt constrained to insert a large number of ellipses indicated by whole lines of spaced periods. The effect was not only a watering down of the text, but its literary and philological interest was thereby significantly reduced. Had the author been consulted by Fischer, he probably would have chosen to let the text stand as it was and risk confiscation.

Switzerland

It was impossible for Panizza to remain in the city that had caused him so much grief. In a vitriolic farewell message, *Abschied von München. Ein Handschlag* (1897, *Farewell from Munich: A Handshake*), he furiously poured out his hatred and contempt for the Bavarian capital. This denunciation is in the usual Panizza form of a historical survey, beginning with the lynching of several dozen Lutherans between 1519 and 1521. All of his hostility toward Catholicism is directed at the city he believes to be controlled by the Vatican; it is the Roman Church which has caused Munich to sink to a level of Latin degeneracy:

> And don't you know that it is your specifically Catholic frame of mind that has brought this about? Your worshipping of Jesus' heart, your enthusiasm for Mary's milk, your religion of bones, flesh, milk, hair and reproductive organs? And you still don't have enough! Are not yet satisfied! More and more bones, more and more purgatory terrors, more and more Jesuit missions and Redemptorist institutions [14].

Renouncing his Bavarian citizenship, he left Munich on 15 October 1896 to gain Swiss nationality in Zürich. With the publication of *Abschied von München* the following year, the second warrant for Oskar Panizza's arrest was issued by a Munich judge; and once again the police were ordered to confiscate and destroy all copies of his latest book. The only difference now was that he had become a fugitive of the law, determined never to return to the country he had learned to despise.

After settling down in Zürich, he embarked on what sometimes appears to have been a frantic attempt to continue his literary career where he had left off. In 1896 Schabelitz published a second edition of *The Love Council*, complete with a *Zueignung* (Dedication) and *Vorspiel* (Prologue), which clearly satirize Goethe's *Faust*. A third edition appeared the following year with a megalomaniacal preface and a revised fourth act. But when Schabelitz refused to publish his Amberg diary, Panizza concluded that the only thing for him to do was to become his own publisher. To this end, he created a self-publishing entity which he called *Verlag Zürcher Diskußionen* (Zürich Discussions Press) with variant spellings.

The first book to be published by the author himself was *Dialoge im Geiste Hutten's* (1897, *Dialogues in Hutten's Spirit*), "in which the discussion of public conditions was attempted in the fresh and unabashed style of the early sixteenth century" (*In memoriam* 15–16). These five dialogues — On the Germans, On the Invisible, On the City of Munich, On the Trinity, A Love Dialogue — were all written in prison and contain much of the old Panizza wit and devastating satire. Few of the works written after his stay in Amberg even approached the quality of his earlier writing. One sentence prophetically charts the trajectory of Panizza's own literary life: "Today, if someone expresses a free thought, he is left with only three choices: the madhouse, jail or exile" (*Dialoge* 19). Within the arc of a single decade, Oskar Panizza would experience all three.

Not only did he feel the need to establish his own publishing firm, but he also decided to start his own journal, since the leading magazines were no longer accepting his articles. Thus, in the spring of 1897, he created the curious journal, *Zürcher Diskußionen. Flugblätter aus dem Gesamtgebiet des modernen Lebens* (*Zürich Discussions: Broadsheets from the Entire*

Spectrum of Modern Life), of which he managed to publish thirty-two issues, mostly containing his own contributions. While a number of articles were signed with Panizza's own name, others appeared under such pseudonyms as Hans Kistemaecker, Louis Andrée, Hans Dettmar, and Sven Heidenstamm. These unusual articles range from "A Psychopathological Discussion of Christ" (I, no. 5) to "The Pig in its Poetical, Mythological and Cultural-Historical Aspects" (III, no. 28) As might be expected, the journal's circulation never exceeded several hundred, and its short life-span was concluded in 1902 with volume III. There is something both ludicrous and pathetic about a well-known writer who feels compelled to establish his own publishing firm and found his own journal for no other purpose than to assure the publication of his own works. An undeniable alienation from his former literary contacts appears to have reinforced his latent paranoia to the point where he was compelled to 'go it alone' or fail trying.

It is difficult to agree with Prescher when he states that "this mind began to dissolve because it was overburdened" (Prescher 254). This explanation seems wholly inadequate in view of the fact that Panizza had been making far greater demands on himself in the years prior to his imprisonment. Nor can we go along with Prescher's tendency to imbue the author with prophetic significance: "Something of the German fate which was to lead to the catastrophe under Hitler flashed through these writings." What does emerge in these writings of Panizza's Swiss period is the author's very gradual mental disintegration, resulting in a preoccupation with insanity.

Evidence of his fear of insanity can be found in the not very funny satire *Psichopatia Criminalis*, written and published in the spring of 1898, and bearing the formidable subtitle: "Instructions for psychiatrically elucidating and scientifically determining the mental diseases recognized as necessary by the court. For doctors, laymen, jurists, guardians, administrative officials, ministers, etc." Panizza summoned his impressive erudition in his discussions of epilepsy, melancholia, softening of the brain and paranoia in an effort to prove that freedom of thought is nothing but criminal psychosis and should be persecuted to the fullest extent. Thus, free-thinkers and liberal writers should be committed to state institutions where they can no longer jeopardize the German monarchy. He also suggests that these dangerous elements should be denied the right to procreate, lest the disease spread and undermine the entire nation.

The booklet concludes with the sarcastic warning:

> The danger is here. It is imminent. And with the constantly progressing tendency of political mental disease in the Western world it will soon become even clearer that we are faced with one of the most dangerous and far-reaching mass epidemics, and that it is time to call out to the monarchs: "Princes of Europe, guard your most holy possessions!" [48].

It is difficult to escape the conclusion that behind this awkward political satire lurks the author's obsession with his own "constantly progressing tendency" toward mental disease.

Further evidence of this tendency can be found in Panizza's last drama, *Nero* (1898), a tragedy in five acts. In a quite superfluous, fifteen-page historical appendix, the author stresses the fact that Nero cannot and should not be judged by Judaeo-Christian moral precepts. He was, the dramatist points out, the most brutal and the most popular of all Roman emperors, a psychopathic ruler who can only be judged from a "world-moralistic" point of view. In this respect, he compares his drama to Goethe's *Iphigenie* and Dürer's portrayal of the Passion. But behind the author's pseudo-historical interest is the obsession with the psychotic breakdown of a great immoralist, the mental disintegration of a daring man who considered himself to be a great artist.

Very little is known of Panizza's personal life during his two-year stay in Zürich, which came to an abrupt end late in 1898. His expulsion was prompted by the complaint of a fifteen-year-old prostitute, Olga Rumpf, whom he had used as a model for some nude photography. The second time she came to see him at his home on Turnerstrasse 32, he showed her his collection:

> [...] of partly anatomical, partly artistic nude pictures, such as can be found among our art dealers, and among which were two nude male photographs, one with the *membrum virile in statu erectionis*, the other with the *membrum virile in statu relaxationis*. For such representations the artists of anatomical folios used to rely solely on their memory, while instant exposures now enable photographic representations to be made directly from nature. These art pictures actually have nothing at all to do with our matter at hand here; but I must bring them up, since Olga casually mentioned these pictures to the police, and because it is important to me that the reader learn everything, even the most minute detail, in order to form an opinion of the true reasons for my expulsion [*Zürcher Diskussionen*, I (1898), no. 12, 7].

Although the Canton of Zürich had outlawed prostitution, Panizza was not charged with any specific crime. He was merely declared an undesirable alien by the Zürich police on 27 October 1898, which amounted to a pronouncement of *persona non grata* and expulsion from the entire country. Coming a month after the assassination of the popular Empress Elisabeth (Sissi) of Austria by an Italian anarchist in Geneva, Switzerland, political motives may well have played a role in the decision by the Swiss authorities to expel Panizza, an uncomfortable and stateless anarchist with an Italian name. In his paranoid frame of mind, Panizza suspected the involvement of the German Kaiser and challenged him, "the great unknown person who in reality had caused my expulsion from Zürich, to declare himself" (*Zürcher Diskussionen*, I [1898], no. 12, 11). Wilhelm II remained silent, and Panizza was forced to repatriate himself for the second time in two years. From Zürich he moved westward to France in mid–November, the country that had held such a strong attraction for him as a young man. Surely the Kaiser would be unable to reach him here in this land which was Germany's traditional enemy. As so often before, his plausible assumptions were again to prove totally false.

The six years which Panizza spent in Paris were not nearly as productive from a literary point of view as the preceding six. He continued to publish his *Zürcher Diskussionen* for another few years, having decided to retain the title which by this time had become a glaring misnomer. Understandably, the number of subscribers diminished with the quality of this little publication, and the editor-publisher was not able to make ends meet without the continued financial support of his family. Toward the end of 1902 he addressed his readers with a forced termination notice, admitting yet another defeat.

Parisjana

It was probably inevitable that a writer of such unorthodox persuasions, forced to live in a Parisian exile after having been consistently persecuted in his beloved fatherland, would conceive of himself as a spiritual kin to Heinrich Heine. Indeed, it was here in Paris that Panizza, in the spirit of Heine, returned to writing poetry after having neglected this genre for virtually a decade. The French capital obviously had a liberating effect on him, and he reveled in the enlightened atmosphere which stood in such sharp contrast to the censorship of Germany and Munich, in particular. A year of relative seclusion in his new home at 13 rue des Abesses enabled him to pen what may well be the most vitriolic anti–German verse written by a German poet in the nineteenth century. By December 1899 he had completed 97 poems in ragged iambic tetrameter. These were collected in a little volume titled *Parisjana. Deutsche Verse aus Paris* (*Parisiana: German Verses from Paris*), which he himself published in an edition of one thousand copies. This was Oskar Panizza's last book, and it certainly fared no better than most of his previous literary efforts. It is dedicated in "cordial admiration" to his old friend M.G. Conrad, whom he lavishly praises as the father of modern German literature. Panizza's *Parisjana* contains a foreword in which he also apologizes for having "stolen" the title from Conrad, who had published a collection of essays, *Parisiana*, back in 1880. The recipient of this dedication expressed his due appreciation in an announcement published in *Das litterarische Echo*: "Dr. Oskar Panizza in Vienna [sic] has, without my knowledge or consent, dedicated a little volume of poetry to me. I herewith reject this dedication" ("Erklärung." 1 Feb. 1900: 672).

Other former comrades-in-arms, who had worked and socialized together with Panizza during the previous decade in the heyday of the GmL, had clearly distanced themselves from him by now. In a satirical collection of literary "wanted posters," Bierbaum wrote that Panizza had gone from trying to exterminate the Jewish race and the pope to being obsessed with getting expelled from everywhere. Bierbaum correctly predicted that Panizza would not last very long in Paris, but that first he would be displayed at the Paris World's Fair "in an ape house specially built for him, where he would without a doubt earn the title of world champion in long-distance spitting at moveable targets. Naturally he only spits at targets depicting the portraits of crowned heads" (Bierbaum, *Steckbriefe* 103f.) Bierbaum scoffed that if Panizza " is not successful in becoming famous that way, he will join the Society of Jesus with the deliberate intention of later becoming first a Jesuit general and later pope."

Panizza himself characterized *Parisjana* as a work "in which the author's personal opponent, Wilhelm II, is portrayed as the public enemy of mankind and culture, and in which the acuity of the train of thoughts and their form of expression were pushed to the extreme limit of the aesthetically permissible" (*In memoriam* 17). He contemptuously portrayed the German Emperor with scatological derision and gleeful disgust. Addressing his readers back in Germany, he wrote: "You have a god with real intestines / and your god makes poop" (#8). Virtually all ninety-nine poems are staunchly anti–German and bitterly denounce the German people's subservience to their vainglorious ruler, Kaiser Wilhelm II:

> A population that allows itself
> To become the henchmen for a stupid boy
> Loses its rights to rule
> And sinks forgotten into the night.
>
> A people of lackeys,
> Content to be natural-born servants,
> Loses the power to lead
> Loses the right to exist, [...] (#9)
>
> Don't come as "God" or "thinker"
> with things that nobody listens to,
> stop whinnying and making a big stink
> and become a person instead of a horse! (#25)

Only one question here has any
meaning left, whether you are a fighter,
then draw your sword and challenge,
as anarchist, as socialist. (#39)

I see the enemy of the German fatherland,
from my Patmos in Paris,
as someone related to a horse,
coupled, foaming at the mouth,
spawned by horse harlotry
and certain of its family tree;
not that I would call it centaur —
this steed is not so noble —
horseshit from its rump in back,
horseshit from its mouth in front! (#42)

Panizza's savage hostility toward his enemies is anything but subtle: "[...] just grab your enemy by the collar,/ and then rip his balls out!" (#74) As the author had surely anticipated, all unsold copies of this work were confiscated by the German authorities. He was formally charged in January 1900 with the crime of lèse-majesté for insulting Kaiser Wil-

helm II, and another warrant for his arrest was issued in Munich by Freiherr von Sartor, the district attorney who had successfully prosecuted him in 1895 for blasphemy in *The Love Council*. What Panizza had not anticipated, however, was that in addition to the issuance of an arrest warrant, on 10 March 1900 his entire estate in Germany of RM 185,000 was frozen, since he was now considered both a "foreigner" and a fugitive from the law. After a year of barely being able to survive in Paris without adequate funds to even pay his rent, Panizza was forced to return to Germany in the spring of 1901. On 13 April 1901, a Good Friday, he surrendered himself to the court in Munich that had issued the warrant for his arrest, and his assets were unfrozen. Once more, Panizza had to endure imprisonment, this time for four months in the detention facility Am Anger. Finally, he was sent to the *Oberbayrische Kreisirrenanstalt München*, a district psychiatric clinic, for a six-week period of observation. This must have been a truly nightmarish "homecoming," for the clinic was the same one in which he had worked as a psychiatrist two decades previously.

The results of the extensive psychiatric

Woodcut by Bruno Paul of Oskar Panizza and his dog, Puzzi, first appeared in Martin Möbius [O.J. Bierbaum], *Steckbriefe*. Berlin: Schuster und Loeffler, 1900.

examinations clearly showed that the patient was suffering from chronic paranoia. After a few more weeks spent in the Munich prison, he was released without any explanation. He subsequently learned from friends that all criminal charges had been dropped against him as a result of Dr. Fritz Ungemach's detailed psychiatric evaluation, which covers some seventy handwritten pages. This psychiatric evaluation and other medical records are quoted extensively and discussed in detail by Jürgen Müller in his psychiatric study, *Der Pazjent als Psychiater*. On August 26, Judge Dimroth ruled that all criminal charges should be dismissed due to the defendant's legal incompetence resulting from his mental illness. Panizza left Munich the very same day and returned to Paris by train.

Once in Paris, he published the last few issues of his *Zürcher Diskussionen* before finally ceasing all his publishing activities. It was not that he had stopped writing, but he was no longer able to secure a printer for his works.

Hallucinating Toward Imperjalja

The years spent in Paris, especially those following the publication of *Parisjana*, appear to have been filled with solitude and very little social intercourse. He saw a few old friends from time to time, but these encounters would seem to have been progressively infrequent. Frank Wedekind, old friend from his days in Munich, is one of the few writers who made a point of seeing Panizza whenever he was in town. In a letter to Richard Weinhöppel, Wedekind tells of dragging Panizza around Paris "with super-human effort" (*Gesammelte Briefe* I, 332). In a later letter to the same friend we find the sentence: "Panizza is perfecting himself more and more in his madness" (335). There is no evidence, nor is it very likely, that this "madman's" path ever crossed that of young Rainer Maria Rilke. He, too, was leading a life of painful solitude in Paris, not many blocks away from Panizza. From Emma Goldman's memoirs we know that Panizza spent some time in Paris with Oscar Wilde, who had also just served a stiff prison sentence on a morals conviction (*Living My Life*, 269–270).

The vacuous two years from November 1901 to November 1903 are referred to in the author's Autobiographical Sketch of 1904 by a dash:—. Much of the time he was trying to deal with his various mental and physical problems, such as frequent nausea, fatigue and intestinal cramps. By far the most troubling aspect of his life was his gradually deteriorating mental health, as he became increasingly paranoid. In his diaries, notebooks and other literary efforts, we see the anguished author, a professional psychiatrist, trying to make sense of his progressive psychotic behavior, particularly the increasingly frequent auditory and olfactory hallucinations dating back to his days as a psychiatric resident in 1885. Panizza tried in vain to order his thoughts, record his symptoms, test his objectivity and analyze his perceptions, even as he was being inexorably overwhelmed by his growing mental deterioration.

Panizza wrote his sister Ida in June 1903, asking her for money to buy a villa in France. The family in Germany, however, was in no position to indulge their black sheep in such an extravagance. The last phase of his Parisian exile began in the fall of 1903 when Panizza, who was now living in the strictest seclusion, began to be tormented by painful auditory hallucinations. He was convinced that the German government was conspiring with a large number of French detectives to make his life miserable. The French government had shown such tolerance to him that they were free from any suspicions. The following excerpt from the author's tortured prose describes himself in the third person and gives a vivid picture of his acute paranoia:

Since he, as previously mentioned, had not published anything in two years, one had to consider the possibility that another party, which was more less [sic] kindly disposed toward the patient's views, might secretly be monitoring his manuscripts, perhaps copying them and, insofar as they corresponded to the views of the new party, publishing them, even using the title, firm, imprint and paper of the defunct *Zürcher Diskussionen*. Only thus could one explain the new hostilities toward the patient, who, at least in a certain place, was considered to be the author and the editor responsible for the supposed publications. Since, that the finding of insanity issued two years previously could be taken seriously — so that any friendly or hostile political party would have been wary of dealing with his manuscripts — that is something patient considered all the less, as neither Frenchmen nor foreigners among his acquaintances had the remotest notion not to consider him to be in complete mental health [*In memoriam* 18–19].

Panizza mentions minor chicaneries such as a temperamental fireplace, the cutting off of his water supply and tampered apartment locks. But these were trifles compared to the shrill, high-pitched whistling sound which painfully stimulated his auditory nerve. The instruments which produced this whistling were everywhere. When he sat at home, he could hear the sound coming from a house across the street on the rue des Abesses. When he went for his weekly Sunday walk in the Bois de Montmorency, the whistling mysteriously followed him. Panizza-the-psychiatrist was sure that these sounds were not psychogenic since they disappeared when he covered his ears. The whistling tormented Panizza in Paris for more than half a year, and as the months passed, so did any final doubts that the hellish noises might actually be auditory hallucinations. During most of the spring of 1904, he was forced to forego exercise and fresh air, remaining locked in his little apartment where the noises were not as severe as outside.

Another "conspiracy," which the author felt might be linked to the above-mentioned one, was believed to be directed by his aging mother in Munich and aimed at forcing the fifty-year-old bachelor into marriage. He saw this plot being carried out by local *concièrges*, chamber maids and other gossips. Once he perceived these intrigues to be under foot, he wrote his mother telling her that he had neither the desire nor the time to think about getting married. This letter seems to have done the trick, for shortly thereafter this second "conspiracy" came to an abrupt end.

In his Autobiographical Sketch, Panizza devotes a considerable amount of space to a justification of his refusal to even seriously consider matrimony. He begins with the rational argument that there are numerous hereditary defects in his family, especially on his mother's side, which would endanger the health of any offspring. Furthermore, he still had the deformation on his right leg, which he — probably erroneously — attributed to syphilis. In view of the fact that psychotics and syphilitics were being urged to refrain from marriage, he reasoned, it would be almost criminal for him as a physician "to frivolously procreate decrepit offspring" (*In memoriam* 21). The other reasons he adduced are less than convincing, namely that his literary activity forced him to spend the greatest part of his days writing in absolute isolation, the rest being devoted to extended solitary walks outdoors, a lifestyle wholly incompatible with marriage.

And even if the products of this literary creation are minimally esteemed by the public and critics, they are not an expression of the patient's whim or caprice, but absolutely essential in relieving his brain. Thus, he must take the safer way and continue in the old proven track in order to maintain his psychic balance and not chase after phantasmata, which are perhaps most useful for others, but which appear as a health hazard to him [22].

It is certainly not hard to understand why a fifty-year-old bachelor undergoing a severe psychotic breakdown would shy away from the thought of being forced into marriage. It might be a more fruitful question to ask why, in the preceding decades, he remained single despite his preoccupation with sex and his liberal-permissive attitudes on this subject. As far as one can judge such things more than a full century later from a few scraps of biographical sources, it would appear that Oskar Panizza may have been bisexual. One anonymous contemporary literary source explicitly referred to his homosexuality ("Oskar Panizza." *Das litterarische Echo* 1 Dec.1904: 349). Panizza was drawn to writing articles about homosexuality, e.g., "Bayreuth und die Homosexualität. Eine Erwägung" (Bayreuth and Homosexuality: A Consideration; *Die Gesellschaft* 1895, 88–92). He also repeatedly condemned paragraph 175 of the German penal law that forbid homosexual activity (*ZD* III, no. 25/26, 13 and no. 27, 8). Dr. Paul Ostermeier, a physician who had known Panizza since they were students together in the 1870s, wrote in May 1901 that "a certain sadistic streak also seemed to be part of his sex life; [...] he related to women with a certain brutality" (Müller 117). Perhaps most telling of all, an almost visceral revulsion against heterosexuality seems to be imbedded in some of his best works, including *The Love Council, From the Diary of a Dog* and a number of his short stories, e.g., "Der Corsetten-Fritz." He does not appear to have *ever* had any intimate, emotional ties to any women outside of those in his immediate family. One need not belabor this point any further, but if Panizza did indeed believe his rationalizations for shunning marriage, it might be a good indication of how limited his awareness had become in 1903.

One of the clearest and most bizarre documents of Panizza's progressive paranoia is his work titled *Imperjalja*, a delusionary fantasy that has rarely been matched in the vast literature of conspiracy theories. Long believed to have been lost, the author worked on this 180-page manuscript between his 1901 incarceration in Munich and his final admittance to a Bayreuth sanatorium in 1904. It was first published in 1993 and depicts the author's full-blown fantasy construct of an international conspiracy, with Panizza playing a central role in unmasking the villainous scheme. *Imperjalja* depicts the deadly struggle between the evil emperor, Wilhelm II, and his nemesis, Otto von Bismarck, the head of a shadow government trying to unite the German-speaking peoples of Europe against foreign enemies. The author employs a variety of sources, including newspaper clippings and photographs, all of which are seen as coded messages concerning Wilhelm II.

As a psychotic case history, it is morbidly fascinating to see how the author weaves an endless web of intrigue, encompassing a huge array of nineteenth-century European social and political figures. These even include the notorious Jack the Ripper, Lord Byron, Charles Baudelaire, Paul Verlaine and Pope Leo XIII, all of whom are revealed to be mere "parallel personages" of Wilhelm II. *Imperjalja* links tabloid accounts of notorious sex crimes with the devious machinations of the Kaiser, who was also viewed as responsible for Panizza's 1895 trial for blasphemy in *The Love Council*. Even Nietzsche and the Bavarian King Ludwig II were seen to be caught up in Wilhelm's murderous scheme, which only Panizza could fully comprehend and which he was heroically struggling to reveal to the world in *Imperjalja*, his grandiose exposé. The author's own deteriorating mental health actually made sense as part of Wilhelm's all-encompassing web of intrigue: Panizza saw himself as being mercilessly hounded in Paris by the Kaiser's undercover agents, who were secretly working to either discredit him or, if that failed, to destroy him by driving him insane.

Return to Germany

Plagued by his perception of "marriage conspiracies" and increasingly frequent hallucinations, especially the incessant whistling that continued unabated despite resolute attempts to distract himself by writing, he was literally at his wits' end by the early summer of 1904. On May 21 he wrote a really alarming letter to his mother, and a second one followed a week later. Frau Panizza thought a sanatorium in Boll might be the right place for her son to find a cure, and she dispatched a granddaughter, Mathilde Collard, to fetch her uncle in Paris. However, he had since moved to a shabby rooming-house on Montmartre and stubbornly refused to see his niece. Panizza simply could not yet admit to himself that he was a very ill individual, and accepting his family's mercy mission would have been tantamount to surrender.

During the following few weeks, the whistling became sharply intensified, and the agony of remaining in Paris was approaching the unbearable. On the evening of June 23, he rather abruptly fled Paris by taking an express train to Lausanne. There he still perceived the annoying sounds, albeit at diminished intensity, but they completely disappeared once he began to rest at Lake Geneva and stroll in the nearby woods. After an unsuccessful attempt at obtaining a modest country home in these pleasant surroundings, he left the following week for Munich via Bern, Zürich and Lindau.

Since his hallucinations began to recur in Munich, he saw no other alternative but to request admittance to the *Oberbayerische Kreisirrenanstalt München*, the Munich district insane asylum where he had worked as an intern in 1885 and where he had been admitted for psychiatric observation in 1901. He could not readily accept that he was mentally ill, he simply wanted to prove to himself and everyone else that he was the unfortunate victim of external persecution. Dr. Fritz Ungemach, however, would not admit him, supposedly due to lack of space. Instead, Panizza was directed to a private asylum, Neu-Friedenheim, an institution which, if anything, only heightened his paranoid feelings. After one brief week of treatment there, Panizza left, allegedly after being harassed by Dr. Rehm and his staff. He still refused to accept the fact that he was suffering psychotic episodes.

Oskar Panizza's last quarter-year as a non-institutionalized citizen was spent in a modest room at Feilitzschstraße 59/II. He assiduously avoided the city and his old friends, preferring instead to take long walks in the refreshing parkland of the *Englischer Garten*. When he asked to see his 84-year-old mother, he was informed that this was impossible, since the feeble woman feared the sight of her son might precipitate a stroke. As the summer passed and the days became cooler, he began to spend most of his mornings sitting in the *Staatsbibliothek* (State Library), either reading or filling his notebooks with poetry and prose. Yet not only did the whistling sounds persist, but they were now augmented by flutes of a distinctly metallic character. His paranoia had grown so acute by September that the police had to investigate several public incidents reported to them, where the author had insulted strangers on the street, accusing them of being police spies and throwing stones at them. Panizza had previously experienced suicidal inclinations in Paris, Lausanne and Neu-Friedenheim, and by the second week in October his depression had again reached suicidal intensity. After having gone without food for over a day, he felt the time was ripe to extinguish his suffering. In a fit of despair, he hastily wrote a will and proceeded to a secluded spot in the *Englischer Garten* in order to hang himself. But once he had climbed the tree, he was overpowered by fear and failed to successfully complete the project. He returned to his room even more dejected and "deeply ashamed" (*In memoriam* 24).

On October 19 he seized upon a less desperate course of action, an eccentric measure which was more in keeping with the true Panizza style. On this day he had been "whistled at" six times on his way to the library and again on his solitary walk through Oberföhring. Taking advantage of the mild afternoon temperature, he returned home briefly, undressed, and at 5 P.M. strolled down the busy Leopoldstraße wearing only his shirt. Naturally he did not get very far on this walk. Outraged citizens apprehended and dragged him into the nearest house, where they awaited the arrival of a policeman. Wilhelm Hirschbiel, Panizza's 74-year-old landlord, had followed him onto the street, but the author refused to recognize him. Instead, Panizza stated his identity as Ludwig Fromann, stenographer from Würzburg. He was taken by ambulance to the police station, given a brief medical examination and transferred to the psychiatric ward of the Links der Isar Hospital. Writing his autobiographical sketch four weeks later, Panizza notes with a certain satisfaction: "The coup succeeded" (25).

His mother, however, refused to provide either a security deposit or clothes for her son's hospital stay. She suggested, instead, having Oskar transferred to a "higher class" insane asylum and appointing a legal guardian for him (Bauer 32). Mathilde Panizza's suggestions were carried out in due course the following year.

The Psychiatrist as Patient

In the Links der Isar Hospital, Dr. Panizza continued to claim that he was Ludwig Fromann, on leave from a mental hospital and about to go swimming in Lake Kleinhessellohe. However, once he was recognized and positively identified, he gave a fluent and lucid oral account of his case history, closely paralleling the previously-cited written one. This time he added a few more details, such as the fact that the Kaiser had died and was being played by a stand-in, and that Chancellor von Bülow was conspiring with the French Minister Delcassé against Panizza.

On 5 November 1904, only a few weeks after Panizza had provoked his own arrest, the Munich district attorney initiated proceedings to have the author declared legally incompetent due to mental deficiency. Three days later, the author was transferred to the new Psychiatric Clinic on Nussbaumstraße and *Justizrat* Josef Popp, a distant relative and an attorney recommended by Panizza's mother, was appointed as his interim legal guardian. Panizza was highly displeased by the choice of this attorney to be his guardian. Nine years previously, Popp had publicly lambasted *The Love Council* as being so sinful that it could only be cleansed by a deluge and had characterized its author as "a faun of the most disgusting sort" (*Augsburger Postzeitung* 7 June 1895: 2. See entire article in Chapter 11). Panizza at first filed an objection, which he withdrew several days later, admitting that he was incapable of adequately assessing his situation. He later wrote his Autobiographical Sketch and filed a deposition on 17 November 1904, stating that he was the victim of an international conspiracy and was being whistled at wherever he went, including inside the clinic by agents posing as patients.

An extended hearing was held in the clinic on 6 December 1904, at which Presiding Judge Seidl, Dr. Fritz Ungemach and others questioned the author about his perceived persecution by painful whistling, as well as about his theories concerning Wilhelm II and those "secret undercover agents." Professor Hans von Gudden, the son of his former supervisor, Bernhard von Gudden, was in charge of examining the patient. He was quite unambiguous in the conclusion to his voluminous psychiatric testimonial of 2 February 1905:

Dr. Panizza's behavior over the past years has sufficiently proven that all his actions and activities have been guided by systematized delusions of persecution, that as a result of these delusions he repeatedly changed his residence, transformed his lifestyle into that of a homeless, hounded refugee, who hardly dared to eat and viewed everyone as his enemy, who perceived and processed all phenomena in a pathological manner [Müller 171–172].

Professor von Gudden concluded his evaluation with the verdict that his patient was incapable of forming judgments about anything that were free of delusions, that in accordance with civil law he was therefore incompetent. His colleague, Dr. Fritz Ungemach, was in complete agreement when he stated that the patient had been suffering from "chronic madness for many years" (Müller 173). On 28 March 1905, Judge Seidl ruled that Oskar Panizza was legally incompetent due to mental illness and was ordered to pay 2,000 RM to cover the proceedings. While Bauer maintains that Panizza, "an author in opposition to the Wilhelmine Empire," was the victim of "a politically motivated proceeding using medical evaluations" (219), Müller notes that even if the authorities and certain relatives indeed appeared eager to institutionalize this black sheep, he was examined at length by some of the best psychiatrists in all of Germany, whose thorough examinations were all in complete agreement: "No doubts remain about his diagnosis" (Müller 196). Müller's lengthy case study, meticulously tracing the author's entire life and his family's mental health history, concludes that what led the Munich court to declare Panizza mentally incompetent in 1905 was not his prickly politics but his progressive psychotic condition: "Panizza had completely lost his relation to reality" (213).

On 5 February 1905, Panizza was transferred from the major Psychiatric Clinic in Munich to St. Gilgenberg, a small private mental asylum for twenty patients in Bayreuth. His derangement, which progressed over the years, was frequently interrupted by long periods of apparently normal lucidity. Thus, after informing the court that it should decide whatever would be in his best interest, he vigorously protested when he lost his legal rights on 28 March 1905. Now he became relegated to a ward of his brother Felix and the loathsome attorney, Josef Popp, toward whom he had long harbored a strong antipathy.

Panizzal continued to create some bizarrely fascinating art during his sojourn in St. Gilgenberg. During his first two years in this asylum, the author produced around four hundred pencil drawings. Several years later, a selection of thirty-four of these drawings was sent to the Prinzhorn Collection of the Psychiatric University Clinic in Heidelberg, a world-renowned repository of art by psychiatric patients. The folder with Panizza's drawings contained a note asking for the artwork to be returned, which it never was. The Prinzhorn Collection still owns these drawings, along with six additional ones acquired later. Dedicated to Léon Gambetta (1838–1882), the staunchly anti–German French politician, Panizza's drawings reflect a number of personal, sexual and political themes that were dear to him, such as Otto von Bismarck in a sarcophagus or Théophile Delcassé, the French Foreign Minister from 1898 to 1905, with his head in a noose. The entire collection of Panizza drawings from the Prinzhorn Collection, as well as ten additional ones collected by Friedrich Lippert, were published in 1989 by Michael Farin.

One of his later poems written in St. Gilgenberg, "A Poet Who Lived in Vain" (1904), shows the author's utter despair at what he saw as his wasted life. It ends with the lines:

> Cursed be my life, writing, dreaming, singing;—
> I have lived in vain — breathing stops.—
> Death takes hold of him, from his pale mouth

The breath of life is expelled from his mind,—
And the echo calls mocking in the round
No kind word after him: "Lived in vain."
(*In memoriam* 54)

Before the St. Gilgenberg asylum was sold in 1908, Panizza was moved to Dr. Würz-burger's Herzoghöhe, then a luxury sanatorium at the edge of Bayreuth, which still oper-ates today as a modern rehabilitation clinic. The author was housed in the facility's newly built and equally luxurious Mainschloss building, where he would remain for the next thir-teen years until his death in 1921. Herzoghöhe was certainly not a mental institution of any kind, but rather an open facility primarily for patients with coronary and circulatory ail-ments. Panizza was apparently accepted there on the basis of a lucrative financial arrange-ment with the author's co-guardians. He alternated between considering himself mentally ill and perfectly sane. When a professor from Erlangen visited him in Herzoghöhe and inquired about what was bothering him, the author answered, "I have hallucinations." Asked to explain his condition in greater detail, Dr. Panizza caustically replied, "You can read about it in any textbook!" (*In memoriam* 31).

One can indeed read about the author's case history in one of the most famous psy-chiatric textbooks of the twentieth century.

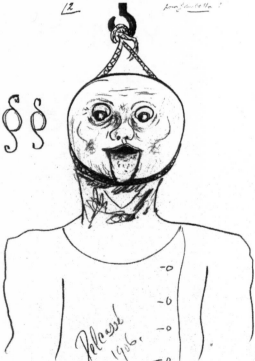

French Foreign Minister Théophile Del-cassé, drawn by Panizza while he was a resident in the mental asylum of St. Gilgen-berg in Bayreuth, 1906. Courtesy of the Prinzhorn Collection of the Psychiatric Uni-versity Clinic in Heidelberg.

At this time [Emil] Kraepelin's binary system of dementia praecox or *circuläres Irresein* was con-tested, and Panizza himself became a personifica-tion of the insufficiencies of Kraepelin's system, leading ultimately to the concept of paraphrenias. In 1921, for the first time, the eighth edition of Kraepelin's textbook of psychiatry contained the concept of paraphrenias. "Systematic paraphrenia" was mentioned in a lecture given in 1916 (in the third edition of Kraepelin's lectures), and Oskar Panizza's history was used as a case report [Müller, *American Journal of Psychiatry* 157, 1 Jan. 2000: 114].

Professor Kraepelin, director of the univer-sity's Psychiatric Clinic in Munich, thoroughly examined Panizza, whom he had known for twenty years ever since they had worked together in 1884 under Professor Bernhard von Gudden. In his textbook, Kraepelin cited Panizza as a prime example of "paraphrenia systematica," closely related to "dementia praecox." Accord-ing to Kraepelin, patients with systematic para-phrenia are characterized by persistent, fairly cohesive delusions, without disintegration of the personality. As the disorder progresses over time, patients increasingly experience auditory, visual and other hallucinations. Delusions of grandeur and memory deficiencies are integrated into their paranoid constructs. Persecutory fantasies often lead to violent attacks against imagined enemies, so that patients usually end up being institutionalized to protect themselves and others.

In October 1907, the Panizza family asked Deacon Friedrich Lippert, the clergyman who had befriended Panizza during his imprisonment in Amberg, whether he would be willing to care for the patient in the privacy of his own home. He wisely declined, stating that he felt the patient's mental condition required institutional care. However, when Oskar's brother Felix died in March 1908, Lippert accepted the responsibility of functioning as the patient's co-guardian. He took this job very seriously, and when he retired in October 1915, he moved to Bayreuth in order to better serve his ward. Lippert appears to have been truly devoted to Panizza, though he was also generously compensated from the author's estate. The following quotation, though not without a trace of vanity, offers a glimpse into how Deacon Lippert viewed this responsibility:

> I performed my duty all the more gladly, since Oskar greeted me as an old friend at our first reunion, and his words, "Now I'm in the insane asylum," moved me deeply. But I also knew that he liked to hear the comfort of the gospel, and I held worship services at least once a month [...] during which Oskar joyfully sang along to the hymns and devoutly prayed "with his better self." After all, these patients are often like children, who feel the divine drive toward religion the strongest [...] my most beautiful reward was when he kissed my hand after services [*In memoriam* 48f.].

Besides being a loyal guardian and friend to Panizza, Lippert has provided us with virtually the only information about the author's last years. He describes how Panizza was unable to complete his ultimate book with the envisioned title *Die Geburtsstunde Gottes: Ein mitologischer Ziklus im Sinne des Sonnen- und Mondlaufes* (*The Hour of God's Birth: A Mythological Cycle Following the Solar and Lunar Orbits*). Panizza's notebooks degenerated into "a witch's brew of Bible, myth, sagas, ghosts, pornography, philosophy, Wagner, murder and manslaughter in German, English, French and Italian" (*In memoriam* 49). Whenever Panizza was hallucinating, he only spoke French; even the daily newspaper he read was French. As the years passed, his hallucinations became more prevalent and his notebooks grew more confused and lascivious. It was only in the last few years, however, that he ceased writing altogether.

There does not seem to have been any effort made to treat the patient, obviously because he was considered to be incurable. Lippert recounts how Panizza progressively withdrew from everyone around him, how he refused to talk to the doctors and only occasionally spoke with his fellow patients, preferring the company of the hopelessly incurable to those who had the potential of being rehabilitated. He drifted further and further away from his family and only reluctantly received any visitors. He was untouched by the death of his brother Felix in 1908 and displayed no reaction to the death of his 93-year-old mother in 1915.

Other accounts of Panizza's years in Herzoghöhe differ sharply from the one given by Lippert. Walter Mehring, in an otherwise inaccurate discourse on Panizza, offers the following conspiratorial version:

> An alleged fit of insanity resulted in his being sent to a private sanatorium. His Munich coffeehouse colleagues claimed he was sent there because his uncle, a Jesuit, intervened at the request of his family, as the Marquis de Sade's mother-in-law had done. He remained in the sanatorium for twenty years, shut off from the outside world and continuing to write until his death in 1922. Like the Marquis de Sade at Charenton, no one was permitted to visit him. I tried in vain to do so [*Lost Library* 65].

Unless one assumes a full-fledged conspiracy involving scores of apparently unrelated individuals, then Mehring's account must be regarded as a gross distortion of the facts. Of greater interest is Max Krell's report of a visit by Frank Wedekind to Herzoghöhe: "In the Torgelstube one evening, Frank Wedekind said, 'I visited Panizza yesterday. He's in excellent shape. He's the most rational person on this earth. And he's working!' (54). Krell goes on to report that

> when Wedekind, the only acquaintance from his past, visited him, he showed him what he was working on: he was translating Aristophanes into German, and he engaged his guest in astonishing discussions concerning dramaturgical craft. Wedekind considered the renditions to be excellent, he showed portions of them to Greek scholars at the university who admitted: simply brilliant. Later these texts disappeared, as did Panizza's earlier publications [57].

Wedekind's visit occurred during the first few years of Panizza's sojourn in Herzoghöhe, when he enjoyed long periods of complete lucidity; whereas by the time Mehring tried to visit him in 1915, his condition had vastly deteriorated. According to Lippert, World War I was an event the author could no longer comprehend.

The last years of his life appear to have been completely devoid of any rational activity. He tore up books that displeased him, smashed windows when he wanted to have fresh air in his room, dispensed medical counsel to his fellow patients and generally behaved in a deranged manner. A stroke suffered on the evening of 28 September 1921 put an end to Oskar Panizza's difficult life. He was buried two days later by Deacon Lippert in the Bayreuth municipal cemetery, following a funeral attended exclusively by asylum personnel. There has never been even a simple marker to designate the plot where he is buried.

Panizza's immediate family and heirs, primarily his nieces and nephews, did nothing to preserve the author's memory or even his literary estate. On the contrary, they seemed eager to obliterate any traces left behind by the family's black sheep. His exquisite personal library, consisting of some ten thousand books valued at 75,000 RM, had been sent back from Paris when he was initially committed in 1904. This prized collection, including many rare volumes that the author had collected for more than a quarter-century, were stored in a barn outside of Bad Kissingen and eventually sold in 1919 to Horst Stobbe, a Munich book dealer. Two years after Panizza's death, Deacon Lippert was paid 40,000 RM by the author's heirs for the his entire literary estate, including early unpublished manuscripts and diaries written during the last decades of his life (Bauer 30f.). These have never been seen again and probably no longer exist.

Chapter 6

Panizza's *Autobiographical Sketch*, 1904

The following *Autobiographical Sketch* is dated 17 November 1904. It was written by Oskar Panizza some four weeks after intentionally provoking his arrest and admission to the Psychiatric Clinic in Munich. He remained there under observation until he was transferred on 5 February 1905 to the St. Gilgenberg asylum in Bayreuth.

Oskar Panizza, born 12 November 1853 in Bad Kissingen, comes from a troubled family. Uncle suffered from partial religious madness and died after a fifteen-year insane asylum stay in the insane ward of the Juliusspital in Würzburg. Another uncle committed suicide at a youthful age. One aunt died of a stroke, another aunt is still alive and is psychologically abnormal, sometimes affectedly witty, sometimes feeble-minded. All these relations are on the maternal side of the family. Mother is still living, hot-tempered, energetic, strong-willed, with an almost masculine intelligence. Father died of typhus, was of Italian descent, passionate, dissolute, hot-tempered and accomplished man of the world, poor household manager. Of the patient's siblings, the two younger ones experienced melancholic episodes, as did patient himself in earlier years. Younger sister attempted suicide twice (perhaps compounded by hysteria). In the entire family there exists a prevalence of mental activity with an inclination toward discussing religious questions. Mother and patient write. Patient himself suffered from the usual childhood diseases, measles, whooping cough, had great difficulty learning to read, showed no aptitude, received the nickname "dummy" from his siblings, had difficulty progressing in high school, had an unproductive but lively imagination and was constantly introverted, so that he was incapable of comprehending the necessity of an orderly, systematic preparation for a profession, devoted himself temporarily to music and finally graduated at the advanced age of twenty-four from the humanistic *Gymnasium*. Experienced a mild sleepwalking episode with the measles at about age twelve: in an unconscious state, he left his bed during the day, ran around in the sickroom and was finally found kneeling and praying in front of his bed and was rescued from his trance. After graduation from the *Gymnasium* he devoted himself with great love and zeal to the study of medicine, became a co-assistant under [Professor Hugo von] Ziemssen, worked under same at the Clinical Institute, received his doctorate in 1880 *summa cum laude* and in the same year received his medical license. As a student he became infected with *lues* which, though treated *lege artis* for years, is still manifest in the form of a massive *gumma* on the right tibia and resists even the most energetic treatment with potassium iodide. After completing his military obligation as resident doctor in the military hospital and promotion to assistant doctor second class in the reserves, patient went to Paris with numerous recommendations from Ziemssen,

119

but visited only a few hospitals, devoting himself instead to the study of French literature, particularly drama, for which he was especially suited with his knowledge of the French language, which had been continuously fostered in his parents' home as the result of his mother's Huguenot ancestry. Having returned to Munich in 1882, he joined the Upper Bavarian District Insane Asylum as assistant doctor fourth class under [Professor Bernhard von] Gudden and served there for two years, having advanced to assistant doctor fourth class [sic]. Impaired health and scientific and other differences with his supervisor caused him to leave this position in 1884 and, with the exception of minor medical services as a general practitioner, now turned definitively to literature, which since Paris had never lost his attention. Partly under the aftereffect of a mental depression, which had begun in the insane asylum and that lasted almost a year, there emerged the volume of lyric poetry *Düstre Lieder* [*Gloomy Songs*] (Leipzig, 1885), which was influenced by Heine. Substantially buoyed and refreshed by this literary release, he visited England in the same year, a visit that had been preceded by an intensive study of the English language and literature under Mrs. Callway, and where he spent a full year on literary work in the British Museum. *Londoner Lieder* [*London Songs*] (Leipzig, 1887) emerged as the fruit of this sojourn. In the following years, learning and studying Italian language and literature under Signora Luccioli in Munich, since intensive occupation with foreign languages and literary production proved to be the best antidote for all kinds of psychopathic moods. Repeated trips to Italy. As a result of the acquaintance with M.G. Conrad, a series of partly scholarly, partly literary and art essays appeared beginning in 1890 in *Die Gesellschaft* [*The Society*], whose founder and editor was M.G. Conrad. In the year 1899 [1890] *Dämmrungsstücke* [*Twilight Pieces*] had been published, a collection of fantastical novellas, which are partially under the influence of the American novelist Edgar Poe. Introduced by M.G. Conrad into the *Gesellschaft für modernes Leben* [Society for Modern Life], patient gave several lectures there, including "Genie und Wahnsinn" [Genius and Madness] (Munich: Pößl, 1891), which resulted in the attention of the authorities, the hostility of the ultramontane press ("Social Democrats in Tuxes") and remonstrations from the district militia commander. Summoned by the latter to leave the Society for Modern Life, patient refused and was relieved with a "simple discharge" of his military status, to which he had meanwhile advanced to assistant doctor first class.

An essay by the patient, "Das Verbrechen [The Crime] in Tavistock Square" (an English reminiscence) in the *Sammelbuch der Münchner Moderne* [*Anthology of the Munich Moderns*] (Munich: Pößl, 1891) led to the legal charge of an "immoral act," which, however, was dropped by the District Court Munich I. A tragiccomical piece, *Aus dem Tagebuch eines Hundes* [*From the Diary of a Dog*], illustrated by Hoberg in Leipzig, appeared in 1892. In the following year: *Visionen* [*Visions*], again partially in the style and spirit of Edgar Poe. In 1893 *Die unbefleckte Empfängnis der Päpste* [*The Immaculate Conception of the Popes*] was published, a theological attempt, in the seemingly most serious style, to expand the dogma of the immaculate conception of the Virgin Mary to include the popes, with all the embryological, anthropological and theological consequences, which, according to the title page, patient had translated from Spanish. As a result of denunciations in Stuttgart, this publication was confiscated by court order and banned throughout the German Empire by means of the so-called objective procedure. This was followed by strong criticisms on the part of the Catholic and Protestant press, as well as public warnings not to purchase the book. *Der teutsche Michel und der römische Papst* [*The German Michel and the Roman Pope*] was published with a foreword by M.G. Conrad in 1894, in which Germany's *gravamina* against Rome are summarized tendentiously in the form of theses, based on historical narratives and using extensive citation of sources. This work was likewise confiscated in the objective process, i.e., after expiration of the deadline for filing a complaint and legal prosecution. The "heavenly tragedy" *Das Liebeskonzil* [*The Love Council*] was also published in 1894 (Zürich, Schabelitz) in which, using a quotation by Ulrich von Hutten, the emergence of syphilis in Italy at the end of the 15th century is portrayed as the result of the licentious behavior at the papal court of Alexander VI, executed in the form of a medieval mystery play with modern illumination. In the spring of 1895, this closet drama brought the patient before the Munich Court of Assize, where he was sentenced in the spring of 1895 for violation of Paragraph 166 of the Imperial Penal Code to one year imprisonment, a sentence which was soon thereafter upheld by the Imperial Court in Leipzig. Patient served his sentence in the Amberg prison, where, after a belated appeal by the defense attorney regarding mental competency (without first asking the prisoner), there ensued a summary examination of same *quoad psychen intactam*—"Are you mentally ill?"—"No."—, which led to a negative conclusion. After serving his sentence, patient took leave of Munich with the little brochure *Abschied von München* [*Farewell from Munich*] (Zürich, 1896), which resulted in confiscation and the issuing of an arrest warrant for the author, who had meanwhile moved to Zürich. Still in the same autumn, patient published the ethnographic study *Die bayrischen Haberfeldtreiben* [*The Bavarian Charivaris*] (Berlin, S. Fischer), in which, at the request of the fearful publisher, several passages from the text, as well as some verses of the original "Charivari Protocols," were replaced by ellipses in the text, which had already been set and was ready for printing; this occurred even though it had been published without objection a few years previously in an essay by the patient in the *Neue Rundschau* (same publisher).

Patient had meanwhile renounced his Bavarian citizenship with the intention of acquiring Swiss citizenship after his two-year residency in Zürich. Since Schabelitz in Switzerland was now also creating difficulties, patient established his own publishing firm, using the same name as the simultaneously founded journal, *Züricher Diskussionen* [*Zürich Discussions*], and published the *Dialoge im Geiste Huttens* [*Dialogues in Hutten's Spirit*], which had been written in the Amberg prison and in which the discussion of public conditions is attempted in the fresh and unabashed style of the early sixteenth-century polemics. In the following spring of 1898, patient wrote the political satire *Psichopatia criminalis* (Zürich, Verlag Zür. Diskussionen), lampooning the prosecution mania of the German district attorneys, while positing a new political mental illness afflicting the German public. This was followed by the drama *Nero* (Zürich, 1898), based exclusively on historical studies. In autumn of the same year, patient was expelled by order of the police, allegedly for having intercourse with a *puella publica* who had just turned fifteen — in Switzerland, having sexual intercourse with girls under the age of fifteen is prohibited, and the tolerance of prostitution had been suspended following a plebiscite; he was labeled a "filthy person" by the Swiss press and, when objection was raised at police headquarters, was immediately told that his expulsion from the Canton of Zürich was tantamount to his expulsion from all of Switzerland. Patient responded to this act of violence in the next issue of *Züricher Diskussionen* with a frank and uncompromising presentation of all the facts in this case, revealing himself and his error committed, but simultaneously pointing to the highest authority in Berlin, whose influence patient believed to have perceived behind the entire proceeding. In Paris, to which patient had meanwhile moved, publication of *Züricher Diskussionen* continued, despite the now anomalous local title, with a more critical slant, especially in political topics, and around Christmas of the following year there appeared, as the fruit of the most withdrawn life and incorporating the freshest, best and most immediate impressions of the French capital, the poetry collection *Parisjana*, in which the author's personal opponent, Wilhelm II, is portrayed as the enemy of mankind and its culture, and where the ideas and forms of expression are pushed to the most extreme limits aesthetically permissible. As foreseen, this publication was confiscated in Germany and a renewed warrant for the author was issued; but, what was not foreseen, his German trust fund was confiscated at the same time, under the most farfetched pretext that he was a fugitive. After holding out for a year, in April 1901 patient found himself in the painful situation of being forced to turn himself in to the court in Munich that had issued the warrant; here he was arrested and, by order of the criminal court, transferred after four months to the Upper Bavarian District Insane Asylum and then, after several weeks, transferred back to the jail and released without the disclosure of any court decision. According to newspaper articles and an unverifiable, private oral statement by the senior district attorney of the Munich I District Court, Baron von Sartor, the case against patient was dropped due to mental illness as the result of an evaluation by Dr. Ungemach, the senior physician at the Munich District Insane Asylum. Having returned to Paris, patient published several more issues of *Züricher Diskussionen* (through no. 32) and in November 1901 suspended his publication activities, but not his writing, for lack of a printer. — In November 1903 there began a series of chicaneries directed against the patient, who lived in the utmost seclusion; the extent of these harassments indicated the collusion of a larger number of agents. And since the French government had shown, if not visible benevolence toward the patient, then at any rate no hostility, thus one could only think of foreign agents, or an order given overseas and carried out by locally recruited French private agents, to make the patient's life miserable. Since he, as previously mentioned, had not published anything in two years, one had to consider the possibility that another party, which was more less [sic] kindly disposed toward the patient's views, might secretly be monitoring his manuscripts, perhaps copying and, insofar as they corresponded to the views of the new party, publishing them, even using the title, firm, imprint and paper of the defunct *Züricher Diskussionen*. Only thus could one explain the new hostilities toward the patient, who, at least in a certain place, was considered to be the author and the editor responsible for the supposed publications. Since, that the finding of insanity issued two years previously could be taken seriously — so that any friendly or hostile political party would have been wary of dealing with his manuscripts — that is something patient considered all the less, as neither Frenchmen nor foreigners among his acquaintances had the remotest notion not to consider him to be in complete mental health. Aside from trivialities, such as snuffing out the fire in the hearth, plugging the chimney, cutting off the water and damaging the apartment locks, the harassment consisted mainly of ingenious *whistling*, calculated to most painfully injure the nervous system, molestations with all kinds of instruments most severely affecting the auditory nerves, some from the house across the street in the rue des Abbesses, some on the street, some even in the Montmorency Forest, where patient regularly went every Sunday. That these were not auditory hallucinations was proven by the simple fact that the whistling stopped the moment patient covered his ears, which surely would not have been the case if they were of cerebral origin. This whistling, which patient considered to be directed at him, later persisted in Munich, where it was also confirmed by reputable witnesses, Ludwig Scharf and Countess Reventlow, who only raised some occasional doubt as to its meaning. However, regarding the latter there was hardly any misinterpretation after three-quarters of a year of suffering and persistence. — Aside from these very targeted attacks, there seemed to be a smaller, less dangerous operation played out in the immediate vicinity and in the subordinate hands of concierges or *femmes de chambre* — an operation from which probably no aging bachelor can escape — that of getting the patient married. As soon as he recognized this activity, he brusquely dealt with the local gossips and then took the occasion to write his mother in Munich — whose liaison with certain Parisian circles was, after all, not impossible — that marriage was out of the question, given the current financial situation of her son, that he had neither the desire nor time for marriage, least of all, if the whistling and other chicanery were ultimately connected to this project, which seemed almost impossible to him, to be forced by such infamous means to choose a marital partner. Following this, the marriage intrigues stopped, while the other molestations continued. Since the former emerged in the most grotesque and scurrilous form once again in Munich, it cannot be overlooked that in the letter to his mother patient had, out of consideration for her and a sense of propriety, concealed the most egregious arguments against entering marriage. The troubling predisposition on the maternal side of the family, which certainly cannot be taken lightly, and the still manifest *lues* in the form of a *gumma* on the *tibia dextra*, would today make frivolously spawning decrepit offspring appear to be criminal, especially for a physician, at a time when it has been proposed to legally prohibit the mentally ill, consumptives and syphilitics from getting married. Furthermore, in the practice of his literary activities, patient must spend the greatest part of the day in solitude and isolation, during good weather take extensive solitary walks, habits that are certainly incompatible with marriage. And even if the products of this literary creativity are esteemed minimally by the public and critics, for the patient they are not the expression of a mood or whim, but are absolutely necessary for relieving his brain. Thus, for the sake of maintaining psychological balance, he must follow the surest path and proceed on the old, well-tried track, and not chase after phantasms that perhaps seem useful for others, but appear to be a health threat for the individual involved.

After more than a half-year's persistence of the molestations described above, which eventually confined the patient to his apartment and caused him to forego the necessary outdoor exercise in the middle of summer, he decided rather suddenly to depart, after intensive occupation with scholarly work did not achieve the necessary distraction, and on 23 June he left Paris with the evening express train from the Gare de Lyon, arriving via Dijon the following noon in Lausanne (Switzerland). To his greatest surprise, the whistling could also be heard in Lausanne, though not nearly to the same extent. This resulted in the compelling conclusion that Paris was not the only source of the animosities. Now the actual reasons for these manifestations remained hidden from him. He recuperated considerably along Lake Geneva and in the surrounding forest where, in contrast to Paris, he had never been harassed, but departed after eight days via Bern, Zürich and Lindau to Munich, as the attempt to find a modest country dwelling had failed. Since the molestations began here as well, he presented himself to the District Insane Asylum in Munich and asked for admittance, in order to prove to himself and others that he was not deceiving himself in the belief that he was dealing with external, systematic hostilities directed at his person; however, he was turned away, allegedly due to overcrowding. He was persuaded by Director Vokke to enter the private insane asylum in Neufriedenheim. But the realization that he was unmistakably being harassed here led to a sharp disagreement with the director, Dr. Rehm, in the course of which the latter asked patient to leave the institution. Patient then rented a modest room on the right at Feilitzstrasse 59/II, where he awaited what was to come. During the subsequent quarter-year, July to October, patient completely avoided the city, regularly went for walks in the English Garden and surroundings, otherwise kept himself completely withdrawn and passive in the knowledge that a change in his external situation could only be brought about by his opponents, as well as himself. His extensive literary works in prose and bound, which had been written while traveling and in Munich, would, unless the patient is very mistaken, not elicit the label of pathological expectorations from any literary or psychiatric expert. An intensification of the situation had occurred, since now, in contrast to Lausanne and even to Paris, serious harassment also occurred at night by far-reaching whistles and flutes of a metallic character, which were most injurious to the auditory organ. After suicidal thoughts had already emerged once in Paris, once in Lausanne and once in Neufriedenheim, there followed on 9 October, in a rapture of despair and hopelessness after quickly writing a will, the beginning of an attempted suicide by hanging in a remote area of the English Garden. But cowardice at the last moment resulted in failure of the decisive jump from the tree that had already been climbed, and patient, who had not eaten in twenty-four hours, returned to his room with the deepest sense of shame. On 19 October patient seized upon a ridiculously dumb remedy compared to the previous one, but which in its consequences was effective. After he had previously been whistled at six times on this day in an unmistakable manner on his way to the State Library and then on his solitary walk through Oberföhring and surroundings, he went home, removed all his clothes except for a shirt, took advantage of the mild weather and at 5 o'clock in the afternoon walked down the Sterneck-Maria-Josefa-Straße onto the Leopoldstraße, with the intention of being seized and, suspected of mental illness, being brought to a public institution and getting examined there by an expert: thus achieving, what he had three months previously failed to accomplish in the Upper Bavarian District Insane Asylum. The coup succeeded. After being apprehended and led into the nearest house, he gave a false name to the policeman who came rushing in, Ludwig Fromann, stenographer from Würzburg. An ambulance was called and patient brought to the police, from where, after a brief examination by the district physician, he was transferred to the municipal Links der Isar Hospital.

Chapter 7

The 1895 Trial in Munich

Oskar Panizza could hardly have been surprised that his publication of *The Love Council* resulted in a trial that will forever be associated with this play. His two previously anti–Catholic publications, *Der unbefleckte Empfängnis der Päpste* (1893, *The Immaculate Conception of the Popes*) and *Der teutsche Michel und der römische Papst* (1894, *The German Michel and the Roman Pope*), had both been legally confiscated and banned throughout the German Reich. Though *The Love Council* is a complex play that contains far more than the anti–Catholic tirades found in these polemics, it does include an assault on traditional Catholic dogma and practice, particularly the various manifestations of what is disparagingly referred to as Mariolatry.

There was perhaps some hope that the author would be spared prosecution because the publication had occurred in Switzerland, outside the jurisdiction of the German Reich. However, there are strong indications that the author consciously provoked what turned out to be the biggest German literary scandal of the 1890s. Once charges were filed, the author still could have easily avoided prosecution by simply leaving Germany, a step he undertook the following year after his release from prison in 1896.

We can rarely ever know with certainty the multitude of complex factors that determine any person's actions. What is clear is that from the very inception of *The Love Council*, the author appears to have been fully aware of being on a collision course with the prevailing German penal code and its powerful enforcement mechanism. He also viewed himself in rather grandiose, unflinchingly heroic terms, apparently ignorant of the heavy toll that a grim year in prison would exact on his already fragile mental health.

Additionally, there was a strong anarchist streak in Panizza, who denied the existence of God and any ultimate reality outside of his own *daimon*, the natural impulses emanating from deep within his psyche. Panizza discussed this concept, largely based on ideas from Max Stirner's *Der Einzige und sein Eigentum* (1844, *The Ego and Its Own*), in his own rather derivative treatise titled *Der Illusionismus und die Rettung der Persönlichkeit* (1895, *Illusionism and Saving One's Personality*).

Finally, it should be remembered that Panizza had always been a rebellious youth, much to the chagrin of his mother. She too, inspired by her staunch Huguenot faith, had frequently challenged governmental authority in religious matters, particularly regarding the education of her children. Her son certainly viewed his decision to stand trial as being consonant with his Huguenot heritage. He later wrote that it "was Huguenot love of opposition and hostility to the state that made me remain in Munich. We Huguenots feel uneasy when we are *d'accord* with the state.... We say: You must educate this thing, your soul, the best thing that you have, to be hostile to the state. Only then do you feel well. Only then are you—you" (Jelavich, *Munich* 60f.).

Paragraph 166 of the *Reichsstrafgesetzbuch* (Imperial Penal Code), which deals with blasphemy or offenses against religion, has undergone various minor reformulations since the nineteenth century. Yet it remains essentially unchanged today, both in paragraph number (§166) and content, in the Penal Code that forms the basis of criminal law in the current German Federal Republic of the twenty-first century. The version adopted on 15 May 1871, under which Oskar Panizza was prosecuted, reads as follows:

> §166. Whoever through insulting utterances publicly blasphemes God, gives offense, or who publicly insults one of the Christian churches or another corporate religious society in the country or their institutions or customs, also whoever commits insulting mischief inside a church or in another place dedicated to religious assemblies, shall be punished with imprisonment of up to three years.

Following publication of *The Love Council* on 10 October 1894, Panizza received a shipment of three hundred copies from the publisher on 17 November. That same day, the very first review of the play appeared in the social-democratic *Münchner Post*, which predicted that *The Love Council* would indeed face difficulties. In a letter written to Schabelitz the following day, Panizza describes how he had been in a great hurry to dispose of these copies of his latest book, so that "if the police come, they will at least only find me and not any *Councils*" (*LK* 1997, 12).

The author did not have to wait very long for the anticipated police to arrive. This first review caught the attention of the Munich district attorney's office, which notified the police headquarters of the matter on 5 December 1894. On 8 January 1895, an order was issued for *The Love Council* to be confiscated and a preliminary investigation of the author was initiated. Four days later, Panizza appeared before a hearing officer in the preliminary investigation and signed the following deposition:

> I declare myself to be the author of the instant publication, *The Love Council*. I wrote it in the spring of 1893 and shortly thereafter gave it to the publisher Schabelitz in Zürich to be published.
>
> I not only did not receive any honorarium for the publication, but I had the cover with the illustration printed here at my own expense and spent about 180 marks on it.
>
> The book was published in October 1894 and, I will not deny it, probably was also distributed domestically. I will not deny that, objectively speaking, in some passages of the publication a blasphemy or insult to the divine Trinity can be found, and that it also contains what can be construed as an insult to the institutions of the Christian churches, such as the veneration of Mary. I will also not disavow that a person who stands on the basis of Christian belief, will, or rather can be, offended while reading the book by the contents of same, i.e., by the objectively present blasphemy.
>
> On the other hand, I maintain that, in a subjective sense, while writing the book no insult to religion or anything similar was intended at all. In my capacity as physician and writer, I was concerned with portraying the origin of syphilis in a drastic manner. This drastic treatment applies to all of the characters featured in the piece and, similarly, to the entire action. The following factors were decisive for me while writing the play: first of all, the historic fact that syphilis first emerged in Naples at the end of the 15th century in the camp of the French King, Charles VIII, at a time when Pope Alexander VI was enjoying a lavish court in Rome while, in contrast to this, Savonarola in Florence was preaching against luxury; then the circumstance that Ulrich von Hutten, reflecting the view of his time, described syphilis as a punishment imposed by God. For the latter reason I came to represent the events in heaven, which otherwise would have been beyond my artistic intention.
>
> Whatever I depicted of the wantonness at the papal court is based on the documentary record by Burchard, which I cited as the source on page 25 of the publication.

Detailed response to contentions regarding particular passages:

a. Regarding the allegation that on pages 1, 6, 8, 9, 10, 11, 12, 14, 18, 21, 22, 38, 40, 42, 43, 44 and 47 of the publication, God the Father is depicted as a frail, decrepit and infantile old man:

I had in mind that the current generation, in educated circles as well as in the lower levels of the population, is more and more turning away from the Christian faith. I wanted to portray the sentence, "The gods are getting old," in a drastic manner by portraying God the Father himself as a frail old man.

That this contains a blasphemy seems indisputable to me. I only wanted to portray my era in regard to its faith.

b. As to the allegations regarding the passages on pages 10 and 12: Cherub as Antinous:

I only wanted to show that God was accompanied by a pretty angel, the way Zeus is by Ganymede in the classical legend. I had no intention of depicting the Cherub as a catamite or anything similar.

c. As to the contention regarding Christ and the Holy Ghost on page 18:

This portrayal resulted from my quandary of being as incapable as anyone else of rendering an image of the Holy Ghost.

d. Regarding the allegation that Christ is depicted as a ridiculous figure and a ridiculous person on pages 17, 18, 19, 22, 39, 40, 42, 43, 44 and 47:

With the portrayal of Christ as an impotent, consumptive person I wanted to depict the devaluation of Christ by the Mariolatry of the Catholic Church. According to the dogma of the Catholic Church, the worship of Christ has receded far behind Mariolatry, which chiefly prescribes the veneration of the Virgin Mary instead of Christ, e.g., as impotent compared to the omnipotent Virgin Mary, according to the teachings of Lignosi and Professor Oswald in Trier.

e. Regarding the allegation that on pages 22, 45, and 72 there is a mockery of the Eucharist and the belief in a savior:

Here I expressed the pessimistic thought that it will be difficult to still believe in salvation from God for a person who perhaps innocently contracts syphilis and views this as a divine retribution.

f. Regarding the allegation that the Virgin Mary is depicted on pages 15, 19, 20, 41, 43, 44, 65, 66, 68 and 69 as a vain, coquettish person, who additionally lacks any sense of feminine modesty, and on pages 39, 41, 45 and 46 is designated as the devil's girlfriend:

If I wanted to express the idea that syphilis was sent by heaven, then I also had to have the persons in heaven speak uninhibitedly about sexual processes; I had this specifically done by the Holy Mother of God because, according to Catholic doctrine, she had gradually evolved from a human person, who had given birth to her child, into an almighty goddess. I remembered the writings of Jesuits, in which the Virgin Mary is repeatedly given the character of an erotic person and in which erotic pictures are also painted. I had extensively cited these writings in the section on Mary in my recently published book, *The German Michel and the Roman Pope*.

I would just like to note generally that in *The Love Council* I treated religious institutions in many sentences and was, therefore, forced to employ certain exaggerations or even mockery [*LK* 1997, 19–22].

Senior district attorney Eugen Baron von Sartor prosecuted Panizza with the relentless urgency of a modern-day terrorism case. Finding someone in Munich who had purchased the play, had read it and was sufficiently offended to file charges did not prove to be a simple matter, however. Even locating a single copy of the play initially was a challenge for Sartor's office. Finally, two book dealers were located who had sold a total of twenty-three copies. The renowned bookseller Karl Schüler was questioned regarding the names of the customers. He reluctantly divulged the names of two purchasers, the naturalistic author Josef Ruederer and the journalist-historian Ludwig Quidde, who in 1894 had been convicted of lèse-majesté and given a 3-month prison term for satirizing Kaiser Wilhelm II. However, even the Catholic author Heinrich Steinitzer was unwilling to declare that he had been offended in his religious sensibilities upon reading Panizza's play.

As the investigation seemed to be going nowhere, Baron von Sartor sent a request marked "very urgent!" to the police headquarters in Leipzig, asking for assistance in locating a witness who might possibly testify in the case against Panizza (Bauer 154). By return mail, the Bavarian prosecutor got what he was desperately seeking: a Leipzig police sergeant named Forstenberg, together with his lieutenant, Erich Wilhelm Müller, who both claimed to have been offended by *The Love Council*. The case could now proceed.

Today we can more clearly appreciate how the Panizza trial played out against the backdrop of a highly emotional, sometimes hysterical debate in the German parliament and echoed in the press regarding real and imagined threats to the future of the young German nation. Germany's belated unification in 1871 under Prussian rule accelerated its burgeoning industrialization, while a surging urbanization and a growing awareness of the "social question" led to heavy-handed attempts by the ruling powers to suppress the growing social democratic movement. In Bavaria, the Catholic Church was making a concerted political comeback against the forces of liberalism, which had been allied for decades with the Bavarian monarchy. After the assassination of the French president Marie François Sadi Carnot in the summer of 1894, a new wave of antisocialist hysteria swept across the German political scene.

In September 1894, the Kaiser seized the opportunity to launch a campaign to protect "religion, morality and order." This campaign included the so-called Anti-Revolution Bill of 1894–95, as well as later trials of socialist leaders charged with violating the Association Laws. Reading through the "Critical Responses to *The Love Council*," reprinted here for the very first time in any language in over a century, one can see how the various commentators in diverse periodicals on the right and left used Panizza's trial to make their points regarding the hotly debated Anti-Revolution Bill. This bill was not unlike the Patriot Act enacted by the United States after the attack on the World Trade Center in September 2001. However, unlike the Patriot Act, and much to the chagrin of conservative legislators, the Anti-Revolution Bill never garnered enough votes to be enacted in the *Reichstag*, the German parliament.

The failure of the Anti-Revolution Bill to gain legislative approval merely emboldened the Kaiser to attempt to circumvent the parliament altogether and try to get reactionary measures implemented in the individual states. He made no secret of his contempt for the *Reichstag*, and he found a ready ally in King Albert of Saxony. In February 1895, King Albert sought to exploit social democratic street violence in the hope of drastically revising the *Reichstag* franchise, such that it would only be comprised of delegates from the various state parliaments (Ratallack 49–92). Thus, it should hardly be surprising that in February 1895 Baron von Sartor sought and immediately found two willing complainants among the police force in Leipzig, Saxony's largest city.

When the preliminary investigation against the author commenced on 4 January 1895, he was originally charged with blasphemy committed on seventeen pages of *The Love Council*. As the debate surrounding the Anti-Revolution Bill heated up and the publicity swirling around the play escalated over the next three months, district attorney von Sartor added another fourteen pages of incriminating violations. By the time of Panizza's trial on 30 April 1895, he was charged with violation of §166 of the Imperial Penal Code in more than ninety instances. Almost half of the twelve-page indictment dealt with the way Panizza had portrayed the Virgin Mary in *The Love Council*, followed by his treatment of the Trinity, the Eucharist, Satan and the doctrine of redemption.

Sometime in mid–March, Panizza appears to have hired two prominent Munich defense lawyers, Bernstein and Loewenfeld, whose brief relationship with their client ended well before the trial began. Perhaps the case had become too controversial for them to publicly defend a Protestant in his blasphemous attacks against the Catholic Church. In any event, the author seems to have relished the idea of martyrdom and eagerly assumed the main burden of his own defense himself. He prepared an exhaustive literary-historical defense plea, which proved to be so lengthy that he was unable to read it in its entirety at his trial. The complete text was published by his Zürich publisher, Johann Schabelitz, later that year and is included in the present volume. Some days before his trial, an undistinguished attorney, Dr. Georg Kugelmann, was found to legally represent Panizza and handle all the procedural formalities of his case.

With the approach of the annual May Day manifestations, political tensions in Munich were visibly heightened at the end of April. The day before Panizza's trial, five thousand social democrats demonstrated against the Anti-Revolution bill (Bauer 156), concerned that social democracy could once again be outlawed as it had been until 1890. Even though Panizza was not involved in social democratic political activities, his writings were considered a threat to established conservative Bavarian Catholic values. Both the prosecution and the jurors at his trial acted as if setting a strong example was urgently required as a deterrent against any further erosion of traditional values and to help prevent what some saw as the threat of a radical power shift to the political left.

Panizza's day in court began early on 30 April 1895 in Munich's Justice Building on Augustenstrasse. At the very outset, Baron von Sartor cleverly set the stage for his jury of largely uneducated Bavarians by ordering the courtroom to be cleared, ostensibly to protect the public from any moral contamination that might ensue from the reading of objectionable passages from the play. Aside from court officials, members of the jury and the press, only five associates of the defendant were allowed to remain in the courtroom. Not only did this clearly signal to the jury the seriousness of the case and the purportedly extreme danger and depravity associated with the defendant, it also magnified the case's deterrent effect that could be expected from the ensuing publicity.

Michael Georg Conrad, Panizza's mentor and the dean of Munich naturalists, took the stand during the trial as an "expert witness." His prepared testimony, which was published together with Panizza's defense plea later in 1895 and reprinted in Chapter 8 for the first time in English, did little to prevent his friend's conviction. In his lengthy and somewhat patronizing statement, Conrad characterized *The Love Council* as an example of naturalism:

> In his work, the author employed those artistic means and those special techniques that we commonly refer to as the most refined and, at the same time, as the most radically "modern" ones. An incomparable intensity and clarity is achieved by these means. At the same time, however, this kind of art produces an existential truth of such intensity or, to use a current catchword, such a relentless *naturalism*, that the ordinary, unprepared reader, who loves to wallow in heavenly blue idealisms and blissful fantasies, will not know how to deal with Panizza's drama, *The Love Council* [Panizza, *Meine Verteidigung* 29f.].

What bothered him the most, Conrad freely admitted, was "an element which borders on the perverse, the pathological" (30). But all in all, he summarized, Panizza's play represented "one of the most powerful and most significant works of art in modern dramatic literature and, considering the difficulty of his topic, perhaps the very most significant work of the last years" (32). The twelve Bavarian jurors were obviously unimpressed. One of them commented to a journalist at the trial, "If the dog were tried in southern Bavaria, he wouldn't get out alive" (KS 6).

Bauer maintains that Panizza's statement at the beginning of his trail, "I declare that I am an atheist," helped to ensure his conviction by the jury (Bauer 17). Ten hours later, as the light began to fade in room 94 of the Justice Building, one of the least surprising events that had transpired was Panizza's conviction on multiple charges of blasphemy. That outcome had been pretty much a foregone conclusion. He sealed his own fate simply by showing up at the trial and then, in the course of the proceedings, freely admitting that he had indeed intended for *The Love Council* to be distributed in the German Empire, thus nullifying any chance of acquittal based on the play's publication outside the *Reich*.

In his summation, Baron von Sartor forcefully charged the jury with defending God, religion and humanity's holiest feelings from the "swinish meanness" emanating from Panizza's pen, thereby explicitly setting an example for the entire modernist literary movement:

> Gentlemen of the jury! I don't ask you, I demand that you show these modernist men by your swift judgment that we in Germany still have laws that forbid treating God, religion and the holiest feelings the way the accused has done. If the modernist men want to brew filth, they should do that alone within their four walls. Thank God we have not reached the point where we have to allow our belief and our religion to be besmirched by such books [*Augsburger Abendzeitung* 1 May 1895: 7].

At 7 P.M., the judges of the Royal State Court Munich I issued their ruling before adjourning:

> In the name of His Majesty the King of Bavaria, the Jury Court of the Royal State Court Munich I, in the case against the author Dr. Oskar Panizza of Kissingen, charged with an offense against religion committed in print, judges as follows: 1. For an offense against religion committed in print, Dr. Oskar Panizza of Kissingen is sentenced to a prison term of one year, as well as bearing the costs of the trial and the sentence. 2. The remaining copies of the publication *The Love Council* by Oskar Panizza, as well as the plates and molds for its production, are to be rendered unusable. 3. An arrest warrant for the accused is issued [Panizza, *Meine Verteidigung* 36].

Panizza's defense attorney had pleaded for a sentence of no more than one month. The sentence of twelve months in prison was less than the eighteen months demanded by the prosecution, but far more than was ever meted out to any other German writer during the half-century of the Second Empire. The judges cited the limited sales and circulation of the book as a reason for limiting the sentence to one year. Ironically, as a result of the widespread publicity generated by Panizza's scandalous trial, sales of the play soared, and after the first printing of one thousand copies sold out in a matter of months, Panizza was able to publish two more editions in 1896 and 1897. One could say that the author's ploy succeeded: the trial he provoked assured him a place in literary history. At the time, he could not be aware of how high the price would eventually be, and what toll it would exact on his long-term health and welfare.

The one unexpected development at Panizza's trial was that the judges issued a warrant for his immediate arrest, claiming there was a high threat that the convicted author might flee the country. In view of the convict's ample assets and Dr. Panizza's praise of Swiss literary freedom, the judges ordered the author jailed on the spot, pending the outcome of any appeal. He was immediately sent to the Am Anger jail and not freed on bail for three weeks, until his mother could raise the enormous amount demanded of 80,000 RM.

His ineffective defense attorney, Dr. Kugelmann, duly filed an appeal on 3 May 1895 with the *Reichsgericht*, Germany's Imperial Court in Leipzig. In his appeal, he noted that the prosecution's charge to the jury had failed to provide proof of Panizza's intention to have his play distributed within Germany. Less than two months later, the high court rejected the appeal on 1 July 1895, citing the fact that "according to the transcript of the trial, the accused declared the distribution of his book in Germany explicitly to be his intention and described transmitting the work to the publisher as the means for it to be distributed anywhere" (KS 25; full text in Chapter 11). Panizza was also obligated to pay for all the state's expenses associated with his trial, the appeal and his twelve months in prison.

Panizza's trial in 1895 brought him short-lived notoriety, but he paid dearly for it with a devastating year in prison, followed by emigration to Zürich in 1896, expulsion from Switzerland the following year, gradual impoverishment in Paris, eventual institutionalization upon his return to Germany in 1904, loss of his legal rights, and steadily deteriorating mental health during the remaining decades of his life.

Chapter 8

Defense and Judgment in the Matter of *The Love Council*[1]

Oskar Panizza's Defense Plea

Before the Royal State Court Munich I.
30 April 1895

> "The concept of God falsified;
> the concept of morality falsified!"
> — Nietzsche, *Antichrist*

Gentlemen of the jury: as a non-lawyer, I cannot address the question of a German court's jurisdiction in this case. I do know from the personal statements of reputable attorneys, men who are competent to evaluate this matter, that they are of quite differing opinions; since there is a violation of a very clear paragraph in the Imperial Penal Code, whereby an act committed abroad, which is not punishable there, cannot be prosecuted domestically. I can only address the purely human aspect, the artistic and aesthetic aspect of the case. And since you, gentlemen, likewise non-jurists, should judge the purely human aspect of the case, I thus believe that we are not that far apart at the outset of our deliberations and will soon come to an understanding.

I believe you can best discern my intention in writing the book at hand if I briefly tell you how I came to the charge.

You know, gentlemen, that in Italy at the end of the fifteenth century, and later on in Germany as well, an epidemic broke out that caused the most terrible injuries to the human body, and which evidently did not spread through sexual contact initially, but which later spread almost exclusively through sexual intercourse, affecting all social classes, high and low, and which was called the "lust scourge" [syphilis]. It was not known where it came from. The effect it had on people's minds was enormous. The chronicles of the period are full of excruciating descriptions of both mental and physical ravages. There was no cure, nor was there any escape. In a certain sense, it was worse than the "Black Death." The course of that disease was known, and one could flee to uncontaminated lands. But here the disease emerged everywhere almost simultaneously. And as it happens when a natural cause is unknown, a supernatural one was constructed. And so the people believed then that the "lust scourge" was a divine retribution. And since the connections between the disease and sexual intercourse were soon discovered, the matter was constructed in such a way, that they said: the divine retribution resulted from sensual debauchery and sexual excesses. Hence the name "lust scourge." And thus we find the following passage from a chronicler, one of the most prominent personages of the time, a pugnacious writer and poet, *Ulrich von Hutten*, from the year 1519: "It hath pleased God, that in our time sicknesses shulde arise, whiche were to oure forefathers as it may well be conjectured unknown. But the divines did interpretate this to be the wrathe of God, and to be his punishment for oure evil livinge."[2] I placed this passage as an epigraph at the beginning of my book, in order to point out from the start what I was getting at: that I was not interested in blasphemous things or obscenities, but rather in presenting the particular situation in which the people of that time found themselves, a situation which was, of course, particularly close to me as a former physician.

Now consider, gentlemen, someone setting out from this point of departure, and who is otherwise familiar with the course of this terrible disease of that time, trying to orient himself historically, and who comes across the curious fact that the court at which by far the most severe sexual excesses took place was the papal one; and that the personage who engaged in the wildest orgies, in the most unbelievable manner, was Pope *Alexander VI*; and this despite the fact that in Florence, only a few miles away, there lived a penitent preacher with the stature of *Savonarola*, who daily brought attention to this life of debauchery. Consider further that this Pope, who, like all in his lineage, is completely suffused in his godliness, calls himself "Son of God," "Christ's Deputy," "God on Earth," "who maintains direct ties to God in heaven," who does not shy away from appointing pimps as cardinals or from publicly supporting three mistresses in Rome, and who finally has Savonarola hanged in order to get rid of him, that uncomfortable preacher, who had turned down a cardinal's appointment. And this while the terrible disease rages throughout Italy, and the people, the scholars, the theologians maintain that it is unleashed by "God's wrath," sent as a punishment for people's immodesty. And on Saint Peter's throne sits the Pope, the head of Christendom, who according to Catholic doctrine "receives orders directly from God," a person who is the worst of these offenders, to whom applying the term "immodesty" sounds almost ludicrous.[3] Now transpose all this material into our present age, filled with skepticism and disbelief. Let this confluence of historical elements as an artistic conceit fall into the hands of someone who — perhaps to his own misfortune — is inclined toward satire, and then I ask you, gentlemen, how would *you* have portrayed the Trinity, what kind of image would *you* have had of the divinities in heaven, who under such circumstances sent the "lust scourge" down to mankind on earth?

I would like to conduct an examination of another kind. There has been, gentlemen, at all times and among all peoples, no lack of attempts to draw the divine into the realm of art and to depict it. And since we are dependent on mundane images from our surroundings, even when portraying the highest and sublime — since we cannot get beyond our own experience — thus all painters and poets and sculptors have always sought models on earth for their portrayal of the divine. *Dürer* made German blondes and *Murillo* fiery Spanish women into Madonnas. *Dante* filled the transcendental realms in his grand sublime epic with Italians, just as French mystery plays endowed their devils with Gallic temperament. And whenever anyone, such as *Klopstock*, tried to depict the divine in the absence of any sensory forms, he got mired in nothing but abstract intellectual forms and purely linguistic effect. — But now, gentlemen, do not contradict me when I say: *satire* is equally justified as any other art form, *pathos* is as justified as *melos*, walking on a *soccus* [Roman slipper] as justified as on a high *cothurn*. And if someone wants to write a satire, a divine satire, a divine comedy, then he is simply dependent on human exemplars, like any other artist. He must transfer the grotesque little traits, which he observes in people, to the divine. Now, I think I have already sufficiently explained how eminently *satirical* the material was, of the syphilis epidemic emerging in the Western world, with the simultaneous behavior of the Pope and the judgment of his contemporaries regarding the causes of the divine retribution; how the reference to the papal behavior and the conception of the divine was inevitable. And then, gentlemen, you will no longer be surprised when the portrayal of the divine in *The Love Council* became so outlandish, as it indeed was the case.— Now, gentlemen, you may perhaps retort: the portrayal of the sublime in the divine is allowed, the portrayal of the comic in the divine is forbidden. I admit that. But you, gentlemen, will likewise have to concede that this is no standpoint for an artist. If such a standpoint had always been followed, then no satire would ever have been written; neither of gods nor of people. For the satires of people were usually much more severely punished than those of gods. Then the *Divine Dialogues* of *Lucian* would not have been written, nor the comedies of *Aristophanes*. The Englishman *Wright* would not have been able to write his *History of Caricature,* nor the German *Flögel* his *History of the Grotesque Comical.* But satire and the *vis comica* have always been one of the most powerful resources in the intellectual realm. I will just remind you of the far-reaching influence during the Reformation in France of *Rabelais*, whose witty airs shaped today's intellectual character of the French, and whose unbelievably ruthless attacks on the divine were even printed with the royal privilege. And think of the brazen attacks by the German satirists at the time of *Fischart* and *Reuchlin.*— You will, gentlemen, perhaps further retort: every artist simply must suffer the consequences imposed by the laws of his own country for his artistic creation. Certainly, gentlemen, that is why I am appearing here before you. But you, gentlemen, will perhaps concede that satire is a trait rooted in human nature and cannot be expunged.

Gentlemen! Our current age is not favorably disposed toward depicting the sublime in the divine. Today, nobody paints colossal religious pictures anymore as, for example, *Hess* and *Cornelius* once did. Our age is oriented more toward skepticism and criticism. Many people may see that as a step backwards. But that was not any different previously. The Christian religion has repeatedly undergone periods of extreme skepticism and deepest disbelief. And especially at times when the Church made inordinate demands on people's hearts and pocketbooks, there emerged resistance and satire in the ranks of the educated. Such an era was, for example, the first third of the eighteenth century in England, when the Methodist congregations were founded. And the artist who lambasted this period with the most ruthless satire was the English caricaturist William *Hogarth.* I will show you some of his most famous copper engravings, which appeared under the name "Credulity, Superstition and Fanaticism." The scene represents the interior of a church. A service is taking place. And while down below among the worshippers — as if the artist wanted people's innermost thoughts to emerge — all kinds of sensual and lascivious abominations and innuendos are visible, up on the pulpit the holy sacraments are lampooned in the most grotesque fashion. And yet our *Lichtenberg* states in his famous explications of *Hogarth's* copper engravings: "Mr. *Walpole* says of this page by our great artist that it is the grandest of deep and useful satire that his pen has ever produced. Even if this praise appears somewhat exaggerated, it still seems that, of all *Hogarth's* engravings, this one deserves to be hung in every house. The sight of it elicits shock and revulsion. And yet everything here is true."[4] Incidentally, the small reproduction which I will pass around to you, and which represents an excellent reproduction, was printed and published here in Munich.— Gentlemen, I am not aware that a *Hogarth* copper engraving has ever been confiscated.

However, gentlemen, when it comes to religious satire, how tame the English are compared to our western neighbors, those frivolous French. The French Revolution was another one of those periods, when scorn for the divine was especially prominent. A long era of freethinking had immediately preceded it, and during the Revolution the aversion against the clergy and Christianity in the land of *Voltaire* had risen to a level of idiosyncrasy against all revealed religion; against a religion that had not been able to prevent the people from being tyrannized on the one hand, and being reduced to utter poverty on the other. At that time the slogan emerged: "Écrasez l'infâme!" "L'infâme," that was Christianity. Incidentally, the expression comes from *Frederick the Great* (in his correspondence with Voltaire). Around that time, gentlemen, in the year 1799, there appeared one of the most audacious poems ever written, by one of France's foremost poets, *Parny,* whom Voltaire called the "French Tibullus." "La Guerre des dieux" caused a huge sensation in France and was received with a storm of applause. It was not confiscated until thirty years after its publication, during the period of French reactionism. In spite of that, it has been reprinted repeatedly to the present day and can be ordered from our better German bookstores. Next to this poem, gentlemen, *The Love Council* pales by comparison. What is so audacious about this poem is the fact that nowhere is the purpose evident as to why the divine personages are made so unbelievably ludicrous. And here, gentlemen, is where I perceive the principal distinction between Parny and the book which is the subject of your aesthetic judgment today. I believe that in *The Love Council* the artistic treatment is thoroughly grounded in the subject matter, and the crass portrayal is contained in the problem itself. For syphilis was something terrible in Italy at that time. And God had sent it as a punishment, while God's representative was one of the worst conceivable libertines the world has ever known. With Parny it is purely a superficial intellectual construct, frivolous exuberance and Gallic wit. I am confident to say, gentlemen, that compared to Parny I look like a veritable moralist. The Olympian gods — to briefly outline the plot — are sitting around feasting and having a good old time, when Mercury, the messenger of the gods, bursts in and reports: a new family of gods is approaching. Great horror and outrage. They deliberate what is to be done. Minerva, the goddess of wisdom, remarks that it is likely that the old family of gods seems day by day to have become more worthless and superfluous to mankind. She is afraid of *Jesus.* Whereupon Jupiter says:

(Gentlemen, I must apologize for reading aloud some very strong passages; but it is within the framework of this little literary-historical discussion, which I ask you to hear.)

> "...Fi donc! Ce pauvre diable,
> Fils d'un pigeon, nourri dans un étable
> Et mort en croix, serait dieu?...
> Le plaisant dieu!..."

> ["...Phooey! This poor devil,
> Son of a pigeon, nurtured in a stable
> And died on the cross, is a god?
> What a funny god!..."]

Now Mercury is sent back to find out more about the situation. He soon returns and reports: Yes, indeed, those are really gods about to ascend into heaven. Renewed rage and despair. While the others are making an assortment of suggestions to intercept the new gods and throw them out of heaven, etc., Jupiter decides to make the best of a desperate situation, dispatches a messenger and invites them — typically French — to dinner. Now the Christian divinities slowly come with their retinue of saints and dine with the Olympian gods. The

Trinity is symbolized by a feeble old man, who has a bleating lamb on his lap and a pigeon on his shoulder. The lamb bleats, the pigeon coos, and the old man wants to make a speech; he cannot manage to say anything, he laughs embarrassedly and finally sits down at the table!

> "Une heure après les conviés arrivent.
> Etaient-ils trois, ou bien n'étaient-ils qu'un?
> Trois en un seul; vous comprenez, j'espère?
> Figurez-vous un venerable père,
> Au front serein, à l'air un peu commun,
> Ni beau ni laid, assez vert pour son âge,
> Et bien assis sur le dos d'un nuage.
> Blanche est sa barbe; un cercle radieux
> S'arrondissait sur sa tête penchée:
> Un taffetas de la couleur des cieux
> Formait sa robe: à l'épaule attachée,
> Elle descend en plis nombreux et longs,
> Et flotte encore par-delà ses talons.
> De son bras droit à son bras gauche vole
> Certain pigeon coiffé d'une aureole,
> Qui de sa plume étalant la blancheur,
> Se rengorgeait de l'air d'un orateur.
> Sur ses genoux un bel agneau repose,
> Qui bien lavé, bien frais, bien délicat,
> Portant un cou ruban couleur de rose,
> De l'auréole emprunte aussi l'éclat.
> Ainsi parut le triple personnage.
> En rougissant la Vierge le suivait,
> Et sur les dieux accourus au passage
> Son œil modeste à peine se levait.
> D'anges, de saints, une brillante escorte
> Ferme la marche, et s'arrête à la porte.
>
> L'Olympien à ses hôtes nouveaux
> De compliment adresse quelques mots
> Froids et polis. Le vénérable Sire
> Veut riposter, ne trouve rien à dire,
> S'incline, rit, et se place au banquet.
> L'agneau bêla d'une façon gentille.
> Mais le pigeon, l'esprit de la famille,
> Ouvre le bec, et son divin fausset
> A ces payens psalmodie un cantique
> Allégorique, hébraïque et mystique.
> Tandis qu'il parle, avec étonnement
> On se regarde; un murmure equivoque,
> Un rire malin que chaque mot provoque,
> Mal étouffé circule sourdement.
> Le Saint-Esprit, qui pourtant n'est pas bête,
> Rougit, se trouble, et tout court s'arrête.

De longs 'bravo,' des battements de main,
Au meme instant ébranlèrent la salle."

["One hour later the guests arrive.
Were there three of them, or maybe only one?
Three in one; you understand, I hope?
Imagine a venerable father,
With a serene brow, he looks a little ordinary,
Neither handsome nor ugly, still young for his age,
And firmly seated on the back of a cloud.
White is his beard; a radiant circle
Surrounds his bowed head:
A piece of silk the color of the sky
Constitutes his robe: attached at the shoulder,
It falls in folds, numerous and long,
And floats beneath his feet.
From his right arm to his left arm flies
A certain pigeon, coiffed with a halo,
Flaunting the whiteness of its plumage,
He gives himself the air of an orator.
On his lap rests a pretty lamb
Who is nicely washed, fresh and dainty,
Wearing a rose-colored ribbon around its neck
And sharing the aura of the halo.
Thus appeared the triple personage,
Followed by the blushing Virgin,
And as the gods crowded forward to see her pass,
Her modest eyes barely lifted.
Angels, saints, a splendid escort
Concluded the procession and stopped at the door.
To his new guests the Olympian
Addresses his compliments in a few words,
Cold and polite. The venerable Lord
Wants to respond, finds nothing to say,
Bows, laughs and sits down at the banquet.
The lamb bleats nicely.
But the pigeon, the family wit,
Opens its beak, and its divine falsetto
Sings a hymn to these pagans,
Allegorical, Hebraïcal and mystical.
While he speaks, surprised looks are exchanged;
Each word provokes an amused murmur,
A barely suppressed snicker makes the rounds.
The Holy Ghost who, after all, is not stupid,
Blushes, becomes embarrassed and stops abruptly.
At this moment, the hall shakes
With long shouts of 'bravo' and applause."]

In the Trinity's retinue come angels, saints, martyrs and the Virgin Mary. The Olympian goddesses find her boring, gauche, her hair badly done, not chic.

> "Fi donc! elle est sans grace et sans tournure;
> Quel air commun! Quelle sotte coiffure!"—
> ["Phooey! She's shapeless and without charm;
> How ordinary she looks! What an awful hairdo!"—]

The male residents of Olympus find her attractive enough, even if she is a peasant beauty, so that a conquest would not seem to be a total waste of time. They enumerate her physical assets in a manner which I would not want to reproduce here, even in French. In the course of the first canto and after dinner, the new divinities explore the accommodations at Olympus. Mary ends up in the dressing room of Venus. In her curiosity, she can't resist trying on one of the fancy gowns she finds there. At this very moment Apollo comes in, he becomes aroused by the sight of the seductively-dressed woman, and she succumbs to the tempestuous entreaties of the god of the muses.——I believe, gentlemen, you can dispense with hearing the contents of the other nine cantos and have already realized that we are dealing here with one of the most audacious works of French poetry. It confirms, incidentally, what I said above: that in the portrayal of the supernatural, the poet relies on the colors and forms of his own experience. Whether one is portraying the sublime or the ridiculous in the divine, the clothing is always taken from the earthly sphere. And in *Parny's* work the Christian gods speak and act in the style of the French salon at the end of the last century.

You will perhaps say, gentlemen: This author of *The Love Council* gets up and even wants to play the moralist; he perhaps excuses himself by delivering even saucier passages from the poem by a French author?—*No!* Gentlemen, with a clear conscience, I differentiate here between the French text and my own works. I *have* degraded the Christian gods and have done so intentionally, because I saw them in the mirror of the fifteenth century; because I observed them from Alexander the Sixth's point of view. Our conceptions of the divine, gentlemen, are contained in our *thought*. You know as little as I do what really happens up there above us. If our notions of the divine are sublime, then they are sublime in our *thought*; and if they are ludicrous, then they are ludicrous in our thought. Now if somebody comes along, such as a debauched pope, and changes our notions of the divine from sublime to ludicrous, then that is a process that takes place in our thinking and has nothing to do with what really exists in the space above us, with the transcendental. If I attacked the divine, then I did not attack that supernal spark that slumbers in the heart of every person, but rather I attacked the divine that had become a farce in the hands of *Alexander VI.*

Now gentlemen, to get back to our French author, perhaps you will counter: but in Germany such grotesque portrayals of the divine never took place. Only the frivolous French and the ruthless English attacked the divine in such a barbaric fashion. At the risk of detaining you a few more minutes, I must provide a sample from the writings of the Swabian folk poet *Sebastian Sailer* (1714–1777), especially from his humorous drama *Lucifer's Fall*, which so greatly delighted *Goethe*. Here we now enter a totally different sphere, the sphere of Swabian dialect poetry; but you will see, the coloring is the same. The first act begins with a choir of angels:

> "Dance, jump,
>   pipe, sing

these are old things in heaven;
    shout yoohoo.
    with shawms
until your belly bursts.

Hop, dance
    those lice and bedbugs
shake them with a currycomb
    currycomb and hair-comb
    out of the temple
when they shout do-si-do."

The plot of the play revolves around catching Lucifer, that insubordinate fellow, and bringing him before God's court of judgment. This effort is finally successful. He is caught in a place which is unmentionable in polite society. The archangel Michael bolts the door shut and Lucifer is caught. Hanswurst [stock clown] had helped in the process. Both rush to God the Father to report their news:

MICHAEL: „Cheer up, Father God! Something new!
                Don't be frightened if I fire my gun.
                Lucifer is captured.
                I'll now describe how it happened."

Then they tell him, and God rewards them with a glass of wine.

GOD THE FATHER: "Michael! Go to the cellar;
                there you have Rhine wine, Muscatel,
                Mosel, Neckar wine, Burgundy
                by the bottle, tons of it;
                Valtellina and Tyrolian
                are good digestives
                when you spit up
                or have a bellyache.
                Tell me, what do you want to drink?"

However, the wine they are offered is so sour that neither Saint Michael nor Hanswurst can drink it. They decide that Lucifer should drink it as punishment for his shameful deeds. God the Father is asked to agree:

GOD THE FATHER: "Alright, I'll give it a try;
                bring him to us quickly.
                Hanswurst! Get out, or else I'll have to laugh;
                I need to put on a serious face."

Lucifer is led in.

LUCIFER: "Pardon, Father God, pardon,
                Do you really know me?

GOD THE FATHER: Of course I know you,
                but now you need to remember.
                What were you up to?
                How far have you gone?

LUCIFER: Pardon, Father God, pardon!

GOD THE FATHER: Hold your tongue! I know you.
                     Saint Michael just gave me some good advice,
                     which will surely get you into deep trouble.
                     Look at this glass of wine,
                     it's from the lake region. Now drink it up!
                     And then for all your sidekicks
                     we'll pour some more from the tap,
                     so that you'll crawl twisted and lame on all fours,
                     or you'll croak like a dog."

But Lucifer says no thanks to this wine. He claims to know where he can find something better.

LUCIFER: "To hell with the sacraments
                     and all seven elements!
                     May the devil take Michael and all his ilk,
                     this I wish, as sure as my name is Lucifer."

Now God the Father orders the boisterous Devil to be ejected down to hell.

MICHAEL: "March, you hellhound, march!"

LUCIFER: "All of you can lick my ass!"

Exit the Devil! The remaining angels join in a hymn of praise to God's glory.

You see, gentlemen, this scene has quite a different effect on us. Compared to the delicately spiced fare of *Parny*, these are genuine German, Swabian beets. But characteristically, whether German, French or English — no people ever miss an opportunity to lampoon their own religion. And all take figures and colors from their immediate surroundings. As surely as the "Messiad" was written by *Klopstock*, so surely such an "Offenbachiad" of divine events emerges from folk life to make us laugh. And what the gargoyles and grotesque animals are on our church doors, that is what the satires and humorous epics are in the religious domain.

Now who was this *Sebastian Sailer*? Perhaps some itinerant ballad-monger, who told a couple of jokes for a few bites of lunch or a glass of wine? Or a so-called "modern" of the eighteenth century, who hoped to make a name for himself with his all too audacious literary production? None of the above. He was the famous preacher and senior Canon in the Premonstrant Monastery of Obermarchthal in Swabia. His fame as a preacher was so widespread that he took to the pulpit throughout the German lands, as was the custom then, traveling as far as France and Moravia, and preaching for the Empress in Vienna. He received the epithet "the Swabian Cicero." He was, to be sure, frequently attacked on account of his plays, and even the clergy moved against him. But his superior, the Bishop of Constance, Cardinal von *Rodt*, took it upon himself to travel on an inspection tour to Obermarchthal, where one of Sailer's plays was performed; he distinguished it not just with his applause, but he also declared the judgments of Sailer's opponents to be false and unwise. Subsequently, Sailer's works were reprinted numerous times and in Württemberg achieved the status of an all-popular chapbook, similar to *The Cousin from Swabia*. My edition, which I have here, is even adorned with drawings from the hand of the well-known *Hebel* illustrator, *Nisle*. And in the scene which I just presented to you, you can see *Lucifer* in the traditional outfit of a Swabian village magistrate with jackboots, large silver buttons and mighty wings pinned to his back. *Michael*, with a large caterpillar helmet on his head, is wearing the uniform of a Napoleonic grenadier. *God the Father*, wearing a floral nightgown, sits in an armchair, his bare feet in loose slippers, on his head a sleeping bonnet with a crown of stars. Engraved on the back of the armchair is the so-called "eye of God," the well-known symbol of the Trinity. Next to the armchair is a spittoon.

You see, gentlemen, humor and satire are two things in human nature that cannot be eradicated, and they have their justification in the religious sphere, just as much as exaltation and rapture.

And do you believe that today the times are inclined to impose a more rigorous censorship in this regard? Gentlemen, it has now been half a century since the publication of *The Life of Jesus* by *David Friedrich Strauss*. You all know how this book, which spread through all educated circles, has become the basis, as it were, for a religious skepticism in Germany. And from the current era I need only mention the name *Harnack*, whose book *The Apostolic Creed*, in which he rejects Christ's supernatural birth as unhistorical, has circulated in some fifty editions through all segments of society. Gentlemen, even if I am speaking here primarily to a group of Catholics, you will still permit me, as a Protestant, to mention those elements which cause my action to appear in a somewhat different light than it perhaps might be in the eyes of a Catholic. You all know, as well as I do, that there are dozens of Protestant ministers in the German Empire today who have been suspended, because they have not in good conscience been able to speak the baptismal text in the traditional manner of earlier times, according to which Christ was conceived supernaturally. And hundreds of other pastors are knocking on the doors of synods, asking for dispensations and concessions for our ever-skeptical generation. Do you believe, gentlemen, that it is appropriate in such an era to summon a religious satire, like the ones previously written, before a court of law?

Gentlemen, I appeal to your liberal sentiments in regard to the country in which the book was published. The book was not published in Germany. It was published in Switzerland. Every German author occasionally has something on his mind that he cannot have printed in Germany, and then he goes abroad. English surgeons who want to practice vivisection go to France, because vivisection is prohibited in England, and after they complete their training they return home. It would not occur to any English court to prosecute them, since the act was committed in a foreign country, where it is not punishable. Now if you treat a book, which was published in another country because it could conflict with the domestic laws, the same way as if it had been printed in the home country, then you reverse the intention of its author and harm him in such a way that he is unable to defend himself, i.e., you do him an injustice. With this in mind, gentlemen, I appeal to your natural, innate sense of justice and *request an acquittal*.

The Judgment

After the Presiding Officer of the Jury Court had pointed out in the course of the proceedings that, in case the accused was not found guilty of distributing the book in Germany, the entire charge of blasphemy would thereby become moot, since it would then be an act committed outside the country, which is not punishable there and according to Paragraph 4, Article 3 of the Imperial Penal Code would also not be a prosecutable offense domestically, the counsel for the defense, Dr. Kugelman, moved to present the jurors with the subsidiary question: whether the author was guilty of distributing the book in Germany. This motion, which was objected to by the District Attorney, Baron von Sartor, was dismissed by the court with the justification that the subsidiary question, regarding the defendant's guilt pertaining to the distribution of the book in Germany, would be contained in the prime question, whether he was guilty of blasphemy. The question then directed to the jurors read:

"Is the accused, Dr. Oskar Panizza, guilty, in that he publicly blasphemed God with offensive pronouncements, caused offense and insulted public institutions and customs of the Christian Churches, in particular the Catholic Church, with the publication *The Love Council: A Heavenly Tragedy in Five Acts*, written by him in spring 1893, published in October 1894 by Verlagsmagazin J. Schabelitz in Zürich and then distributed in Munich, Leipzig and other cities within the German Empire?"

Text of the Judgment:

In the name of His Majesty the King of Bavaria, the Jury Court of the Royal State Court Munich I, in the case against the author Dr. Oskar Panizza of Kissingen, charged with an offense against religion committed in print, judges as follows:

1. For an offense against religion committed in print, Dr. Oskar Panizza of Kissingen is sentenced to a prison term of *one year*, as well as bearing the costs of the trial and the sentence.

2. The remaining copies of the publication *The Love Council* by Oskar Panizza, as well as the plates and molds for its production, are to be rendered unusable.

3. An arrest warrant for the accused is issued.

Justification

On 20 March 1895 the Royal State Court Munich I initiated a proceeding before the Jury Court and charged the author, Dr. Oskar Panizza of Kissingen, with an offense against religion, committed in print.

Consequently the matter came to a public trial today.

After the opening statement for the prosecution by the Royal District Attorney, the case for the defense was presented by Dr. Kugelman and the accused.

The accompanying question was given to the jurors for their answer.

The declaration of the jurors to the question posed was: yes, with more than seven votes.

The Royal District Attorney requested a prison sentence of 1 year and 6 months, destroying the remaining copies of the publication, as well as the plates and molds for its production, issuing an arrest warrant and bearing all costs.

The counsel for the defense proposed a prison sentence of one month.

The court ruled that a conviction exists according to Paragraph 166 of the Imperial Penal Code, Paragraphs 2, 20 and 21 of the Imperial Print Act of 7 May 1874, whereby the action in question represents an offense against religion, committed in print.

The sentence was in accordance with Paragraphs 166 and 16 of the Imperial Penal Code and compounded by the fact that the content of said publication is capable of deeply offending the religious and moral feelings of others, furthermore that the insults in the publication cannot be excused by authorial freedom, but instead represent an inappropriate abuse of same.

Mitigating the sentence was the consideration that, given the offensive content of the publication, it probably was rejected by decent people and therefore had limited distribution.

Therefore, the sentence given above was adjudged appropriate.

Considering that the sentence given and the personal circumstances of the accused make him prone to flight, an arrest warrant for him was issued. (Paragraphs 112 and 124 of the Penal Procedural Ordinance.)

Since the entire content of the publication written by the accused is actionable, it was ruled according to Paragraph 41, Section 1 and 2 of the Imperial Penal Code that all copies of same, as well as the plates and molds for its production, are to be destroyed.

As part of the sentence, the accused was ordered to cover the costs of the proceeding and the sentence in accord with Paragraphs 496 and 497 of the Penal Procedural Ordinance.

Everything is by application of the above-mentioned legal paragraphs.

Thus adjudicated and announced in a public session of the Jury Court at the Royal State Court Munich I on 30 April 1895 at 7 P.M., in the presence of: Royal *Oberlandesgerichtsrat* [Senior State Judge] Quante, presiding, the Royal Justices Baron von Dobeneck und Ziegler, associate justices, the Royal District Attorney, Baron von Sartor, the Royal Secretary Pasquay as court recorder.

Signed: *Quante, Dobeneck, Ziegler*

Panizza's Notes

1. The following defense plea was not delivered in its entirety and not always verbatim as it was prepared in advance and is written here. The kind of proceeding, which entailed answering the hearing by the judge in the morning and that of the district attorney in the afternoon, also forced the defense to divide up its arguments. To provide a complete summation at the end was a hopeless undertaking in the face of the jurors' disposition. Thus, the passage about Parny was entirely left out. Similarly, other material that occurred extemporaneously has been omitted here. However, the speech set forth here corresponds in meaning and wording to most of the arguments introduced at the trial. [All footnotes by Panizza]

2. Ulrich von Hutten, a German knight, *On the French Disease or Syphilis*, 1529.—*Hutten's Writings*, edited by Böcking, Leipzig, 1859–69. Vol. V, 399–401.

3. In the scene where I describe one of the typical evening entertainments of the Pope, I have naked young men appear, who in front of the Pope and his ladies engage in wrestling matches, at which the winner receives one of the naked courtesans, with whom he disappears behind the scene. But the historical account is much worse. I toned down the scene, not out of consideration for the popes or the sensibility of Catholics, but for artistic reasons; because I always had the theater in mind, because I always thought about the possibility of a performance; and because the above scene could conceivably be performed, under certain conditions. The real scene, as it is documented in historical reports, would have been an impossibility, even in a closet drama. According to the account by *Burchard*, the papal Master of Ceremonies, and confirmed by the reports of envoys living in Rome, the following took place: "In sero (dominica, ultima mensis octobris, vigilia omnium sanctorum)— 31 October 1501—fecerunt cenam cum duce Valentinense in camera sua, in palatio apostolico, quinquaginta meretrices honeste, cortegiane nuncupate, que post cenam coreaverunt cum servitoribus et aliis ibidem existentibus, primo in vestibus suis; deinde nude. Post cenam posita fuerunt candelabra communia mense in candelis ardentibus per terram, et projecta ante candelabra per terram castanee quas meretrices ipse super manibus et pedibus, nude, candelabra petranscentes, colligebant, Papa, duce et G. Lucretia, sorore sua presentibus et aspicientibus. Tandem exposita dona ultima, diploides et serico, paria caligarum, bireta et alia pro illis qui pluries dictas meretrices carnaliter agnoscerent; que fuerunt ibidem in aula publice carnaliter tractate arbitrio presentium, dona distribute victoribus." (*Burchardi Diarium* [1483–1506] ed. L. Thuasne. Tom. III. p. 167. Paris, 1885): "In the evening (on the 31st of October, the eve of All Saints) fifty notable whores, called courtesans, dined with the Duke of Valentinois (Cesare Borgia, the Pope's son) in his room in the papal palace, and danced after the meal

with the servants and others present; at first in clothes, later naked. After the meal, the burning candelabra from the table were placed on the floor and chestnuts were thrown under the candelabra, from where the naked girls snatched them up, scurrying between the lights on their hands and feet. The Pope, the Duke and his sister, Donna Lucrezia, were present and watched. Finally, prizes were distributed, silk robes, boots, capes, etc., to those who could have intercourse the most times with the aforementioned girls. They were then sexually taken in the prescribed manner in front of the spectators and judged by those present, with prizes distributed to the winners."— This activity was something quite ordinary. The Venetian envoy, *Giustiani*, reported home on 30 December 1502: "Yesterday I dined with his Holiness in the palace and stayed until the early morning at the entertainment, which constitutes the regular diversion of the Pope, and at which women participate; the Pontiff cannot conceive of any festivity without them. Every evening he has girls dance for him and gives parties of a similar nature, at which courtesans perform." (Yriarte, Ch., *Les Borgias*. Paris, 1889. Tom. II, p. 40).

4. G.C. Lichtenberg's *Explication of Hogarth's Copper Engravings*. First series. Göttingen, 1809. p. 55.

Chapter 9

Twentieth-Century
Trials

Panizza's most important work survived him, sometimes serving as a catalyst for further legal battles involving freedom of expression. Throughout the twentieth century, *The Love Council* has continued to be the focus of sporadic criminal prosecutions, courtroom trials and far-reaching legal controversies, with widespread ramifications for the entire European Union and beyond.

After the third edition of the play was published in 1897, the book went out of print and none were publicly available for the next sixty-three years. Early in the twentieth century, a tiny collectors' edition of only fifty copies of *Das Liebeskonzil*, based on the third Swiss edition of 1897 and with nine original pen illustrations by Alfred Kubin, was printed in the Netherlands and published by the *Gesellschaft Münchner Bibliophilen* in 1913 (reprinted 1991, ed. by Michael Bauer, Munich: Edition Spangenberg). In view of the strict censorship prevailing at the time, each copy had the name of its future owner printed on a separate page at the end of the book.

The second and somewhat larger publication of *The Love Council* in twentieth-century Germany, the first in the current Federal Republic, ran into considerable opposition from the law. Dietrich Kuhlbrodt, formerly of the Hamburg district attorney's office, one of the co-authors of the *Liebeskonzil* screenplay and a Panizza scholar in his own right, describes the plight of publisher Peter Jes Petersen in his thoughtful essay, "Panizzas Gegenwart" (*Filmbuch* 145–158). The 26-year-old Petersen, who had been impressed by Georg Grosz's seminal painting "Widmung an Oskar Panizza" (Dedication to Oskar Panizza, 1917/18) in the Staatsgalerie Stuttgart, obtained permission from Panizza's niece in Münster for his own Petersen Press to reprint 300 copies of *The Love Council*.

Shortly after the books were published and began to be distributed, on 1 July 1962 two criminal investigators from nearby Flensburg, armed with arrest and search warrants, raided Petersen's house in the tiny north German town of Glücksburg (Schleswig-Holstein), on the border with Denmark. They rifled through his library and picture collections, confiscated books and arrested the young publisher. After an outcry of protest arose in the German press against this heavy-handed police action, all charges were dropped against Petersen in November 1962. A few months later he moved to West Berlin, where, despite occasional run-ins with the law (Höge, *taz* 14 Dec. 1996: 36), he continued his notable career as a publisher and gallery owner until his death in 2006.

The year 1960 marked the appearance of a seminal French translation by Jean Bréjoux of *The Love Council*, with an insightful introduction by one of the main founders of surrealism, André Breton. According to Klaus Rarisch, the German poet who staged the first public reading of the play in 1962, Mexican film director Luis Buñuel was inspired by Bréjoux's translation to want to make a film version of *The Love Council*, a project which unfortunately never materialized. The first twentieth-century German edition of the play for general distribution followed shortly thereafter in 1964. Credit for this "rediscovery" of Panizza goes to Hans Prescher, a scholar and journalist, whose perceptively edited "best of" collection introduced new generations of readers to this "madman" from Bad Kissingen.

Two years after the very low-key 1967 world premiere of the "heavenly tragedy" took place virtually unnoticed on a small Viennese stage, the lavish French production introduced *The Love Council* to a much larger and more sophisticated international audience. This historic production of *Le Concile d'amour*, under the direction of Jorge Lavelli at the Théâtre de Paris in 1969, occurred some seventy-five years after the play had first been published in Switzerland. In the course of the next dozen years, major theatrical productions followed in London (1970), Hamburg (1973), Rotterdam (1976) and Rome (1981).

It is certainly understandable that a work of art containing such a fierce plea for freedom of expression should encounter an equally strong move to suppress it. The 1981 production of *The Love Council* at the Teatro Belli in Rome was to form the basis for one of the most important, yet little publicized, censorship cases in postwar Europe.

How the Teatro Belli production of *Il concilio d'amore* was transformed into the *Liebeskonzil* feature film, which premiered in February 1982 at the Berlin Film Festival, is carefully documented in the *Liebeskonzil Filmbuch*. German producer Peter Berling caught the last performance of the play in a small theater not far from the Vatican walls on a Friday night in April 1981. That same night, he got the idea to use this theatrical production as the basis for a film and, later that same night, secured the financial backing from Hanns Eckelkamp, then head of the large Atlas-Film company in Germany. Perhaps most important was his choice of director, Werner Schroeter, widely considered to be one of Germany's "singularly most influential filmmakers" (Corrigan 171), a principal figure of the New German Cinema of the 70s. Within twenty-four hours, Schroeter had arrived from Germany and cinematographer Jörg Schmidt-Reitwein flew in from Baghdad. At the time, Schmidt-Reitwein was best known for his outstanding cinematographic work in films by Werner Herzog, Alexander Kluge and Herbert Achternbusch. The Italian portion of the film was shot in nine consecutive all-night sessions.

The film *Liebeskonzil* (no definite article in the film's title) is by no means identical with the Panizza play. The entire second and fifth acts, containing the most graphic scenes with nude courtesans and sex play at the Vatican court of Alexander VI, were not part of the Teatro Belli stage production and hence do not appear in Schroeter's film. Executive producer Berling assumes that, instead of any self-censorship, there were physical and economic exigencies for this omission. Instead, Schroeter's film is framed by scenes depicting Panizza's 1895 trial at the beginning of the film and by his sentencing at the end. Antonio Salines, the Teatro Belli director who plays the role of the Devil, also plays Dr. Panizza in the framing scenes, which were later shot in Berlin during the summer of 1981. Schroeter explained his choice of the framing scenes as follows: "There is the ever-unresolved problem of the Church's claim to secular power, against which Panizza fought so hard. The Church is a mechanism of suppression. [...] The action in the frame makes clear what happened to the man's life. His attack against society is as current as ever, since nothing has fundamentally changed." ("Sauberpapst aus Polen — Out of Competition," *berlinale-tip*, No. 10, 1982: 6.)

**Painting by George Grosz dedicated to Panizza, titled "Widmung an Oskar Panizza, 1917/18."
Courtesy of Staatsgalerie Stuttgart. Copyright © Staatsgalerie Stuttgart.**

Though it did not do well at the box office and has yet to be distributed in video or DVD formats, Schroeter's *Liebeskonzil* did win the Critics Award at the 1983 São Paulo International Film Festival. According to the distributor, the film's theatrical run with only eight prints was extremely brief for a variety of reasons: "Panizza is unknown to the public, the movie was considered a theatrical film, the provocative advertising didn't work" (Eckelkamp, 30 Sept. 1996). The unabashedly provocative advertising involved using the picture of a Neapolitan satyr, whose huge and "visually attention-grabbing, stunningly erect penis" was cause for some local advertisers to move toward a drastic cover-up ("Nonnen gegen *Liebeskonzil*," *Der Spiegel* 22 Mar. 1982: 188). "In some newspaper ads his masculinity is omitted or pasted over on posters. [...] Anticipating concerns, the distributor planned ahead: included with the advertising poster is a sticker, a fig leaf."

Other than the provocative advertising that was not always considered acceptable for public display in newspapers and theater window cases, the distributors had little reason to assume their film would encounter any legal obstacles. *Liebeskonzil* was limited to viewers over the age of 16, and the *Spitzenorganisation der Filmwirtschaft*, the umbrella organization of the motion picture industry based in Wiesbaden, issued the necessary approvals (*Unbedenklichkeitsbescheinigungen*) for the feature and its trailer. The mandatory pre-distribution evaluation by the film industry's oversight group concluded unambiguously: "There are no substantial concerns regarding the public showing of the feature film *Liebeskonzil* in the version submitted" (Sandfort & Hanisch 2).

The prospect that the film could possibly lead to a public disturbance of the peace struck these legal authorities as both far-fetched and rather ludicrous:

> A person professing Christianity may be offended by the film but, considering the situation in our times, will not be provoked to react tumultuously to this distortion of his convictions, let alone go to the barricades. Nor will he be affected by the film to the extent that, after public screening of the film, he will fear a limitation of his freedom of faith or even an anti–Christian influence of other citizens, since in his modern enlightenment he has a good sense of one-day flies (here an edgy film in 1982 — there the worldwide, almost 2000-year-old institution of Christianity) and is also aware that the inviolability of his religious standpoint is guaranteed by the constitution of our government of laws [Sandfort & Hanisch 7].

Among the film's more sympathetic reviewers was Karena Niehoff (1920–1992), one of Germany's leading film critics. Niehoff had been charged with high treason and sent to a concentration camp during the Third Reich and later testified against Nazi film director Veit Harlan ("Jud Süß") in 1950. She praised the "exceptionally intelligent and informative" press brochure accompanying *Liebeskonzil* and noted that Nazi literature was treated "far more leniently" by postwar West German authorities than Panizza's works had been (*Der Tagesspiegel* 12 Mar. 1982: 4). Niehoff likened Jörg Schmidt-Reitwein's camera work to "penetrantly gripping fangs" and pointed out Salines' intense yet calm portrayal of both Panizza and the Devil, noting his successful portrayal of extreme loneliness "with his marvelous sadness." She thought that all the outraged commotion surrounding *Liebeskonzil* was quite unjustified, especially since Panizza's graphic depictions of debauchery at the Vatican were entirely missing from Salines' stage production and from Schroeter's film.

This point of view, however, was certainly not shared universally. The more conservative Catholic reviewers were decidedly less complacent in their evaluation of *Liebeskonzil*. One Catholic film journal referred to Panizza's characters as "ridiculous figures in a crude farce. [...] So far over the top in terms of staging and acting that it results in ludicrousness, and the verbal salvos largely miss their mark" (Graf 20).

Roberto Tesconi as Christ in the 1982 *Liebeskonzil* film directed by Werner Schroeter. First published in *Liebeskonzil Filmbuch*, ed. Peter Berling. Munich: Schimer/Mosel, 1982. Courtesy of Dr. Franz Ringel. Copyright © 1982 Schirmer/Mosel Verlag, Munich.

This same attitude was also in evidence among more conservative circles in the neighboring Republic of Austria. An official publication by the Education Ministry in Vienna plagiarized portions of the above review from the Catholic *Filmdienst*: "The staging and acting are so far over the top that ludicrousness is often the result. However, the intention to disparage religion and the Church is obvious and amounts to blasphemy" (R.E., *Multimedia* 1984/4: 1).

Schroeter's Liebeskonzil film had short and uneventful cinema runs in Vienna, Graz and other Austrian cities. On the other hand, the situation in Tyrol was a different matter altogether. In the spring of 1985, the Otto-Preminger-Institut für audiovisuelle Mediengestaltung (OPI) in Innsbruck decided it would present Schroeter's *Liebeskonzil* film at its Cinematograph Theater in Innsbruck for six evening showings, beginning on Monday, May 13 at 10 P.M. The announcement was inserted in the OPI newsletter, sent to its 2,700 members and placed in various display windows in Innsbruck: "In Schroeter's film, God's representatives on earth, adorned with the insignia of secular power, completely resemble the heavenly protagonists down to their last hair. Trivial pictorial images and excesses of Christian faith are parodied, and the relationship of articles of faith and mechanisms of secular repression are explored" (Twele 2). The newspaper advertisement also noted that the film was prohibited for persons under the age of seventeen.

On 10 May 1985 the Innsbruck diocese of the Roman Catholic Church requested the local district attorney to institute criminal proceedings against OPI's manager, Dietmar Zingl, for planning to disparage religious doctrines, an act prohibited by Paragraph 188 of the Austrian Penal Code (*öStGB*). The district attorney's office cooperated fully with the request in accordance with the federal prohibition against blasphemy, which reads:

> Whoever publicly denigrates or derides a person or object worshipped by a domestic church or religious community, or an article of faith, a legally permissible custom or legally permissible institution of such a church or religious society, under circumstances that are apt to elicit justified offense, will be punished by up to six months in prison or a fine amounting to 360 days of income [*öStGB*, § 188 Denigration of Religious Doctrines].

The Innsbruck district attorney not only fully cooperated with the diocese's request, but it sprung into action with a remarkable swiftness. On May 12, a Sunday, the OPI's Cinematograph movie theater was ordered to hold a private screening of the film for the Innsbruck district attorney, Hautz, in the presence of duty judge (*Journalrichter*) Kandler. The local newspaper reported the event with mild amusement: "God the Father flickered across the screen as a doddering old geezer. Mary was portrayed as a slut. And Jesus was assigned the role of an infantile, inept bumbler. The Pope was portrayed next to a naked woman's buttocks and even the Holy Ghost made an appearance as a dove on the head of God the Father" (G.G., *TT* 15/16 May 1985).

The officers of the court decided that the sole intent of the film was to be blasphemous: "Overall, the film in its whole presentation only has the purpose of reviling God the Father, Mary and the Trinity" (Landesgericht Innsbruck, *Protokoll* 1). Immediately following the private screening on May 12, the district attorney petitioned for the film's seizure under Paragraph 36 of the Austria's Media Law. This application was granted by the Innsbruck *Landesgericht* (regional court) that same Sunday. When Dietmar Zingl was informed of this situation the following day, he voluntarily cancelled the six scheduled public screenings and sent the film back to its distributor, Czerny, in Vienna. It was, in fact, seized there by law enforcement officials four weeks later on June 11.

The small audience that showed up on the evening of May 13 was treated to a public reading of three texts: the judge's decision ordering seizure of the film, the OPI's letter of protest against this court order and Act III of *The Love Council*. The national press was highly critical of the actions taken to suppress the film, which were described with obvious sarcasm in *Kurier*: "Shortly before 10 on Monday, May 13, two discretely dressed gentlemen appeared in the lobby of the Cinematograph in Innsbruck to protect about 40 adult Austrian citizens from an offense to their religious feelings" (Schöpf, 16 May 1985).

Referring also to the fate of Herbert Achternbusch's film, *Das Gespenst* (*The Ghost*), which had been banned in Austria not long before, commentator Alois Schöpf posed a series of pointed rhetorical questions:

> Why is the screening of a film that was shown without objection in Vienna and Graz suddenly criminal in Tyrol? Why is the screening of this film criminal, but not the public reading from the far more explicit play, *The Love Council*, which bears the same name and has for years been for sale in every bookstore, even in "Catholic" Tyrol? And who in our secular country protects the "community" of those who, as agnostics or descendents of the Enlightenment, reject or antagonistically oppose traditional religions? Don't they have a right to express their worldview in the arts? [Schöpf, 16 May 1985].

One day after canceling the film screening, the OPI board of directors issued a strongly-worded press release, denying any criminal intent and lambasting the actions taken by the court and the district attorney. The board pointed out that the main targets of the film were secular, not clerical authorities: "Here parallels are drawn in a dramaturgical fashion, in the form of a prologue and epilogue, between secular and heavenly judges. [...] The board of directors of the Otto-Preminger-Institut has also reached the conclusion that the film rather serves to criticize secular conditions" ("Pressemitteilung," 14 May 1985).

Not surprisingly, the left-wing press was most critical of the court's move to impose artistic censorship. Writing in *Volksstimme*, the central publication of the Austrian Communist Party, Uli Eisner reflected on the parallels between Panizza's 1895 trial in Munich and the situation in Austria a century later: "And now, as if ninety years had not passed, in Tyrol they are again self-righteously blowing the hunting horn. [...] One thing above all else is holy to the Tyrolean officials: the right to employ the anachronistic, arbitrary instrument of cultural censorship" (4 June 1985).

The court order to seize the film was duly appealed by the OPI's board at the end of May 1985. This appeal was denied by the Innsbruck *Oberlandesgericht* (appellate court) on 30 July 1985, which ruled that "artistic freedom is limited by the obligation of the state to guarantee an orderly coexistence of citizens based on tolerance" (4.) Preserving the constitutionally guaranteed right to freedom of artistic expression was decidedly less important than protecting the feelings of the majority of "average" persons with "normal" religious sensibilities. The court confirmed that the film had been properly seized, "since the massive lampooning of religious feelings weighs more heavily than the arguments of artistic freedom" (9–10).

Again, it was the leftist press that registered the strongest outrage at the ruling of the *Oberlandesgericht*:

> Oh, my poor, sanctimoniously Christian Austria! No proper Christian feels injured when masses of innocent people are slaughtered. [...] Further in the text: "The fact that the overwhelming majority of average Christians must perceive the film to be particularly disparaging and degrading is decisive by itself." However, the "average Christians" are hardly sitting in the movie theater. And if so, then in "Rambo." [...] Judges are deciding what constitutes art. Has it really come to that again? [Eisner, *Volksstimme* 16 Oct. 1985: 9].

Since the film was never publicly shown in Innsbruck and was surrendered to the court as ordered, the case against Dietmar Zingl, suspected of attempted blasphemy, was finally dropped five months after it had commenced. However, the tenaciously argued case surrounding the legality of this film's seizure was to occupy the highest Austrian and international European courts for the next decade.

The effort to challenge the banning of the *Liebeskonzil* film in the courts was supported by the membership of the OPI in Innsbruck, as well as by a special fund established by the *Interessengemeinschaft österreichischer Autoren* (Association of Austrian Authors) in Vienna. In a letter to its membership dated 24 December 1985, the organization's executive director, author Gerhard Ruiss, called on its members to support the creation of a new "solidarity fund of Austrian artists and writers to finance model lawsuits as well as take all legal steps to assure 'freedom of art' in Austria — including appealing to international courts" ("Zum Entscheid" 2).

Ruiss was responding not just to the seizure of *Liebeskonzil*, but to actions taken by Austrian authorities against other literary works, such as the book and film by Herbert Achternbusch, *Das Gespenst* (1983, *The Ghost*), and Thomas Bernhard's novel, *Holzfällen. Eine Erregung* (1984, *Woodcutters: An Excitation*). According to Ruiss, "This fund will not only raise money for pursuing ongoing cases, but will also provide resources for research and other expert studies for clarifying the legal situation" (Ruiss, *Solidaritätsfonds* 2). The rather ambitious general goal of this initiative was, "along with supporting incriminated art and artists, reappraising the current judicial and statutory conditions in order to eliminate legal uncertainties, as well as introducing further legislative measures to further the intentions of Article 17a of the Constitution." Dr. Frank Höpfel, OPI's attorney who later became a law professor at the University of Vienna, handled the case on a *pro bono* basis through 1994, which kept the overall costs to a minimum.

On 10 October 1986 a trial took place before the Innsbruck *Landesgericht* (Regional Court). Both the judge and the district attorney stated that they personally considered the film to be a work of art, but that the average religious Tyrolean person could be offended in his religious feelings. The judge was very clear about his reasoning: "The only decisive point is that undoubtedly the overwhelming majority of average Christian believers must perceive the film as being disparaging and debasing" (Landesgericht Innsbruck, *Im Namen der Republik*, 10).

The film had again not been shown to the court in open session, a fact lamented in a commentary by the local newspaper, because "it is thus difficult to judge whether art in its presumed freedom has actually crossed the line of religious sensitivity" (Lutz, *Tirol Kurier* 11 Oct. 1986). The commentator proceeded to speculate as to who, if anybody, was really threatened by the film: "An anonymous 'average person' had to serve as the basis for the confiscation. Who is this ominous being — and how do the district attorney and the judge know so precisely what he thinks and feels?"

In his judgment issued the same day, Judge Walter Krabichler ordered the forfeiture of the previously seized *Liebeskonzil* film. In his decision, Dr. Krabichler ruled that the film, in his opinion, was "primarily a provocative and conceptually anti-clerical film" that was criminally blasphemous as set forth in § 188 of the criminal code (Landesgericht Innsbruck, *Im Namen der Republik*, 12). His reasoning to limit artistic freedom and to now ban the *Liebeskonzil* film from ever being shown again in Austria invoked the familiar justifications:

> Artistic freedom is not to be understood as being without any limitations. The limits of artistic freedom are firstly found in other basic rights and freedoms guaranteed by the constitution (e.g., freedom of religion and conscience), secondly in the necessity for an orderly living together of people based on tolerance, and finally in the blatant and extreme offenses to other legally protected entities [...] [12].

It is noteworthy that artistic freedom of expression had recently been expanded in 1982, just four years prior to this ruling, by the addition of Article 17A to the Austrian constitution: "Artistic creativity, the transmission of art as well as its teaching, are free." Nonetheless, the court's decision apparently gave this constitutional guarantee less weight than the traditional prohibition against blasphemy. As one Viennese newspaper insisted: "If the 'honesty of the artistic work's originator' is beyond doubt, then jurisprudence should be based on the principle 'In dubio pro arte,' and not [...] try to reduce art to a measure that might satisfy 'the average Tyrolean person'" (Bandhauer, *Wiener Zeitung* 7 Nov. 1986).

Not surprisingly, the OPI strongly criticized the court's ruling as being based on a double standard: "'Equal rights for all' becomes an empty formula when film scenes in one city are more apt to create a public nuisance than elsewhere" ("Pressemitteilung," 10 Oct. 1986: 2). The court's ruling in Innsbruck was seen by the OPI as a continuation of the travesty of justice depicted in the film's framing courtroom scenes: "Perhaps the action that Schroeter depicted in the framing scenes will continue in reality. [...] The entire prosecution appears as a pomaded caricature of infallibility, which ironically does not become credible by its depiction in the film, but only by the fact that the authorities want to move against the film" ("Pressemitteilung," 10 Oct. 1986: 3).

The judgment of the regional court was appealed by Dietmar Zingl, who claimed that §188 had not been interpreted in line with the guarantee of artistic freedom set forth in Article17a of the Austrian constitution. His appeal included a declaration signed by some 350 persons, who protested that they had been denied free access to a work of art by the court's seizure of the film. On 25 March 1987 the Innsbruck Court of Appeals declared the appeal inadmissible, ruling that Zingl had no standing since he was not the copyright owner of the film.

Shortly after this ruling was issued, Dr. Höpfel, OPI's attorney, asked Hilde Hawlicek, Austria's federal Minister for Education, Art & Sports, for help in obtaining a plea of nullity. Dr. Hawlicek obliged and sent a letter on 18 May 1987 to the Viennese attorney general, Otto F. Müller, asking him to explore obtaining a plea of nullity for safeguarding the law. In her view, the Innsbruck court's ruling was "difficult to reconcile with the principles of a pluralistic society based on tolerance, which are also recognized by Article 10 of the Human Rights Convention" (2). Her suggestion was to shift the point of view away from the average citizen, whoever that might be, to that of a more open-minded, artistically oriented public. However, this approach was unproductive. Citing the Austrian Supreme Court's previous decision concerning Herbert Achternbusch's film *Das Gespenst* (*The Ghost*), the attorney general decided on 26 July 1988 that there were no grounds for filing such a plea of nullity (ECHR *Judgment*, paragraph 18).

Even before that decision was announced, the Otto-Preminger-Institut had decided to take the important step of contesting the seizure and subsequent forfeiture of the *Liebeskonzil* film before the European Commission on Human Rights in Strasbourg. On 6 October 1987 the OPI lodged an application (no. 13470/87) with the Commission to obtain a decision as to whether Austria had violated its obligations under Article 10 of the European Human Rights Convention. The OPI was clearly aware of the precedent-setting nature of its action. In the press release accompanying the application to the Commission, the OPI stated: "After exhausting all legal appeals in Austria, for the first time ever a case involving seizure of art under § 188 of the Penal Code finds its continuation in Strasbourg" (8 Oct. 1987).

In view of the recent favorable rulings in previous cases, the owners of the Cinematograph were optimistic about their chances of gaining a favorable ruling from the Strasbourg court: "Repeatedly [...] the authorities have emphasized that the protection of freedom of speech also applies to ideas that can offend, provoke or shock." Commenting on his legal action, attorney Frank Höpfel emphasized that artistic freedom not only benefited the individual artist but also society as a whole: "It is often overlooked that prosecutorial measures against artists and purveyors of art also encroach on the rights of the interested public, since 'artistic freedom' also means 'free access to art by the public'" ("Wie frei ist die Kunst?" 2).

The European wheels of justice were grinding very slowly in the late 1980s. Because of a huge backlog of cases, the European Commission on Human Rights did not begin to discuss the case of the *Liebeskonzil* film for almost four years after it had been submitted. The case was formally admitted on 12 April 1991. The fourteen members of the Commission finally took up the case and screened the film for the first time on 5 July 1991 (*TT* 9 July 1991). The European dimension of this case did not go unnoticed back in Tyrol: "It is certainly of interest throughout Europe that the Human Rights Commission is dealing with freedom of art for the first time" (Licha, *Tirol Kurier* 5 July 1991). Attorney Frank Höpfel saw the guiding principle in his case as being one that was essential to a free democracy: "The 'Cinematograph' is not any movie theater into which one stumbles unprepared. Rather, it is an art cinema in which an open-minded audience is also prepared to deal with provocative works. That must be possible in a democracy."

Actually, Höpfel's assumption ultimately proved wrong, at least if the democracy is Austrian. But before the European Commission on Human Rights finally reached its decision in 1993, there were two important theatrical productions of Panizza's *Love Council* in Austria. The first one was directed by Stephan Bruckmeier in Vienna in 1991 at the Ensemble Theater am Petersplatz. According to Lothar Lohs, Bruckmeier's production was admittedly conceived as a provocation, but one intended to produce insight instead of scandal (*Der Standard* 11 Nov. 1991: 12). He praised the production as "the best theater presented by a free troupe in a long time" (*Falter* 47, 1991).

The second notable Austrian production of *The Love Council* during this period was at the Tiroler Landestheater in 1992 under the aegis of its new Swiss *Intendant*, Dominique Mentha. Ironically, the regional Landestheater is just blocks away from the Cinematograph in Innsbruck, where law enforcement authorities had come to seize the film version seven years previously. Directed by Dieter W. Hübsch, this new production was generally well received, though not without a certain amount of controversy and outright opposition. Innsbruck Bishop Reinhold Stecher saw no reason to take any legal action this time against the play, "because the piece condemns itself" (Linde, *Tirol-Kurier* 6 May 1993). Notably Armin Benedikter, a law student described by one newspaper as "a militant Catholic who considers believers and priests adhering to Vatican II to be heretics," tried to halt the production by filing a complaint of blasphemy, but this time the district attorney declined to take action (Steinkeller, *Salzburger Nachrichten* 1 Oct. 1991: 23).

The leader of the conservative ÖVP youth group in Innsbruck, Egon Saurer, complained that the play was "anti-religious" and railed against what he described as a "mockery of Christian religion subsidized by tax-payers' money" (*Oberösterreichische Nachrichten* 28 Sept. 1992: 19). In contrast to Saurer, the local press was generally supportive of this production:

> Everyone has the right to demand protection of one's religious feelings. However, this protection can also be obtained by "self-administered justice": by not allowing oneself to be provoked and not watching the play. Just as nobody is forced to watch comparatively demeaning, actually brutal theatrical and TV films or to play psychologically deforming computer games. [...] There are also people in Tyrol who would like to watch a play like *The Love Council*. In an enlightened society they should not be prevented from doing so by a performance ban [Lepuschitz, *TT* 3/4 Oct. 1992].

Despite a small demonstration outside the theater, the premiere in Innsbruck went off without a hitch. Under the title "No Council Problem," a regional paper noted laconically: "In Innsbruck, the premiere of *The Love Council* took place without any threatened incidents. The performance of the play [...] was met with strong applause. Only a few Catholic traditionalists demonstrated" (*Oberösterreichische Nachrichten* 5 Oct. 1992: 18).

Maria Deppermann, a professor of comparative literature at Innsbruck University, described the enthusiastic reception of the play: "While a kneeling prayer demonstration took place in front of the theater, an enthusiastic audience paid tribute to the director, the set and the ensemble with standing ovations mixed with shouts of hallelujah and bravo" (16). As a literary historian, she recognized that Panizza's "criticism of the characters of God the Father, Christ and the Virgin Mary were not directed against their divine essence, but rather against the crudely distorted image that people have made of them" (15).

Celestial and Vatican entourage surrounding Renzo Rinaldi, center, playing both Pope and God in the 1982 _Liebeskonzil_ film directed by Werner Schroeter. Courtesy of Dr. Franz Ringel. Copyright © 1982 Schirmer-Mosel Verlag, Munich.

In view of the successful production of *The Love Council* in Innsbruck in 1992, when the long awaited and much anticipated decision by the European Commission of Human Rights in Strasbourg was finally handed down on 3 April 1993, there was little cause for shock or surprise. The Commission ruled 9 to 5 that the original seizure of the *Liebeskonzil* film by Austrian authorities in 1985 had violated the guarantee of freedom of expression contained in Article 10 of the European Convention on Human Rights. Furthermore, the Commission ruled 13 to 1 that the subsequent forfeiture and country-wide ban of the film upheld by the Austrian courts was also in violation of Article 10.

The Otto-Preminger-Institut, the plaintiff in this case, was naturally pleased by the decision. Attorney Frank Höpfel summarized the objective of his legal actions, which at this point had extended over eight years: "From the very beginning, the aim of the lawsuit was to establish that it must be possible in a democracy to also present possibly provocative works of art to an interested audience — at least as long as nobody is forced to view the work and appropriate introductory information about the contents is offered" (*Presse-Info*, 5 May 1993).

Panizza had now been the object of controversy in Austrian cultural life for eight years: "Since May 1985 Oskar Panizza's play *The Love Council* has provided for unrest in Tyrol" (Steinkeller, *Salzburger Nachrichten* 7 May 1993: 17). One Tyrolean daily newspaper began its story with the following upbeat statement: "How the times have changed" (Glantschnig, *TT* 6 May 1993: 4). Although time would prove this statement to be chimerical, at least as far as censorship in Austria is concerned, there was widespread optimism that legal change of major proportions was taking place. It was acknowledged by Amnesty International, the U.S. State Department and others that Austria had a fairly good human rights record. However, Austria did have an above-average number of complaints lodged against it with the European Human Rights Commission, especially regarding freedom of expression in the media and the arts (Kamolz, *Profil* 7 June 1993).

After its April 1993 ruling that Austria had violated Article 10 of the European Human Rights Convention by seizing and banning the *Liebeskonzil* film, the Commission then referred the case to the European Court of Human Rights for a final ruling. The ECHR, the highest court in Europe and from which no appeal is possible, is also located in Strasbourg. It received the case of Otto-Preminger-Institut v. Austria (11/1993/406/485) from the Commission on 7 April 1993. Attorney Höpfel and his clients had high hopes that the ECHR would confirm the Commission's ruling and establish a major precedent for ensuring freedom of expression throughout Europe: "The decision in Strasbourg could have consequences not only for Austrian jurisprudence, but it can also provide an important clarification for cultural life and artistic freedom throughout Europe" (Linde, *Tirol-Kurier* 6 May 1993).

On 2 September 1993 the ECHR granted leave to two non-governmental organizations, Article 19 — International Centre Against Censorship and Interights — International Centre for the Legal Protection of Human Rights, to submit written observations on specific aspects of the case. Both London-based groups submitted their comments jointly. After surveying the law regarding blasphemy and insult to religious belief in ten European countries and the U.S., they concluded that "courts in eight of the ten countries [excluding Italy and England] not only would be likely to refuse to find that the showing would constitute a crime but also the seizure could not be justified since the interest in freedom of expression and art would clearly outweigh any possible harm of showing a film under these circumstances" (Coliver & Schiffrin, 20f.).

The hearing before the nine ECHR judges in this case to determine whether "seizure and forfeiture of a film found to be blasphemous" (ECHR *Judgement* iii) violated Article 10 of the European Human Rights Convention was held in Strasbourg's Human Rights Building on 24 November 1993. On the previous day, the court had screened the *Liebeskonzil* film at a private showing. Commenting on the hearing, at which Austria was represented by legal officials from the Federal Chancellery and from the Ministries of Justice and Foreign Affairs, a national newspaper sounded optimistic that freedom of expression would finally prevail in Strasbourg: "The still outstanding judgment should again be a condemnation of Austria" (Lahodynsky, *Die Presse* 29 Nov. 1993).

It was, therefore, a major surprise when the ECHR's final judgment of 20 September 1994 turned out to be a crushing defeat for freedom of expression in Europe at the end of the twentieth century. The court ruled 6 to 3 "that there has been no violation of Article 10 of the Convention as regards either the seizure or the forfeiture of the film" (ECHR *Judgment*, paragraph 57). The ECHR based its ruling on Section 2 of Article 10 of the European Convention on Human Rights, which restricts the broad guarantee of freedom of expression contained in Section 1:

> The exercise of these freedoms, since it carries with it duties and responsibilities, may be subject to such formalities, conditions, restrictions or penalties as are prescribed by law and are necessary in a democratic society, in the interests of national security, territorial integrity or public safety, for the prevention of disorder or crime, for the protection of health or morals, for the protection of the reputation or rights of others, for preventing the disclosure of information received in confidence, or for maintaining the authority and impartiality of the judiciary [ECHR *Judgment*, paragraph 42].

The majority of the judges on the ECHR clearly held that freedom of expression needed to be restricted in order to preserve what they described as "religious peace" (paragraph 52) in a part of the country where 87 percent of the population is Roman Catholic:

The Court cannot disregard the fact that the Roman Catholic religion is the religion of the overwhelming majority of Tyroleans. In seizing the film, the Austrian authorities acted to ensure religious peace in that region and to prevent that some people should feel the object of attacks on their religious beliefs in an unwarranted and offensive manner. It is in the first place for the national authorities, who are better placed than the international judge, to assess the need for such a measure in the light of the situation obtaining locally at a given time. In all the circumstances of the present case, the Court does not consider that the Austrian authorities can be regarded as having overstepped their margin of appreciation in this respect.

No violation of Article 10 [of the European Convention on Human Rights] can therefore be found as far as the seizure is concerned [Paragraph 56].

In their strongly worded dissenting opinion, the judges from Finland, Poland and Sweden stated: "There is a danger that if applied to protect the perceived interests of a powerful group in society, such prior restraint could be detrimental to that tolerance on which pluralist democracy depends" (paragraph 4 of the Joint Dissenting Opinion). The dissenters maintained, "The Convention does not, in terms, guarantee a right to protection of religious feelings. More particularly, such a right cannot be derived from the right to freedom of religion, which in effect includes a right to express views critical of the religious opinions of others" (paragraph 6). They further pointed out that the Cinematograph's Innsbruck audience had sufficiently been warned beforehand about the nature of the film "to enable the religiously sensitive to make an informed decision to stay away" (paragraph 9). The dissenting judges cited substantial case law to strongly affirm that freedom of expression "is applicable not only to 'information' or 'ideas' that are favorably received or regarded as inoffensive or as a matter of indifference, but *particularly* to those that shock, offend or disturb the State or any sector of the population. There is no point in guaranteeing this freedom only as long as it is used in accordance with accepted opinion" (paragraph 3; emphasis in original document).

That very same day, the shockwaves of this ruling literally went round the world via a major international wire service story. Erroneously referring to Panizza as an Austrian writer, the 285-word United Press International story accurately summarized the ECHR ruling, "that Austrian authorities did not violate rights of freedom of expression in banning a film that is allegedly offensive to many Christians" (20 Sept. 1994).

European commentators were quick to respond. Perhaps the most dismissive was the journalist who conflated the Commission with the ECHR and equated it with the Catholic Church: "Whoever has such a Human Rights Commission that argues on the level of Wilhelmine justice (which harassed and censored Panizza almost a hundred years ago) no longer needs the Catholic Church" ("Unterm Strich," *taz* 21 Sept. 1994: 12). Even the commentator in the fairly conservative Innsbruck daily newspaper was highly critical of the court's decision: "The film is being locked up instead of the author. [...] In the meantime, *The Love Council* was allowed to be shown on the stage in our country. A weak consolation for those who assume that the right to freedom of thought is generally applicable in democratic Europe" (Lepuschitz, *TT* 21 Sept. 1994).

Another Austrian daily, in an editorial titled "The Inquisition is Alive," was even harsher in its denunciation of the ECHR's verdict, stating that it "only helps those who are always in favor of forbidding" (Stainer, *Oberösterreichische Nachrichten* 21 Sept. 1994: 17). The editorialist noted the hypocrisy behind the ECHR's rationalization that Austria was justified in banning the film in order to preserve "religious peace": "Word has evidently not reached Strasbourg that the holy land of Tyrol survived the live performance of the play

[...] in 1993, without a religious war having erupted." Not surprisingly, Terezija Stoisits and Friedrun Huemer, members of the Austrian Green Party, warned that the ECHR's judgment would only "encourage intolerance toward people with differing views" ("Zum *Liebeskonzil*-Urteil: Grüne bedauern EGH-Entscheid." *Wiener Zeitung* 23 Sept. 1994). This view was also reflected in the more conservative Austrian provincial newspapers. Christa Dietrich lamented: "According to this particular case of censorship that only applies to Austria, the judgment must be seen as a sign of intolerance and ostracism of those with differing points of view" (*Vorarlberger Nachrichten* 24/25 Sept. 1994).

One of the most detailed analyses of the ECHR's judgment was in a London *Times* article by David Pannick, a practicing attorney teaching at Oxford. He totally rejected the Strasbourg judgment, asserting that "it is no business of the judiciary to assess whether a film makes a 'contribution to any form of public debate capable of furthering progress in human affairs.' The central purpose of freedom of expression is to allow readers and viewers to make up their own mind about the value of a work" (8 Nov. 1994). Pannick pointed out that "the court fails to understand that social development, in art as well as in politics, has often proceeded from the assertion of ideas that cause offence, sometimes outrage, to established thought. Freedom of expression is of limited value if it covers only that which does not upset received opinion." He shares the view of most academic and media commentators who opposed any kind of blasphemy laws whatsoever, invoking the time-honored words of Emperor Tiberius (b. 42 B.C.), that "insults to the gods are the affairs of the gods."

There is a further weakness in the ECHR's judgment, according to Pannick, "for judges to assess artistic merit, and to penalize dissent, is especially dangerous in the context of established religion, which demands uncritical devotion from many of its followers, and so enjoys considerable power in religious societies." He recognizes that freedom of speech should not depend on public acceptability: "In such a climate, dissenting voices will struggle to make themselves heard. It is the task of the court to ensure that they are not silenced." Certainly Jesus, Luther, Nietzsche and many other great men and women were initially considered by their contemporaries to be strong threats to the established authorities. "No doubt Galileo, Copernicus and Spinoza greatly offended religious feelings in their day, and were considered to be making no useful contribution to human knowledge." Citing U.S. Supreme Court Justice Harlan's observation in 1971 that "one man's vulgarity is another man's lyric," Pannick concluded by strongly admonishing: "Judges, whether in national courts or in Strasbourg, should resist the temptation to act as arbiters of good taste."

Writing about this landmark judgment in the *St. John's Law Review*, Brian Walsh, himself a judge on the ECHR and a former justice on the Irish Supreme Court, noted that the *Liebeskonzil* trial "marked the first time the European Court ever heard such a case" (77). He further stated that "the holding of the European Court is quite significant, considering that the God in question is the God not merely of the Jewish and the Islamic people, but of the Christian people as well. With ramifications throughout the world, the decision could easily give rise to public disorder, which is one of the reasons in favor of an intervention." He also points out that "the European Convention has not been adopted as part of the domestic law by a majority of the thirty-three member States. One reason is that in certain areas, the national law of the member State provides better protection than the European Convention."

One country where the national law would appear to provide better protection for freedom of expression is Switzerland. For the century-long trials of Oskar Panizza did not end

Bernhard Michel, left, and Sandra Utzinger as angels in Barbara Frey's 1997 student production of *Das Liebeskonzil* at the Schauspielschule in Bern. Courtesy of Leonie Stein, Institut für Transdisziplinarität, Hochschule der Künste, Bern. Copyright © 1997 by the photographer, Michael Schneeberger.

in Strasbourg in September 1994. Three years later, on 13 December 1997, about fifty people associated with the religious group *Christen für die Wahrheit* (Christians for Truth) assembled in the courtyard in front of the *Berner Schauspielschule* (Bern Acting School, today's *Hochschule für Musik und Theater*, Graduate School for Music and Theater). Carrying signs proclaiming "The Gospel of Jesus Christ is no Cheap Play," the demonstrators tried to engage theatergoers in conversation and distributed leaflets asking: "Why such theater during Advent? Without those being mocked, there would be no Christmas!" (Koslowski 167). At issue was the performance of *The Love Council* by the graduating class of the Acting School under the direction of Barbara Frey. Despite the distraction caused by the demonstrators loudly singing Christmas carols outside, the performance went off without a hitch and the police reported the peaceful dispersal of the demonstrators later.

Subsequently, on Christmas Eve, Christians for Truth took the students, faculty and administration of the Bern Acting School to court for their production of *The Love Council*. They were charged with violating Article 261 of the Swiss Penal Code, which governs the freedom of religion and worship. Nor surprisingly, among the most vehement opponents of the theatrical production was the anti-immigrant, far-right Schweizer Demokraten (SD) party. They demanded "an immediate performance ban on the perverse and blasphemous play" (*SD Pressemitteilung*, 19 Dec. 1997). Citing the prior decision by the ECHR, SD politicians vowed to cut funding for the offending acting school: "Bern SD city-councilman Bernhard Hess wants to obtain information through a parliamentary inquiry regarding why the Bern Acting School ignored the performance ban that was confirmed anew in 1994 by the European Court. With so much favor toward bad art, at least the SD will even more vigorously combat the sometimes princely subsidies of the arts."

Most of the press, and presumably the public as well, considered the case to be something of an anachronism:

> It seems like a reminiscence from bygone times when art was still able to able to spark scandals and was punished with censorship: This coming December the theater director Barbara Frey and Leonie Stein, the director of the Bern Acting School, will have to face the judge in court for a theater production. [...] The defendants named were the director as well as the nine actors and actresses who had presented the play in December '97 as their capstone work [von Bergen, *Berner Zeitung* 24 Sept. 1998].

The uniqueness of this six-hour trial, which took place a year after the performance on 10 December 1998, did not go unnoticed: "For the very first time in Switzerland, a theater performance has resulted in a trial before a judge on charges of disturbing the freedom of religion and worship" (Leis, *Der Bund* 11 Dec. 1998: 9). The Swiss press emphasized the weighty historic dimensions of this case:

> Artistic freedom is rarely debated in a court of law. Yesterday's trial was all the more significant. That could be seen from the huge crowd of spectators: for the first time, a simple criminal case before a single judge was moved to the large Assizes Hall of the Bern Municipal Building, Judge [Lienhard] Ochsner spoke of a record crowd. The Bern trial marks the first legal proceeding against the performance of a play in Swiss legal history; and one of the rare cases being judged according to Article 261 of the Penal Code, which deals with disruptions to the freedom of religion [von Bergen, *Berner Zeitung* 11 Dec. 1998].

The judge agreed with the defense that blasphemy itself was not a punishable offense: "In explaining his acquittal, Judge Ochsner agreed with Hänni, that not the blasphemy itself is punishable, but rather its malicious application against religious peace." The acquittal in this case was seen as an affirmation of artistic freedom of expression: "The charge is anachronistic and could have most severely damaged artistic freedom. If a hundred-year-old theater classic may no longer be performed, then the floodgates would be open to ideologically motivated censorship," wrote Sandra Leis ("Kommentar," 11 Dec. 1998: 9). The dangerous threat of artistic censorship, such as was carried out in Innsbruck and upheld by the ECHR in Strasbourg, was averted by the decision of this latest *Love Council* trial in Bern. As her editorial in *Der Bund* warned: "Everyone has the right to confront art, or not to. It gets dangerous when one declares one's own opinion to be the only correct standard and dictatorially postulates the right to make up other people's minds for them."

The German press also took note of this landmark trial in Bern. Reinhardt Stumm pointed out in the *Frankfurter Rundschau*: "Blasphemy is not the criminally relevant act, but rather the disturbance of the public peace. If that were charged, then proof of the intentional violation of the basic rights of others would have to be submitted. That, however, would not have been possible at all" (19 Dec. 1998: 8). Stumm describes how the judge in this case traced the principle of tolerance back to Henry IV's Edict of Nantes in 1598. Religious freedom guaranteed today also includes the freedom to believe anything or nothing at all: "Atheists and agnostics have the same basic rights — they can believe in one god or several gods or none at all, the state has to protect them as well from the intolerance of others."

While the 1998 Bern acquittal was certainly a victory for freedom of expression, at least within the tiny Swiss Confederation, some on the far-right continued to rail at what they viewed as the evils of artistic freedom. Writing for the right-wing Eidgenössisch-Demokratische Union (EDU) party, Thomas Feuz asserted: "With the Bern verdict it seems that religion has lost and art has won. Remember, when the revision of the Bern constitution was being discussed, that the EDU opposed the constitution, not least because of the stipulation of 'artistic freedom'? The current development has proven that those concerns were, in the truest sense of the word, 'right'!" (*EDU-Standpunkt*, 6 January 1999).

For more than a century now, Oskar Panizza's infamous *Love Council* has functioned as a kind of prime litmus test for freedom of artistic expression in Germany, Austria, Switzerland and beyond. In its satirical, farcical presentation of a deadly serious topic, the origin of sexually transmitted syphilis, the play questions many fundamental assumptions regarding free speech and censorship that have often gone unexamined. The play's various productions have provided unique opportunities for proponents and opponents of artistic freedom to test the judicial system's ability to balance the fundamental right to freedom of religion with the equally fundamental right to freedom of expression. A historic review of the trials of Oskar Panizza and his *Love Council* has shown how precarious this balancing act proved to be throughout the entire twentieth century.

PART IV: RECEPTION AND PERFORMANCE

Chapter 10

M. G. Conrad's Evaluation, 1895

From the Expert Testimony of Dr. Michael Georg Conrad

Esteemed court! I have been asked the question whether I consider the book *The Love Council* to be a work of art or a blasphemous diatribe.

I consider it to be a work of art for the plain and clear reason that it was produced by an *artist* and is written in *one of the strictest literary genres*, as a drama. This dramatic form, when applied to a book that will probably never be performed onstage, is thus exclusively intended to be read; it is considered by knowledgeable people to be both the least fashionable, most unpopular book form, as evidenced by the fact that of all the works of fiction, none find less appeal and fewer buyers than the closet drama, which, gentlemen, any bookseller will confirm to you. It has also previously been stated in the book dealer's testimony that Panizza's book, *The Love Council*, had virtually no sales. A dozen or so buyers don't amount to any sales revenue. Someone who wants to write and disseminate an effective polemic will certainly not begin by choosing a form that limits distribution from the start and, given the current taste of our educated readership, almost completely excludes distribution. I am convinced that the gentlemen who are summoned here as jurors to judge the accused book have never to this hour seen it at all and have only learned of its existence from the prosecution. Not even in the daily press could anything be gleaned about it, because the few reviews of *The Love Council* to appear in the last four or five months since its publication were exclusively in specialized literary magazines with limited circulation.

However, in my estimation the indicted book is a work of art not only for its form, but basically also for its content and mode of presentation, in which the thought of any one-sided bias is completely in the background, at least for really educated art lovers. In his work, the author employed those artistic means and those special techniques that we commonly refer to as the most refined and, at the same time, as the most radically "modern" ones. An incomparable intensity and clarity is achieved by these means. At the same time, however, this kind of art produces an existential truth of such intensity or, to use a current catchword, such a relentless *naturalism*, that the ordinary, unprepared reader, who loves to wallow in heavenly blue idealisms and blissful fantasies, will not know how to deal with Panizza's drama, *The Love Council*. Here I want to say at the outset that I personally occasionally detect in Panizza's artistic method an aspect that borders on the perverse, the morbid. For me, that explains the Baroque, tasteless, crudely grotesque elements, with which especially the first act of this drama is suffused. However, I am not in a position to perceive these personally repugnant instances of tastelessness as alleged blasphemies. For if tastelessness regarding religious concepts and figures always amounted to blasphemy, then popular religious art, specifically in Catholic and especially Latin countries, would be teeming with blasphemy. What atrociousness have I not seen in innumerable pictures of hell and purgatory, in depictions of crucifixions, etc., with which church walls and cemeteries of Catholic towns are decorated in pious naiveté. Not to mention the saviors on the cross in Italy and Spain, onto whose heads real human hair is glued or whose wounds are smeared with genuine blood. And these painters of saints and wood carvers of the Lord God were also not scrupulous in their choice of physiognomies, since the first best confiscated, criminally ugly face was good enough for their Lord God or for their Christ. Has anyone ever seen blasphemy in that? Or a denigration of the Virgin Mary in the fact that she is dressed like a fashion doll in churches of Rome or Naples, decorated with rings on her fingers and ears and bracelets on her arms? It is known that in addition to the Madonnas by Raphael, there are also quite different ones that leave something to be desired regarding their holiness. But it did not ever occur to any good Catholic to take any offense. If hair or a beard is growing on a picture of Christ, it is not taken to be a blasphemous scandal or humbug, but rather an amazing miracle.

The Bible teaches that "God is a spirit." If this spirit is humanized or personalized, the particular people's taste will express itself in this image. "Man paints himself in his gods." There is no dogma in the Church which dictates that we have to imagine God or Jesus or Mary or the devil in such and such a manner, with such a head, such eyes, such physical characteristics, such a hair color, such an expression, etc. Absolute freedom of choice reigns here. Interpreters of the Bible relate a passage of the Old Testament to Christ, which says: "He had neither form nor beauty." Thus, it is Biblically sound to conceive of Christ as ugly. Who wants to draw the line and say that over here is permissible humanization and over there begins blasphemy? Strictly speaking, since God is a "spirit," according to Biblical doctrine, any depiction would have to be proscribed. But nobody is further away from this sublime concept than the Church and its representatives. Thus, the Church and whoever else represents clerical or religious interests cannot forbid anyone from imagining God to be young or old, robust or fragile, etc.

In the author's vision, the traditional heaven and what goes on there assumes a form that is thus actually beyond any discussion. The author envisioned it as he had to see it, from the artistic necessity of his creative imagination, period. You can accept of reject his vision, but you cannot legally transform it, you cannot punish it. The sole forum to which writers and artists have to answer is aesthetic criticism. The question cannot be judged by theological value or lack of it, but rather solely by artistic merit. And if the question is framed this way, then Panizza has created with his *Love Council* one of the strongest and most significant works of art in modern dramatic literature and, given the difficulty of the topic, perhaps the very most significant of recent years. As a physician, psychologist and satiric author, Panizza has chosen a topic which nobody else among our modern authors, and certainly none of the older gentlemen of the literary profession, would have felt capable of treating, and has shaped it with such genial courage, with amazing energy and consistency. And since the subject of his *Love Council* is a *historic* one, he has treated it with all the critical irreverence and relentless incisiveness that is characteristic of modern historiography. Like the modern historian, the modern dramatist is beyond all self-pity, beyond all unmanly consideration for the sentimentalities and emotionalism of the general public. And this attitude of the historian and author, which is the only correct one in scholarship and art, is naturally taken by certain people to be brutal and crude as soon as a topic is treated that is traditionally sacred to them, such as the Christian heaven in *The Love Council* and the Roman papacy at a time when the epitome of all vice and criminality sat on St. Peter's throne, when the Vatican state and its neighboring countries were the scene of the most unbridled debauchery and the murderous *syphilis* epidemic emerged.

And that is now the problem, which in my opinion Panizza saw as the challenge in his *Love Council*: How can the emergence of the syphilis epidemic into the European cultural sphere (historically documented date of spring 1495) be imaginatively demonstrated and explained out of the spirit of that time, using a large tableau and a historically authentic basis, utilizing the popular belief in gods and the devil? And like every authentic and great dramatist, Panizza saw all of this in one *vision*, in a fabulous interaction of earth, heaven and hell in the sense of the medieval-papist world view, and he shaped this vision with the superior means of modern dramatic technique. The modernity of the artistic techniques alone would have caused the scenes in heaven to have a sharply satirical bent, and the true German, un–Roman and un-papist spirit of the author and his scholarly, critical and creative prowess led unintentionally, purely unconsciously to the scenes in the Vatican being fashioned with such explosive power. Individual details are of overwhelming greatness, such as the depiction of the demonic procreation of the syphilis carrier, and even in the episodic passages one discovers elements that we are only used to encountering in the greatest literary works.

The personages in heaven do not come off very well. Yet, if the earthly representative of the Trinity in the Vatican is such a notorious abomination, then that must reflect back on one's appraisal of heaven. As the servant is, so is the master. A monster such as Borgia, being God's representative, does not go with a pure, majestic heaven, and vice versa. But is that the author's fault? Is the author criminal, if he is psychologically and historically *logical and honest*?

In conclusion: Panizza's *Love Council* is a work of art, and it would be a defamation to want to view biased blasphemy in it. However, if a special moral bias is discernable outside of the author's artistic intention, it could objectively only be based on the book's dedication: "To Hutten's memory." Hutten, the glorious German torch-bearer and intellectual warrior, the knightly precursor of those heroes who gave us the splendid Reformation Age, he succumbed to the tragic fate as one of the first victims of that terrible, mysterious disease from Italy. If a free German and modern author wants to contribute a worthy memorial to his compatriot and intellectual relative, Ulrich von Hutten, then he won't do so in sentimental or didactic verse, but rather in a dramatic work of art of such powerful intellectual and psychologically liberating force, that all who dwell on the heights of humanity are shaken by it, and that even God's representative on earth feels a shock from it. And *The Love Council* by Panizza is such a worthy votive offering, since it is, as I have tried to demonstrate, despite certain aesthetic flaws, an authentic, German, modern work of art.—

Chapter 11

Critical Responses to
The Love Council, 1895–1897

Compiled by Oskar Panizza and published as an appendix in the third, revised edition of *Das Liebeskonzil* (Zürich: J. Schabelitz, 1897).

Irma von Troll-Borostyáni in ***Der Freidenker***, Milwaukee (America), 30 December 1894: ...Compared to his earlier writings, the author has gone one step further here, in that his angry outrage is now directed against Christian mythology itself. And we state unequivocally that, as far as wit and sheer force is concerned, Panizza's sarcasm has not been surpassed, indeed has not even been equaled, by the most famous satirists in world literature....

Neue Bayerische Landeszeitung, Würzburg, 17 January 1895: ...This is even greater filth than the other book by the same author, *The German Michel and the Roman Pope*. His canvas is only painted with dung, spinach and "rhinoceros oil" [laxative]. It is no pity if such books are confiscated and burned.

Magasin International, December 1894: ...*The Love Council*. Although it is labeled a "Celestial Tragedy," this latest work is not exactly made to please believers. What is sometimes perhaps outrageous is the powerful irony, the sharp humor which the author uses to show that, as a facetious angel says in the first act, "The throne of the eternal father is falling apart."

Heinrich von Reder (from a letter to the author of 19 November 1894): Your book is partly below, partly above any criticism. Below, because reviewers will refrain from quoting excerpts for fear of the district attorney; above, on account of its personal peculiarity regarding material and form. It's just a Panizza, and one should let the old bird chirp as he pleases.

Dr. **M. Schwann** (from a letter to the author of 8 December 1894): ...I feel your *Love Council* got bogged down in the idea. That was not a dramatic, but rather an epic-fantastic subject. Just look at your stage directions in small print, which tell me that you yourself perceived the subject matter as epic and not dramatic. And then: verses! Glistening verses! Alexandrines! Ariostian verses! Blinding, shimmering, glittering!—This brilliant idea in such a Baroque form really hurt me!

Hermann Bahr in ***Die Zeit***, 24 November 1894: Christian mythology is treated here the way that classical mythology was treated by Offenbach. This insolence is this work's charm, which suffers from the long-winded passages. If one is going to risk such blasphemies and presumptuousness, they need to have some Byronic verve in order to have an effect.

Maurice von Stern (in a letter to the publisher): ...The most cynical book I have ever read!

The North-German Patron [Baron Otto von Grote] (in a letter to the author of 10 October 1894): ...Aren't you at all afraid that, following the intervention of the holy district attorney, the auspices will make their move against you with the no longer uncommon medical examination? Santo Cazzo! That will be a scream!

Rudolf Tambour (in a letter to *Vorwärts*, Berlin, 10 November 1894): ...But doesn't this German Voltaire belong in the madhouse? Why is something like this even allowed to be printed?...

Robert Reitzel in *Der arme Teufel*, Detroit, 17 November 1894: Without being satisfied by the whole play — the scenes in heaven, although drastic and brazen, don't appeal to me — too much symbolism — I still have to say: my respects! The second act certainly surprised every reader with its dramatic force, which already manifests itself in the composition. This German Michel, who calls himself Oskar Panizza, has more going for him than his literary friends suspected. And everything becomes a sword *contra Romam* for him. With this second act it is impossible not to think of K. F. Meyer's *Angela Borgia*. These are two painters whom one must have next to each other.

Detlev von Liliencron (in a letter to the author of 20 November 1894): ...The second act and Satan's selecting the women are absolutely colossal!! The *de profundis*, etc., right into the orgy! Again: absolutely colossal!

Otto Julius Bierbaum (in a letter to the author of 17 November 1894): ...I'm almost amazed that in your latest book you maltreat God the Father so *artistically*, since you like to put the artistic last. *The Love Council* is your most complete, artistically most rounded work. If you can, on the one hand, keep it up (regarding this whole side of your talent) and, secondly, finally leave the basically irrelevant Vatican empire aside, in order to focus on wider (but for us nearer) circles, then we may hope to view in you our Aristophanes. But you must leave the country, for now they will lock you up.

Ernst Kreowski in *Der Gesellschafter*, Hamburg, No.7, 1895: ...We should deeply pity the author for such an aberration....

Dr. M.G. Conrad in *Die Gesellschaft*, January 1895: ...Let the country's religious folk be warned! The great hypocrisy dance by the moral dervishes will soon get going. We will wait with a review until the comedy of critical virtue has had a good retch....

Julius Schaumberger, Munich (personal communication to the author): ...The first scenes in heaven are pure madhouse....

Franz Servaes in *Neue deutsche Rundschau*, February 1895: Panizza is a strange bird. The "pleasure at stinking" is probably not as well developed with anyone today as with him. But it is more the physician's coarse cynicism and the high spirits of the visionary than Zola's aesthetic-objective conscientiousness that endows him with this strange predilection. Panizza stinks with wit and humor — though not always, often just out of Teutonic bearish crudeness, for which he will surely gladly point to Luther's example. His "heavenly tragedy," *The Love Council*, which appeared in Zürich's Verlags-Magazin (thus beyond the borders of the Reich), is a rather unfermented mixture of philistine ridicule and demonic wit. I could have dispensed with his rasping and spitting dear God — Bierbaum has given us the old fellow with far more endearing humor — but I must compliment him for his Devil. When he thumbs through his menu of sweeties and finally stops at Salome, the daughter of Herodias, in order to conceive a daughter with her named "Lues," who shall afflict sinful mankind at God's command ... that's the stirring of a true satanism, a brand, as everyone knows, in great demand today.

Anna Croissant-Rust (in a letter to the author of 19 November 1894): ...You should know: your *Love Council* is the most significant work you have written so far. A work of *one* pitch, of such power and artistic unity, strutting with marvelous images and obscene audacity.... If only one could see it! Truly, I would give much for it; to have money, actors, sets!...

Allgemeine Zeitung, Munich, 12 January 1895: *The Love Council,* the much-discussed book by the author Oskar Panizza, published in Zürich by J. Schabelitz, has been confiscated by the office of the Royal District Attorney.

Else Erdmann, Braunschweig (in a letter to the author of 12 February 1895): ...The powerful effect of your work, which for many has opened up a new awareness, can no longer be expunged from the world through an act of barbarity....

Neues Münchener Tagblatt, 29 April 1895: On April 30, the famous author Panizza will have to defend himself before the local jury court against *no less than 93 charges of blasphemy*. These crimes were found in Panizza's book *The Love Council*, in which Catholic dogma is mocked. Dr. Panizza has not been able to find an attorney who will take on his defense.

Dr. **Sigl** in the *Bayerisches Vaterland*, 30 April 1895: ...The accused is said not to have been able to find an attorney until the last moment; that's how much holy respect our lawyers have for religion!— We wish the sinner, who otherwise is quite a "nice guy," a happy acquittal, that he mend his ways and live long! Because simply locking someone up is not going to convert anyone.

Judgment of the Royal State Court Munich I, 30 April 1895: In the name of His Majesty the King of Bavaria, the Jury Court of the Royal State Court Munich I, in the case against the author Dr. Oskar Panizza of Kissingen, charged with an offense against religion committed in print, judges as follows: 1. For an offense against religion committed in print, Dr. Oskar Panizza of Kissingen is sentenced to a prison term of one year, as well as bearing the costs of the trial and the sentence. 2. The remaining copies of the publication *The Love Council* by Oskar Panizza, as well as the plates and molds for its production, are to be rendered unusable. 3. An arrest warrant for the accused is issued.

Neues Münchener Tagblatt, 1 May 1895: Since this author with a writing mania imagines himself to be at least an Ulrich von Hutten, he rummages around in old books to find new "material." In a moldy piece of pigskin he found an account that syphilis raged in the fifteenth century, and that the people viewed the terrible disease as a scourge from God for the corruption of mankind. Panizza did not say to himself, as the historic research showed, that the disease was brought in and spread to Italy by French mercenaries, but he thought, as he cannot do otherwise in his manner or rather un-manner, that the Roman popes and particularly Alexander VI caused the misery, because it is widely alleged that the greatest depravity and debauchery reigned at the papal court during the 15th century. The sublime idea inspired a new work; immediately he grabbed his filthy pen and scribbled a five-act heavenly tragedy, *The Love Council*, which presents itself as a chain of blasphemies of the most ghastly kind. We could have assumed that the "author" of this vulgar concoction, which is targeted at and based on the hubris of degenerate minds, might be in some insane asylum, if we had not seen him today in the courtroom. The public was excluded, since the public would have indeed been grossly offended, had it been subject to all the filth that was dished out. With unbelievable cleverness, the author in whose *Love Council*— for which he could not find a German publisher, so that it saw the light of day in a well-known Swiss smut magazine — was able to mock God the Father and Son, the Virgin Mary and all the saints and to drag them through the mud. In addition to suffering from a rabid desire to destroy everything divine and holy, he also suffers from megalomania, since he naïvely and unself-consciously responded to the considerate and serious questions from the judge, that he has developed his syphilis idea into an artistic problem, that he has written a satire on the papal history of the 15th century. In reality, however, he has worked without humor and wit, with a tastelessness that can hardly be stomached even by those contemporaries who enjoy blasphemy. — Panizza's "artistic problem" involves relating syphilis to the depravity and debauchery at the papal court, and presenting it in a plot unfolding in heaven as God's punishment. In so doing, he depicts God himself as such a despicable caricature that one can scarcely comprehend how he can still find words for his own justification. He invokes Ulrich von Hutten, Erasmus of Rotterdam, Reuchlin, Fischart and maintains he has not done anything differently from what was done by the turbulent minds of the Reformation age, though he errs decisively, since nowhere can it be shown among the humanists of the Reformation age that they attacked, insulted and mocked the personage of God. Although in his monstrous writings he casts himself as their judge, how little Panizza understands about the Catholic Church and its institutions is proven by his naïve assertions: "The Pope receives direct orders from God, he calls himself the son of God, Christ's deputy; according to the doctrine of the Church, the Pope and the divinity are one; how can I attack the Pope without attacking God? But if I am allowed to attack Pope Alexander VI, then I also have to be allowed to portray God the same way the Pope was. If I present God as a punishing serious judge, then my book will be serious, but I want to write a satire. I simply wanted to attack the concept of God that the Catholic Church had in the 15th century. Furthermore, the uneducated reader will lay the book aside, incomprehensible and therefore unread, and say to himself: I don't understand anything, but the author must have had something in mind." — Panizza is brazen enough to draw a parallel between his hideous product and Byron's *Cain*, obviously another argument for his megalomania; he cites a slew of additional works, even folk books, which supposedly were models for his blasphemous "satires." — The defendant's horrible blasphemies, i.e., his entire "literature," were read and can impossibly be reproduced; however, it may be claimed that never among Christians have the deity and all the saints been so blasphemously and hideously dragged through the mud. — Dr. Conrad, another modern author, testified as an expert: "Panizza's *The Love Council* is an outstanding and quite unique work of art, perhaps the very most significant in modern literature, with a brilliant composition. To be sure, a few tasteless passages in the first act frighten off the non-artistic reader; but these are overcome by reading on, and then one is gripped by an artistic feeling." — The royal District Attorney, Baron von Sartor, represented the prosecution in the most forceful fashion, and after he had dissected the frightful contents of the incriminating work in detail and illustrated its entire hideousness for the jury, he expressed his outrage to the defendant. — The defense attorney, Dr. Kugelmann, refrained from attempting to justify the contents of the book. He limited himself to formal exculpatory reasons for his client. — The jurors agreed with the arguments of the prosecutor, who had said: Thank God we have a law in Germany, according to which blasphemy can be punished. If the moderns want to brew filth, they should do it within their own four walls and not carry it out into the public. — The judgment declared the defendant guilty of having committed a public offense by mocking God and insulting the institutions of the Catholic Church. — In view of the severity of the crime, *the prosecution requested a prison sentence for Panizza of one year and six months, as well as issuing a warrant for his arrest*; since Panizza has said that in Switzerland a free author could still write something, and there was the danger that he would take his pen to that free country in order not to return. Panizza was *sentenced to a prison term of one year, and a warrant for his arrest was issued.*

Oral statement from one of the jurors to a Munich journalist at the trial: If the dog were tried in southern Bavaria, he wouldn't get out alive.

Oral statement from the Director of the State Library, Dr. Laubmann in Munich, to Dr. Kugelmann, attorney in Munich: In 300 years it will be as hard to understand that in our day someone was sent to prison for a book, as it is for us today to understand that 300 years ago someone was burned for a book.

Kölnische Zeitung, 2 May 1895: The author Dr. *Oskar Panizza* has been sentenced to a year in prison for violation of §166 of the Penal Code (blasphemy and insulting a church). The subject is a tragedy, *The Love Council*, which Panizza had published with Schabelitz in Zürich. The *Vossische Zeitung* writes: 'The piece deals with the greatest monster who ever disgraced the papal throne, Pope Alexander VI, the honorable father of the honorable off-spring Cesare and Lucrezia Borgia." We are not familiar with the play and therefore are not able to judge whether the author exceeded the accepted norms in individual passages. How-ever, Panizza is an author who combines wit and intelligence with a great knowledge of history and Catholic dogma. As far as we can judge from other works by Panizza with which we are familiar, it cannot be a matter of a lowly diatribe; but we certainly would not put some sharp words against ultramontane nonsense past him. Incidentally, according to a report in the *Frankfurter Zeitung*, the district attorney declared that despite his investigations, nobody in Munich could be found who was outraged by *The Love Council*; then came a police report from Leipzig about an outrage there. A book dealer there had given the book uncut to a police officer, who read it and asked a member of the police commission whether he shouldn't be outraged by it. The latter also read it and was likewise outraged. In Munich only fifteen copies were sold. The author Dr. Conrad testified as a literary expert that the book contained some examples of tastelessness, but was an outstanding, if not the most outstanding, literary product of the last years. The defense attorney pointed out that Panizza believed the book would not be distributed in Germany. Concerning the testimony that Panizza gave before the court, the following is reported from Munich on April 30: Dr. Panizza explains that he wanted to treat the origin of syphilis as an artistic problem and had involved the deity, because the population at that time had viewed the disease as a pun-ishment from God. A life of unprecedented depravity and debauchery had reigned at the court of Pope Alexander VI. Now the Pope was God's representative on earth and, accord-ing to the teachings of the Roman Church, receives direct orders from God. It was thus the purpose of this closet drama, which he had set for himself, to have the deity viewed through the papal lens of Alexander VI, and which other satirists of the time had also treated, such as Erasmus of Rotterdam. He portrayed the deity as it would have appeared to any satirist at the end of the 15th century. Granted, the paint was applied heavily, yet the basic idea was artistically and satirically correct, any *mala fides* was completely foreign to him. He admits that some descriptions contain blasphemies, but he denies that he wanted to attack the notion of God inherent in good people; rather, he simply wanted to attack the Chris-tian Church's notion of God at that time. — We do not want to leave unmentioned the fact that the judge felt it necessary to give the author a lecture on how he might have solved the artistic problem without causing an offense.—Dr. Panizza strenuously denies that his closet drama does that, even among the less educated.—With such a judgment, passed according to the still valid §166, one wonders why the Center Party is still trying to make this paragraph even stricter. We hope that this sentence will not just be the last blow against the Anti-Revolution Bill, but will also help to strengthen the movement against §166.

Vossische Zeitung, Berlin, 2 May 1895: *Freedom of Art*. A petty criminal who has stolen silver spoons, a racketeer who has financially cut the throats of dozens of people, a vandal who smashes mirrors will make off with a short sentence if he has a previously clean record. But a writer who has published a satirical tragedy, offending a Leipzig police officer and a Munich court, has been sentenced to a full year in prison. We have reported the sentence for Dr. Panizza; we cannot even say that we are surprised. But we also are not surprised when the Social Democrats find ever more supporters in educated circles, when such sentences are handed down "from the right."—Panizza has published a series of spirited satires, which admittedly pleased neither the district attorney nor the ultramontanes, unless they appreciate jokes and value wit. The writer is filled with high spirits, it fizzes and brews in him, and the cup sometimes bubbles over. But the must promises to turn into a good wine. And this man of the pen gets locked up like a dishonorable counterfeiter or arsonist, because he is said to have attacked the papacy or even insulted the dear Lord. Breaking into religious feelings is prosecuted more severely than perhaps breaking into a jewelry store. And then is anyone surprised that Herr Rintelen introduces his bills? Or maybe the surprise is justified after all, since his bills seem superfluous?—It's just good that in today's German lands there is no Luther, no Hutten, no Voltaire. For in the face of §166 of the Penal Code they would only get out of prison in order to immediately get locked up again. And that would be all the more understandable, since their writings circulated in much broader circles than Panizza's do. In all of Munich, that pious city, fifteen copies of the criminal *Love Council* were sold. It thus does not follow that the farmers in the southern Bavarian highlands are reading modern dramas and being poisoned by them, and a chubby prior will be able to read them without suffering any damage to his soul. Did it have to be there that the writer received a year in prison and was immediately arrested?—The jurors need only to dutifully ask whether, in their conscientious conviction, the accused violated §166. They did not write the paragraph. They also do not impose the sentence. Back in the year 1888, under the leadership of school principal Oskar Jäger, over 30,000 Protestant men petitioned parliament to abolish this crime. This wish has recently been repeated. The Supreme Court has decided that even the Trierers' unsewn skirt is protected by §166. After the jurors had affirmed the question of guilt, the court was only left with sentencing. But it is barely comprehensible, at least outside of Germany, that the district attorney requested one-and-a-half years in prison, and the judges decided on a year.—We share neither Panizza's political nor his literary point of view. But it does seem to us to be a harshness that is neither necessary nor useful, when on account of a tragedy, no matter how questionable it might be, a writer is locked up like a common criminal for a year behind bars. The writer will serve his sentence, and then what? Then he will presumably go abroad, where freedom is not a prison flower, and will avenge himself with all the more passionate attacks on the *Reich* and will get much more attention, have much more success than would have been possible without his sentencing. Is that the way it has to be? Even if one assumes that he has gone astray, does one have to use such means to force a fresh, young, great talent — into worse aberrations? — Perhaps the hope is justified that the involvement of respected German writers on behalf of their brother in Apollo will bear fruit. Ernst von Wildenbruch just published a gripping legend in the *Deutsche Rundschau*. It is a narrative about the history of the Christians under Nero. The Christians are worshipping the scorned cross: "They knelt down before it, they worshipped it. It might have seemed exaggerated — but that is the way it really was. Was there ever a more disdainful mockery of all moral tradition and a more audacious insurrection against the existing world order?" The writer is not talking about the Anti-Revolution Bill, nor about §166. But maybe he will put in a good word for Panizza, whose criminal play another writer in court labeled "a first-rate work of art, perhaps the very most significant of modern German literature."

Fränkischer Kurier, Nuremberg, 5 May 1895: The sentencing of the author Dr. Panizza in Munich to one year in prison is stirring up a big commotion everywhere. We cannot judge whether a conviction was necessary, since we are not familiar with the publication; in any case, the punishment is a very strikingly severe one, which would not be any tougher if we were already under the regime of the Anti-Revolution Bill. For the year in prison, Dr. Panizza could almost have injured someone with a deadly outcome. The *Vossische Zeitung* covers the case with the following detailed report (the above article from the *Vossische Zeitung* is reprinted).

Germania, Berlin, 4 Mai 1895: *Liberalism in the Struggle for "Intellectual Freedom."* — The *Reichsbote* writes about the Panizza case: "What certain authors think of art these days is shown by a trial that recently took place before a jury court in Munich, where the author Dr. Panizza was sentenced to one year in prison. As reported in the *Vossische Zeitung*, which naturally deplores the sentence, Dr. Panizza himself explained 'he wanted to treat the origin of syphilis as an artistic problem' (!!), and had placed the notoriously depraved court of Pope Alexander VI at the center of his play, including the deity as seen through the lens of Alexander VI. In so doing, he committed blasphemies of such a serious nature that even the naturalist author Dr. Conrad, summoned as a literary expert and whose own novels contain the most unbelievable cynicisms, declared that Panizza's book contained certain instances of tastelessness. (Panizza also had trouble obtaining a defense lawyer.) We believe that we can *completely do without* any art that takes the origin of syphilis as an artistic problem, and in the interest of morality it is urgently necessary to remove such monstrous aberrations." — The *Vossische Zeitung*, however, writes: "After the jurors had affirmed the question of guilt, the court was only left with sentencing. But it is barely comprehensible, at least outside of Germany, that the district attorney requested one-and-a-half years in prison, and the judges decided on a year. — We share neither Panizza's political nor his literary point of view. But it does seem to us to be a harshness that is neither necessary nor useful, when on account of a tragedy, no matter how questionable it might be, a writer is locked up like a common criminal for a year behind bars." — But did *Archbishop Count Ledochowski* not have to spend two years in prison, and he would have had to spend several more years there if he had not been summoned as a cardinal to Rome, and an extradition for his "violations" had been permissible? Doesn't the *Vossische Zeitung* remember *Archbishop Paulus Melchers*, who was listed as *"Melchers, basketweaver"*? Why was that? Because in June 1873 in Prussia certain acts *suddenly became illegal*, which until then nobody had challenged, and which were a *matter of conscience*. And thousands of years of prison and hundreds of thousands of marks in fines were imposed in the *Kulturkampf*. Graying bishops and priests were deposed and exiled for *discharging their duties*! — The *Vossische Zeitung* also has this to say about Herr

Panizza: "And this man of the pen gets locked up like a dishonorable *counterfeiter* or *arsonist*, because he is said to have attacked the papacy or even insulted the dear Lord." — Doesn't the *Vossische Zeitung* remember that during the *Kulturkampf,* on account of a May Law violation, a priest was imprisoned in Trier alongside a *Jewish extortionist* who had made people miserable, and that the Jewish cutthroat was permitted to have his own food, but not the physically weak clergyman, so that he too, along with many *aging* priests, also had to sacrifice his health in prison due to a completely different diet and lack of exercise? And all that on account of such laws that *punished* acts in June 1873 that had been permitted in May and which were largely *permitted again* under the laws of 1886 and 1887. The *Vossische Zeitung*, however, that old cultural warrior, criticized the latter laws, approved the former ones, and now gets worked up when a morally depraved poet, quarreling with God and the whole world, is punished for dozens of the worst violations against longstanding laws! Unrestrained freedom for disbelief and immorality, bondage for religion and Church.

Kölnische Volkszeitung, 11 May 1895: *Concerning Dr. Panizza*, the *Strassburger Bürgerzeitung*, whose literary colleagues belong to the "moderns," writes that it succeeded in rounding up one more copy of *The Love Council*. It states that Panizza was "surely not aware of the legal ramifications of this ingenious *piece of garbage*"; "the blasphemies alone in this book are beyond all words. We ourselves, who are neither prudes nor bigots and allow all people to get to heaven in their own fashion, have to admit that we have rarely read anything more cynical. If German literature has lost its way along such paths, it is high time that a *psychiatrist* examines it." — And this guy is lovingly defended by publications of our "educated bourgeoisie."

Berliner Börsen-Courier, 9 May 1895: It was reported to us from Munich regarding the *Panizza trial*: As proof that there were numerous instances of similar satire in the past, during his trial Panizza cited a book that had appeared in *Ulm* by the Swabian dialect poet *Sebastian Sailer*, a reference which the prosecution sought to downplay with the questionable observation that the book had appeared in 1840, that *today* the author would likewise probably *need to have it published in Switzerland.*

Vorwärts, Berlin, 5 May 1895: In his essays on Shakespeare, Heinrich Heine makes the observation: two things had always annoyed and amazed him. How did the business-minded people of Frankfurt ever come up with their Goethe, and how did the global merchants of England ever get such a magnificent poet as Shakespeare? What might have been most annoying about the British for Heine, that great lover of freedom and beauty, was their small-minded prudishness, the rigid convention of English "society" and their malicious hypocrisy, which persecuted every openhearted person and declared them anathema. Whoever failed all too humanly, whoever deviated even a single step from what was outwardly correct, had to suffer under the furious hatred of the perpetually correct, as Lord Byron's fate proves. And in this world such a grandiosely openhearted soul as Shakespeare was able to grow up, a confessor of naked truth, who pointed with naïve genius to the most secret things with which human vanity, human weakness loves to cover itself, without any anxious timidity? — Even if one disregards the powerful English Renaissance period, in which a Shakespeare was fortunate to live, there still remains a strong one-sidedness in Heine's judgment. As derisively as the good English society's sense of mockery manifests itself, as repulsively it expresses itself toward those whose private life does not strictly stay on track. One thing the British lords have always respected: they damn the man who, in their limited social view, was an evil-doer, but they respect his talent, his intellect. They were indignant at the views of free and all-too-free spirits, but they did not measure them with the yard-stick of a constable, who with fervent zeal would like to render the sinner and his sinful work harmless.—In recent days there were two trials of writers in London and Munich. They have nothing in common, and yet they allow a characteristic insight into English and German views regarding the spirit of a work. In London the subject was the dirty or sick *personage* of Oscar Wilde, the greatly renowned poet, in Munich it was the *book* by the writer Oskar Panizza. What has caused a great offense in "the best circles of London's society" is the scandalous story, whose sad hero has become the foppish, vain and perverse Oscar Wilde, a man who for years has known how to draw attention to himself with his conspicuously fantastic dandy attire. The deeper someone gets stuck in tartuffery, the wilder he tends to flail about; and thus it happened that individuals approached the judge in the Wilde trial and insisted that Oscar Wilde's books be examined for their depravity or "perverse content." However, the judges, who naturally also move in England in the ideological circles of the ruling elite, resisted this pressure. They did not deny, for instance, that Wilde's works reek of pitch and sulfur and taste like sin, they admitted their complete commonality with the country's decent folk, but they justified their dismissive attitude toward those scouts who wanted to drag in evidence of his transgressions from Oscar Wilde's writings. They pointed to certain English authors of the 17th and 18th centuries and stated that their content was immoral, so despicable, that no decent person could be expected to read them; but what did that have to do with the lives of these novelists or playwrights; and some of these writings were still valuable and respected cultural monuments.—Oskar Panizza in Munich belongs to the younger generation of authors. He has never appeared to covet scandal, has worked modestly and lived modestly. At most, he has disturbed the bourgeois peace by committing himself to spreading modern ideas in art and literature. He was never greedy for the honors of a metropolitan super-idol and never swaggered about with aberrations, which can only be explained as pathological, as did the "criminal" Oscar Wilde. Even someone who otherwise tends to become enraged and turns beet red in the face at any talk of art and literature by the moderns, our friend Sigl from the *Bayerisches Vaterland*, rates him as a "good guy," and now this "good guy" has been sent to prison and immediately arrested to prevent him from absconding. On account of a play whose performance on a living stage the author could never have imagined! If he were not concerned about artistic seriousness, if he were merely a frivolous speculator, wouldn't he then have preferred children's porridge literature or the dramatic genre that combines prurience with sentimentality? This is where material gain alone flourishes. If it appealed to him to place a tragicomic monster of world history, as Pope Alexander VI once was, in the center of a drama, if a problem occupied him, which only the strong dared approach and which promised him neither reward nor thanks, given the current anxious German philistinism, then at least one could not reproach the author with frivolity. The district attorney in Munich also had to look for a long time until he found someone who had honestly been offended by Panizza, the dangerous criminal. But the people of Munich don't easily work themselves up into choleric rancor over books; and so there was nothing left but to prescribe the necessary outrage from Saxony; from the state whose Association Act is not that government's only "jewel," as Count Hohenthal remarked. It also has other jewels. So, in Saxony a police officer was found, whose soul was deeply troubled over the godless blasphemer Panizza; and now that one knew how pious souls could be wounded by Panizza's nefarious book, they went to work with holy zeal to condemn him. The scoundrel has to suffer, even if his artistic intentions were ever so serious.—That is the difference previously mentioned. The English judge respects the special intellectual life in a work of art, in the literary work, even if it were tenfold repulsive according to his entire education, according to his sense of decency. And if a prudish or bigoted society calls out to him: "Stone the sinner!"—his compliance with this society does not extend so far as to move him to any condemnation other than the one that is correctly and honorably exercised by the community, even when dealing with a person as unlikable as Oscar Wilde. If some sinner in our country is to be prosecuted for his literary, not his personal vice, then one scours around the city and countryside to see if some policeman's soul might have been disturbed.—Where such examples speak so eloquently, where one is so tenderly concerned to avoid offending any constable's morality, who needs any big guns like the infamous Anti-Revolution Bill, for whose sake the battle will be unleashed again this week? May Day leaflets are confiscated from the proletariat, only to be returned to them after the holiday by order of the court. Anyone is a miscreant who takes that amiss and does not recognize that the police action resulted, as it were, from benevolent precaution. The atmosphere on May Day is charged, anyway. Why make the blood boil even more with pathetic illustrations and fiery essays? If the policeman's point of view is already trump in this country, why try to overtrump it?

Armer Teufel, Detroit, Michigan, America, 4 May 1895: *Oskar Panizza*, the physician, researcher, poet and satirist, has been sentenced to one year in prison for writing an "immoral" book. The work is *The Love Council*, this historical and fantasy tableau, conceived with the powerful strokes of a Michelangelo, which is also an indictment of the Roman papacy, more powerful than has ever been wrought. Readers of the *Armer Teufel* know Panizza's kind of writing from many samples, thus it cannot surprise them that he also gets thrown in jail, in order to secure the sweet morality of the Church from the vandal.—I send the warrior, who now has really become indomitable by such punishment, a greeting to his jail cell. We will talk about this more later.

Neues Münchener Tagblatt, 28 May 1895. The jury court judgment against the author Panizza, who was sentenced to one year in prison for his pornographic achievement and who is only temporarily free on bail of 80,000 marks, has not just exercised the simmering outrage of social democratic and populist publications, but has also moved left liberal papers like the *Voss. Ztg.* to make statements to the effect that the freedom of German literature is embodied and raped in Herr Panizza's concoction. Under these circumstances it might be of interest to learn how a thoroughly liberal paper, the *Berliner Nationalzeitung*, judges the book and the judicial finding. The newspaper writes: "Consequently, we procured the book and can only say that it is the crudest and meanest mockery of the Christian religion, and thus of the feelings of the large majority of the German people, for whom the Penal Code was designed to protect against such insult; there is no mitigation whatsoever of this impression from an artistic aspect; because in this book the author never gets beyond a mindless and awkward babble. As for the question of sentencing — the maximum under §166 is three years imprisonment — let's just let the matter rest, as in other cases; but regarding this conviction, we feel obliged to say to one part of the press: the accused did deserve a severe punishment.

Badischer Landesbote, Karlsruhe, 11 May 1895. They worshipfully sing Georg Neumarck's deeply felt hymn, "Just Let the Good Lord Dispose"—and summon district attorneys and policemen to protect the good Lord. They have learned and firmly believe: "God is almighty," and He who says: "Mine is the vengeance," of whom it is equally said: "God is love." He, the almighty, is supposed to be protected by policemen, who otherwise have the job to go after burglars, bums and drunks. We once read the tasteful notice: "The highest lords and ladies went to church to thank the highest." Verily, nowhere are things stranger than on earth, particularly in Germany. A hundred years after the flight of genius by Lessing, who asks in his glorious work *Nathan the Wise*: "What kind of a god is it who needs others to fight for him?" A hundred years after the Enlightenment's golden rays shone on Germany, for the powers that be this Enlightenment has become something that can only be approached with a broom, like litter to be swept up. With fervent zeal they strive to achieve a condition for the entire nation like the one that the infamous Wöllner Religious Edict under Kaiser Friedrich Wilhelm II created for teachers and clergy in Prussia: any spoken or written deviation from the orthodox belief should be punished.—But why the effort to strengthen the laws to protect the good Lord? It is hardly necessary. In Munich they just sentenced the highly talented author, Dr. Panizza, to a year in prison because his criticism of the popes is said to have offended the dear Lord. One year in prison! An extremely severe punishment, as is normally meted out to burglars, counterfeiters or swindlers, is given to a highly educated author and poet on account of his forthright treatment of that divine being, of whom it is said that one carries him in one's heart, according to one's own feeling and one's own understanding, not according to the officially stamped doctrine of the Church. Such a punishment for blasphemy in an age when the concept of God is struggling more and more to free itself from emotionality and is being more and more comprehended and corrected by critical reason! Yet, how can we proudly speak of "our age"? Do we have any right to such pride? After all, the accused and ultimately convicted Munich author cited in his defense that the same expressions for which he is being charged were already contained in a book that was published in 1840 in Ulm and were unobjectionable then. To which the district attorney replied: "Yes, 1840, that was a very different time." Indeed, like a bright lightning bolt this pronouncement by a representative of government authority illuminates the sad state of our intellectual freedom today, the steps backward that we have taken. To what degree of zealotry must we have already advanced, when educated judges dictate a year in prison for a man on account of a literary work intended for educated people, a work which could hardly diminish the belief in God among the readership for which it was intended?—And in the face of such a shattering event, in the face of such severe punishment for "blasphemy" under the rule of the current Penal Code, now, if things go according to the will of the Center Party, blasphemy will be treated even harsher. Up until now, proof was required for a "blasphemy" conviction that it had caused someone to be offended. This proof is no longer to be required. That would mean a brutal suppression of criticism against dogmatic Church belief. But it would not do any good anyway: "the light of the sun cannot be draped in purple robes or dark frocks." Religion that is the result of clear conviction after careful critical examination is more valuable and conducive to morality than the religion of force and binding subordination to dogmas lacking consistency and inner truth. In the early Middle Ages, "blasphemers" were punished with great torment, but not for God's sake, but rather for profit. There was the superstition that hunger, earthquakes, the plague and other scourges had come to certain regions as punishment for blasphemies, and thus blasphemers were severely punished to ward off such threats of divine retribution. People later moved away from this dishonorable notion, and new legal codes in the Pre-March Era [1815–1848] totally ignored blasphemy. But gradually that religious view again became powerful and influential, which sees in blasphemy a serious moral depravity. And today?—Yes, today we have really come wonderfully far!

Augsburger Post-Zeitung, 7 June 1895. *Oskar Panizza, a Modern Writer*, by J. Popp.— For the psychologist there is hardly a more interesting time than the present and the study of the "modern psyche." Weigand, himself a modern, sketched it in his brilliant study of Nietzsche: "The modern psyche resembles a jungle, into which some curious researchers just set foot: strange monsters suddenly lumber toward the sunlight, alien sounds emerge from the darkness, a wondrous vegetation blooms and wafts up from the dangerous depths: everything is a secret, twilight, most fateful process of becoming."— Oskar Panizza is one such forest monster. He has been the focus of much discussion lately, ever since he received a year in prison for his latest brainchild. This caused the most diverse judgments of Panizza's literary qualities to be expressed; nobody could claim that they are objective: friend and foe were too close to the immediate impression of said trial. On the other hand, Bierbaum's essay, which he published in *Die Gesellschaft*, seems to be honest, thorough and artistic; let him be the source for our essay!— Panizza, the "person," may be a good guy, as he is generally described to us; the author Panizza , however, is a faun of the worst kind: cynically impudent, full of madness and desire for orgies, without timidity regarding morality or religion, overflowing with mockery, the victim of an immense imagination. The man seems sick to us; we agree with the doctor who said, after reading *The Love Council*: "Panizza belongs under observation in an institution; his book has only pathological value." It seems abnormal that a highly talented intellect, as Panizza undoubtedly possesses, should only be interested in the dark side of human life.— The following verses from his "Holy Antinous" could headline his literary work:

> Whoever looks for beauty and tenderness here,
> Let them be warned!— in these pages
> Slumbers many a horror, and from the letters
> There often grins what looks ugly and wicked.

Panizza had already injected this bad seed into his first lyric poetry. About his poetry, Bierbaum has this to say: "Perhaps the best way to express the genre is to compare it with medieval German woodcuts: recalcitrant, angular in form, the content coarsely original, full of all kinds of allegorical allusions, with unbridled, at times indecent power, above all honest and sensitive despite the crudeness, here and there a bit tasteless, bizarre and twisted — but never banal." That says a lot, coming from one of Panizza's friends.— "The form is usually very deficient; ... its rhythm (of the poetry) is like machine hammering, blustering, forceful, choppy, jarring."— The ideas of the poems are a "tumultuous swarm of wild waves and motions"— the brain, from which they emanate, a "witch's cauldron."— With Panizza, one can too easily still discern his previous profession: doctor for the insane. That is why he has such little sense for a healthy mind and healthy mental nourishment; he himself is infected, at least by suggestion. We therefore find it quite probable, what Panizza jokingly often told his circle of friends, that some visitors to the institution also considered him to be one of the fools. If the predisposition for mental illness first manifests itself in the imagination, then our view is strengthened by a further factor: Panizza's imagination is often mere fantasy. Even Bierbaum refers to this: "He can't have enough of the wild racket, and it is a pure orgy of unfettered, screaming, whirling, fuming, twitching phantasma."— This imagination even feels better in the depths of the human psyche than in its upper regions. Panizza is a naturalist of the worst sort: in thought, execution and form. He sometimes has such "wonderfully tender tones and elusive, delicate colors," but his preference is for "strong colors" and "street scenes." Bierbaum writes: "Since Luther, nobody has made such extensive use of vulgarities in German writing as Panizza is now doing. Compared to him, Johannes Scherr is a little orphan child." — Even more of that applies to Panizza's prose writing. Those are weird, intricate books, hellish Breughels of a mad burlesque phantasma. They are not compilations of good manners; their readership is very limited (!) — Especially characteristic for him is his work *From the Diary of a Dog*. The man loves above all to choose a rather obscure point of view from which the whole world appears to him in monstrous foreshortening. The reader must be able to assume this perspective, otherwise it will all remain incomprehensible. From this art of the "dog's" standpoint we now also understand Panizza's cynicism. — He is the master of description, at least of the unusual. — He is also significant as a satirist, although he is lacking "the high point of view with a broad perspective" for true greatness. If Bierbaum calls *The Immaculate Conception of the Popes* a "perfect work of art" or "one of the most significant satirical works of art, that we possess," then that is his business. It bored us to death, since it is pure nonsense, regardless of whether the reader is a Christian, Jew or heathen. The book was overestimated by our side, since such urgent warnings against it were issued. Whoever does not read it out of cultural-psychological or literary-historical interest will toss the book in the corner after a few minutes. His achievement, however, is unheard of regarding blasphemies: Panizza is generally big at this. Among the modern atheists at most the unfortunate Nietzsche is comparable. — Finally, Panizza has a true mania to have everything play over into the sexual realm. That too is sick. Whoever is familiar with his characterization of *Parsifal*, for example, has no doubt about this; he even introduces anatomical images into his critical lectures. — Furthermore, he lacks just about everything necessary for a critic; he generally takes things from a reverse perspective. — All in all: Panizza is a symptomatic phenomenon of the times. Such writers only find publishers, readers — and admirers in an epoch of decline. Hand in hand with a decline of ideals goes a moral decadence; anarchy of the intellect follows that of morality. With his demonic hatred of God and his lascivious digging in smut, Panizza is the terrible "Menetekel." — One could also have drawn a different conclusion other than locking the man up for a year! — Especially concerning immorality, our law enforcers have their work cut out for them; an afternoon browsing through the display windows of some Munich book dealers would turn up books that are even more dangerous than Panizza, since they provide veritable instructions for sin. — That Frenchman got it right: Après nous le déluge! — Only a deluge can wash away the massive sin from such literature and create a new earth for new life.

Deutsche Zeitung, Vienna, 5 May 1895. ...Well, it's a fact: Panizza will be imprisoned for a year and was immediately arrested to prevent him from escaping. Panizza did not steal, did not commit any sex crime, did not swindle, did not embezzle, commit libel, but he did write a satirical tragedy, and §166 is a flexible and useful paragraph in the German Penal Code. Who is Panizza? One of the most brilliant satirists of our time, his attacks are devastating, his wit knocks down the brashest. His *Love Council*, which has not yet made its way here, is declared to be valuable and significant by an authority such as Conrad. The work therefore garnered the attention of the most incomprehensible of all critics, a constable in Leipzig. The police officer has great examples and famous models. Herr von Köller, the dashing government minister showed how powerless German literature is when the police sabers rattle, how infinitely higher that incomparable yardstick is, which the policemen are swinging over Parnassus. A pathetic spirit is wafting over from Free-Germany, the spirit of the "great subjugation" from the pre–Reformation era; the great achievements of the years 1870 and 1871 have been used up in the mania for minimizing and distorting history, the old course is dead, and the young, talented ruler who guides and leads Germany's fortunes probably has strength and resolve, but so far has not had an excess of luck. It must be a rough-and-ready court administration that has nestled into the German imperial capital; the case of Kotze, and tangible hints that only recently were set forth in a major anonymous Bismarck novel, have curiously highlighted the intrigues and rumors that surround the young, heroic German Kaiser. — In brief, an un–German spirit is blowing these days in central and southern Germany. The Anti-Revolution Bill was so un–German that we cannot explain who would want to burden his conscience with it. — It is true, the Anti-Revolution Bill has become futile, its fate is sealed. But that is not even cause for joy anymore. It is sad that this bill could indeed make it as far as the parliament. — And now comes the Panizza case! With all the German ideals, where is the German Empire drifting off to, toward what depths is it rushing? It is throwing itself into the arms of reactionism, it is becoming a police state par excellence, in which nothing is free and beautiful anymore. — No, that is not the future of German culture, those are not the ways to salvation for our people. Foreign cliques, Roman mischief, social democratic swindling is at play there, unrestrained and unpunished, and what is still free and open and has an honest German heart and masculine courage, that is being — oppressed by police fists. In the land of freedom, in the land of songs! Freedom of art, freedom of speech, freedom of criticism is undermined, a people of intellectual serfs under the Roman whip is to be bred again. — And it will not happen. The young German Kaiser's high-mindedness can and should not tolerate that, he is not the man who wants intellectual servitude, he does not want a people of timid slaves under his scepter. He has proven that a hundred times and now, in the moment of greatest danger, he has to do so once more. And if he does, then the last hour for Herr von Köller [Interior Minister] in the German parliament will also have tolled. — Germany stands at the grave of Gustav Freytag and before Panizza's prison. With Freytag, one of its most noble disciples of freedom has passed, with Panizza's arrest the old enemy of all intellectual freedom has stepped onto the field. — But Gustav Freytag's legacy is not forgotten, Panizza's dungeon will not become an intellectual dungeon for the young Pan-Germany!

Otto Baron von Völderndorff in the ***Augsburger Abendzeitung***, no. 152, 1895. ...Sometimes literary gentlemen move a bit too self-confidently and unabashedly into areas where they don't belong, so that from time to time one has to make clear to them that not every immature, not every sick and depraved fantasy may rub up against what is sacred and holy to people. Herr Dr. Panizza has published a book that certainly is not suited to lift the dignity of mankind, as Schiller said, otherwise the artist wouldn't have to be locked up for an entire year. For his pretty story, "The Crime in Tavistock Square," in the 1891 Munich almanac of the moderns, he would have had to "tread water" [similar to waterboarding] for me three days a month during this time, if this punishment specialty still existed. Incidentally, Panizza must be even more precious than his *Love Council*, since the Munich State Court assessed this modernist 80,000 marks for freeing him on bail, which two dozen of them aren't worth....

Ernst Baron von Wolzogen in the ***Magazin für Litteratur***, Berlin, 1895, no. 24. ...It is Oskar Panizza's ideal to be a champion of Lutheranism in Germany with the pen of Fischart or Rabelais. Sometimes he has succeeded quite well at it. But generally the point is missing from his barb, and above all he is lacking literary potency. So it happens that he utters Gallic cynicisms and witty mischief, but one misses the full artistic personality that would justify this cynicism and mischief.... Then *The Love Council* was written. The sensation was there. A book that the general public normally would have noticed as little as they did the author's earlier works, a book that is barely more than the belated sophomoric escapade of a grumpy, ignored and misunderstood man, has become the talk of literary tea parties, it indeed became the event of the season, even if nobody viewed it as a literary accomplishment, they still regarded it as a Herostrates action.— He was sentenced to a year in prison. That's no wonder here with us in Bavaria. A word of mockery toward God the Father could still have slipped by, but one thinks too Catholic here to let even a shadow of an insult against the Virgin Mary go unavenged. Furthermore, the jurors were all farmers.— Now, to be sure, moral impropriety and blasphemy are irrelevant artistically. The Leipzig policeman would surely be offended by the classical Walpurgis Night [in Goethe's *Faust, Part Two*], if he understood it. But *The Love Council* seems to me without a doubt to be a literary misdeed. The dear Lord does not need a defender; but art often needs one badly, especially since its judges are so incompetent. On the many pages of this book we experience no bitterness, a dull picture is painted with dull colors, repulsive figures are carved out of rotten wood and fashioned into lifeless scenes devoid of content or style. What good is all the courage and openness with which the author defended his work before the judge, if this courage and openness is devoted to a work that is artistically so weak?

Dr. **Arthur Seidl** in ***Deutsche Wacht***, Dresden, 12 May 1895. *The Panizza Case.* We have meanwhile had an opportunity to familiarize ourselves with the contents of the controversial drama that has become so fateful for its author, *The Love Council*, and now completely understand the court testimony of Dr. Conrad, that in spite of some tastelessness the book represents one of the most outstanding literary achievements of recent years. But we also particularly agree with the judgment of the author by Otto Julius Bierbaum: "A great talent has been shamefully wasted!" No doubt we find artistic design here, a substantial poetic and philosophical power, a great satire — but the basic tendency of this one-sided, wild imagination is pathological through and through. Without any question, from the perspective of a Christian government, this author's activity poses a grave threat to public order; but nothing more strikingly illustrates the practical intellectual impotence of this selfsame police state, as well as the need for reforming our views of psychiatry, than the helpless and clueless summoning of the district attorney and the purely mechanical reverting to the formal paragraph from the letter of the law, which in this instance is incomparably cruel. In our considered opinion, such a man belongs not in prison but, if he is locked up at all, then at least in a progressive sanatorium, or sent out of the country altogether with his writings; this is not something to be punished but to be cured — it is the only way to restore our errant art scene back to health, permanently and from the inside out. The way things are now, the modern state will have assured that a person, having been isolated with this imagination for a year, will leave the prison incurably insane, and this in our estimation would border on judicial murder.

Dr. **Hans Schmidkunz** in ***Der socialistische Akademiker***, Berlin, 15 May 1895. ...The latest book by our Vatican satirist, another piece of fiction, begins with a strong set-up of artistic problems that could hardly be conceived more audaciously; in the course of which he has us vacillate back and forth between worldly-wise imaginative power and miniature episodes, instilling us full of admiration or shock at the unprejudiced breadth of his imagination, yet at the same time with the perception of how these passing images have left us with several striking passages, but otherwise they have evaporated. Nevertheless, *The Love Council* probably belongs to the best that recent creative literature has to offer.

Der Kunstwart, Dresden, no. 18, 1895. We are obliged to speak to our readers about this book (*The Love Council*), since they have a right to inquire about how monstrous something must be to bring its author, amid the furor of the literary world, one year in prison for blasphemy. We also have located our review copy. However, first we have to state our position on such sentences in general. The law justifies it, demands it, thus the individual judge could only be reproached at most for the length of the sentence, if a "blasphemy" in the sense of the law has occurred. But we admit: we don't believe that a progressive culture will uphold the current legal concept. If I seek to uncover what to me appears to be reprehensible in another religion, using the weapons not only of seriousness but also of derision, then I can be guided by the profoundest moral motives. That certainly was the case with the derisive Luther and some of his good comrades, as with some derisive comrades of the Counter-Reformation, and in such cases opponents always accused their opponents of blasphemy. As mentioned, we think future legislation will have to decide differently, since the terms "insult" and "mockery" simply have no firm contours. They will need to distinguish between religious insults from which the believers cannot remove themselves, abuses with which they are *being pursued*, and those that the believers, *for their part, have to seek out* before they can be insulted by them. The latter will almost always apply to books. And especially writings like Panizza's *Love Council*, which no religious Catholic will leaf through after just seeing the title page, unless he *wants* to be annoyed. If one must combat them (which we do not want to discuss at all today), is it appropriate to immediately hit them with severe punishments, as with public violent crimes? — Now to the book itself. To summarize its plot, God, outraged by the activity at the court of Alexander VI, hires the devil to bring a scourge to earth, which will destroy bodies but leave their souls capable of redemption, and to that end the devil and Salome conceive a "Woman," syphilis. The idea has nothing that at the outset would make it objectionable for a satire, it could very well have been the subject of a serious literary treatment. And we admit that there were some really literary, even great aspects, both in Panizza's historically documented portrayal of the life of debauchery at the papal court of that period, as well as in this or that other depiction, e.g., the act that takes place in hell. Difficult to understand, however, is the treatment of God, Mary and Jesus, as well as the whole heavenly sphere in general, which is reminiscent of Offenbach's Olympus with its flat operatic jokes. It must be a wondrous kind of religious feeling, to whose heights this miserable splattering of filth insultingly rises. We at least, who still retain some religious feelings, were not affected in that regard, but the matter of good taste was something else. Instead of the martyr's crown, Panizza really deserves the question: Do you belong in a mental institution because you have some perverse drive toward such degradations, or are you blind to the immense values of the powers that you deride here as trifles? In the first case a mineral spa cure, in the second case a public discussion at least might possibly have benefited the man and us. — For this also is beyond question: *not a single paper* in all of Germany, not even a social democratic or an anarchist one, would have printed *these* mockeries of Panizza's on its own. Now, however, the situation is thus: the state must act as if it had to protect people who ought not to encounter that which offends them at all, unless they *seek it out*; the critics have to focus more on the sentencing and thereby advertise the book more than they would like.

Freidenker, Milwaukee, Wisconsin, America, 2 June 1895. *A distinguished German author* writes to us about the *Panizza* case: "A while back, the publisher of Panizza's drama *The Love*

Council, for which the author was sentenced in Munich to a year in prison, showed me the manuscript with the request for my opinion about it. I replied: '*Without any doubt, the piece is a work of art of the very first order*, even if disfigured at first sight by certain abominations. But even in these abominations it is so grand, so brilliant, that one can only admire it in its entirety! If it is marketed in Germany, it will immediately be confiscated and banned.'—I never would have dreamed that the author could be punished with prison on account of it, and immediately after pronouncement of the verdict he was arrested to prevent escape, even though the renowned M.G. Conrad had described the high quality of the play as a literary expert at the trial, almost as I just did. Most recent newspaper accounts report that Panizza has appealed the verdict and for the time being is out on 80,000 marks bail. That naturally won't help him much, since the higher court will likewise condemn him. But what must happen on the part of the world of German writers, at least in order to open the public's eyes, would be a declaration in the entire German press under the heading 'Literary Notice,' or a classified announcement in those papers that refuse to cover it, to the effect that literary experts consider the fateful play to be a first-rate work of art. M.G. Conrad would have to gather signatures for this declaration, and even if Panizza himself could not benefit from such a publication, the impressive names brought together in this fashion would certainly give the public a lot to think about, as well as provide sympathy, encouragement and support to the author himself in his terrible predicament. Can there be a more disorienting and reprehensible condition than for a brilliant author to be sentenced to a year in prison on account of his brilliant work, because this brilliant work offends a — senseless breed of priests and potentates?!"

Mrs. **E. Meyer-Brenner** in *Berner Tagwacht*, 1895, No. 40: ...And what crime did the author commit in his book, what is he accused of? My gosh. He is said to have committed blasphemy in it! Who is that laughing? Punishment for blasphemy at the end of the 19th century.—The afterpains of earlier times!—now, when the existence of a personal God can only be an unprovable hypothesis for every thinking person.—If Panizza had been convicted by uneducated, naïve people, well then, they simply would have misunderstood him. But that is not the case! No, his judges are educated men who themselves do not even believe in the crime of blasphemy with which he was charged, but who want to strike a blow against Panizza, the man of truth, the man of freedom, and therefore set his conviction in motion. This is the tragic element of the trial! The scorn of our dishonest society, to which we only say, trembling with disgust, Phooey!—There was probably nothing further from the author's mind than a frivolous mockery of true, genuine religiosity. That is obviously clear as daylight. He just wanted to combat superstition and dogmatism, not unlike Goethe in his *Faust*. And like him, Panizza threw down the gauntlet to *all clergy*, whether Catholic or Protestant, using coarse mockery to lampoon their bosom friendship with the inscrutable. Whoever interprets his sallies against the "Highest" differently has totally misunderstood the serious, profound thinker who is not at all inclined toward casual joking or frivolous mockery.— For the rest, *The Love Council* is a nerve-shattering, grandiose negation of that much-touted reason, that divine justice, which is supposed to document itself in the whirl of the universe, in the history of mankind dripping with blood. Panizza's tragedy is a shrill-sounding, painful scream of the tortured creature in the face of the countless unheard-of brutalities of life!— I got this and nothing else out of the book under attack.—Poor Panizza! Have you forgotten that, like a workhorse, mankind has to set the gears of its masters in motion, so that they can lead a comfortable life! Didn't you know that the attempt to liberate the poor animal from its miserable situation represents a punishable act? Or have you forgotten that in the house of the hanged man, one may neither speak of him nor of the rope? Why did you plead in such an impermissible fashion and so impertinently for freedom of thought in a Catholic state?! That is why they put you behind lock and key!—A hundred years from now—who knows!—perhaps *The Love Council* will be produced onstage without any objection, and with a smiling expression it will be recounted that the author paid for his heinous deed in prison *anno domini* 1895.

Imperial Court Judgment, July 1895. *In the Name of the Empire.* In a session on 1 July 1895 in the criminal matter against the author Dr. Oskar Panizza of Kissingen for an offense against religion, the Imperial Court, First Penal Senate, in which participated: as judges: Chief Justice von Bomhard and the Imperial Justices Dr. von Buri, Stellmacher, Schmidt, Dr. von Zimmerle, Braun, Dietz; as official of the district attorney's office, Superior State Court Councilor Zweigert; as court recorder: secretarial assistant Gläsemer, has ruled as follows in the defendant's appeal after oral proceedings: the appeal of the judgment by the Jury Court of the Munich I State Court of 30 April 1895 is rejected. The accused will bear the costs of the appeal. By right of law. *Reasons*: The question submitted to the jurors contains the action with which the accused is charged, according to its legal criteria, with determination of the circumstances necessary for its decision, and thus corresponds with §§292, Paragraph 1, and 293 of the Criminal Procedure Code. The lack of one criterion belonging to the elements of an offense can only lead to a negation of the question of guilt, but can never be determined, however, by means of a subsidiary question, as has correctly been articulated in the decision to reject the subsidiary question submitted by the defense.—Rather, it could only ask whether, at the time he submitted his manuscript to his Swiss publisher, the accused was aware that the book would be distributed in Germany—which the defense wanted to be determined by the subsidiary question, to be incorporated into the main question. Granted, such an awareness is a prerequisite for culpability, according to general legal principles. However, since it is not explicitly listed among the elements of the offense in §166 of the Penal Code, it would only need to be explicitly determined if it were disputed. This was not the case, rather, according to the transcript of the trial, the accused declared the distribution of his book in Germany precisely to be his intention and described transmitting the work to the publisher as the means for it to be distributed wherever it might be. Subsequently, a special determination regarding the awareness in question was not necessary at all, and the court omitted it without an error in law.—Thus, the appeal is rejected.—Signed von Bomhard. Dr. von Buri. Stellmacher. Schmidt. Dr. von Zimmerle. Braun. Dietz.—Leipzig, 1 July 1895.

Otto Julius Bierbaum, in a review rejected by two journals on account of the threatened trial. Spring 1895.

Without a doubt, the most confiscable of all living German authors is Oskar Panizza in Munich. His favorite sport is stepping on the corns of the district attorney, in order to determine how far this official can go in tolerating pain. But it is peculiar: while ordinarily his prosecutory eminence is so hypersensitive that he feels the slightest touch of a fingertip as painful and unhesitatingly responds with promptly filed charges,—the brave Oskar never succeeds in discountenancing (he would spell it: diskongtenangsing) him. It is similar to stinging-nettles: if you timidly grab them or just lightly brush against them, they sting something terrible, but if you grab into the stickers with a hard fist, they do not hurt in the slightest.

I must admit that Panizza's sport seems rather odd to me. The first impression he makes on me is that of the wondrous Englishman who anxiously stood for three hours under a balcony that he knew was not attached firmly and would surely fall down sometime. It is just that I understand the Englishman better than I do Panizza. The Englishman was a person of leisure, having nothing else to do with his twenty-four free hours; Panizza, however, is a great literary talent, one of the most original, imaginative minds we have in Germany, at the same time an exceedingly hard-worker, who certainly does not need this mortally dangerous sport with the district attorney's corns in order to pass his time.

So, perhaps it is more than just sport? So, it is *serious*, and he is more interested in the *issue* than the district attorney?

But what is the issue?— His holiness, the pope.

That is his target, as if he were one of the angry Protestant pulpit-blusterers "against the Antichrist in Rome" at the time of the Reformist deluge in Germany. But we now write the year 1894, and the hand twitches with completely different pains, and our thoughts swirl around a somewhat broader plane than that between Rome and Wittenberg.

Thus, Panizza's entire assault against the Vatican appears somewhat atavistic, and his pope-murdering books can have no other value for us than as curiosities, unless they possess some inherent artistic value.

Up till now this kind of artistic value was minimal in Panizza's works, and Panizza himself probably did not intend to create any works of art with them.[1] The situation is different with the third book in this vein, *The Love Council*, a "heavenly tragedy in five acts," which has just been published by Schabelitz in Zürich.

This work purports to be a quality piece of literature, and it is one.

Of course, it is a special kind. Moritz Carrière, I fear, would not have considered it art. One has to jump back very far to find anything similar. It is a jump, which in two leaps leads back to Aristophanes.

The first leap lands us in the middle of the Storm and Stress period at the turn of the previous century, when those hotheads following Rousseau's call "retournons à la nature" wanted to smash the ideal of a Germanness glorifying power and whose style is reminiscent of the *beginning* of our most recent German literary movement, which then, as far as it coalesced into two "directions," assumed quite contrary characteristics. The language in Panizza's *Love Council* is not seldom reminiscent of *Klinger's* and *Lenz's* ecstatic phraseology, which out-superlativizes the superlatives, and yet plays its favorite trump card by suddenly coming crashing down from the greatest heights to the lowest reality. There is also some of that German Storm and Stress in its inner disposition. All perspectives lead into eternity, and in such perspectives only the larger-than-life things have any place. And if a dung heap is required at some point, then it too piles up larger than life. The second leap backwards brings us to the writers of the Rabelais-Fischart stripe, who made crudeness acceptable in literature and for whom the most vulgar material was just the right one to knead into art. As risqué for our age as his outrageousness is, Panizza does not approach the gigantic uninhibitedness of these two, and next to *Aristophanes* he seems almost pious. Compared to our bashfulness, his piousness is, to be sure, already a devilish impudence again, and I am almost afraid of even hinting at the contents of this heavenly tragedy.

The title page is dated 1895, and this not just on account of the well-known practice in publishing to pre-date publications in the winter. For it is a kind of inverted anniversary publication. Note the time of the action: "Spring 1495, date of the first historically documented outbreak of syphilis...."

But the plot itself ... I am embarrassed.... No matter how I twist and turn it, I do not have the courage to retell it. Since, no matter how I might do it, what would remain would only be the naked, wicked contents, bared of everything artistic that surrounds it and thereby also makes it bearable even for someone who considers it abominable. Only so much need be said: it portrays the emergence of lues in a fantastic manner.

It may appear difficult to comprehend that such a subject could withstand a literary treatment. But it only depends on what one considers to be literature.

Who is the greater author: the blessed [Oskar Freiherr von] *Redwitz*, who wrote "Amaranth" and to whom the countesses erected a monument, or the prophet *Ezekiel*, on whose account some pious mothers lock up the Bible in the poison cabinet? Where is the greater artistic power: with Miss [Elisabeth] Bürstenbinder, who writes for *Gartenlaube* magazine, or with *Aristophanes*, who created the *Thesmophoriazusae*? No doubt: the Amaranth-Redwitz and Miss Bürstenbinder are both incomparably more respectable than the prophet Ezekiel and the cynic Aristophanes, but art is beyond what is decent or shocking, art is immoral through and through. Elsewhere, say in France, it is not necessary to stress this truth, but in Germany one has to shout it again and again to the public, which here is only too glad to just look at the subject of a work of art.

With a work such as Panizza's *Love Council*, the cry of "Why?" will be heard from all sides. Why mobilize heaven, earth and hell, God, devil and pope to ultimately depict the creation of syphilis? What does this huge array of wit and fantasy and passion and imagery, and finally also dung, have as its *purpose*? Will *The Love Council* topple the pope? Will it shake faith in God and Christ and Mary? If such a "devilish" book ever ends up in their hands, will it not rather move believers to unite in holy wrath? And then: who can be pleased by this sinister accumulation of cynicism and blasphemous audacity? Isn't it merely harmful? Isn't the whole thing an assassination attempt?

But with the same right one could ask: why mobilize heaven, earth and hell, God, devil, pope and emperor, in order, after all, just to create the framework for the seduction of a German virgin named Gretchen? What is the purpose of the giant edifice of *Faust*? Does it make men who are in love more moral, and girls in love — more cautious? Has *Faust* "improved or converted people"? Isn't the phalanx of literalist believers today more united, arrogant and stronger than it ever was at the time of Goethe? And then: this "godless poem by the stateless heathen Goethe, the patriarch of all liberals and atheists," what offense did it give to all the pious? Isn't it basically an attempted assassination?

I truly do not want to compare *The Love Council* with *Faust*, but this much is certain, that one cannot confront *every* work of art with such non-artistic questions. This also applies *mutatis mutandis* to every priggish and pious work of art. I perceive shallow piety in art and wishy-washy moralizing as an assault on my freer and higher faculties, and I feel very injured when atavistic demands are made on me by means of art; but when it occurs with real art, then I don't hold back from enjoying and gratefully worshipping it:

> The dove nested in many a cathedral,
> The world knelt down before the legend,
> In the Middle Ages, the charburner's faith,
> I know it well, was also poetry —

says Arno Holz in the splendid dedicatory epistle to his still undervalued *Book of Time*.

No, nobody who values walking without crutches should ask the question about the purpose of art anymore. Teleology in art is just as much an antiquated remnant of antediluvian times as it is in philosophy. Whoever sits down on this old, sunken-in grandfather's chair logically ends up tracing all poetry back to didactics.

There are people who boil red rose petals, mix the extract with vitriol and verdigris, and thus obtain a black ink. These people could maintain with the same right that the purpose of roses is in the fabrication of ink, just as the purpose-seekers in art set forth a purpose in art, say, in morality or in some other goal. Each according to his own taste. One person simply delights in the red roses without associating any practical thoughts with them, another person cooks them into tincture: one person delights in art and its formation, another stuffs it into the catechism.

Heavens, who is grabbing me by the throat! What ferociously triumphant eyes are in front of me! "We've got you! Now you're trapped! What? Isn't there a purpose in your immediate hearty delight in art? Miserable hedonist that you are!"

Am I really stuck on the precipice of hedonism? I don't believe that it is a precipice.

For this seems to me to be self-evident and only sophistically refutable, that indeed the purpose inherent in art is to provide *artistic* pleasure. For this purpose is to increase life's energy, that is to say: to create pleasure is inherent in all living endeavors, and what does not have this purpose is disease.

It is precisely this unique, self-evident purpose, however, this end in itself of art, which excludes any secondary purposefulness, or at least it is damaged if commingled.

The purest work of art is one which streams out of the untarnished creative joy of a great personality, which at least lets us enjoy a reflection of the creative joys with which it was produced. In response to a very great work of art, we don't just exclaim: what a work! but also: what a person!

Where have I ended up! From *The Love Council* to the favorite party game of German art theoreticians, the question-and-answer game about the purpose of art. Let's leave it as quickly as possible.

To apply my concluding remark to the author of *The Love Council*, there is this to say: we do not see a *great* person behind this work, but rather someone who is limited in more than one respect. But he is an extraordinarily interesting person and an extraordinarily talented artist.

However, if we want someone who treated a similar theme, the theme of a dead God, as a great person and a *superb* artist, then the creator of *The Antichrist* towers above us: Friedrich Nietzsche.

But what did Goethe write in the second "fragment" of his "Eternal Jew"? This very great poet, who was even a Storm and Stress author, spoke thus:

> The greatest person remains a human child,
> The greatest heads are only, what others are.
> Just mark this: they do it upside down,
> They don't want, like other poor earthlings
> To walk on their feet — they walk on their heads:
> Disdain what others honor —
> And what outrages common sense
> Is honored by uninhibited song;
> They haven't made it all too far:
> Their non plus ultra any time
> Was mocking God and praising filth.

Dr. Kausen in the ***Ausgburger Postzeitung***, 6 July 1895. The Panizza case has reached its final conclusion this week; a year in prison on account of blasphemy will remain. It was evident to anyone knowledgeable that the Imperial Court would uphold the conviction handed down by the Munich Jury Court, unless important procedural errors could be identified. And that was not the case. The 93 blasphemies which the jurors found in *The Love Council* must be atoned with 365 days' sojourn in Nuremberg's Hotel Baumgärtl. Dr. Panizza can't complain about the harshness of the sentence; since it does not amount to even four days for each violation, while a drunkard who utters offensive words easily gets 14 days for each offense.— To be sure, Dr. Panizza may not have expected a sentence of a year in prison; since without special attentiveness one can notice that insulting a policeman generally is punished more severely than blasphemy. But the purported "work of art" was just so filled with blasphemies that the court could not well have acted otherwise. If I say: Dr Panizza may not have expected such a severe sentence, then I arrive at this view from a reading of his defense speech, which has now been published. It is the address of a man who is exalted by the lofty consciousness that is so nicely expressed by Berliners with the words: Nobody can touch us!— with the mental reservation: at least not lock us up for more than a month.— Otherwise it would hardly be possible for the accused to stand up before the jurors and say: "I *have* degraded the Christian gods (Dr. Panizza knows of Christian *gods*!) and have done so *utterly intentionally*, because I saw them in the mirror of the fifteenth century." But who says that an author who wants to produce a "work of art" needs to see things through the self-fabricated mirror of the 15th century? And did he see correctly? At best, the mirror of the 15th century shows him depraved people, such as his comrade Ulrich von Hutten was, but not God, the holy and just, as worthy of degradation. Ulrich von Hutten is certainly an expert in the field of syphilis, to which he succumbed; but as a Christian he is not credible when treating the Catholic Church and the pope. In this regard, Ulrich von Hutten deserves about the same credibility as Dr. Panizza himself. He, the translator of the disgraceful pamphlet *The Immaculate Conception of the Popes* by Brother Martin O.S.B.— if the publication did not actually emerge from Panizza's own dung heap, which cannot be ruled out — should have some idea how Hutten's *Chronicles* came about.— In the treatise translated or freely invented by Panizza — I'm not familiar with the original Spanish version — about the "immaculate conception of the popes," the translator or author already revealed of what a mindset he is. He evidently was emboldened by the press reviews of this libelous work. He evidently did not glean from the reviews that the author is being sought in an insane asylum, that he lacks the capacity to think about Catholic things, not to mention absolute judgments about Catholic publications. He has evidently not learned anything and, therefore, believes he can outdo himself with an even more obnoxious "work of art." Indeed, his defender, the "expert" Dr. Conrad, said: "As a physician, scientist, psychiatrist and satirical author, Panizza has chosen a topic that perhaps none other of our modern authors, and surely none of the elder gentlemen of the literary profession, would have felt up to. And since the subject of his *Love Council* is a historical one (what isn't!), he has treated it with unrelenting harshness and a total lack of reverence." That is not exactly what the trial showed. Panizza shows a great lack of reverence, but only in regard to religion. For criticism he does not need to reach very far, he takes the filth from wherever he can find it, and handles it with joy and glee. Because his great ideological comrade, Ulrich von Hutten, succumbed to syphilis, because this Hutten made up the lie that syphilis came from the papal court, Panizza had to "honor" the great pamphleteer with a chain of blasphemies. That is the logic of the moderns. I will gladly admit that *The Love Council* is a memorial worthy of Hutten,

a monument made of coprolite. But one does not form a work of art out of coprolite.—
With his two libelous tracts, *The Immaculate Conception of the Popes* and *The Love Coun-cil*, Dr. Panizza has amply demonstrated that he is neither out to create literature nor to
conduct research, but rather that he believes he needs to misuse his little bit of wit against
the Catholic Church, specifically the papacy. It would be better for him to perfect himself
in the Protestant catechism, instead of honoring Hutten, so that it does not happen again
that he speaks of "Christian gods," he, who refers to Harnack in order to deny the divine
nature of Jesus. How muddled, befuddled and tangled it must look like inside this writer's
brain! Since, however, it is not to be expected that he will use his ample leisure time in
Nuremberg for a serious study of his catechism, nor that he will attain the insight that the
papacy actually does not in the slightest concern him, the Protestant, the Baphomet believers can count on further additions to the book market by Dr. Panizza. The melancholy
monotony in the Nuremberg hotel, his anger at the depressing simplicity will stimulate his
laudable capacity for outrageousness to its greatest potency, and Dr. Conrad will have such
a thrill that he will not be able to find any more words for it, having already declared *The
Love Council* to be the most outstanding work of art in the second half of our century.

Münchener Freie Presse, 12 September 1895. ...One may think whatever one wants to about
Panizza's book, one may judge his bizarreness ever so strictly, but the harsh sentence of year
in prison for a man who arrived at negating the customary concepts of heaven and the
divine, either out of sheer artistic exuberance or following rigid scientific deductions of given
premises, is a far greater crime than that for which he is being punished. Neither art nor
science belongs before the district attorney, and if some artist or scholar ends up on trial,
then either art is about to go bankrupt or science or—the sevenfold holy justice system....

Berliner Zeitung, 28 August 1895. *The Love Council*, conceived in dramatic, artistic form,
is the work of a strong, original talent, filled with Aristophanean wit, with the naturalness,
accuracy and pictorial coarseness of a Rabelais. It is the work of a true satirist, whose hand
was led by the insight of a historian and the excitation of a poet. One can make artistic
objections here and there against this saucy work of Panizza's—but that would now be
moot, since the court has found 93 blasphemies and *The Love Council* has been confiscated....

Heinrich von Stümke in *Neue Litterarische Blätter*, August 1895. Panizza is neither purely
a satirist nor purely a dramatist—he is too fanatical for that, especially in the area of religious dogma, which he treats with the most diverse interpretations—*The Love Council* being
one example. There is something satanic in him, a demonic irony and satire—and yet something sober. What is missing is warmth, an emotional involvement. No blood or nerve is
there. He is a relentless dissector, who focuses all his attention on the operation, on the
wound, and does not want to get distracted by emotional involvement, in order to avoid
any wrong cut. I must admit that I miss this emotional involvement; I want it, even if the
hand is trembling with excitement and sometimes makes a wrong cut. One can sense that
Panizza is a physician in all of his literary works. This medical—actually, more of a surgi-
cal—orientation is even present in his poetry, although there, especially in his first collection, a rather profound mood predominates.

    The ironic-satirical basic idea of the present work comes across loud and clear, but
often in an unfortunate way, unfortunate because the characters of God, Christ and Mary
are not ironized, but rather caricatured, and that not always wittily, since the author caricatures external features instead of internal ones; that is a way to suggest the weakness and
transience of these figures, but not of the spirit inherent in them; this is not the way to show

that they have been inwardly overcome, but only that they possess a fragility that manifests itself in the most unattractive manner; the symbolic aspect of these figures is not treated, the human aspect, which has been draped around this symbolism — and I think that is a mistake. To have focused on uncovering this false symbolism would have been commendable.

And yet a grand theme runs through this work, a fanatical zeal opposing dogmatism and blind faith — one could call it a business- or anal-belief. But it is a fanaticism without passion, actually a contradiction, but a contradiction that is followed through in Panizza. Blood, blood, nerve, nerve, flowing blood, twitching nerve — that was always my wish. But I found only the cold, unrelenting steel scalpel — and again, that is the mistake of this otherwise great and powerful work, which is nevertheless among the good and readable ones.

Stauf von der March, in a review for an Austrian publication that had already been set to print but was then retracted after the intervening trial: ...The first impression that this work made on me was one of extreme amazement. I do not recall ever having read anything so demonically blunt, reveling in the most glaring contradictions. Not just that the author opens up gaping wounds —: he also has to twist the knife — covered with some unknown caustic — into these wounds, the way one handles a drill. It would not surprise me at all if someone from the black International, moved by holy zeal and pain from the martyrdom suffered, would like to make the claim: the book was blown into Panizza by the † † † himself, any more than it would surprise me if another, braver "man of God" had him advance to the personified Satan. The proof would not be very difficult at all. One would not require any subtleties à la Lainez [theologian, 1512–1565]. The devil's claw cannot be overlooked anywhere, neither in *Visions* and *Twilight Pieces* nor in *The Immaculate Conception*, but here in *The Love Council* you can grasp it, as it were, with your own hands. Woe to him, whom this claw seizes! — Is the work — a work of art? In my opinion: yes! And if perhaps not in all sections, then certainly in the great majority of them. Scenes in which Satan is reviewing his supply of women, or: the one where Syphilis appears, can only have been created by a great artist. And the great scene in heaven? One would have to spend a long time researching all of world literature to come across anything with even a hint of this spirit. — It did not surprise me that this book was confiscated, since I call Austria my fatherland, but that the author should be sentenced after such a splendid defense, that was rather surprising to me. 93 blasphemies — a nice bit of work for the district attorney! Did he perhaps confuse God with Pope Alexander, *le porc* Borgia? It seems that way, at least to me. — Messrs. *Lucian, Juvenal, Persius, Rabelais e tutti quanti* can consider themselves lucky that they did not have to live at the end of the 19th century! The same goes for the gentlemen of the district attorney's office, in that they do not have anything to do with these "individuals" — with so many blasphemies they might have ended up becoming blasphemers themselves! — Well, they may strive to save the state as long as it is still possible, this salvation business. We live in an age of bankruptcy from which nobody is immune....

Bayerischer Kurier, 14 January 1897. *Antichristian pamphleteers.* There is a big difference between an opponent of something, even if he is satirical, and a pamphleteer. The former we must take seriously or at least respect, the latter is best compared to an arsonist who shuns daylight to best pursue his dangerous craft in the dark of night. Christianity has encountered both kinds of opponents — beginning very early on.

The heathen philosopher *Celcus* is the Church's best known literary opponent from the earliest time, by no means the only one. His diatribes, with which Christian authors could well compete, largely reflect the malicious libels and accusations that were popular among the masses, according to Jewish sources. They include *the same* reproaches which *modern* opponents direct against the supernatural birth of the Lord, against his divine nature, against his resurrection and ascendance into heaven — and all these old weapons only prove by their age how — rusted the weapons of the modern enemies are.

In between these attacks, the learned philosopher does not shy away from dishing out the *most ridiculous* fairy tales aimed at the ancient Christians; for example, fairy tales like onolatry (worship of donkeys) or consuming a child during the love-feast, which were believed about as seriously as, say, many gullible Catholics *unfortunately* believed in the signature of the devil *Bitru*, which Mr. Leo Taxil invented. Here, too, the mocking heathens resemble their modern colleagues, who incorporate in their pamphlets all kinds of ludicrous fables, which blind hatred has spawned. And if *Celsus*, therefore, was not wholly lacking in purely logical accusations and scientific rebukes and in *this* sense is related to Renan and Strauss — but only in this sense — he still must be counted among the list of scurrilous pamphleteers, since he waded into the lowest swamp of obvious libel.

Emperor *Julian Apostata* can be viewed as a satirist in an entirely different sense. He did not regard Christianity as something ridiculous, as Celsus had, from his point of view as a freethinker he regarded it as a folly and a danger. He spoke and wrote satirically, but when he wanted to create the *greatest satire* by overlaying more noble Christian features onto the grotesque face of Graeco-Roman paganism, the hated Nazarene put a stop to him.

From Julian until today, the opponents of Christianity have been legion. Their *material*, their *intention* and their *tone* have remained pretty much the same. As far as serious research or a significant critique of Christianity is concerned, they have accomplished next to nothing: however, they have wreaked havoc seducing thousands of Christian hearts, and they were able to do that because the human heart resembles a boat that is blown about by the four winds.

One glance at *contemporary* literature shows us the slew of opponents in full-blown attack against the Church perched atop the cliff. We may not deny that at least half is due to modern *science*, which informs the army of enemies and — godless as it is — must consistently lead to alienation from God. But — the other half is the more or less professed "*aesthetic*" *literature*, which has taken up the war against any revealed religion. We certainly are *not* going too far if we designate the entire "modern," realistic and naturalistic literature as hostile to revelation — and there is hardly a respected author of this movement who contradicts us; however, we neither deny those publications the right to exist nor deny them artistic or even moral value, *insofar as they maintain a decent opposition*, since we know that disbelief from inner conviction and without ill will need not be immoral. But those writings are unquestionably immoral whose *purpose* is to *disparage* the opponent's holiest convictions, to *ridicule* Catholic dogma, to *insult* Church's institutions. We do not call the *opposition as such* mean, but rather the *spirit* that guides it, the *methods* it uses, the *language* which it articulates and the *intention* it pursues.

Those who use pamphlets as weapons are certainly not the *least talented* minds in our contemporary German literature. Whoever claims the opposite is deceiving himself. But that is precisely a sign of our time, that talents often grow up without morality and — often manifest themselves *immorally*. Two years ago we read an epistle "*in rebus amoris*" by *Scharf*,[2] which, referring back to the unfortunate memory of Pope Alexander VI's personage, just for the sake of its form makes us regret the cynical content. And if at *Oskar Panizza's* trial a noted author such as *M.G. Conrad* characterizes the infamous *Love Council* in a certain sense as a "*work of art,*" this should not be surprising at all: a literary work can well observe the formal rules of aesthetics and still be despicable for us. It is *not so easy to see through* the devilish face of *this* art.

It seems to us that the activity of the "anti–Christian pamphleteers" is dangerous to much more than the belief in God or our Christianity — to *good taste,* as well. And that has truly astonished us far more than the infernal hatred of the Church by these gentlemen: *that such writers seek and find their community in those circles who supposedly — have good taste.*

It stinks — not just among these modern Celsians, but unfortunately also quite a bit among the "modern" Christians!

Die Geissel, Munich, No. 33, 15 August 1896.

Oskar Panizza

Behind *iron curtains*
You were put away,
Because you had lifted the *curtain*
And uncovered what was hidden.

Just keep following your path
You will win in this crux,
But employ some caution —
Write in *free Switzerland.*

Panizza's Notes

1. They are: *Die unbefleckte Empfängnis der Päpste. Von Bruder Martin O.S.B. Aus dem Spanischen von Oskar Panizza* [*The Immaculate Conception of the Popes. By Brother Martin O.S.B. Translated from Spanish by Oskar Panizza*]. Zürich: Schabelitz, 1893, and *Der teutsche Michel und der römische Papst. Altes und Neues aus dem Kampfe des Teutschtums gegen römisch-weltliche Überlistung und Bevormundung* [*The German Michel and the Roman Pope. Old and New Material from the Battle of Germandom against Roman-Secular Treachery and Paternalism*], Leipzig: W. Friedrich, 1894.

2. *Seiner Heiligkeit Papst Alexander VI. Bulle: "In rebus amoris."* [*His Holiness Pope Alexander VI's Bull: "In rebus amoris."*] Translated into German by Ludwig Scharf. Published by Giambattista Casti, the Reverend Canon of the Montefiascone Cathedral. Zürich: Verlags-Magazin (J. Schabelitz), 1894. 60 Pf. = 75 Cts.

Chapter 12

Performances around the World, 1962–2008

Indeed, we must acknowledge that the spirit of sedition is brought by him to such a pitch and so bluntly, and he treats forbidden things with such insolence that, even today, it is likely that the reaction of an audience would require the curtain to be rung down before the end of the first scene.

—André Breton, 1960

To do justice to the roughly one hundred productions of *The Love Council* around the world in the past half-century, one would certainly need to devote an entire book to this fascinating slice of theater history. In addition to numerous productions in German, Panizza's play has also been performed in Dutch, English, French, Italian, Portuguese, Serbo-Croatian and Spanish. These productions were principally by professionals but also by adult amateurs, public school children and senior citizens. They were initially staged in basement clubs and later in commercial, state-supported or municipal theaters, featured at drama festivals, inside city hall restrooms, outdoors in amphitheaters and even in a farmer's barn loft. This chapter will provide only some broad outlines that are far from complete. Despite these limitations, what already seems clear is that these productions are generally perceived as being liberating by those involved in staging *The Love Council*, a sentiment also shared by a growing number of theatergoers who continue to experience the play in one language or another.

It is hardly surprising, and actually quite fitting, that the very first stage production of *The Love Council* did not take place until the 1960s, the decade of the profound cultural revolution that is popularly associated with "sex, drugs and rock 'n' roll." More than two generations after Panizza had written his "heavenly tragedy" and published it in Switzerland, it was rediscovered in France by Jean Bréjoux, who read about it in Walter Mehring's 1951 account of his father's *Lost Library*. Published at the beginning of the decade in 1960, Bréjoux' French translation, *Le Concile d'amour*, appeared with an insightful and frequently quoted introduction by André Breton, the co-founder of surrealism and its major theoretician. Its reception was decidedly muted at first, but by the end of the decade, there had been diverse productions of the play in Germany, Austria, France and England.

As previously noted, the German rediscovery of Oskar Panizza was largely the work of Hans Prescher. His doctoral dissertation (Munich 1956) had focused on Kurt Tucholsky, the anti-establishment author who had been a great admirer Panizza's work and who had allegedly been blocked by Oskar's sister in his attempt to publish the late author's complete works. In 1961 Prescher wrote an article in a Frankfurt newspaper commemorating

Manfred Manger, left, and Kurt Reitner during public reading of *Das Liebeskonzil* in the restrooms at city hall in Schweinfurt, 2003. Photographer unknown. Courtesy of Manfred Manger, Mainberg.

the fortieth anniversary of Panizza's death. The following year, the popular German newsweekly *Der Spiegel* published a lengthy feature on Panizza (3 Mar. 1962: 81–87). Extending over twelve columns and including six photographs, this article marked the very first time since the mid–1890s that Panizza's seminal play was discussed in the German mass media. While this article presented a wealth of information about the playwright and his work, the prediction that *The Love Council* "will probably never be performed" (81) was soon to be proven very wrong. Prescher persevered in his pioneering efforts to bring the author's work to a larger audience with his publication of *Das Liebeskonzil und andere Schriften* (1964), which included the play and a selection of other works by Panizza. To appreciate how much German culture had indeed changed by the mid–1960s, we need to realize that this marked the very first time that Panizza's controversial work was *ever* freely made available to a German readership.

During the early 1960s, cultural repression was still widespread, and anyone associated with distributing *The Love Council* in Germany faced legal retaliation. A whiff of scandal and a wealth of publicity had been generated following Peter Jes Petersen's facsimile publication of 400 copies of *Das Liebeskonzil* in July 1962, the first reprint of the play in Germany since the private printing half a century earlier in 1913. Petersen was immediately charged with distributing obscene literature. Following a police raid on his premises in the

Klaus M. Rarisch reading during the early 1960s at Massengrab, the underground literary café in Berlin where he conducted the first public reading of *Das Liebeskonzil*. Photographer unknown. Courtesy of Klaus M. Rarisch, Berlin.

tiny town of Glücksburg in rural Schleswig-Holstein, he was arrested, photographed and fingerprinted. After a public outcry in the German press against the Flensburg district attorney's actions, all charges were eventually dropped later that year, and Petersen soon moved on to the less restrictive city of West Berlin.

Berlin 1962

In the wake of the scandal caused by Petersen's *Liebeskonzil* reprint in Glücksburg during the summer of 1962, Vier + 4 (Four + 4), the largest literary society in West Berlin, undertook the historical and somewhat risky step to schedule the very first-ever public reading of excerpts from the play. Founded in 1957, the Vier + 4 literary society originally started with eight members. These eight comprised two quartets of friends brought together by the group's co-founders, the author/bookseller Dieter Volkmann (b. 1934) and the author/archivist Klaus M. Rarisch (b. 1936). Rarisch probably first learned of *The Love Council* from Walter Mehring's *The Lost Library*, whose German edition appeared in 1952.

This seminal work was a uniquely personal chronicle of German literary developments during the past half-century. Rarisch and his circle were undoubtedly attracted to Mehring's accounts of Berlin's Dadaism, literary expressionism, surrealism and futurism of the 1920s. The importance of Mehring's work for Panizza's legacy was that it contained an entire chapter devoted to *The Love Council.*

Between July 1961 and the end of 1963, the Vier + 4 literary club grew to 1,700 members and organized 133 literary soirees in a basement venue they named *Das Massengrab,* the mass grave. This club site at Schillerstraße 40 in Berlin-Charlottenburg was a converted coal and potato cellar that had also been used as an air raid shelter during World War Two. It was certainly an appropriate spot for a pacifist literary group opposed to West Germany's rearmament and closely linked to ultimism. Volkmann and Rarisch were among the leading ultimists, a group that viewed themselves as the successors to the Dadaists of 1916: Hugo Ball, Tristan Tzara, Richard Huelsenbeck and Hans Arp, who had come together in Zürich to oppose the massive destruction wrought by the Great War. The ultimists of the 1960s saw themselves as apocalyptic visionaries, ridiculing and provoking bourgeois society while creating "ultimate" art in the face of the impending nuclear catastrophe. The Vier + 4 literary soirees at the *Massengrab* focused on past and present avant-garde authors of all political persuasions, including selections from their own work and that of Albert Camus, Lucian, Detlev von Liliencron, August von Platen, Mikhail Bakunin, Carl Einstein, Joris-Karl Huysmans, Hanns Heinz Ewers, Karl Hans Strobl, Otto Weininger and even a reading of Joseph Goebbels' dissertation on Wilhelm von Schütz, the forgotten romantic dramatist.

This initial public reading of *Das Liebeskonzil* on 6 October 1962 was a members-only event, titled *Hochamt in Schwarz,* High Office in Black. The event featured selections not just from Panizza's play, but also from his short stories and poetry, including number 92 from his vitriolic *Parisjana* (1899). This poem begins with a call to stop venerating the Weimar classicist, perceived by Panizza and many of his contemporaries to be an effete, opportunistic Philistine:

> Räumt endlich auf mit Eurem Goethe —
> das ewige Papperlapapp!
> [Finally get rid of your Goethe —
> that eternal poppycock!]

Rarisch introduced the event with a reading of a sonnet he had just written the previous month, titled "Oskar Panizza" (later published in *Die Geigerzähler hören auf zu ticken,* Hamburg: Wohlleben, 1990: 21). He also read a German Press Agency (dpa) dispatch in which U.S. Surgeon General Luther Terry characterized the tripling of American syphilis cases and a worldwide increase in venereal diseases as "primarily a moral and less a medical problem" ("Alarmierende Nachricht: Geschlechtskrankheiten nehmen wieder zu," *Der Kurier* [Berlin] 7 Sept. 1962). The various roles in the play were divided among Rarisch, Volkmann and their friends. The part of the Virgin Mary was read by the historian Ilsedore Half, who later became Rarisch's wife for a period.

Since the invited journalists failed to attend, there are no newspaper reports of this event, but Rarisch personally recounts that the *Massengrab* club, which normally had a capacity of sixty, enjoyed an overflow audience of about eighty that evening. In the wake of Petersen's scandal in Glücksburg earlier that summer, Rarisch describes the event as a "sensation," since the district attorney in Schleswig-Holstein had not yet dropped the charges or released the confiscated facsimile edition of the play. "After the reading there was an intense and controversial discussion about Panizza that lasted until 2 A.M. the next morning. One Protestant minister distinguished himself as an ideological opponent," Rarisch wrote in an unpublished account of the event (9 Oct. 2008).

Rarisch, who broke off his university studies to earn a living as an archivist, organized numerous subsequent literary events in Berlin. From 1975 through 1986 he administered the literary estate of the noted naturalist author Arno Holz. Today he views himself as the last of the ultimists, continuing to publish poetry, essays and literary reviews. Dieter Volkmann, the co-founder of Vier + 4, suffered a complete neurological breakdown at the age of fifty in 1984 and has been institutionalized ever since.

The Love Council thus did not initially emerge on the public stage as a full-blown production, although the Vier + 4 literary society intended to produce a stage version at a later date, which never materialized. In the course of the 1960s, what began with selected readings from *The Love Council* in a private Berlin basement club (1962) would progress to readings of the entire play in academic and cabaret basement theaters in Munich (1965); from there to a full staging in an experimental Viennese basement theater (1967), before finally emerging out of the cellar onto the stage of a large, established boulevard theater in Paris (1969).

Munich 1965

The first public reading of the complete play took place on 9 December 1965 in the Studiobühne Theater of the Ludwig-Maximilians-Universität München. The theater critic for the Munich *Abendzeitung* welcomed the event and noted its "significance for theater history" (13 Dec. 1965). Even though this production was limited to a dramatic reading by nine student actors, it was described as being "lively, at times sparkling, building up to a graphic visualization." Citing André Breton's prediction that a full-fledged production would be so volatile ("a detonation") that it would be shut down before the end of the first scene, the reviewer was nonetheless impressed by the explosive power of Panizza's diction:

> The text is one of incisive clarity, the dialogue full of explosive contemporaneity. Even the language is surprisingly modern, concise, expressive and without the least bit of fat. When one considers how quickly satirical products turn yellow with age, how soon yesterday's outrage succumbs to a benevolent smile, especially how fatally the pathos of the 1890s became rancid, one must admire the explosive power of Panizza's diction.

While the reading was not shut down before the end of the first scene, this initial public reading of the entire play did elicit a swift and powerful reaction from incensed Catholics within the university. The scandal erupted as soon as the premiere was over. Even though the dramatic reading of *The Love Council* had been preceded by a half-hour introduction to the author and the historical context of his work, describing the play as a "document of a hyper-satirical spirit at the turn of the century" and not a reflection "of its own intellectual programs," the AStA (General Student Association) was forced to discontinue the subsequent scheduled performances under threat of legal action and withdrawal of funding from the Catholic Student Association (von Uslar, *Abendzeitung* 18 Jan. 1966: 6).

The battle against any further readings of *The Love Council* was led by Klaus Moersdorf (von Uslar, *Die Zeit* 22 Feb. 1966: 34), professor of Catholic theology and Church law, who had no first-hand knowledge of the play but had read about it in the 1962 article in

Der Spiegel. Professor Moersdorf claimed that the Imperial Court's judgment of 1895 was still valid seventy-five years later in the German Federal Republic. When AStA learned that Professor Moersdorf had already contacted the Munich district attorney's office, it quickly caved in and cancelled the readings scheduled for December 15 and 16. Rupert Frania, the student in charge of AStA's cultural affairs, was also the student delegate from the Catholic theological faculty and today serves as the parish priest in Bad Tölz. Neither the university's administration nor the academic senate took any action as AStA sought to avoid a larger scandal by discontinuing ticket sales, tearing down posters and freezing the student theater's funding. A larger scandal was averted when the district attorney refused to press charges, saying that Professor Moersdorf's complaint was baseless, because he had not attended any performance of *The Love Council.*

In the face of such academic repression, there ensued a heated debate in the student parliament. The upshot was that the Liberaler Studentenbund Deutschlands (LSD), the official university student organization affiliated with the FDP party from 1950 to 1969, agreed to sponsor *The Love Council.* The LSD had some experience with turning unpopular events into successes, having previously sponsored Günter Grass in a number of campaign appearances. The LSD took on the responsibility of moving the readings to Munich's Rationaltheater, an eighty-seat cabaret that had just been established in 1965 by Reiner Uthoff. When the dramatic readings became a "rousing, demonstrative success" (von Uslar, *Die Zeit* 22 Feb. 1966: 34), it was decided to donate the profits to the defense fund of cabaretist Wolfgang Neuss, then in deep legal trouble for publicly revealing the murderer in a popular TV series. The LSD also organized a panel discussion of *The Love Council* with author Walter Mehring and the noted German literary scholar, Werner Vordtriede. Professor Moersdorf, however, declined the invitation to attend, dismissing it as a "cynical request."

Vienna 1965

The actual world premiere of *The Love Council* has remained one of the best-kept secrets, even within the esoteric field of Panizza scholarship. All three major Panizza biographies omit the correct production, and even thirty years after the event took place, the Parisian production of 1969 is routinely and erroneously listed as the play's world premiere. Since the appearance of Sylvia Vogler's exceptional master's thesis at the University of Vienna in 1993, we now know that the actual honor for the first stage production goes to the Experiment Theater am Liechtenwerd. This 49-seat theater proudly proclaims itself to be the oldest and smallest of the Austrian capital's various little theaters. Since its founding in 1956, it has produced over 250 plays and no less than 43 world premieres, among them *Das Liebeskonzil* on 1 June 1967 under the direction of Reneé Heimes.

Those responsible for producing this world premiere of *The Love Council* in 1967 were fully aware of the historical step that they were undertaking. As with the reading of the play two years previously at the Ludwig-Maximilians-Universität München, there was a conscious effort to place sufficient distance between the explosive content of the play itself and those responsible for producing it. Using almost identical language to the previous introductory disclaimers in Munich, the Viennese program notes emphasized that the play's intentions were solely those of the playwright:

> Panizza's heavenly tragedy must therefore be evaluated as a suppressed document of an overly satirical spirit in Germany at the turn of the century, as an insolent, imaginative and revolutionary

act of liberation from the stultifying ghetto of the Wilhelmine throne and altar atmosphere prevalent at that time. The staging of *The Love Council* is thus nothing more than a document of historical satire and not a documentation of our own intellectual programs [Pikl 2].

Vogler reports that the premiere took place without incident, except for a phone call by an outraged lady from Prague (97). The production with a troupe of unexceptional actors is described by the theater's own chronicler as having been flat and occasionally bumpy. While largely ignored by the mainstream press, it was reviewed in the daily *Kurier*, as well as in the working-class *Arbeiterzeitung* and the communist *Volksstimme*. Certainly none of these publications, nor the Austrian media in general, were aware that any kind of histor-ical event was taking place at the Experiment Theater am Liechtenwerd. Even though the *Kurier* reviewer, Rudolf Uwe Klaus, had some praise for the production and the actors, he noted that the play itself was "something that perhaps should better have remained unper-formed. [...]Without a doubt it is still offensive today, and attendance is not advised for those who are religiously inclined. [...] Part of the audience was just as ostentatiously silent as the others who applauded" (3 June 1967).

Harald Sterk's review in the *Arbeiterzeitung* only mentioned one actor by name and hardly discussed the production at all, focusing instead on the changing nature of sexual and religious censorship: "Although sexual taboos have not disappeared, they have been inte-grated by society; a certain tolerated permissiveness detracts from the fact that they still exist" (3 June 1967). In Sterk's view, the main value of the play was as an historic artifact. "Surely strict Catholics will still find Panizza's blasphemies disconcerting. [...] Thus, the belabored production in the Experiment only has the appeal of a theater museum."

Even the staunchly communist *Volksstimme* warned that attending *The Love Council* was "only recommended for people with a strong constitution" (3 June 1967). Edmund Kauer also asserted that the inducement behind the play had disappeared, that Panizza's attack against Church and Empire was a distraction from the primary "rebellion against the sys-tem." He maintained that "the anger and the cynicism, the bitterness of our grandfathers has become foreign to us — we blaspheme more objectively, we don't allow our rage to be misguided toward heaven any longer."

Paris 1969

Vogler is certainly correct in concluding that the "Experiment Theater created the mediocre premiere of a play that cannot be optimally transferred to a small stage" (99), in part due to the requirements of an enormous cast. This challenge was overcome two years later with the hugely successful production in Paris of *Le Concile d'amour*, still widely mis-taken to be the play's world premiere. This French production opened on 7 February 1969 at the Théâtre de Paris and was indeed historic, since, for the first time, a dazzling produc-tion brought Panizza's *magnum opus* to the attention of an international audience in a major world capital.

This Parisian production avoided the small-stage, wooden and two-dimensional stag-ing that had plagued earlier efforts in Germany and Austria. For the first time, *The Love Council* appeared in a major theater with a large and accomplished cast in a well-funded production. Under the highly imaginative direction of Jorge Lavelli, the play was a theatri-cal spectacle that enjoyed both critical and sustained box office success during the 1969 the-ater season. The Argentine-born Lavelli, who had come to prominence in the 1960s with his baroque productions of works by Witold Gombrowicz, Copi (Raul Damonte Botana) and Fernando Arrabal, saw Panizza's play in relation to these playwrights:

> I feel related to them: their plays attack, insult, shock. They deal with the relationship of orthodoxy to freedom of thought. They address issues which — especially in Catholic countries — are still taboo. Thus, I had the production rights for *The Love Council* for years, but no theater in France wanted to produce it, all the public theaters declined" [Kulschewskij, "Böse Komik" 11].

Declaring himself to still be a Catholic, Lavelli characterized the way he related to *The Love Council* as being "sensual, religious-affective." He also viewed the play as "the work of a Christian, but that of a disappointed Christian. The Christian hierarchy is still anchored in people. Panizza's ideas run counter to popular concepts."

Guy Dumur compared the impact of Lavelli's production to some of the greatest avant-garde works of the mid–twentieth century, describing the powerful effect of the play as one "which plunges us into one of those theatrical atmospheres that only Beckett and, in his better days, Arrabal knew so well how to create in their plays" (*Le Nouvel Observateur* 17 Feb. 1969: 3). Lavelli's staging also benefited from live music, from the lavish sets and especially from the opulent costumes designed by Leonor Fini (1907–1996), the Argentine (post-)surrealist artist. Her exquisite designs offered colorful, extravagant and fanciful costumes with ample flashes of nudity. Fini's designs for *Le Concile d'amour* in the form ink drawings, posters, color paintings and etchings have since become prized and highly priced collectibles in the art world. A selection of Fini's ink drawings and striking stage shots by the noted Russian-Australian photographer Nicolas Treatt appeared in Pucciani's 1973 English edition of the play, *The Council of Love.*

Of course, not all reviewers were impressed by the spectacular production at the Théâtre de Paris,

François Maistre as Pope Alexander VI and Viviane Everly as his daughter, Lucrezia, in Jorge Lavelli's 1969 production of *Le Concile d'amour* at the Théâtre de Paris. Copyright © 1969 by the photographer, Maria Cristina Orive.

and the more conservative ones were positively aghast. Writing in *France Soir*, Jean Dutourd could only think of one word, garbage, to describe the play: "I call garbage a spectacle that shows me the God that I believe in with the features of a senile, cataract-ridden man on crutches. I call garbage a spectacle that shows me the happy Virgin Mary as a crazy vamp. I call garbage a spectacle that mocks our Lord Jesus Christ" (9 Feb. 1969).

Conversely, *Le Figaro*'s Jean-Jacques Gautier could hardly find enough adjectives to describe his disgust: "This is stupid, tedious, unseemly, obscene, repulsive, despicable, wretched, sickening, outrageous, offensive, foul, vile, scandalous and disturbing," he wrote (10 Feb. 1969: 20). Comparing those involved in this theatrical production to the Roman soldiers who crucified Jesus, he denounced them as "people [who] affirm their taste for spittle, their predilection for the world of spittle. They too would have spit in His face." He dismissed the play and its appreciative audiences as "a filthy undertaking which, as all that is base, will find a clientele for whom nothing revolting provokes nausea."

Left-wing criticism of the play did not fault the play's content, but instead felt that Panizza's revolutionary message was overwhelmed by the opulent staging and extravagant costumes. Writing in the French Communist Party's *l'Humanité*, Phillippe Madral lamented: "Unfortunately, Jorge Lavelli tried to do too much of a good thing by transforming this important work into a baroque and precious production, more suited to appeal to the eye and the senses than to the intelligence" (14 Feb. 1969: 8). On the other hand, he was impressed by Paul le Person's captivating portrayal of the Devil as a "simple and intelligent man." He generally had high praise for the actors who "had the courage to perform in this difficult and 'accursed' play."

To be sure, *Le Concile d'amour* did not premiere in a vacuum but rather in a highly charged political and artistic environment. It was a mere nine months after the Events of May 1968 had culminated in raging streets battles between thousands of demonstrating Parisian students and equally massive contingents of club-wielding police. And three years before *Le Figaro*'s Gautier compared those involved in the production of Panizza's *Le Concile d'amour* to Christ-killers, the same theater critic had denounced as irresponsible and toxic a controversial play by Jean Genet. *Les Paravants* (*The Screens*), which opened at the state-subsidized Odéon theater in April 1966, touched a raw nerve in its epic account of the Algerian War of Independence, polarizing the public as well as critics and eliciting the ire of the far-right Occident group. Encouraged by the extreme denunciations and the widespread publicity provided by *Le Figaro* and other conservative publications, this militant organization felt empowered to launch violent demonstrations outside and even inside the Odéon, temporarily halting a performance while bottle-throwing demonstrators were forcibly removed by the police.

When *The Love Council* opened in 1969, the small militant Occident group had already been formally disbanded by order of the police, but its leaders organized demonstrations against Panizza's play that threatened to repeat the violent outbursts of 1966. Lavelli's actors were quick to issue a public declaration in support of the production, questioning the vehemence of its most extreme critics and pointedly emphasizing that Panizza's play merely uses humor to expose various forms of secular and clerical oppression. The actors' declaration was distributed to the press by Gilles Guillot, the actor portraying the role of Christ. It concludes with the statement that Panizza's "truth is expressed by means of humor, and that is what enrages our inquisitors, who can't bear seeing the public laugh. The actors in *Le Concile d'amour* are honored to participate in such an event" (*Le Nouvel Observateur* 17 Feb. 1969: 38).

The dazzling Parisian production of *Das Liebeskonzil* did not go unnoticed in the German-speaking press. At one extreme were reviewers who felt that Panizza's text was too insignificant to justify the theatrical effort involved in the staging of it. One mainstream Viennese critic referred to the "slimness" of *The Love Council*, dismissing both the play as a "pamphlet designed for a momentary effect" and Lavelli's production as a symptom of the "current decadence of Parisian Theater" (Metken, *Die Presse* 19 Feb. 1969: 4). Some German reviewers agreed with their French colleagues that Lavelli's spectacular production had perhaps overwhelmed Panizza's play. Christian Ferber, the critic in the conservative daily *Die Welt*, pointed out that enthusiastic audiences were simply applauding the "flashy, pretentious" production, the "bombastic show," rather than Panizza's play, which he also dismissed as "a little piece of political dynamite" (20 Feb. 1969: 21).

More conciliatory was Werner Bökenkamp, who concluded that the main question in the play was "thoroughly Christian, namely the problem of evil in the world" (*FAZ* 28 Feb. 1969). While recognizing that the piece "theatrically approaches modernism," he would have preferred "a critical, [...] Brechtian interpretation" to the more opulent staging by Lavelli. He wrote that the "orgies at the Borgias" offered little more than the burlesque revues staged at the nearby Casino de Paris nightclub, only dressed up better for the theater by the artist Leonor Fini. Bökenkamp also ridiculed the small group of demonstrators from Occident, who "sought to save Christian civilization by creating a ruckus." The added publicity could hardly have been entirely unwelcome on either side. However, Bökenkamp expressed surprise at the level of public outrage in the press: "In Paris — where this iconoclast's satire was preceded by a long tradition from the Enlightenment to Victor Hugo, where one should have been used to heresy by Genet, Arrabal and, to a certain extent, also by Beckett — one would not have imagined such outrage."

All in all, the play was a major theatrical hit in Paris, and whatever outrage it elicited hardly created more than a minor scandal. Frantz Vossen summarized the circle of outrage that Panizza's play elicited: "There are three kinds of reactions: outrage at the play; (progressive) outrage at this (reactionary) outrage; and finally, reverse (ultra-reactionary) outrage at the fact that *The Love Council* had not caused sufficient outrage" (*Süddeutsche Zeitung* 27 Mar. 1969).

London 1970

In contrast to Lavelli's Paris production, the first English-language staging of Panizza's play was not very successful at all. The play was extensively adapted by English television actor and comedian John Bird (b. 1936). It opened on 24 August 1970 at the 660-seat Criterion Theatre on London's Picadilly Circus, which suggests that the promoters were hoping to duplicate the box office success enjoyed the previous year by *Le Concile d'amour* in Paris. Bird's adaptation in two acts was titled *Council of Love* and was co-directed by first-time director Jack Gold and choreographer Eleanor Fazan. In his error-ridden program notes, for instance, Bird alleges that Oscar (sic) "had been brought up in the family tradition of the Hernhüfer" [= Herrnhüter], supposedly "an extreme Huguenot sect," and that "Panizza went to jail more than once because of what he wrote — he served time for blasphemy when *Das Liebeskonzil* had its premiere" (Bird 11). However, Bird did accurately delineate:

Entertainment at the Vatican during Act II of Lavelli's 1969 production of *Le Concile d'amour* at the Théâtre de Paris. Copyright © 1969 by the photographer, Maria Cristina Orive.

> [...] what in the present version of the play is Panizza's and what is mine. The overall subject is his and so too (for the most part) is the sequence of scenes. The content, characterizations, and the words are mine. The cosmology, if I can use that epic term, is mine as well, and has attempted to reconcile (not for the first time, I must add) the Jehovah of the Old Testament with the Lemaitre–Gamow "Big Bang" theory of the Universe [Bird 11].

To most viewers and critics, Bird's cosmology was far less evident than his blatant use of sex. Clive Barnes, drama critic for the *New York Times*, compared *Council of Love* to "*Oh! Calcutta!*": "But after 'Oh! Calcutta!' what? Shock is one of the sacred implements of the theater; how is it to be used in a determinedly unshockable society? [...] In a most strange play called *Council of Love* at the Criterion Theatre here, an elaborately staged orgy is only one aspect of the play's earnest desire to be, in a most intellectual way, shocking" (12 Sept. 1970). John Barber noted that the co-directors confronted "the old theatre problem of showing an orgy of wild indulgence on the stage. They tackle it head-on but hardly solve it brilliantly. Young ladies in see-through nighties bare their breasts to the men, and even to one another, while four hard-breathing wrestlers throw one another about with intense seriousness. But on the whole, you have to take the depravity on trust" (*The Daily Telegraph* 21 Aug. 1970: 10). One outraged theatergoer actually filed a complaint of obscenity with Scotland Yard, which apparently declined to take any action due to lack of evidence (Exner, *Frankfurter Rundschau* 27 Aug. 1970: 4).

In addition to liberal doses of nudity and simulated sex, Bird's adaptation "modernized" some of the characters in extreme ways. Thus, Mary offers to sacrifice her virginity to conceive a second savior. In another instance, the fourteen-year-old former schoolgirl-turned-angel in the original play's first act is transformed by Bird into a twelve-year-old, newly-minted saint, whom grateful monks have submitted for canonization after violating her 284 times. Christian Ferber chided Bird both for his "meager" talent and his "tastelessness" (*Die Welt* 25 Aug. 1970), while John Barber concluded that the production was "designed for theatergoers who do not mind a very slow story and a great deal of profanity."

Perhaps most damning of all to this West End production was the fact that it was not considered to be great entertainment. Clive Barnes admitted that "some of the play is undeniably funny, and although the humor is sophomoric for the most part, it is also liberating about things never previously joked about. [...] Unfortunately, the story is feeble, and once the nature of the jokes has been established, their lack of range and variety becomes a little monotonous." Christian Ferber was far less kind: "A permissively raised High- or Low-Church audience watches this, getting mildly irritated and later very bored. [...] Poor Panizza. He went to prison for this play, he died in an insane asylum. The oven has gone out. The short, crackling fire of Paris will never burn again."

Hamburg 1973

Today we know that, although the production at London's Criterion Theatre did indeed not last very long, the "fire of Paris" has continued to burn, fueling a hundred more productions around the world. To be sure, not all of them have met with success. Jorge Lavelli had set the bar very high with his 1969 smash hit at the Théâtre de Paris, which even he was unable to replicate. His subsequent staging of the first full-fledged theatrical production of *The Love Council* in Germany was a great disappointment. This premiere on 30 August 1973 at the Ernst Deutsch Theater in Hamburg had been eagerly anticipated for some time, but the critics were virtually unanimous in their judgment that the German production lacked the energy, polish and conviction of the French production.

The Hamburg production was anything but a shocking event. Ralf Kulschweskij summed up the experience: "The Ernst Deutsch Theater had announced the German premiere of Oskar Panizza's *The Love Council* to open the Hamburg season, and it was anticipated with some excitement. [...] We too have now finally gotten to see the play in Germany. No big deal" (*Theater heute* 10 Oct. 1973: 12).

The leading German theater magazine, *Theater heute*, devoted a major portion of one issue (10 Oct. 1973) to this long-anticipated German premiere, including an interview with Lavelli (Kulschewskij 11), an extensive comparison of his two productions and a reprint of *Das Liebeskonzil* in its entirety. Lavelli acknowledged similarities between the two productions but stressed that the Hamburg version was "not a reprise, for that I have too poor a memory" (Kulschewskij 11). Comparing the actors in the two countries, he ventured to generalize that German actors are "serious and straight. They lack the contradictions" of the "Latins." Perhaps more important was Lavelli's own limited knowledge of the German language. Mechthild Lange charged that Panizza's "text was generally treated by Lavelli rather casually" and suggested that "one should have provided the foreign guest with a competent German dialogue coach" (*Frankfurter Rundschau* 6 Sept. 1973: 16).

In general, the German production seemed to be less of a lavish spectacle than its French predecessor. Klaus Wagner felt that the play was actually a closet drama never

Rehearsal for the 1973 German premiere of *Das Liebeskonzil* at the Ernst Deutsch Theater in Hamburg. From left: Günter Witte, Manfred Reddemann, Kyra Mladek and Jorge Lavelli. Courtesy of the Ernst Deutsch Theater, Hamburg. Copyright © 1973 by the photographer, Jutta Ungelenk-Stamp.

intended for performance, and that this production was little more than a hellish farce without a sting, "reduced to the format of a blasphemous Christmas fairy-tale" (*FAZ* 6 Sept. 1973: 11). He noted that "the design by Max Bignens seemed to be adapted to German conditions. The 'Casino de Paris' effects are missing, the orgiastic excesses at the court of Renaissance Pope Alexander VI are stylized to a masked ballet of ceremoniously manipulated marionettes, with a wrestling match thrown in as a Teutonic-barbaric interlude." It was generally agreed that audiences could experience far racier fare in the nearby St. Pauli red-light district. Still others complained that Panizza's religious and social criticism was passé, so that the production had arrived "not only late, but eighty years too late" (Hanjo Kesting, "Christus ist müde," *Vorwärts* 13 Sept. 1973).

Ralf Kulschewskij especially missed the beauty, the aesthetic pleasures that had marked Lavelli's Parisian production, where the visual splendor, irony and vulgar diction was of such intensity as to sustain an entire evening's performance (10). His perceptive review also noted a theatrical flaw inherent in the structure of *The Love Council*, which, in his analysis, ends too abruptly after a very strong exposition. He describes how the play's medieval cosmology provides insights into a dusty heaven, where a senile God suffers both superfluity and immortality; an opulently degenerate Vatican; and a sparsely furnished hell, which is presided over by a lonely Devil, an intellectual who has yet to lose any of his imaginative powers:

The play's strength, its powerful, original exposition, determines its most sensitive dramatic weakness: the all too rapid ending is irritating. The scenes in Mary's chamber and in the Borgia chapel are too episodic to assume any weight of their own and barely suffice as a transition — but where to? In the last scene — the Devil's mission to "the Woman" — there is hardly anything at all to act. The open ending that leads toward the audience is merely verbal, the frontal shock effect is missing [10].

Kulschewskij also noted a letdown on the part of disappointed spectators:

While those attending the premiere, after brief indecision, heartily applauded the workmanlike effort, the "normal" audience in one of the subsequent performances, following "the Woman's" final walk down the ramp, clearly expected a continuation. Appropriately conditioned by film and TV movies, they wanted (a glance at the clock) after only two hours to know what would happen with this Renaissance Candy.... [12].

Reutlingen 1974

The production of *The Love Council* that took place the following year in Reutlingen, a city of 110,000 in southern Baden-Württemberg, seems to have been more of a crowd-pleaser than the much anticipated German premiere in Hamburg had been. The play opened on 15 June 1974 under the direction of Walter D. Asmus, who led a group of semi-professionals that were called the Theater in der Tonne, Theater in the Barrel. This was a popular ensemble originally established by a taxi driver in the basement of a private home, which later moved to its current location in the vaulted basement under a 14th-century church. The troupe performed the Panizza play in an abandoned factory hall, where the actors splashed about in a swimming basin erected for the performance. The heavenly tragedy was staged as something of a cross between a passion play parody and a student farce. The headline in the local paper said it all: "*The Love Council* a Great Crowd-Pleaser. Nobody Felt Shocked by the Spectacle" (H. Steinhäuser & R. Weible, *Reutlinger Nachrichten* 18 June 1974).

Stuttgart 1975

Performing any play that pleases both critics and audiences is always a formidable challenge. The parameters within which most productions fall are well known: performances, like the people who stage them, can be criticized as being flat, wooden and boring at one extreme. At the other extreme, they can come across as being flashy, superficial and showy. Certainly *The Love Council* is no exception, as this survey of its reception on the stage clearly shows. Perhaps worst of all is the criticism of being both flashy *and* boring, as was the case with several of the productions already discussed. Additionally, the size of the stage, the number of actors and the size of the production budget can be crucial with a play written for over a hundred characters. While major state-subsidized theaters in large cities may have the necessary resources to stage *The Love Council* as written, most theater companies are forced to put on severely scaled-back versions of the play by deleting characters, entire scenes or even whole acts.

A good example of this was the production at the Altstadttheater in Stuttgart. It premiered on 26 February 1975 under the director of Franziskus Abgottspon, who had previously played Jesus in the Viennese world premiere in 1967. His production was referred to as a *Kammerspiel* or chamber-drama version of the play, dictated by the limitations of Stuttgart's Altstadttheater. As had been the case in previous productions, reviewers wondered if the entertainment value derived from showy effects was what the playwright had in mind: "So, this play can be amusing. But is that what Panizza wanted?" (Skasa-Weiss, *Stuttgarter Zeitung* 28 Feb. 1975: 34). With so much humor written into his satire, it seems hard to imagine that Panizza did not intend for his play, whether read or performed onstage, to both amuse and entertain audiences, even as it reflected the hypocrisy and deadly contradictions of certain sacred beliefs and institutions.

Cambridge, Massachusetts, 1976

The American premiere of *Das Liebeskonzil* took place on the Loeb Mainstage at Harvard University on 29 April 1976. Based on the translation by Oreste Pucciani, *The Council of Love* was directed by an undergraduate student, Richard Peña, today a professor of film studies at Columbia University and for the past two decades the program director at the Film Society of Lincoln Center and the New York Film Festival. He first learned of the German author from reading a reference by André Breton, but it was the cinematic nature of Panizza's spectacle that most attracted him to the play. In answer to a recent personal query, Peña wrote:

> I liked the idea of theater as spectacle, and the play offered me lots of opportunities for visualizing things like heaven and hell. Also, as I was already much more intellectually involved with cinema, I had this "theory" that *The Council of Love* was a work of cinematic imagination — Panizza imagined the cinema, or what the cinema could do, without having the actual apparatus.

There were some formidable obstacles to staging the play at Harvard, Peña recalls: "The administration of the Loeb, which had to approve student productions, was against it; happily, the faculty advisory committee backed the production and we were able to do it." Producing this play was certainly an ambitious undertaking. With no less that 53 people on stage, Peña notes that this was "the largest production in terms of the number of actors ever put on by the Harvard-Radcliffe Drama Club."

Pre-performance announcements in *The Harvard Crimson* were sketchy, at best. The announcement by student reporter Gay Seidman, today a sociology professor at the University of Wisconsin, described the upcoming historic event as follows: "The American premiere of Oscar Panizza's fairly bizarre play about the arrival of syphilis at the papal court. Sounds orgiastic, but may be good" (29 Apr. 1976). The following week, she wrote: "One of the actors in this play described it to me as 'more of an orgy, sort of, than a play.' This is its American premiere, and as far as I can tell it deals with syphilis coming to the papal court in the 17th century. Or something. An allegory for heaven knows what, by Oscar Panizza" (6 May 1976).

The play was reviewed in *The Harvard Crimson* by Anemona Hartocollis, who has since become a distinguished journalist at the *New York Times*. She prefaced her review with some provocative reflections on the role of religion in modern life:

> For most people in our times the really perplexing questions of sin and redemption turn up in a secular context. Religion tends to be a perfunctory kind of activity, if you bother with it at all,

James Doherty, Pat Dougan and Kevin Grumbach of the Commedia dell'Arte troupe in Richard Peña's 1976 production of *The Council of Love* on the Mainstage of the Loeb Drama Center, Harvard University. Copyright © 1976 by the photographer, Laura Jean Zito.

or an eclectic sort of scholarly pursuit. Everyone has mystical moments, or gets tangled up in emotions, fazed by situations that are hard to sort out in a rational way. But 20th-century life demands a pretty pragmatic and scientific frame of mind. Christian love, Eastern serenity, contemplation — they're all right, but too often you have to squeeze them into your spare time, maybe as an after-thought. Perhaps religion affords an out when you're down and confused, but it hardly rates as opium for the masses anymore, if it ever did [7 May 1976].

While this rather dismissive view of religion may have been typical of Harvard undergraduates in the mid–1970s, it is a far cry from our post–9/11 world, replete with ever-popular televangelists, burgeoning megachurches, resurgent religiosity in the former Soviet bloc, overcrowded pilgrimage sites, a seemingly endless supply of eager suicide bombers and religious fundamentalists of every imaginable persuasion, not to mention mainstream worshippers the world over.

Ms. Hartocollis' review, perceptively titled "Lovesick," characterized Panizza's depiction of the heavenly principals as something of a family portrait:

God might as well go by the name of The Father, it's plenty descriptive and doesn't wrench a person outside the bounds of ordinary human experience. Mary, the Eternal Woman, is indeed typical, for she cannot deal straightforwardly with sexuality, and her virginity has nothing to do with her reservations and furtive denial of desire. Christ is rarely lucid. Perhaps the burden of sin makes him appear half-witted a lot of the time, and his body is wracked by hoarse coughing and as wasted as a consumptive's.

The reviewer's sympathies seem clearly to be with the Devil. She describes him as viewing the "heavenly world" in the following manner:

> [...] the way the playwright does — as a fraud. He's an intellectual type, consigned for his shrewdness to menial tasks and thwarted revolutions. He's sort of sympathetic in his weakness [...] It might be going too far to call him a prole, but he works hard [...] There are hints that the devil's domain isn't so unpleasant, it smells of earth and spice, while there's a notable stench in heaven.

The key role of the Devil was played by Kenneth Demsky, today a psychotherapist in London, who recalls that the high point of his performance was the "outburst of rage" at the very end of the play: "I attempted to be in a near-manic state of ferocity for those few lines, because I felt it was in them that the character showed the pain of the tremendous alienation that had been imposed on him. For the rest of the part he was calculating and in control. I felt it was not possible to be excessive in conveying the intensity of his wish for revenge" (e-mail to the author, 27 Dec. 2009).

Ms. Hartocollis incisively remarked that "the script has technical faults which director Richard Peña failed to recognize. Sometimes the metaphor of syphilis becomes obsessive, which makes the devil's session before God too long, redundant and plain boring." She further added that the "movement of minor characters is much more skillful than their acting." She wrote disapprovingly that the actors "show a lot of skin, but excess is rarely titillating. The gold costumes of the bare-assed angels, their short aprons secured by thongs, don't need to be so banal." Demsky also vividly recalls the near-nudity, especially of Syphilis, the woman sent to infect the Vatican, who "wore very little, if anything, underneath a diaphanous purple gown with lilacs at the scooping neckline; her breasts and nipples could easily be discerned by members of the audience." He added that although "no comments came to me about the religious aspects of the play, a few people commented to me afterwards about how revealing the costume was: not offended or scandalized to any degree, but struck by how cutting-edge it was."

Ms. Hartocollis had high praise for the carnivalesque aspects of the play, describing the court scenes as "a frenzied brew of comic motion, alternating between medieval Italian dance, bouts of wrestling and the Commedia dell'Arte's pantomime. [...] Even the courtesans playing cat's cradle and pat-a-cake provide an instant's interest for the roving eye." Mr. Peña recalls that he "included a lot of tango music," as he "thought it lent itself to the play's sense of decadence."

While this American premiere was in many ways successful as a wildly entertaining spectacle, Ms. Hartocollis pointedly concluded that it was "unfortunate that this production draws you in for the sights and stumbles over the ideas." This lament is echoed frequently by reviewers of other productions of *The Love Council*. Finding just the right balance is indeed one of the principal challenges in staging Panizza's play.

Rotterdam 1976

Like Jorge Lavelli before him, the Flemish director Franz Marijnen was a young expatriate Catholic director who succeeded in bringing his vision of *The Love Council* to a number of different countries. For both men, the play provided an opportunity to creatively confront their own religious heritage. Asked why he had left his successful work with the American troupe Camera Obscura to direct *The Love Council* in Rotterdam, Marijnen replied:

Because the author of this play got a
year in prison, because he suffered
an attack against his estate and
because the court judgment destroyed
him. [...] They tried to bring him
down. The man who attacked the
power of the Church was flattened
by secular power. Panizza's action
was directed against an existing order,
and he was destroyed by this order.
[...]

I always had dealings with the
Church and not always in the best
sense. Then I freed myself from
that. I welcome a play like this so I
can make that perfectly clear and visible.

I have nothing against faith. I do
have something against institutions
that represent God on earth. And
that's not something minor. It's what
the popes have managed to do in the
Vatican. How the institution reveals
itself as aggressive. The Inquisition,
the sectarian wars, the expansion of
economic power. A pope who
remains silent during the Second
World War, while so many Italian
Jews are being deported.

The current pope, who celebrates a
public mass before the death of
Franco, one of the greatest murderers
of our time, a pope who remains
silent while a religious war is raging
in Lebanon, a pope who refuses to
deal with abortion. That's why directing *The Love Council* also reflects my
personal beliefs [*Provinciale Zeeuwse
Courant* 31 Dec. 1976: 15].

**Kenneth Demsky as the Devil and Kim Romano as
the Woman in Richard Peña's 1976 production of *The
Council of Love* on the Mainstage of the Loeb Drama
Center, Harvard University. Copyright © 1976 by the
photographer, Laura Jean Zito.**

The 33-year-old director insisted that he was not an atheist: "I'm a religious person,
but it's difficult to describe what I believe. The ethics and morality that I have retained make
up my personality, and I can't personify that in a godly figure who is separate from the masses.
I don't believe in the Trinity, the Virgin Mary, angels and saints. I'm beyond all that" (*PZC*
31 Dec. 1976: 15). His depiction of heaven in *The Love Council* was designed as "a fantasy,
which I directed with a generous amount of pity, not with hatred. [...] Heaven is a reflection
of the condition on earth. That's the way Panizza intended it to be. That's why I directed
it this way. Not to be blasphemous."

Marijnen also revealed that he had wanted to be the first director ever to stage *The
Love Council*, and how upset he was when he learned in 1969 that Lavelli had beaten him
to the punch. He refused to see the productions in Paris, London and Hamburg in order
to avoid being influenced by them in any way.

Preparations for his own production took a year-and-a-half. One of the challenges was to assemble a huge cast in Rotterdam, which he describes as a theatrical "garbage pit." While the script contains scores if not hundreds of different parts, depending on how many angels, Sisters of Mercy, Vatican dignitaries, musicians, soldiers and the like can fit onto the stage, there are only three or four principal roles. Molding a cohesive ensemble for the Schouburg production required many months which, he claims, could not have been accomplished in his native Belgium: "I avoid Belgium like the plague. It's a nice place to live, but a terrible place to work. It's a country with latent forms of censorship and a cultural policy that seeks to be all-controlling" (*PZC* 31 Dec. 1976: 15).

Marijnen's highly innovative production of *Het Liefdesconcilie* deviates considerably from Panizza's original script by inserting additional scenes and characters. Thus, the playwright Oskar Panizza and the philosopher Friedrich Nietzsche are included in this production as characters who appear onstage and in the audience. The two are portrayed together in additional scenes crafted by Marijnen that are set in a brothel, in a café and at the author's trial, using court transcripts and occasionally evoking overtones of Kafka.

The principal action takes place on a stage that is divided into three physical levels: the action in heaven takes place high above the stage floor, hell is on the lowest level, while the scenes at the Vatican are set in between the two. A huge trampoline is set onstage at mid-height, allowing the actors, in various states of undress, to mingle and bounce around from one level to another. After the playwright is convicted in his trial onstage, the actor playing Panizza assumes the role of the Devil. In the final Vatican scene, what had begun as a devout Easter mass suddenly flips over into a frenzied black mass, at which point some of the most conservative audience members would leave the performance, if they had managed to stick it out till then. For Marijnen, the former altar boy and Catholic boarding school pupil, this production definitely seems to have served as a form of self-liberation.

Shortly thereafter, Marijnen planned to take his stunning production on tour to a number of other Dutch and Belgian cities from 17 October 1976 to 15 January 1977. However, at the last moment, he was forced to cancel long-scheduled performances for Eindhoven, Ghent and other Belgian venues. These cancellations were ostensibly "for technical reasons," but likely under pressure from authorities in Belgium, where the issue was debated at the parliamentary level (Cultuurraad 15 Feb. 1977).

Hamburg 1977

Marijnen brought his spectacular production of *The Love Council* to Germany on 17 January 1977 for a guest appearance at the Deutsches Schauspielhaus in Hamburg. His reputation in the Hanseatic city had already been established by appearances there with his American troupe, Camera Obscura, as well as by his production of *Grimm!* Despite protests by Jesus People in front of the theater, the event was well attended and enthusiastically received by a predominantly young audience. Klaus Wagner characterized the production as an act to exorcise remnants of Marijnen's "childhood belief in Beelzebub (and thereby also in God)" (*FAZ*, 21 Jan. 1977: 21). For Wagner, Marijnen's addition of Panizza as a stage character provided the critical link between the action occurring on the three stage levels: heaven, earth and hell.

> Just as the one-year prison sentence had evidently broken him, so the Panizza character (Lou Landré, standing out from the rest of the Rotterdam ensemble) similarly transforms himself

diately following his conviction. From then on he assumes the role of the Devil, who pursues the planned "divine poisoning," intentionally cast by Panizza as a blasphemous symbol.

Rome 1981

The 1981 production by Antonio Salines of *Il Concilio d'amore* at the Teatro Belli is perhaps best known for providing the basis for Werner Schroeter's film, *Liebeskonzil*, which premiered in February 1982 at the Berlinale film festival in Berlin. In the film, described in greater detail in Chapter 9, a severely abridged version of the play is framed at the beginning and end by scenes of Panizza's 1895 trial in Munich. Salines played the role of Panizza, in addition to that of the Devil in the play itself. The production is beautifully documented by Schroeter's film, with fine camera work by Joerg Schmidt-Reitwein, as well as by a film book containing eighty color still photographs from the film (*Filmbuch*).

Unfortunately, the Teatro Belli's production inexplicably omitted all the scenes set at the Vatican court, whose raucous and carnivalesque character had provided the material for such spectacular productions by Lavelli, Marijnen and others. A graphic portrayal of these wild and sensual excesses would seem to be absolutely necessary to explain the level of outrage perceived by God the Father who, in his enraged response, is willing to consider totally exterminating all of mankind. In the end, he settles for "merely" subjecting humans to a devastating punishment in the form of a pandemic, lethal venereal disease. For all its nuance, wit and beauty, the truncated production by Salines remains somewhat sterile and dramatically deficient.

Austin 1983/1989

Credit goes to Jim Fritzler for two completely different productions of Panizza's controversial play, in Texas no less. Titled *The Council of Love*, the Raw Materials production premiered in Austin's Capitol City Playhouse on 9 June 1983. "The cast," wrote Kevin Phinney, "will incur the wrath of every Christian from Harold O'Chester [pastor for 35 years at Austin's Great Hills Baptist Church] to the Almighty, but they have a smoldering night of theater on their hands" (*Austin American-Statesman* 10 June 1983). Phinney had nothing but praise for the play's courageous director: "Jim Fitzler earns kudos as Austin's answer to Fellini. Now the question remains whether Austin is looking for anything as bold as what he offers. Experimentation is what theater is all about, and he has taken a giant gamble and made it pay dramatic dividends." Fritzler's production appears to be the first one of many to follow which explicitly link *The Love Council* with AIDS. His Satan produces a "social disease, a Pandora's box of syphilis, herpes and acquired immune deficiency syndrome, all disguised as feminine beauty."

Apparently, the audience reception in Austin was positive enough so that six years later Fritzler brought a "sharpened revival" of *The Council of Love* back to Austin, with a Big State Production that premiered 18 June 1989 at Synergy Studios. According to reviewer Michael Barnes, *The Council of Love* had morphed into a "fierce and unsettling satire of Austin's most public moral crusader," Mark Weaver (*Austin American-Statesman*, 20 June 1989). Although the characters in heaven are strongly lampooned as set forth in Panizza's original text, Fritzler added scenes that "could have been lifted from one of Weaver's pamphlets":

[...] the most poisonous satire is saved for an earthly preacher. With the help of cartoonish assistants, this preacher triumphantly parades "filthy" pictures in order to disgust the public and condemn the practice. Then he presents a silly moralizing skit, complete with comic phallic devices, and as the scene builds to a voyeuristic frenzy, we witness the kind of unforgiving burlesque that would make Aristophanes proud [Barnes, *Austin American-Statesman*, 20 June 1989].

Barnes clearly admired the work of the Jim Fritzler, a man he termed "Austin's badboy genius":

Perhaps *Council of Love* is too clear a mirror. It portrays religious zealots as inhuman "others," which requires the same kind of meanness that is usually reserved for full-time hatemongers. There is much that is repulsive, as well as attractive, in this production. It alienates while it challenges. [...] Fritzler will never allow us to remain merely tolerant of anything we deem important.

Vienna 1984

Vienna, which had been the site of the world premiere in 1967, experienced a second production of *The Love Council* in 1984. This production by the theater troupe Narrenkastl was co-directed by Justus Neumann and his dramaturge, Joseph Hartmann. They encountered considerably more obstacles and outright harassment from the authorities than anything faced during the first production in the Austrian capital seventeen years earlier. Perhaps since the play was now better known, it proved difficult to even find a venue willing to house the production. According to Günther Baumann, the producers first approached the Moulin Rouge, a popular establishment on the Walfischgasse since 1894, which had a long history of hosting a wide variety of shows ranging from serious theater and concerts to cabaret, vaudeville, burlesque, striptease and disco. When asked about staging *The Love Council* inside the Moulin Rouge, "the owners feared they would forever scare off their regular customers. Then a church was sought as a venue, a deconsecrated one, of course. No way: there is no such thing in Vienna" (Baumann, *Kurier* 31 Aug. 1984).

Elisabeth Loibl recounts how the producers had tried to engage the Church by offering to have a public discussion of the issues raised by *The Love Council*, which could have had some educational value in diffusing the tension surrounding the play: "The invitation to a discussion of *The Love Council* split the Austrian Church into different camps, and it then retreated; [...] potential advertisers — companies and banks who usually like to play the role of sponsors — refused any support with the explanation that they would lose customers if they were associated with this Panizza production" (*Falter* 24 Apr. 1985).

The Narrenkastl production ended up being staged in the Arena St. Marx, a gritty venue in a section of town dominated by gas storage tanks and similar industrial facilities. Alfred Pfoser describes the troupe's director, Justus Neumann, as "one of the most colorful Viennese actors. He has declined to accept a tenured position as an actor, preferring instead to pour his creativity and organizational talent into independent productions. *The Love Council* is one of his most ambitious projects, not just financially" (*Salzburger Nachrichten* 11 Dec. 1984). Pfoser credited Neumann with having given the Austrian capital "a splendid, attractive theater evening." In addition to directing, Neumann also played the roles of Devil, the Cherub and Cesare Borgia. Overall, Pfoser was impressed by the dazzling production:

Sensuality is trump. In the celebration of a baroque heaven-earth-hell Catholicism, every imaginable medium is justified, from ugly papier-mâché monsters to a live snake. Dance, music, ever-changing pink tubes, exotic costumes that look like they come from oriental palaces, and Mary's Fellini-esque regalia provide a spectacle, against which the satire sometimes has difficulty asserting itself.

Heinz Schirnovsky, the reviewer for the Socialist Party newspaper, was even more outspokenly critical. He concluded that despite the enormous personal financial expenditure on the part of Neumann, the play was a failure, "but its failure is more interesting than the success of most others" (*Arbeiterzeitung*, 27 Nov. 1984). Although he granted Panizza some limited historical significance as Herbert Achternbusch's predecessor, he felt that Panizza's satire was sexist and neither terribly shocking nor particularly relevant anymore. Despite Neumann's "exciting process of surrealistic actionism: sensuous physical rituals reduced to small, bizarre gestures," despite "the digestive process demonstrated by a giant coffee machine with ears," despite "the sexual intercourse between Salome and a disemboweled electronic billy goat," he found the production to be boring and "almost reactionary."

Lothar Lohs later reported that several bomb threats had been received at the end of 1984 during rehearsals for the Viennese Narrenkastl production, but this was not confirmed independently (Lohs, *Der Standard*, 11 Nov. 1991). What is certain is that on 30 January 1985 Neumann was issued a summons and fined 2,000 Schillings for four administrative infractions involving improper use of the Arena building, which allegedly was not zoned for theatrical performances. One of the violations involved not having a coat check room, so that patrons had to put their coats and jackets on the floor. Rather than serve a sentence of four days in jail, Neumann paid the fine (Vogler 103).

London 1986

Hell's Angels, which opened on 6 January 1986 in London's Royal Court Theatre, is a work of musical theater loosely based on *The Love Council*. Performed by the Opera Factory London Sinfonietta, it was directed by

Jeff Ellinger as the Devil and Janelle Buchanan as the Woman in Jim Fritzler's 1983 production of *The Council of Love* at the Capitol City Playhouse, Austin, Texas. Courtesy of Jim Fritzler. Copyright © 1983 by the photographer, Bill Leissner.

Paper and cardboard figures from the 1986 production of *Das Liebeskonzil* at the Figurentheater Gerhard Weiss, Munich. Photographer unknown. Courtesy of Gerhard Weiss.

David Freeman, who also wrote the libretto, with a mixture of instrumental and electronic music composed by Nigel Osborne. Osborne explained how the *Hell's Angels* "opera" evolved:

> [... from] a play by Oskar Panizza, which is the story of how God punishes the Borgia Pope and his court for their dissolute excesses. It's a marvelous piece of theatre, and also very lively and provocative [...] Then we extended this in Freeman's text to include a kind of modern version of the story concerning a recent Vatican intrigue.
>
> The idea is that the opera is about myth and superstition. It has not got a single message but has very many messages: we are setting a number of different things in resonance. We call the contemporary myth a fiction, though it could very well be true. It's a serious piece, but also very comic. It may strike some people as being outrageous at times, but the intention is fundamentally serious [Dominic Gill, *Financial Times* 8 Jan. 1986: 11].

The "busy and colorful" production, consisting of twenty short scenes in two acts, was moderately successful, although the music appeared to be subordinate. According to Dominic Gill, "It is not first and foremost a musical experience." He referred to the production's "scatological context" and mused: "The manner of the first act crosses the Benny Hill Show with *Life of Brian* and a spice or two of Woody Allen—a savage, jokey satire, unevenly sharp, which collects together on the stage at the end of the first act, at least, far more naked men and women at once than either Benny Hill or Monty Python could ever hope to have achieved."

Munich 1986

The carnivalesque, vaudevillian aspects of *The Love Council* frequently led to busy and colorful productions, which reviewers both admired for their theatricality or criticized for detracting from the play's text. An example of the latter was Gunnar Petersen's 1986 production in Munich's Studiotheater auf dem Alabama. Jan Bielicki wrote that the dazzling production was too concerned "with elaborate staging — instead of with the text" (*Süddeutsche Zeitung* 30 July 1986). His review describes how the "sets are constantly being built up and rearranged, scaffolding is moved around and covered with cloth panels, toy cars are driven around and a heavenly elevator descends to the stage; there is roaring, screeching, whispering, actors twist into and back out of ecstasy ... what for, anyway? It's never clear in what direction Petersen wants to take *The Love Council*." In the same vein, Bielicke also criticized the elaborate costumes by Reiner Wiesemes, whose "veritable costume orgies stick the young actors into monstrous creations of fabric and leather, which render the actors almost immobile — and yet have nothing to say about the play, on the contrary, they put themselves between the text and the audience, noisily and colorfully hiding the fact that Petersen has not engaged with Panizza."

Mexico City 1987

One of the most creative, courageous and enduring interpreters of Panizza is Jesusa Rodriguez, frequently referred to as the "most important woman of Mexico." This director, actress, playwright, performance artist, entrepreneur and social activist has produced several different versions of *El concilio de amor*. These include productions of Panizza's heavenly tragedy for various venues, such as Mexico City's Shakespeare Forum (1987), a solo performance in New York's Theater for the New City (1987) and a prize-winning performance with her company, El Grupo Divas, at Montreal's Festival of the Americas (1989). She has also presented a version of *El concilio de amor* for many years at Mexico City's Teatro de La Capilla and El Habito cabaret, which she founded in 1990 with her partner, the Argentine musician/actress Liliana Felipe.

Rodriguez not only updated Panizza by replacing syphilis with AIDS, which others had already previously done, but she went considerably further in re-imagining the entire play. Thus, the traditional Devil was transformed into a post-feminist, bisexual Miss Devil, a role she expanded and acted with apparent relish. Modern and postmodern touches abound. For example, when Jesus visits Miss Devil in hell to obtain more knowledge about the disease, she instructs him in the proper use of a condom. Jean Franco describes Rodriguez' solo performance for a New York audience in 1987:

> [...] the devil kept his horns, his bloodstained mouth and wings covered with cobwebs and graffiti, but at times he was also one of Macbeth's witches, and at times a trickster. Naked as only an archangel can be naked, the devil crouches at one point like Rodin's *Thinker* on top of a pedestal that later turns out to be a toilet. The toilet is surrounded by the devil's adepts, whom she names as (among others) Reagan, Pinochet, and, of all people, Grotowski, each represented as a paper dunce cap.
> With scatological gusto, the witch devil drinks her own potion, shits powerfully, and produces an offspring — a blond doll that she immediately baptizes Barbie, as a tribute to Klaus Barbie. The devil as mother nurses her child and slaves over a washboard, though Barbie turns

out to be a nasty little creature, a true child of the age of mechanical reproduction who can mass produce itself. When Barbie tries to strangle her maker, the devil turns executioner and tries to guillotine the doll, finally chopping her in pieces to begin the experiment anew [Franco 1992, 50].

What impressed Franco the most was the performer's exuberant inventiveness and the expressive use of her own body:

> The remarkable thing about these performances is not only their polymorphous nature, their infinite and baroque metamorphoses, not even the gusto with which Jesusa dances, moves, sings, speaks, mimes, but how she uses her body. She is not so much nude as naked, and it is a nakedness that gives the body a power of expression that we normally associate with the face alone. She plays the body like a virtuoso — dancing feet in tennis shoes suddenly imitate Chaplin's stuttering shuffle, hips undulate invitingly only to sag suddenly with age.

Jesusa Rodriguez remains Mexico's leading cabaret and political performance artist. As Oskar Panizza had begun to do in the nineteenth century, her political projects creatively cross genre boundaries, combining popular art with Greek tragedy, modern cabaret with pre–Columbian indigenous art, opera with vaudeville. More recently, she organized numerous cultural activities for the millions of voters who gathered in the streets of the Mexican capital following the highly contested 2006 presidential election.

Jesusa Rodriguez as the Devil in her 1995 production of *El Concilio de Amor* in Paris. Courtesy of Jesusa Rodriguez. Copyright © 1995 by the photographer, Adolfo Pérez Butrón.

Ulm 1987

Franz Hummel's opera *Luzifer*, subtitled *A German Song in Memory of Oskar Panizza*, only very loosely incorporates elements of *The Love Council*. This opera, with a libretto by Christian Fuchs and choreography by Hummel's wife, Rosamund Gilmore, met with a storm of protest when it premiered in the German city of Ulm in 1987. Letters to the editor and ads in local newspapers demanded that the opera be cancelled before it even opened. Some of the more conservative politicians threatened to cut public funding for the Ulm theater, whose general manager, Pavel Fieber, received hate-mail telling him to go to hell and wishing syphilis on him.

In addition to the basic plot configuration of syphilis being concocted in hell and sent from heaven to punish a sexually overactive humanity, Hummel's opera contains "biographic fragments, political pamphlets, medical findings, lyrical outpourings and

Jesusa Rodriguez as the Devil and Daniel Jimenez Cacho as Christ in her 1988 production of *El Concilio de Amor* at the Foro Shakespeare in Mexico City. Courtesy of Jesusa Rodriguez. Copyright © 1988 by the photographer, Pablo Ortiz Monasterio.

extremely private confessions" ("Hummel und Hölle." *Der Spiegel* 1 June 1987: 226). The opera includes four different characters named Oskar, variously played by a boyish countertenor, a baritone, a tenor and a dancer. According to the Bavarian composer, traditional opera music would not be appropriate for depicting Panizza, whom he characterized as "the cruelest hermaphrodite that this culture has ever produced" (227). The anonymous reviewer in *Der Spiegel* found Hummel's experimental music to be up to the task, since "the crazy story is the story of a crazy person."

Regensburg 1988

Regensburg, formerly the permanent seat of the *Reichstag* of the Holy Roman Empire, first adopted the Protestant Reformation in 1542. It has a beautiful medieval center and a number of illustrious past residents, including the astronomer Johannes Kepler, Oskar Schindler, the subject of Spielberg's film "Schindler's List," and Joseph Ratzinger, the current Pope Benedict XVI. When author and director Joseph Berlinger staged his audacious production of *The Love Council* in Regensburg University's Studenten-Theater in January 1988, he was not met with protests of moral outrage. As a matter of fact, Manfried Stuber maintained that contemporary audiences no longer perceive Panizza's play as shocking: "The provocations of the [nineteenth-century] modernists are no longer inflammatory, because the jaded audiences immediately accept any outrage" (*Mittelbayerische Zeitung* 19 Jan. 1988).

Hannes Langer as Christ, left, Christoph Maltz as the Devil and Harald Dichmann as God in Joseph Berlinger's 1988 production of *Das Liebeskonzil* in Regensburg. Courtesy of Joseph Berlinger. Copyright © 1988 by the photographer, Hubert Lankes.

However, Berlinger's production of *The Love Council* did provoke Stuber to reflect on the nature of blasphemy:

> What is blasphemy? As a rule, the self-anointed inquisitors proceed according to the same principle that a U.S. Supreme Court justice [Potter Stewart] applied to the definition of pornography: "I know it when I see it." But this perspective doesn't get us very far. Artists like Achternbusch, Kroetz and Panizza are not trashing God, but just simply those images that man has made for himself of God. The Old Testament's prohibition against graven images did indeed make sense. All too often, the loss of genuine religious feeling is compensated by replacement fetishes, by identification templates. The graven image is not the idea. The image contains neither God nor the gods, only our own reflections. A religious feeling that has not distorted the ideal of God into a worldly idol [...] is, by its very nature, invulnerable.

What Stuber admired most about Panizza was that the playwright had "placed the undeniable double morality of the Christian West, the dishonest sanctimony that emerges again and again in Catholicism, into its own symbolism." In his opinion, "Panizza finishes off [...] the religious myths on their own game-board. The entire construct of our metaphysical hierarchy is brought to the ground of our realities: Those are the gods who suit us."

Kurt Fander lauded Berlinger for his "splendid production" and noted that the issues raised in the play were still very much current, in view of today's widespread belief, "not just by narrow-minded lay Christians," that AIDS is really a "scourge from God" (*Landshuter Zeitung* 22 Jan. 1988). According to Helmut Hein, the sold-out performances were greeted by audiences with enthusiastic "applause and stomping that seemed not to want to end" (*Die Woche*, Regensburg, 21 Jan. 1988). Hein called *The Love Council* "an enormous success," Berlinger's "best and most effective staging," going so far as to claim that the production was "very much better than Panizza's play or Schroeter's film." What Hein liked most was Berlinger's focus on the play's carnivalesque aspects, the "circus-like spectacle, the total work of art, in which every stimulus is justified." He viewed this as a form of "postmodernism, in which, thanks to the media [...] everything that was ever thought, felt or done is present here and now." Using English terms, Hein viewed the overall effect as "a 'show' that is diversified and 'up-to-date.' What was once an existential catastrophe and a political provocation is now a multi-referential, 'witty,' 'saucy' evening's entertainment, which even middle-class audiences experience as 'stimulating' and no longer as offensive."

In order to help preserve a record of this successful production, two years later Berlinger published a limited-edition book (100 copies) containing every page of his working script, complete with the director's scrawled notes and sketches filling the margins, along with production photographs, historical texts, encyclopedia entries and other pertinent materials.

New York City 1988

A rare New York City production of Panizza's heavenly tragedy premiered in November 1988, directed and designed by David Kaplan. His all-male version of *The Council of Love* was staged at the HOME for Contemporary Theatre and Art, an avant-garde theater in New York City's Tribeca district, where playwrights such as Tony Kushner and Chuck Mee premiered their work. (The organization moved to SoHo in 1993, where it is now the HERE Arts Center.) Robert Massa noted that Kaplan staged *The Council of Love* as "an attack on the moralists of our own time" (*Village Voice* 29 Nov. 1988: 122). Using an all-male cast and homoerotic imagery, the analogy with AIDS was certainly made quite evident. However, the production was severely truncated by cutting two full acts, so that only the scenes in heaven were performed, while the action on earth was represented in fleeting silhouettes. The play evidently suffered from this crucial omission, as it had in the 1981 Roman production by Antonio Salines. Massa harshly criticized this excision: "These cuts blur Panizza's original intentions; what remains at worst buys into the terms set by the moralists, at best seems just a trivial romp with sacrilege — particularly because of the screeching, purple, non-acting style."

Nuremberg 1988

One of the more successful of the various 1988 productions of *The Love Council* was the one that opened on June 18th in the ruins of St. Catherine's Church in Nuremberg. Under the direction of Hansjörg Utzerath, his summer production made full use of its dramatic setting in this bombed-out church, which the set designer, Christian Göbl, utilized to his best advantage. The ruined church might have suggested the ruinous religiosity that

Asa Dupuy Watkins as God and Michael Winther as Mary in David Kaplan's 1988 all-male production of *The Council of Love* at the HOME for Contemporary Theatre and Art in New York City. Photographer unknown. Courtesy of David Kaplan, New York.

had once been housed within its crumbling walls; the non-existent roof exposed a clear view to the sky above, the scene of Panizza's heavenly tragedy. Ulrich Hammerschmidt credits Utzerath with serving up a fiery performance, "setting off explosives, verbose and angry, coloring Nuremberg's nocturnal sky with some real fireworks and a hellish pyrotechnic inferno" (*Theater heute*, 9/88: 23). Even though he no longer considered the play to be seriously shocking, he concluded that the production, with its liberal use of pop songs, was staged "with effect and affect, entertainment and horror: a black mass of really dangerous lust, man's animal lust for naked force."

Michael Skasa focused more on the kitschy, even campy aspects of this production, whose musical numbers included the Nuremberg Gay Men's Choir singing a doo-wop version of Ave Maria. He effusively describes the production as a riotous "blasphemical":

> [...] the Pope's Renaissance brood: lecherous, half naked, boozing and groping. Between Latin liturgical hymns and crowds of cream-smeared bodies, a ghastly, beautiful smut-orgy that stinks to high heaven. Writhing bishops, with pot bellies and loin cloths, fall splattering on top of each other, trying to wrestle for courtesans; a petite, stark naked Negress emerges from a giant white cake, then dances about, covered with white cream, now the raspberry blood starts to flow, oozing out syrupy-thick from a white stuffed lamb, which the Pope (here: a fat Popess) slaughters above the Negress leaning back: kitsch and gore, ritual and bacchanal — or: how Borgia becomes orgia. Drenched in red, hoisted aloft by three ephebes, the ebony girl is bedded down on the white altar linen — and just before it gets to be too much, the Popess throws off her violet robe and becomes a tuxedo-clad emcee, with the choir of drag queens crooning: "I wanna be loved by you" [*Süddeutsche Zeitung* 21 June 1988].

Utzerath's production ends in an equally imaginative fusion of disharmonious inventions:

Hansjörg Utzerath's 1988 production of *Das Liebeskonzil* in the ruin of the bombed-out Katharinen Kirche in Nuremberg. Courtesy of the Staatstheater Nürnberg. Copyright © 1988 by the photographer, Marion Bührle.

Then the Devil, with dark brown-red tan and black body fur, splashes around in a pool of mud, wallows around furiously and, as he wracks his brains to find the proper punishment, rolls onto a side altar throne, whereupon little yellow-white flames light up everywhere, the altar, the steps, the side alcoves, red blazing behind all the window vaults: everything is ablaze, the altar block opens via remote control and spits out a tub of naked women: With one of them he will conceive syphilis. Fireworks, wild crackling, stench of powder and the glint of naked flesh, chorales by Händel and the Beatles, rejoicing also in heaven: Satan enters the heavenly realm dressed as a pin-striped agent, holding in one hand his syphilis-daughter — beautiful as sin — and in the other a metal case: "U.S. Department of Health," oh well, aha. Then disease, contrition and salvation can get started.

Now there is singing high above, "All you need is love ... it's easy" — and more and more the audience dares to applaud [*Süddeutsche Zeitung* 21 June 1988].

Berlin 1988

The final production of *The Love Council* in the year 1988 took place in Berlin's Schiller Theater on New Year's Eve. Judging by the immense production costs and the high caliber of the people involved, this promised to be an immensely entertaining interpretation of the play. Instead, it met with tepid applause from audiences and was universally shredded by the critics. This well-funded state theater had hired the Belgian Franz Marijnen to once again direct Panizza's *magnum opus*. Pop singer and songwriter Konstantin Wecker was commissioned to write original music and songs, the British Paul Staples designed the lavish sets and the American Rick Atwell was responsible for choreography. Additional framing scenes were written by the Schiller Theater's resident dramaturge, Knut Boeser, who also meticulously edited a lavishly illustrated, 150-page program booklet. His additional scenes include excerpts from Panizza's trial, as well as some far-fetched conversations between Panizza and the philosopher Friedrich Nietzsche, who by 1895 had already become mentally and physically incapacitated, possibly from syphilis.

Despite the high production values, what bothered critics the most was that Panizza's stinging indictment of secular and religious impotence, of hypocrisy, corruption and brutality, had been reduced to a two-and-a-half-hour variety show, bland enough to be shown on public television. Wolfgang Hammer dismissed the production as "a mixture of stupidity and cynicism" (*Frankfurter Rundschau* 14 Jan. 1989). Hans Ulrich Kersten, a correspondent for the Viennese daily *Die Presse*, lamented that with all the singing and dancing there was "not a trace left of Panizza's original 'issues'" (12 Jan. 1989). Jürgen Beckelmann, finding the musical to be "about as much fun as an inflated condom," considered the play itself to be dated, "[...] no, the play is no longer provocative. ARD and ZDF [public TV stations] can be much more obscene. This stage spectacle only has historical, antiquarian value; it's a kind of philosophical cabaret from an age when this small art form did not yet exist" (*Stuttgarter Zeitung* 10 Jan. 1989).

Wilfried Rott echoed the conviction that this Berlin production, despite its massive attempt to entertain, had extinguished any sparks contained in the original play: "The sumptuous theatrical efforts suffocate the play, or what's left of it — since up to the intermission there is scarcely any of Panizza's original text" (*Der Standard* 2 Jan. 1989). Rott also found the songs superfluous and annoying: "Wherever a scenic flow might occur, a song is inserted, not always for the better. Despite massive electronic amplification, Wecker's additions are unmistakable, yet rarely intelligible, they are arbitrary, uninspired background noise." Friedrich Luft complained that the devilish piece that had brought Panizza a one-year prison sentence had been totally tamed and transformed: "The angry barbs have almost all been clipped off. Protest and insurrection are gone. It becomes a bland New Year's Eve show. Hairs don't stand on end. An expensive state theater co-opts the poor, wild Panizza. [...] The effort expended is stupendous. The effect (amazingly) is rather calming. [...] Poor Panizza!" (*Die Welt* 2 Jan. 1989).

Münster 1989

As had been the case with a few earlier productions, 1981 in Rome and 1988 in New York, the 1989 production of *The Love Council* by Anita Ferraris at the Wolfgang Borchert Theater in Münster omitted all the scenes that take place on earth. She did explicitly include references to AIDS, which had now become commonplace since the mid–1980s. Despite the omission of the raunchy Vatican scenes, Ferraris' production caused a mild uproar in this predominantly Catholic city. Among her supporters, Gunda Maimann praised "the skilled hand of Anita Ferraris," the director:

> [...she] choreographically balanced the characters and found images to reduce the heavenly host to a rather profane size. When the Trinity is seated on the shaky aluminum throne, surrounded

Thomas Schendel as God, left, and Mircea Mihalache as the Cherub in Franz Marijnen's 1988 production of *Das Liebeskonzil* at the Schiller Theater, Berlin. Copyright © 1988 by the photographer, Anneliese Heuer.

by angels munching chips and watching a screen to follow the action on earth, then the earthly cesspool has finally been reduced to a lower-middle class, petit bourgeois TV show [*Münstersche Zeitung* 27 Feb. 1989].

The review ends on a note of both praise and caution: "The audience that dared to attend had a hell of a lot of fun with this successful production. Those people who want to protect their religious sensibilities don't have to attend — and that is everyone's perfect right."

Aside from the fine quality of the ensemble acting and the conspicuous absence of all Vatican material, the Münster production was also characterized by its unusual treatment of the play's opening scenes. For the first quarter-hour, the play took place in total darkness, punctuated by occasional flames from matches and sparklers, while the audience was forced to concentrate on voices delivering Panizza's words. Although this treatment appealed to some critics, others felt that it went on far too long.

Johannes Hasenkamp was outraged by the play as a whole, terming it "offensive and insulting" (*Westfälische Nachrichten* 27 Feb. 1989). He accused the director of staging the play in order to boost ticket sales:

> Obviously, Anita Ferraris wanted to shock. Some of the jokes were mediocre, others were repulsive. The play is basically a theater corpse from the 19th century, in a way it stinks and is mostly just silly and tasteless. Wasted time and wasted theater work [...]. The Borchert Theater has lowered its standards, because it is intellectually bankrupt. To quote from Cicero: whose benefit is served? That of the box office?

Hasenkamp further alleged that the play's depiction of heaven was "not only insulting for Christians," comparing it to "Salman Rushdie's obvious vilification of Islam." That accusation prompted a rebuttal letter to the editor by the theater's dramaturge, Cornella Naumann:

> [...] the dictator Khomeini is bent on the unscrupulous, cold-blooded exercise of power politics with the tools of the Inquisition that were employed by the popes in the 15th century. The alliance between church and government, which is not a given, is reinforced as an instrument of power and repression, not just in Iran. Precisely that is what Panizza was all about. The reviewer missed this, as well as the fact that the play is a parody. The height of blasphemy is the call for murdering a writer. That is why Rushdie's *Satanic Verses* are also on display in the Wolfgang Borchert Theater [*Westfälische Nachrichten* 3 Mar. 1989].

Sparked by this production of *The Love Council*, newspaper readers in Münster continued for some time to publicly debate the worldwide repercussions of blasphemy and censorship.

Hamburg and Trennewurth 1990

Three productions of *The Love Council* took place in or near the north German city of Hamburg in 1990. The first was performed in March by students at the Monsun Theater in Hamburg-Ottensen under the direction of a 29-year-old native Austrian, Barbara Neureiter. Helge Hopp favorably compared this local student production to Jesusa Rodriguez' recent performance with the world-touring Mexican Divas, which she derided as "hectic dance-ritual that degenerated into colorful razzmatazz" (*Hamburger Rundschau* 8 Mar. 1990). Hopp noted that the Monsun production reflected the students' "delight in acting, the burlesque elements of Panizza's script and a surprisingly precise stage choreography. Thus, the play about morality and sin seemed fresh again, freed from the heavy burden of absolutely having to be shocking."

Rather than simply eliminating all the Vatican scenes that place such extraordinary demands on a small troupe with their over forty speaking roles, Neureiter re-imagined the second act by making it thoroughly contemporary. Hopp describes the change in positive terms: "The unquestioned high point of the evening is a procession of the most diverse types, from dominatrix to nun, accompanied by barrel organ music, which in rapid succession leads crisscross through the everyday history of the late 1980s, a breathtaking burlesque parade, which the performers work to great effect with their subtle yet haunting gestures."

The Vatican scenes were very much in evidence again in July, when *The Love Council* was performed in Hamburg's Magnus Hirschfeld Centrum, an institution with a century-long history of combating homophobia through sexual research, education and counseling. Performed by the troupe Nuringenich under the direction of Uwe Sirsch, this production depicted the Vatican hotbed of sin with everything "from dry ice to explicit, graphic love scenes as shadow-play behind screens" (aw, *Die Welt* 10 July 1990). Another innovation by Sirsch was to provide multiple reversals of the competition between the Virgin Mary, played by a man, and the Devil, played by a woman. Whereas in the original version of the play the Devil emerges victorious, spreading disease among the wicked sinners, in Sirsch's version he is clearly beaten by Mary, who, with occasional sips from her flask, maintains a firm grip on everyone, including her whiny son and a senile, impotent God.

The third production of 1990 in the Hamburg area took place in one of the more unusual venues, namely in a cold barn located in Trennewurth, a village of 230 inhabitants in the county of Dithmarschen, Schleswig-Holstein. The two performances there of *The Love Council* in chilly December again featured students from Hamburg's Monsun Theater Institute under the direction of Barbara Neureiter.

Beatrice Sadek as Salome, left, Angelika Thomas as Mary, and Burghart Klaußner as the Devil in Franz Marijnen's 1988 production of *Das Liebeskonzil* at the Schiller Theater, Berlin. Copyright © 1988 by the photographer, Anneliese Heuer.

They had been invited by Uwe Böttjer to stage the play there in conjunction with a two-day conference on "Genius and Madness," organized by Koog-Haus, a psychiatric social institution headquartered in Brunsbüttel and directed by Böttjer.

The performances on December 6 and 7 effectively utilized different levels of a large barn belonging to Wiebke and Lothar Köhler. Neureiter had shortened the play into four acts, replacing syphilis with AIDS and again substituting the Vatican scenes with updated ones depicting "'normal' life on earth with a hippy, a greedy moneybags, a dominatrix, a punk, a nun, a housewife" (Böttjer 106). Several days before the first performance, rumors surfaced in the press that the folks putting on the play were part of some obscure sect that might be performing satanic rituals. When asked what he thought about all the commotion surrounding the play to be performed in his barn, farmer Köhler, a Roman Catholic,

Scene from Barbara Neureiter's 1990 production of *Das Liebeskonzil* staged in a barn in Trennewurth (Dithmarschen). Copyright © 1990 by the photographer, Sönke Dwenger.

replied: "I don't know the play, but I still think that theater should be shown. I have no problem with that, and I'm sure the people of Trennewurth don't either and will come to the performance" (106). After the performance, he commented: "What was finally shown is almost understated, when you see our population explosion and then hear the Pope still speaking out against the pill" (96).

Unperturbed by sensationalist media coverage fanning ominous rumors, Barbara Neureiter's rural production went off without a hitch. Although the unheated Köhler barn was actually quite packed for the two performances, the main complaint seems to have been the cold temperature. However, the audience particularly "enjoyed the changes of scene on different levels and the look into the sinful world of powerful oppressors, dominatrices and bundles of money" (104). Bettina Rathje, a 25-year-old editorial secretary from Brunsbüttel, actually found the play transformational:

> Since I've seen the play, I have another relationship — another perspective — to God. It used to always be God who watched over everything and was responsible for the world, who could separate good from evil. But in *The Love Council* it was no longer a God whom you would like to hold on to when you need help. I can't hang on to a coughing, miserable weakling who can't even take care of himself [97].

The following year, Uwe Böttjer published a lavishly-illustrated book that extensively documents the production of *The Love Council* in Trennewurth. It includes essays, interviews, newspaper reviews and scholarly articles dealing with Panizza, genius, madness and

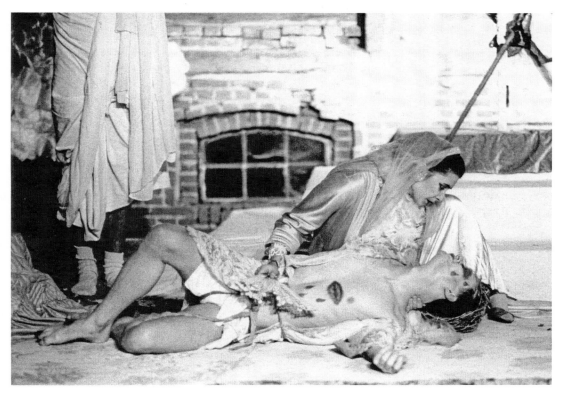

Scene from Barbara Neureiter's 1990 production of *Das Liebeskonzil* staged in a barn in Trenne-wurth (Dithmarschen). Copyright © 1990 by the photographer, Sönke Dwenger.

creativity: *Oskar Panizza und die Folgen. Bilder und Texte zur Wiederaufführung seines Liebeskonzils* (1992, *Oskar Panizza and the Consequences: Pictures and Texts from the Revival of his* Love Council). This volume also contains a collection of erotic collages by the Bruns-büttel artist Jens Rusch, which he exhibited in conjunction with the Trennewurth perform-ance. Some of these collages contain images from Werner Schroeter's 1982 film, while others incorporate sketches made by Panizza himself after he was institutionalized.

Braunschweig 1991

One of the very first secondary school productions of *The Love Council* was staged by Albrecht (Ali) Schultze, who still runs an amateur theater, teatr dach, in the village of Meer-dorf, Lower Saxony. As a teacher in Braunschweig's Wilhelm-Brack-Gesamtschule, in 1991 he directed a production of Panizza's play with twenty teenage students, which was so suc-cessful that it toured other cities in Germany and Switzerland. One of Schultze's innova-tions was to stage the scene in hell in a different room next to the main auditorium, thus providing added elements of intimacy and apprehension for the audience members, who are led there by the Devil and a female assistant. The choice of appropriate pop music added to the comic effect, as when the winged messenger in Act I, scene 4, arrives in heaven to report on the terrestrial cesspool of sin, to the accompaniment of "Let's Talk About Sex" by the female hip-hop group Salt-n-Pepa. The enthusiastic reviewer in the *Braunschweiger Zeitung* commented on the winning combination of passion and humor:

> The caricature of religiosity and sex is a hit, evidently providing the actors with a hell of a lot of fun. [...] Lusty exaggerations of all kinds. Veil dancing in front of the clergy, with effective musical accompaniment, martial wrestlers wearing adult diapers, the Holy Ghost floating above the heads of the audience, court ladies lustily munching on potato chips and much more. Once again, Ali Schultze has dumped his full box of gags onto the stage. Everything seems possible [hilp, 15 June 1991].

After the troupe's guest performance in Olten, Switzerland, the student actors engaged in a public discussion with the audience. Barbara Peters wrote that the young actors were amazed that their performance had not been perceived as being more provocative, which was evidently the result of the overwhelmingly liberal Swiss audience. She also noted that the director "did not need to replace syphilis with AIDS, the parallels are clear enough as is. That was certainly due to the audience, not the play or its staging — it would certainly be interesting to smuggle this production into a municipal theater subscription series!" (*Oltner Tagblatt* 15 May 1992).

Vienna 1991

That indeed did occur later in the year at the Tyrolean State Theater in Innsbruck, but it was preceded by yet another independent Austrian production, this one in late 1991 at Vienna's Ensemble Theater am Petersplatz, under the direction of Stephan Bruckmeier. The director chose *The Love Council* to conclude his "Culture of Destruction" trilogy, dealing with the themes of power and impotence, sexuality and violence, which had included Pier Paolo Pasolini's *Orgia* (1968) and Albert Drach's *Das Satansspiel vom göttlichen Marquis* (1929, *Satan's Play about the Divine Marquis*).

The aspect of Bruckmeier's production that provoked the most critical discussion was his decision to substitute a dance number for the carnivalesque Vatican scenes in Act Two. Lothar Lohs characterized it as a "hard to define ritual ballet of oppression, which six women perform in front of a monstrous boogeyman of power" (*Falter*, 47/1991). He concluded that the play was "the best theater that has been performed by an independent troupe in a long time." Wolfgang Freitag came to the opposite conclusion, stating that the dance was "an amateurishly designed and executed pantomime" (*Die Presse* 15 Nov. 1991). In his opinion, there was no trace "of the 'satanic greatness' which contemporaries ascribed to Panizza's work."

For Ronald Pohl, the "Baroque" dance scene in front of the Pope was reminiscent "of the Romanian dictator Nicolai Ceaucescu; girls pay homage to a sexless idol (Eva Hosemann) wrapped in sable, who, half Venus in furs, half old man at the Kremlin Wall, functions as the priest of a yet to be defined ritual" (*Der Standard* 14 Nov. 1991). Referring to Schiller's characterization of the theater as a moral institution, Pohl concluded that "with a vision like this, the theater has finally abdicated as a moral institution. To be sure: The good was never beautiful, the true was never good, and the beautiful was never true."

Innsbruck 1992

Barbara Peters' wish to see *The Love Council* presented as part of a regular subscription offering in a major public theater was soon realized in Innsbruck, one of the more conservative areas in predominantly Catholic Austria. It is where the *Liebeskonzil* film was prevented from being shown in 1985, leading to a ten-year legal battle that resulted in the decision to seize and forfeit the film being upheld by the ECHR. In 1992 the staid Tyrolean State Theater opened its fall subscription season with Dietrich W. Hübsch's new production of *The Love Council*. The decision to open the season with Panizza's provocative play was made by the theater's new *Intendant* (general manager) from Switzerland, Dominique Mentha. He had been hired to re-energize the theater and appeal to a younger audience, following the 25-year tenure of Helmut Wlasak. Mentha was convinced that it is "better to be provocative in the theater than to be rampaging in the streets" (ni, *ff* 9 Oct. 1992: 35).

Since Innsbruck was the city where the scheduled screening in 1985 of Werner Schroeter's *Liebeskonzil* had led to a total ban of the comparatively tame film throughout the entire Republic of Austria, the press coverage prior to the premiere was both extensive and intense. Hübsch made it clear that, while he was willing to resist censorship and provoke controversy, he was not aiming for a cheap scandal: "Scandal is also made by a naked bosom in the wrong place, but that's lacking in substance. I have absolutely no interest in a scandal that is provoked by the media. Panizza was not out to attack faith, but rather its misuse" (35).

Further publicity was generated when a lawsuit charging blasphemy was filed by Armin Benedikter, a university student from southern Tyrol. The suit went nowhere, but it helped ensure that the premiere on October 3rd was sold out. Film critic Robert Benedikt remarked

Norbert Aberle starring as the Devil in Dietrich W. Hübsch's 1992 production of *Das Liebeskonzil* in the Tiroler Landestheater, Innsbruck. Courtesy of the Tiroler Landestheater, Innsbruck. Copyright © 1992 by the photographer, Rupert Larl.

that "with Oskar Panizza's *The Love Council,* Dominique Mentha has lured rare visitors into the Tyrolean State Theater, for instance, red-haired punk girls and 'Greens' in loden jackets" (*Die Presse* 5 Oct. 1992). Although city politicians cautiously avoided the controversial premiere, District Attorney Rudolf Koll was in attendance to determine if a charge of blasphemy might have any merit. Before the premiere, Koll stated that "if the performance is a mockery of faith, then I have to charge the Intendant, the director or even one of the actors" (ni, "Gotteslästerung," *ff* 16 Oct. 1992). A conviction could have resulted in a fine and six months in prison, though Koll noted that "not everything that goes against the grain of an arch-conservative Catholic is punishable." That was the case with this performance, since afterwards he remarked that he was in no way upset, "either as an individual or as a Catholic." Koll dismissed the entire issue as "much ado about nothing."

Before and after the performance, a private group of traditionalists, Young Christians of Tyrol, demonstrated in front of the theater. They prayed on their knees and handed out leaflets calling on theatergoers to express their outrage with protests. However, a large police contingent both outside and inside the building had no trouble maintaining order. Equally ineffective was the threat by some local representatives of the Austrian People's Party (ÖVP) to retaliate by slashing the theater's public funding. Bishop Reinhold Stecher, whose archdiocese had initiated legal action against the much tamer *Liebeskonzil* film seven years previously, announced after the performance that he would refrain from pressing charges, noting that "what is holy is always stronger than its mockery" (ni, "Liebeskonzil," *ff* 16 Oct. 1992).

Despite all the publicity surrounding this production, the performance itself appears to have been somewhat lackluster. Jutta Höpfel liked the imaginative sets and opulent costumes, which provided for a "veritable orgy of visual pleasure" (*Wiener Zeitung* 6 Oct. 1992). The innovation mentioned most frequently was Hübsch's addition of the fiery Florentine preacher Savonarola who, every time the curtain falls, stands up in a loge and exhorts the audience to repent.

The production was a success in that it achieved Mentha's aim of provoking the public and stimulating thoughtful public discussion. Robert Benedikt reported that during the intermission "there were heated discussions," and "after the curtain had fallen, for a long time one could see little groups around the theater square involved in discussions." In addition to these private conversations, there were no less than four organized panel discussions in the weeks that followed the Innsbruck premiere of *The Love Council*: the first one in the State Theater itself, the second one at the Innsbruck University, the third one at the public television station and the fourth one again at the theater. This final one, titled "Art, Freedom and Censorship," was moderated by local radio host Günther Nenning and included Viennese theologian Robert Prantner, Panizza researcher Sylvia Vogler, journalist Franz Stocker of the *Innsbrucker Kirchenzeitung*, Franciscan Father Felix Gradl and OPI-attorney Frank Höpfel. Mentha and Hübsch were also present, although Irene Heisz describes their participation as largely limited to mime, either "smiling approvingly or frowning" (*TT* 2 Nov. 1992).

Berlin 1993

It is clear that successful productions of *The Love Council* do not depend on the availability of well-established public theaters with their generous budgets, huge casts, impressive choreography, lavish sets and star power. One of the more imaginative presentations of the play was presented in 1993 by young students at the Maria Körber Actors Studio in Berlin under the direction of Austrian Thomas Reisinger. Petra Braendle claimed that "even though Panizza's free-wheeling treatment of divine dignitaries could hardly cause a scandal anymore today, *The Love Council* remains a biting, extremely funny work, bleak as well, with a contemporary relevance, considering the current Pope's views on AIDS" (*taz* 8 Feb. 1994). She likened Reisinger's version of the Trinity to a down-and-out family as might be found in Berlin's bohemian Kreuzberg section of town:

> God, a whining and farting old geezer with woolen socks, is totally annoyed by his asthmatic, post–Beatle softie-son, as well as by Mary, who is just as power-hungry as she is bitchy and vain. Wonderful slapstick develops, spiced by saucy scenes with the angels. Mary, for example, grabs the spotlight from God and greedily stuffs the body of Christ, a loaf of bread, into her hamster cheeks. Christ is continually mimicking kitschy images of himself, as autistic angels drone on with a mercilessly Tyrolean "Motherofgodprayforus."

Braendle saw this bold production as being "both imaginative and precise, which updates Panizza's irony. The director replaced antiquated scenes at the court of Alexander VI with a live report from the current Pope's 1968 visit to Germany. The production playfully transports Catholic pomp into modern kitsch aesthetics."

Susanne Heyden agreed that Reisinger's production was "a clever mixture of cabaret, biting satire and poetry that simply knocks your socks off," a "salutary shocker that should not be missed" (*Tagesspiegel* 18 Dec. 1993). One of several major challenges for anyone staging *The Love Council* is to find and create a dramatic high point in the absence of any obviously climactic scene in the play. Some productions have fallen flat without presenting any such scene, while other directors have sought to create various dramatic climaxes and distribute them throughout the play's five acts. Breitinger created such a scene in Act IV, when the Devil, played by an actress, presents Mary with the deadly "package" that she had commissioned:

> Maryfullofgrace finds in a gigantic Christmas package, like a Pandora's box, first a few tabloids, an automatic assault rifle, then a little bag of heroin and finally a framed portrait — the Devil's daughter, bearing syphilis. Mary is rather shocked by this, and the Devil sarcastically remarks: "Wasn't this what you ordered?" And "Silent Night" waltzes along as it always has. Thomas Reisinger's production keeps hurling out references that all hurt, as intended, and yet are chillingly understated rather than overblown [*Tagesspiegel* 18 Dec. 1993].

Los Angeles 1996

When Ron Sossi established the Odyssey Theatre Ensemble in a Hollywood storefront back in 1969, one of the first plays he intended to stage was *The Love Council*. Instead, the company established its reputation with a successful series of innovative productions of plays by Bertolt Brecht, along with works by other, less frequently performed German-language playwrights such as Georg Büchner, Carl Sternheim and Peter Handke. Three decades later, Sossi finally realized his plan to stage Panizza's play at his Odyssey Theatre, which had since moved to a three-theater complex in West Los Angeles. Sossi used Oreste Pucciani's 1973 English translation as the basis for his script, which he further developed together with his ensemble. Thus, excerpts from Panizza's own legal defense at his 1895 trial were inserted into the text. Don Shirley lauded "Sossi's amusingly carnal and richly detailed spectacle," which "keeps the audience wide awake, regardless of opinions and the play's thesis" (*Los Angeles Times* 6 Nov. 1996).

However, Don Shirley openly cautioned his readers: "Anyone easily offended by caricatures of Christian icons or by sexually graphic action should steer clear." In another cautionary note of political correctness, it was also pointed out that "this production used no government funds." Shirley concluded that "the ending is sobering. The play's comic charge and sexual buzz fade away, and the satirical intent is muffled — as if Panizza began to believe that his fantasy might be true."

Bern 1997 and Kiel 1999

Barbara Frey's 1997 production of *The Love Council* at the Berner Schauspielschule (Bern Acting School) was less noteworthy for its creative staging than for the closely-watched historic trial that ensued in 1998. As discussed elsewhere in this book in Chapter 9 on twentieth-century trials, this was the very first time in Swiss history that a theater performance resulted in a trial before a judge on charges of disturbing the freedom of religion and worship.

An even more innovative student production took place in 1999 at the University Theater in Kiel under the direction of Jens Raschke and Dietmar Fiedler, titled *Panzerkreuzer Panizza Liebeskonzil* (*Armored Cruiser Panizza Love Council*). The angels in Act I were hand puppets who "brilliantly" depicted their characters as "gay motormouths" (was, *Kieler Nachrichten* 11 Feb. 1999). The son of God is portrayed as "a self-pitying Christ, for whom Mary Magdalene scrubs the floor. And his formerly immaculate mommy (Dana Matzen), holding up a vibrator, must first be dragged off the stage, only to then throw herself at every potential partner — even the Devil." The heavenly family is so shocked by watching a priest unconventionally lifting the sins from the celebrated whore, Josefine Mutzenbacher, that they decide to summon help from Lucifer.

Readers outside the German cultural orbit may be interested to know that Mutzenbacher is widely known to German audiences as a tell-all prostitute, whose fictitious memoirs have sold over three million copies since they were first published anonymously over a hundred years ago: *Josefine Mutzenbacher: Die Lebensgeschichte einer Wienerischen Dirne, von ihr selbst erzählt* (1906, *The Life Story of a Viennese Prostitute, as Told by Herself*). She is also featured as the heroine of a dozen popular adult films that have been released since 1970. The original memoir covered only Josefine's childhood sexual experiences, beginning at age five and ending with puberty, when she decides to become a prostitute. These childhood memoirs contained a veritable laundry list of sexual taboos, including incest, rape, group sex and homosexuality. Arthur Schnitzler, the noted Austrian author and dramatist, was originally suspected of having penned this widely-translated work, though scholars now generally attribute the erotic bestseller to Felix Salten (1869–1945). Ironically, Salten is best known as the author of *Bambi: A Life in the Woods* (1923), for which Walt Disney acquired the film rights before producing his children's classic in 1942.

Describing the divine response to viewing the priest and Josefine Muntzenbacher, the reviewer writes how "God's fury is released — brilliantly conceived — as a kind of 'thunder cloud ex machina' with sinister rumbling" (was, *Kieler Nachrichten* 11 Feb. 1999). The Lord of the Underworld is then asked to concoct a harrowing, truly diabolical punishment, yet he must still leave the soul capable of being saved, "otherwise it would just be superfluous."

With the help of Salome, infamous for her cruelty, he spawns a kind of superwoman, also played by the same actress, to infect mankind. The reviewer enthusiastically summarized the overall theatrical experience as follows:

> The performance sparkles with nonstop absurdities as well as with sharp, subtle points, which lead one's train of thought around the corner before delivering the punch-line. A hundred years ago, Oskar Panizza spent a year behind bars for blasphemy and insulting the Church. For their version of *Panzerkreuzer Panizza Liebeskonzil,* Jens Raschke and Dietmar Fiedler would then have presumably been personally strangled by the Pope [was, *Kieler Nachrichten* 11 Feb. 1999].

Vienna 2000

One of the most original productions of *The Love Council* was Bert Gstettner's fusion of choreography and spoken theater. Performed by his Tanz*Hotel troupe in Vienna's Werkstätten- und Kulturhaus (WUK), Gstettner invited his audiences to mingle among his living tableaus, thus dissolving the space between actors and audience, while allowing viewers to select and change their points of view. Oliver Werner wrote that this production was "perfectly wrought: it comes across as very tight, concentrated, pictorial, rich in references and associations" (*Neue Kronen Zeitung* 11 Sept. 2000).

Heidrun Hofstetter-Hambach pointedly remarked that today the play should more appropriately be titled *The Sex Council* ("Let's talk about sex," *Tanzaffiche* 103, Oct.–Dec. 2000). She observed that "black-robed monks making advances on bare-breasted angels provide the first evidence of sanctimony and carnal lust hiding under the mantle of celibacy and asceticism propagated by the Church."

There were markedly differing opinions as to whether Gstettner had successfully met the challenge of choreographically interpreting Panizza's play. One reviewer, for instance, found that concepts like "society, politics, morality and sensuality had found their choreographic structure, humorously decorated with linguistic barbs" (stelz, *Die Presse* 11 Sept. 2000). On the other hand, Brigitte Suchan wrote that the performance was "an interesting exper-

Boy Kramer as Christ in the 1999 student production of *Panzerkreuzer Panizza Liebeskonzil* by Jens Raschke and Dietmar Fiedler in Kiel. Courtesy of Jörg Lippmann. Copyright © 1999 by the photographer, Firas El-Saleh.

iment," but that the spoken scenes "seemed a bit long-winded" and "choreographically contributed too little to approaching the topic" (*Wiener Zeitung* 11 Sept. 2000).

Wolfgang Kralicek was even more outspokenly critical, maintaining that the production did not even amount to dance theater, but rather "a surprisingly text-heavy (if greatly shortened) theater production with dance interludes" (*Falter* 15 Sept. 2000). He also felt that "the dancers in the ensemble were overtaxed by their speaking roles." Another reviewer noted that the climax of the production was "a danced orgy, in which God the Father is outed as a dirty old man [...] together with a choreographed multiple orgasm" (wald, *City* 38/2000). Kralicek's opinion of this climax was less than enthusiastic: "The orgy staged without words and as copulation choreography is — pardon me — not very sexy" (*Falter* 15 Sept. 2000). He concluded that "the play is not a tragedy, but rather the parody of a tragedy. Its bitter joke is that the actual tragedy does not begin until the play ends. A more successful staging would need to communicate the notion that behind Panizza's anarchic wit lurks pure despair."

Dana Matzen as Mary and Marta Pawlik as the Woman in the 1999 student production of *Panzerkreuzer Panizza Liebeskonzil* in Kiel. Courtesy of Jörg Lippmann. Copyright © 1999 by the photographer, Firas El-Saleh.

Braunau 2000

Another Austrian millennial production of *The Love Council* was staged at the municipal cultural center in Braunau, the birthplace of Adolf Hitler. Employing a sixteen-member ensemble of local amateurs and visiting professionals, Viennese director Justus Neumann moved even further away from presenting the play as a heavenly tragedy and staged it with plenty of slapstick as a "heavenly comedy" (Aigner, *Braunauer Rundschau* 9 Nov. 2000: 5). Neumann was very clear about his reasons for emphasizing the humorous aspects of the play: "It is liberating to laugh at God, at Mary, at the whole heavenly host. Laughter has no place at all in the Church, there is really no joy at all in that sense." Neumann certainly recognized the seriousness of the issues behind Panizza's humorous critique of the Church: "The criminal history of this institution is obvious and has not stopped. Every day God-awful things happen in the name of God. The Church continues to be the richest mafia in the world." He stressed how extensive the human psyche has been damaged by our underlying belief system: "The entire

Scene in Heaven from Bert Gstettner's 2000 production of *Liebes*Konzil* in the Tanz*Hotel im WUK, Vienna. Courtesy of Bert Gstettner. Copyright © 2000 by the photographer, Otto Jekel.

basis of our thought is built on guilt and fear." Despite Neumann's outspoken criticisms of the Church, he portrayed Christ in a less ridiculous light than Panizza had done, depicting God's son as "a strong force of love," thus "counterbalancing the stupidity of the old God."

Hermine Aigner also wrote that Neumann had succeeded in providing his audience with "divine amusement" by presenting "a panorama of human weaknesses" (*Braunauer Rundschau* 11 Nov. 2000). While the Holy Ghost blithely chirps away on a clothesline, Mary sips drinks from her flask as she flirts with the Devil, who himself is eventually seduced by a belly-dancing Salome. One of Neumann's most interesting innovations was to completely reverse the location of the actors and the audience. Thus, the spectators filled the chairs arrayed on the stage, while the action all took place in the semi-circle of rising rows in the auditorium that had been cleared of seats. Neumann even used the sound and lighting control room as a space where God, Mary and Christ can be seen behind glass at the end of Act I, watching what is happening down on earth.

For weeks on end, the local newspaper carried letters from readers commenting on the play. The favorable comments were from theater-goers who had loved the liberating effect of Neumann's wildly imaginative and humorous production, while the negative comments were principally from readers who had not seen the play. Some in the latter group asked for religious tolerance instead of mockery, pointedly wondering what the public reaction would have been if a play had been presented making fun of Jews or Muslims.

Laubach (Württemberg) 2001

One of the more spirited outdoor productions of *The Love Council* took place in the summer of 2001 in the woods outside the castle at Laubach, Württemberg, not far from the city of Schwäbisch Gmünd. Under the professional direction of Rainer Lohr-Berlin, the play was presented on three stages representing heaven, hell and earth. The performers were all members of the well-established amateur troupe Kulturverein Schloss Laubach, founded in 1985 and consisting of twenty actors and three times as many financial backers and technical supporters. This production is another example of how successfully Panizza's play has fared over the past forty years, in both professional and non-professional productions, before a wide variety of audiences:

> What licentious fun [...] Ribald dialogues and a good mixture of satire and deadly seriousness fling the spectators to and fro between fun and the possible insult to well-developed religious structures [...] Colorful costumes and convincing theatrical performances [...] heighten the audience's expectation of what is yet to come [...] And it does come [...] [*Aalener Nachrichten* 27 June 2001].

According to Tobias Ullersperger, the „high point is a fashion show with unbelievable articles of clothing" (*Gmündner Tagespost* 22 June 2001). Wolfgang Nussbaumer was equally impressed by the zesty production:

Erich Knoth as the Devil and Ursula Schopf as Salome in Justus Neumann's 2000 production of *Das Liebeskonzil* in the Theater im Gugg, Braunau. Courtesy of Alois Mandl, Kultur im Gugg. Copyright © 2000 by the photographer, Wolf Dietrich Weissenbach.

> The troupe sparkles with their unbridled joy of acting. It makes a great impression on the audience when "The Woman" scoops someone up out of the audience; when, during a frivolous clerical fashion show put on for clerics and their no-less licentious mafia relatives, a well-formed butt flashes through the robes under the nun's habit, just like at the "Love Parade" [*Gmündner Tagespost* 26 June 2001].

Nussbaumer, who felt that it was "really courageous for an amateur troupe" to stage such a controversial play that had landed its author in prison for a year, was certainly not unaware of Panizza's "fundamental critique": "What kind of God is it who punishes people in this way? From the author's point of view: either weak or even obsolete." As in most productions of *The Love Council*, the show was stolen by the actor portraying the lead role of the Devil, in this instance a veterinarian.

Inge Kollra and Gerd Hendricks cast as dual Devils in Götz Lange's 2002 production of *Das Liebeskonzil* at the Seniorentheater in der Altstadt, Düsseldorf. Courtesy of Holm Gottschling. Copyright © 2002 by the photographer, H.D. Schäfer.

Kulmbach 2005

Another very successful production of *The Love Council* dominated by the character of the Devil took place four years later in Kulmbach. Directed by Bianka Zeitler, this is but one of a number of wildly exuberant productions by school groups to meet with critical acclaim. Far from being a new institution, the Markgraf-Georg-Friedrich-Gymnasium proudly traces its roots back to a medieval Latin school, founded in 1393. The modern-dress production, which took place in the Kulmbach Stadthalle (Civic Center), was accompanied by an extensive sixteen-panel exhibit on Panizza's life and the history of religious criticism. This exhibit had been assembled with pedagogic thoroughness by Dr. Christian Henning, a teacher at the school and also a professor at the University of Erlangen, who served as one of the faculty advisors for the production.

Horst Wunner headlined his review with the unmistakable headline: "Brilliant Production of Panizza's *Love Council*." Calling the production a "bull's eye," Wunner was clearly transported by the play:

The audience is fascinated by the performance from the very start: the actors are wholly in their element and perform with such intensity, with such an abundance of pleasure, that it becomes a real experience for the audience. And yet they know exactly the limits of what is permissible, merely hinting at lust and vice, yet in so doing revealing more than pure sexuality would show.

Thus, the action always represents a tightrope walk for the young actors, a real ride on the razor blade. However, the actors master this with youthful nonchalance, without neglecting the depths [*Bayerische Rundschau* 20 June 2005: 9].

Zeitler visually presented the sick state of affairs in heaven by portraying it as a hospital ward, with the figures of God and Christ both seated in wheelchairs, while their attendant angels are clad in nurses uniforms. Mary is attired in an even skimpier white uniform, perched atop her "throne" that more resembles a bar stool, as she leafs though a copy of the women's magazine *Madame*. Wunner credits the director with having a strong sense of how to strike just the right balance between seriousness, sex and humor:

Dietrich Brechler as Christ in Götz Lange's 2002 production of *Das Liebeskonzil* at the Seniorentheater in der Altstadt, Düsseldorf. Courtesy of Holm Gottschling. Copyright © 2002 by the photographer, H.D. Schäfer.

Bodies lying on top of each other, knots of people in steamy proximity, an air pump as a swelling penis and finally a gigantic phallus as the sole eye-catcher on the stage: lust is constantly palpable. Yet the limits are known, the pupils are aware of the danger of drifting into pure obscenity. Nevertheless, the deplorable historical evils are frankly presented, without any taboos. The action leads to the inevitable punishment, from which none of "those up there" are spared. Following the hierarchical sequence from the pope to the cardinal down to the abbot and the simple priest, all succumb to the deadly disease.

As might be imagined, portraying God almighty as an old fool, Mary as a sexy slut, Jesus as a dimwitted patient in a wheelchair and the Holy Ghost as a light bulb might elicit outrage in a certain segment of the public, as indeed it did. In a panel discussion organized by the Markgraf-Georg-Friedrich-Gymnasium, the limits of profaning the divine were discussed by the school's principal, along with other teachers, clerics and authors. The strongest criticism came from a teacher, Herbert Schneider, who both publicly and in a private letter to the principal (19 June 2005) claimed the play was one unremitting blasphemy

Final scene from Bianka Zeitler's 2005 student production of *Das Liebeskonzil* at the Mark-graf-Georg-Friedrich-Gymnasium in Kulmbach. Courtesy of Hans-Werner Fischer, Oberstu-diendirektor. Copyright © 2005 by the photographer, Werner Fischer.

mocking Christians and their faith. He expressed concern that parents would refrain from enrolling their children in a school where such offenses were committed and condoned. He also raised the issue of how such a play might have been received in a Muslim country, to which several panelists responded that "it is precisely a strength of Christian societies that such a play could be performed at all" ("Was darf die Kunst?" *Bayerische Rundschau* 22 June 2005). Thus, as so often before, a production of Panizza's *The Love Council* served to entertain the public, as well as to stimulate serious reflection and discussions regarding the benefits and possible limits to freedom of expression.

Bayreuth 2006

Bayreuth is a city with an especially close proximity to Oskar Panizza. He first visited here in 1891 during the Richard Wagner Festival to write a review titled "*Tristan und Isolde* in Bayreuth" (*Moderne Blätter* 1/19, 8 Aug. 1891: 2–5). It is here that he spent the last sixteen years of his life after being declared mentally incapacitated, first in a mental institution and

Sophie Ringel as Syphilis and Florian Bittermann as the Devil in Bianka Zeitler's 2005 student production of *Das Liebeskonzil* in Kulmbach. Courtesy of Hans-Werner Fischer, Oberstudiendirektor. Copyright © 2005 by the photographer, Werner Fischer.

then in a sanatorium. Finally, it is here that his remains lie in an unmarked grave in the municipal cemetery.

Clearly referring to Panizza's institutionalization in Bayreuth and drawing inspiration from *Marat/Sade* by Peter Weiss, the innovative production by director Birgit Franz unfolds in a madhouse. The play was performed outdoors in the crumbling Roman Theater of the Eremitage, built in a splendid park at the edge of the city in 1744 by Joseph Saint-Pierre for the Margravine Wilhelmine. Contrasting with the faux Roman ruins, the play is set in an early twentieth-century mental hospital, where the newly-committed Dr. Oskar Panizza starts a hospital revolt and ends up staging his own play. He forces the hospital director, Dr. Würzburger, into a straight-jacket and assigns roles to be played by the various patients. A blind patient in a wheelchair gets to play God, while the head nurse is assigned the role of Mary and Dr. Würzburger that of the Pope. Dr. Panizza naturally gives himself the role of the Devil, masterfully performed here by Frank Müller, a clinical physician when not onstage. The spectacle thus simultaneously invoked at least half a dozen different temporal dimensions: a twenty-first-century Dr. Müller in an eighteenth-century, faux 2,000-year-old Roman theater, playing Dr. Panizza in a 1906 Bayreuth hospital, playing the Devil at the Vatican Court in 1495, in a play written by Oskar Panizza in the 1890s.

Panizza aside, performing *anything* on an open-air stage in Germany is risky business.

Some may have perceived a sign of divine displeasure when a veritable deluge poured forth from the skies at the May 27 premiere, while Kathrin Erbacher noted with admiration that "on Saturday the members of the Studiobühne not only proved their excellent acting talent but also their physical perseverance, as there was a heavy downpour for the entire duration of this outdoor performance" (*Bayerische Rundschau* 30 May 2006). Spectators who witnessed subsequent performances under dry skies were treated to an outstanding theatrical experience. As so often was the case in previous productions, the real show-stealer was the figure of the Devil. Valerie Hänisch noted that "Frank Müller euphorically plays the role of Oskar Panizza, who seems to share many concerns with the Devil. Both suffer at being excluded from society. The Devil's books were banned, just as those by Panizza were" (*Bayerischer Anzeiger* 21 June 2006). Monika Beer wrote:

> The depressive Dr. Panizza joins the ladies and gentlemen with falling sickness, gambling addiction, washing and polishing obsessions, Tourette's syndrome and narcolepsy; as in Werner Schroeter's film version, he soon causes a furor as the Devil. Frank Müller masters the transformation magnificently, spitting poison and bile with *grandezza* and speaking the perhaps most important line of the evening, eliciting goose bumps: "If someone is thinking and is no longer allowed to communicate his thoughts to others, that's the ghastliest torture of all" [*Fränkischer Tag* 20 June 2005].

Frank Müller as Dr. Panizza in Birgit Franz's 2006 open air production of *Das Liebeskonzil* in the Roman Theater of the Eremitage, Bayreuth. Courtesy of Birgit Franz, Studiobühne Bayreuth. Copyright © 2006 by the photographer, Regina Fettköther.

Ralf Sziegoleit agreed that "Frank Müller is Panizza and — naturally — the Devil in a grandiose manner. He doesn't simply desire evil, but freedom of thought, as well" (*Frankenpost* 14 June 2006). He also noted perceptively that in the play, "the world is a madhouse — sardonically wicked but also full of melancholy." In an interview with Wolfgang Lammel, director Birgit Franz stressed that "for me, the main theme is freedom of thought, which in the play is explicitly demanded by the figure of the Devil, the antagonist of the decadently drawn figures of God the Father, Jesus Christ and Mary. He wrote without censoring himself. That's what makes the play current" (*Sonntagsblatt* 28 May 2006). She also noted how performing *The Love Council* enabled the actors to re-examine their own convictions: "For many it was an intensive exploration of their own beliefs. As a preparation, we brought along our own hymnals and confirmation verses, which we then discussed." Although their faiths were diverse, they shared Franz's unwavering conviction: "I believe that no work of art should be banned."

Fürth 2007

This same conviction was also reflected a year later in the production staged by Jürgen Herrmann at the Helene-Lange-Gymnasium in Fürth. In order to contextualize this

Frank Müller as the Devil in Birgit Franz's 2006 open air production of *Das Liebeskonzil* in the Roman Theater of the Eremitage, Bayreuth. Courtesy of Birgit Franz, Studiobühne Bayreuth. Copyright © 2006 by the photographer, Regina Fettköther.

student production, Herrmann's troupe included materials from Panizza's 1895 trial, as well as an additional monolog to relate *The Love Council* to current events. Writing in *Helga*, the school newspaper, Tilman Adler describes how they mined Panizza's court records for:

> [...] authentic dialog, supplemented by a monolog of Panizza's, which directly addresses today's audience. He clearly states there that obviously the play was performed in order to provoke. However, the aim in doing so was not to condemn the Catholic Church or any similar institutions. Rather, he wanted to focus on freedom of speech. Nowadays, freedom of speech is hardly more than a casually uttered phrase. And yet our society is based on freedom of expression in word and writing [http://helga-online.de/?pageid=10&articleid=203].

Other difficult questions relevant to a school environment were also raised: "Who may decide how far art — i.e., theater and, in particular, a school theater — may go? The state, in the form of its judges? The Church? The school administration? The group of actors?" By deciding to produce this play, they perhaps contributed their own answer.

As in several other productions using gender-reversals, in Fürth the role of God was played by a female instead of a male. Another innovative casting feature was that the Pope and the Devil were played by the same student, whose performance, according to Adler, was "unsurpassed." He contrasted this actor's "subtly decadent" portrayal of the Pope with that of the Devil, who was "simultaneously superior and evil, conniving and darkly brilliant, who collapsed into a desperate, malcontent being, only to rise again like a Phoenix, even meaner and more brilliant."

Adler characterized the overall quality of the acting as "almost flawless and at the highest, inimitable level. If you had been sitting in the municipal theater instead of in the auditorium of the HLG, you would certainly have thought you were watching a professional company." Particularly in Act II, the audience became "witness to an orgy of pleasure and decadence, which is surely why the lower grades were not permitted to attend." It is hard to imagine *The Love Council* being performed anytime soon in an American public high school.

Regensburg 2007

A second Regensburg production of *The Love Council* was staged in the Alte Mälzerei, a former malt house that now serves as the city's alternative cultural center for progressive musical and dramatic events. It was actor Hans Schröck's first venture at directing in what was decidedly a low-budget production. Some of what he lacked in financial resources he made up with a wealth of performing talent and innovative staging. The actor playing God still belongs to the acting company directed by Joseph Berlinger, whose 1988 production of *The Love Council* in the Regensburg University Theater remains vivid in many a local theatergoer's memory. The long-haired Devil plays in a heavy-metal band, the women from the Realm of the Dead (III, 2) are professional dancers, the various musicians are all part of the regional jazz scene and the angels are members of the local gay men's choir, who also sewed the costumes.

Florian Sendtner lauded the production's "enormous energy and almost overflowing imagination, an elaborate, meaningful set and, above all, excellent actors" (*Mittelbayerische Zeitung* 23 Nov. 2007). He also noted that "the Devil is practically the only likeable character" in the play, which he compared to Goethe's *Faust*, but a Faust "who has read Nietzsche."

Hans Camin as the Devil, left, Barbara Zepf as Mary, Werner Rösch as God, and Peter Leitner as the Cherub in Hans Schröck's 2007 production of *Das Liebeskonzil* in Regensburg. Courtesy of Hans Schröck. Copyright © 2007 by the photographer, Hubert Lankes.

The two-story set was indeed rather elaborate, with the celestial action all taking place on the upper level, while the other scenes were all appropriately set on the lower level.

At the beginning of the play, the Lord is conveyed up to the celestial level by an elaborate process reminiscent of first erecting a cross or raising a May pole. God in his wheelchair is finally enthroned under a huge wooden statue that is part cross and part gallows, wearing a yarmulke and with a golden Star of David at his feet, a motor rug on his lap and a computer screen at his side. The Cherub at his feet regularly puffs on an enormous water pipe, and, after the Devil has discretely provided her with a little plastic bag, Mary clandestinely dispatches occasional pinches of cocaine up her nose.

However, Panizza connoisseurs waited in vain for the carnivalesque Act II to unfold at the Vatican court. Sendtner clearly lamented "the complete updating of the second act. Whereas Panizza entertainingly portrayed the vice-ridden activities at the court of Borgia Pope Alexander VI, with Hans Schröck the venial sins are gone. It's the joyless, ascetic Opus Dei tyranny that enrages the holiest Trinity" to the point of wanting to punish mankind with deadly disease. Instead of the original vaudevillian performances by Italian comedians, wrestlers and courtesans, Schröck totally rewrote the act to include texts by Pope John Paul II for the beatification of Josemaría Escrivá, the founder of Opus Dei. Other contemporary allusions abound, including references to former Regensburg resident and theology professor, Joseph Ratzinger (now Pope Benedict XVI), Chile's late General Pinochet, weapons dealers and the millions in payments by the Church to victims of pedophile priests. Masturbation and other sexual activities are suggested behind a shadow screen. Toward the end of the second act, a Church dignitary drops his trousers and simulates the rape of a young ministrant.

One of the clear strengths of Schröck's staging was his creative use of music and dance. The gay men's choir not only provided comic relief, it also functioned in the manner of a Greek chorus with a critical commentary on the main action. In Act III, the interviewed women from the Realm of the Dead, in this case Helen, Agrippina

Hans Camin as the Devil in Hans Schröck's 2007 production of *Das Liebeskonzil* in Regensburg. Courtesy of Hans Schröck. Copyright © 2007 by the photographer, Hubert Lankes.

and Salome (Phryne and Heloise were cut), were accomplished dancers who performed to the eerie melodies of a lone saxophonist at the side of the stage.

Kaiserslautern 2008

The most recent German production of *Das Liebeskonzil* was staged by Johannes Reitmeier in Kaiserslautern's municipal theater. Even before the premiere just one week prior to Christmas 2008, the play had created more controversy than any other production at the Pfalztheater. The entries in the theater's online guest book ranged from residents strongly opposing any onstage depictions of God, let alone something satirical or critical, to those staunchly defending the right to freedom of expression. Susanne Schütz discussed the pre-premiere controversy and noted that the play's opponents "obviously don't think much of artistic freedom — Article 5 of the Constitution" ("Zur Sache: Empörung im Internet." *Die Rheinpfalz* 15 Dec. 2008).

Mainstream theater critics were hardly shocked and actually sounded disappointed that the play was relatively tame and not even more provocative. Jens Frederiksen wondered "how earlier generations could see any dangers to Western civilization" in Panizza's "overwrought, somewhat silly grotesquery" (*Mainzer Allgemeine Zeitung* 17. Dec. 2008). Noting the clash of pomposity and garishness in the scenes set in heaven, Frederiksen felt that the cabaretistic and somewhat slapstick presentation tended to trivialize Panizza's critical intent.

The scenes in the Vatican were staged by Reitmeier as one gigantic hot-tub party, with all the Catholic dignitaries exuding a forced gaiety as they cavorted in their swimming regalia,

Reinhard Karow as God, surrounded by celestial attendants, in Johannes Reitmeier's 2008 production of *Das Liebeskonzil* at the Pfalztheater in Kaiserslautern. Courtesy of Christina Alexandridis, Chefdramaturgin. Copyright © 2008 by the photographer, Hans-Jürgen Brehm-Seufert.

replete with bishops' hats. Even the final scene, where the Devil's irresistibly seductive daughter, Syphilis, is surrounded by a sea of bodies even before she drops all her clothes, hardly produced much of any shock value in a German audience grown accustomed to ubiquitous nudist beaches and pornography on public television. Frederiksen noted laconically: "But that was all there was to it — nothing more of a scandal." Susanne Schütz also wondered "whether the play might not be too flat to speak to us today," noting that the Monty Python film, The Life of Brian, "offers a sharper religious critique" ("Viel Lärm um Nichts," *Die Rheinpfalz* 15 Dec. 2008).

Once again, this Kaiserslautern production points up the importance of delicately balancing the old and the new, authenticity and innovation, tragedy and comedy. For all its comic elements, Panizza wrote a "heavenly tragedy," one dealing with the anguish of widespread venereal disease suffered for more than five hundred years. What omnipotent deity could possibly be responsible for this massive suffering, where millions of people are consigned to devastating venereal epidemics, where whole populations and entire continents are ravaged by seemingly endless cycles of excruciating misery and pain?

Ultimately, though, *The Love Council* is not exclusively about disease, any more than it is just about divine responsibility for inexplicable, catastrophic misery resulting from earthquakes, famine, tsunamis or other "natural" disasters. As this survey of some of the one hundred productions of *The Love Council* over the past half-century has shown, the play also focuses on expanding freedom of expression by exposing hypocrisy at the highest levels among secular and clerical authorities, often working together. It pushes the limits of freedom of thought by forcing us to confront and question our most sacred, time-honored beliefs.

Finally, it illuminates organized systems of power and control that have historically been used to subjugate, exploit and silence masses of believers. *The Love Council,* brilliantly conceived by its author as part medieval mystery play, part vaudeville, part parody of *Faust,* part boudoir farce, part Commedia dell'Arte, part black mass, seeks to expose the corruption and hypocrisy of those who would continue to rule by brute force and threat of punishment. That all this can be accomplished with huge dollops of satire, verbal puns, crude slapstick, wrestling matches, striptease, ballet, liturgical (and now pop) music is a credit to the modernist in Oskar Panizza. His play has had a liberating effect on diverse artists and their audiences of all ages on several continents, challenging them to imbue his play with ever-new creative manifestations of free thought and expression.

Appendix A: Theatrical Productions of *Das Liebeskonzil*

1962, Berlin, 6 Oct. First public reading by Klaus M. Rarisch. Vier + 4 literary club. Kulturkeller das Massengrab.

1965, Munich, 9 Dec. First complete public reading. Studiobühne der Universität München. Thereafter in Münchner Rationaltheater. Dir. Maria Reinhard.

1967, Vienna, 1 June. World premiere. Experiment am Liechtenwerd. Dir. Renée Heimes.

1969, Paris, 7 Feb. *Le Concile d'amour*. Théâtre de Paris. Designed by Leonor Fini. Dir. Jorge Lavelli.

1970, London, 24 Aug. *The Council of Love*. Criterion Theatre. Adapt. John Bird. Dir. Jack Gold and Eleanor Fazan.

1972, Sainte-Thérèse (Québec). *Le Concile d'amour*. Collège Lionel-Groulx. Dir. André Montmorency.

1973, Lyon. *Le Concile d'amour*. Théâtre de l'Eldorado. Compagnie de la Mouche. Dir. Bruno Boëglin.

1973, Hamburg, 30 Aug. Ernst Deutsch Theater. Dir. Jorge Lavelli.

1974, Reutlingen, 15 June. Theater in der Tonne. Dir. Walter D. Asmus.

1975, Stuttgart, 26 Feb. Altstadttheater. Dir. Franziskus Abgottspon.

1976, Cambridge, MA, 29 Apr. *The Council of Love*. Loeb Mainstage. Harvard-Radcliffe Drama Club. Dir. Richard Peña.

1976, Rotterdam, 2 Oct. *Het Liefdesconcilie*. Stadschouburg. RO Theater. Dir. Franz Marijnen.

1977, Hamburg, 17 Jan. Guest perf. from Rotterdam. Deutsches Schausspielhaus. Dir. Franz Marijnen.

1981, Rome, Apr. *Il concilio d'amore*. Teatro Belli. Dir. Antonio Salines. Filmed:

1981, Rome & Berlin. *Liebeskonzil* Film. Premiere: Berlinale, 21 Feb. 1982. Screenplay by Dietrich Kuhlbrodt, Roberto Lerici, Horst Alexander. Dir. Werner Schroeter.

1983, Austin (Texas), 9 June. *The Council of Love*. Capitol City Playhouse. Raw Materials. Dir. Jim Fritzler.

1984, Vienna, 25 Nov. Arena St. Marx. Narrenkastl. Dir. Justus Neumann and Joseph Hartmann.

1985, Alès (F). *Le Concile d'amour*. Théâtre d'Alès. Zinc Théâtre. Dir. Gilbert Rouvière.

1986, London, 6 Jan. *Hell's Angels*. Royal Court Theatre. Musical by Nigel Osborne. Libretto and Dir. David Freeman.

1986, Munich, 11 Jan. Figurentheater Gerhard Weiss. Dir. Gerhard Weiss.

1986, Hannover, 23 May. Theater an der Glocksee. Hochschule für Musik und Theater. Dir. Peter Meinhardt.

1986, Munich, 29 July. Studiotheater auf dem Alabama. Dir. Gunnar Petersen.

1987, Ulm, 29 May. *Luzifer. Ein deutsches Lied in memoriam Oskar Panizza*. Ulmer Theater. Opera by Franz Hummel. Libretto by Christian Fuchs.

1987, Mexico City. *El concilio de amor*. Shakespeare Forum. Dir. Jesusa Rodriguez.

1987, Hannover. Mittwoch: Theater. Dir. Hans-Hermann Scharnofske.

1988, Regensburg, 15 Jan. Studenten-Theater der Universität. Teater Compagnie. Dir. Joseph Berlinger.

1988, Nuremberg, 18 June. Katharinenkirche Ruine. Städtische Bühne. Dir. Hansjörg Utzerath.

1988, New York, Nov. *The Council of Love*. HOME for Contemporary Theatre and Art. Dir. David Kaplan.

1988, Grenada. *El concilio de amor*. Centro Dramático Elvira de la Universidad de Granada. Dir. Ignacio Calvache and Friedhelm Roth-Lange.

1988, Berlin, 31 Dec. Schillertheater. Music by Konstantin Wecker. Dir. Franz Marijnen.

1989, Münster, 25 Feb. Wolfgang Borchert Theater. Dir. Anita Ferraris.

1989, Austin (Texas), 18 June. *The Council of Love*. Synergy Studios. Big State Productions. Dir. Jim Fritzler.

1989, Montréal. Festival of the Americas. El Grupo Divas. Dir. Jesusa Rodriguez.

1989, São Paulo, 16 Nov. Centro Cultural São Paulo. Dir. Gabriel Villela.

1990, Hamburg, March. Monsun Theater. Dir. Barbara Neureiter.

1990, Hamburg, July. Magnus-Hirschfeld-Centrum. Gruppe Nuringenich. Dir. Uwe Sirsch.

1990, Graz, 21 Aug. Schauspielhaus. Sommerschule für Theater. Dir. George Isherwood.

1990, Trennewurth (Dithmarschen), 6 Dec. Köhler-Hof. Koog-Haus. Dir. Barbara Neureiter.

1991, Braunschweig, 5 June. Wilhelm-Bracke-Gesamtschule. Braunschweiger Theater AG. Dir. Albrecht Schultze. Addtl. perfs. in Braunschweiger Staatstheater; 19 Nov. 1991 at the cabaret Die Kugelblitze, Magdeburg; 21 Feb. 1992 Lindenhof, Braunschweig; 8 May 1992 Olten, Switzerland.

1991, Schaffhausen, 7 Aug. Schaffhauser Sommertheater. Freilicht. Dir. Jordi Vilardaga.

1991, Vienna, 12 Nov. Ensemble Theater am Petersplatz. Theater-bureau. Dir. Stephan Bruckmeier.

1992, Munich, 6 Mar. Aldente Theater. Dir. Peter Spiel.

1992, Innsbruck, 3 Oct. Tiroler Landestheater. Dir. Dietrich W. Hübsch.

1992, Göttingen. Theater im OP. Dir. Astrid Hickmann.

1993, Munich. Theater im Hansa.

1993, Magdeburg, 28 May. Probebühne. Freie Kammerspiele. Dir. Kay Wuschek.

1993, Neuss, 18 Sept. Rheinisches Landestheater. Globe-Theater. Dir. Hansjörg Utzerath.

1993, Berlin/Neukölln, Dec. Fliegendes Theater. Maria-Körber-Schauspielstudio. Dir. Thomas Reisinger.

1994, Bordeaux, June. *Le Concile d'amour*. Théâtre en Miettes. Dir. Jean Claude Parent.

1994, Ferrara, Aug. *Il concilio d'amore*. Il Teatro dell'Asino. Dir. Marco Felloni.

1994, Cologne. Mimikry Figurentheater. Dir. Petra Wolfram.

1995, Fellbach, 24 Juni. Theater im Polygon. Dir. Peter Hauser.

1995, Venice. Biennale. Goldoni Theater. Dir. Jorge Lavelli.

1996, Los Angeles, 20 Nov. *Love Council*. Odyssey Theatre. Dir. Ron Sossi.

1996, Rio de Janeiro. *O concílio do amor*. Casa da Gavea. Dir. Gilberto Gawronski.

1996, Avignon. Festival. *Le Concile d'amour*. Les Saltimbanques. Dir. Benoît Lavigne.

1997, Bern, Dec. Schauspielschule Bern. Dir. Barbara Frey.

1997, Coyoacán (Mexico). *El concilio de amor*. Teatro de la Capilla. Dir. Jesusa Rodriguez.

1998, Avignon, 11 July. *Le Concile d'amour*. Théâtre Le Cabestan. Dir. Angélique Piat.

1998, Brussels. *Le Concile d'amour*. Théâtre les Tanneurs. Dir. Francine Landrain.

1998, Oberhausen. Bertha-von-Suttner-Gymnasium. Dir. Waltraud Szyperski.

1999, Kiel, 9 Feb. *Panzerkreuzer Panizza Liebeskonzil*. Studententheater im Sechseckbau. Theater-gruppe Gnadenhammer. Dir. Jens Raschke and Dietmar Fiedler.

1999, Montréal, 18 June. *Le Concile d'amour*. Théâtre du Nouveau Mond. Dir. Jean-Philippe Monette.

1999, Lanester (F), 27 Nov. *Le Concile d'amour*. Théâtre Salle Jean Vilar. Dir. Marcel Labouiller.

1999, Rennes. *Le Concile d'amour*. Théâtre National de Bretagne. Compagnie au Grand Huit. Dir. Patrice Bigel.

2000, Lausanne, 25 April. *Le Concile d'amour*. Théâtre du Vide Poche. Dir. Michel Demierre.

2000, Paris, 25 April. *Le Concile d'amour*. Théâtre de la Tempête, Dir. Serge Sàndor.

2000, Vienna, 8 Sept. *Liebes*Konzil*. Tanz*Hotel im WUK—Werkstätten- und Kulturhaus. Dir. and choreographed by Bert Gstettner.

2000, Braunau, 9 Nov. Theater im Gugg. Dir. Justus Neumann.

2000, Barcelona. *El concilio de amor*. Teatre Artenbrut. Dir. Joan Raja.

2001, Laubach (Württemberg), 22. June. Theater im Schlosspark. Dir. Rainer Lohr-Berlin.

2001, Paris, June. *Le Concile d'amour*. Crypte Montparnasse.

2001, Kassel, 7 September. Kulturfabrik Salzmann. Theaterpädagogisches Zentrum, Theatergruppe Jezzaba. Dir. Monika Heyder.

2001, Paris. *Maladie d'Amour*. Théâtre de Ménilmontant. Dir. Pascale Lievyn.

2002, Düsseldorf, 7 Nov. Seniorentheater in der Altstadt. Forum Freies Theater im Juta. Dir. Götz Langer.

2003, Belgrade, 12 Jan. *Sarcastikus ili Rodjenje virusa* (= *Sarcasticus or the Birth of a Virus*) Adapt. Plavo Pozoriste. Rex — Kulturni Centar. Dir. Nenad Colic.

2003, Porto Alegre (Brazil), 5 Feb. *O concílio do amor*. Theatro São Pedro. Beginning 14 Mar. Teatro Renascença. Dir. Néstor Monasterio.

2003, Schweinfurt, 28 Sept. Public reading by the Schweinfurter Autorengruppe in the City Hall restrooms as part of the "Night of Culture."

2003, Bremen. Brauhauskeller des Bremer Theaters. Dir. Volker Erdmann.

2004, Saint-Étienne (F), 23 Mar. *Le Concile d'amour*. Comédie de Saint-Étienne. Dir. Frédéric Révérend.

2005, Kulmbach, 15 Apr. Stadthalle. Markgraf-Georg-Friedrich-Gymnasium, Theatergruppe Eigen-Sinn. Dir. Bianka Zeitler.

2005, Cadenet (F), 3 June. *Le Concile d'amour*. La bande d'art et d'urgence. Dir. Marie Anne Etienne and Frédérique Merie. 20 Nov. Pertuis, Théâtre Municipal. 6ème Festival de Théâtre Amateur.

2005, Le Mans, 6 June. *Le Concile d'amour*. MJC Plaine du Ronceray. La Malle de Pandora. Dir. André Lenoir.

2005, Eymoutiers (F), 12 July. *Le Concile d'amour*. Place des Coopérateurs. Compagnie 7AC. Dir. Marc-Henri Lamande.

2005, Rumeln (Duisburg-Rheinhausen), 24 Sept. Theater Trotzdem. Dir. Marc Breitenbach.

2006, Ostend (Belg.), 28 Apr. *Het Liefdesconcilie*. Zaal Malpertuis. Dir. Rik Labeeuw.

2006, Bayreuth, 27 May. Theater der Eremitage. Studiobühne. Dir. Birgit Franz.

2007, Sassenage (F), 19 June. *Le Concile d'amour*. l'Entra'Actes du Théâtre en Rond. Compagnie Les Brigands de la Plume. Dir. Patrick Seyer.

2007, Fürth, 26 June. Helene-Lange-Gymnasium. Dir. Jürgen Herrmann.

2007, Lannion (F), 13 Sept. *Le Concile d'amour*. Chapelle St Anne. Cie Maldoror. Théâtre en Trégor. Dir. Marc de Saint Laurent.

2007, São Paulo, 22 Sept. *O concílio do amor*. Teatro Irene Ravache. Dir. Ivan Feijó.

2007, Regensburg, 21 Nov. Alte Mälzerei. Dir. Hans Schröck.

2008, Kaiserslautern, 13 Dec. Pfalztheater. Dir. Johannes Reitmeier.

2009, Quimper (F), 10 Mar. *Le Concile d'amour*. Opera for voice, instruments, marionettes & machinery by Michel Musseau. Théâtre de Cornouaille. Coproduced with Angers Nantes Opéra, Compagnie Les Ateliers du Spectacle, Massalia — Théâtre de marionnettes. Dir. Jean-Pierre Larroche. Tour incl. **Besançon**, 25 Mar. Théâtre de l'Espace; **Nantes**, 5. Nov. Théâtre Graslin; **Saint Nazaire**, 8 Nov. Université Inter-âges; **Angers**, 13 Nov. Grand Théâtre; **Meylan**, 24 Nov. Théâtre Hexagone; **Toulouse**, 26 May 2010. Théâtre National de Toulouse

The dates given are those of the premieres. Additions and corrections are always welcome, as this list is continually being updated on the author's website: http://www.newpaltz.edu/~brownp/panizza

Appendix B: Chronology of Oskar Panizza's Life

1853

Leopold Hermann Oskar Panizza is born November 12 in Bad Kissingen as the sixth child of the Catholic hotelier Karl Panizza (1808–1855) and his Protestant wife, Mathilde, née Speeth (1821–1915).

1855

Oskar's father dies of typhus November 26 after signing a document permitting Mathilde to raise their children in her faith. She assumes responsibility for running the Hotel Russischer Hof and promptly has all the children re-baptized Protestant.

1856

18 February. Karl's Catholic priest, Anton Gutbrod, pursues legal action against Mathilde in the Kissingen district court, challenging her late husband's deathbed permission to raise their children Protestant. Legal battles ensue for years, eventually resulting in Oskar and his siblings being raised in the Protestant faith.

1860/1861

Oskar begins to receive private instruction.

1863

10 April. He is enrolled in the Pietist Brethren Community boys' school at Kornthal in Württemberg.

1868

Receives his confirmation in Kornthal and transfers to the *Gymnasium* in Schweinfurt.

1870

Transfers to a *Gymnasium* in Munich, which becomes his principal base for the next 25 years.

1871–1872

Drops out of school due to poor grades.

Attends trade school to study business, private tutoring in other subjects, while studying voice at the Music Conservatory.

1873

Mathilde brings Oskar back to Kissingen to work in her hotel. May-August, he interns at the Bloch & Co. bank in Nuremberg before returning to Munich.

1873–1874

Drafted into one-year military service in the 7th Company of the 2nd Bavarian Infantry Regiment. Pursues program of extensive reading, composing and sketching in his leisure time and during frequent disciplinary detentions.

1874

Returns to Munich following military discharge to resume his music studies.

1875

Decides to go back to school to complete his secondary education. Reviews academic subjects with private tutors before being readmitted to *Gymnasium* in Schweinfurt.

1876

After receiving his *Abitur* degree upon graduation from the *Gymnasium*, Panizza enrolls at the Ludwig Maximilian University in Munich, where he studies medicine until earning his doctorate in 1880.

1878

Spring vacation trip through Italy, where he claims to have contracted syphilis, allegedly resulting in the deformity of his right leg. The persistent curvature of his right tibia was more likely due to an improperly-splinted shin following a childhood fall.

1880

Receives his Dr. med. degree *summa cum laude* with a dissertation *On Myelin, Pigment, Epithelia und Micrococci in Sputum,* supervised by Prof. Hugo von Ziemssen, director of the Municipal Clinic links der Isar.

1881

Completes military obligation in a field hospital before spending half a year in France.

1882

Begins two-year assistantship at the Oberbayerische Kreis-Irrenanstalt, the district insane asylum in Munich, working under Professor Bernhard von Gudden, physician to Bavarian King Ludwig II. Mathilde sells Hotel Russischer Hof for 600,000 marks, of which Oskar and his siblings each receive 120,000 marks. Unsuccessful suicide attempt by Oskar's younger sister, Ida.

1884

Growing fear of insanity from interacting with psychotic patients and following the death of his uncle, Ferdinand Speeth, who suffered from "religious madness" in Würzburg. After extended depression and panic attacks, Panizza quits his clinical position at the Oberbayerische Kreis-Irrenanstalt and turns definitively to creative writing as "the best antidote for all kinds of psychopathic moods." Begins drawing a lifetime annuity of 6,000 marks.

1885

First literary publication of poems, *Düstre Lieder (Gloomy Songs).* Briefly opens a private medical practice in Munich. Travels to London in October, where he remains for an entire year.

1886

Returns to Munich in October.

1887

Second volume of poetry published, *Londoner Lieder (London Songs).*

1888

Moves to a new apartment at Krankenhausstraße 5, whose name is later changed to Nussbaumstraße.

1889

Third volume of poetry published, *Legendäres und Fabelhaftes (Legends and Marvels).*

1890

First book of four stories published, *Dämmrungsstücke (Twilight Pieces),* which attracts the attention of the circle of Munich's "moderns." Chief among them is Michael Georg Conrad, editor of the movement's influential journal, *Die Gesellschaft (Society).* Conrad helps Panizza launch his journalistic career and publishes scores of his articles over the next six years in *Die Gesellschaft.*

1891

Joins the governing board of the Gesellschaft für modernes Leben (GmL, Modern Life Society), founded by Conrad and other artists. Delivers lecture on "Genie und Wahnsinn" (Genius and Madness) in March. His publication of a short story, "Das Verbrechen [The Crime] in Tavistock Square," results in his expulsion from the Bavarian militia reserves. *Modernes Leben (Modern Life),* the GmL's yearbook, is confiscated by the police.

1892

Publication of *Aus dem Tagebuch eines Hundes (From the Diary of a Dog).* Begins writing *Das Liebeskonzil (The Love Council).*

1893

Publication of a collection of stories, *Visionen (Visions),* as well as his anti–Catholic satire, *Die unbefleckte Empfängnis der Päpste (The Immaculate Conception of the Popes),* which is later confiscated and banned by court order. Completes writing *The Love Council.* Begins to develop his idiosyncratic, hyper-phonetic spelling.

1894

Der teutsche Michel und der römische Papst (The German Michel and the Roman Pope) published, also banned by court order. Publication of two plays: *Der heilige Staatsanwalt (The Holy District Attorney)* and *The Love Council,* published in Zürich on October 10.

1895

Das Liebeskonzil confiscated, preliminary charges filed and investigation of the case against the author opens on January 4. Panizza deposed on January 12. A Leipzig policeman is located February 27, whose religious feelings were allegedly offended by reading the play, thus establishing the legal basis for charges against Panizza under §166 of the Imperial Legal Code. Author prosecuted by Eugen Freiherr von Sartor in jury trial on April 30, closed to the public. Convicted and sentenced the same day to one year in prison, then arrested and held for three weeks before being released on 80,000 marks bail. Appeal denied July 1 by Imperial Court in Leipzig. Begins serving sentence in Amberg penitentiary on August 8. Befriended by the prison chaplain, Deacon Friedrich Lippert. Premiere October 11 in Leipzig of *Ein guter Kerl* (*A Good Fellow*), only play of Panizza's performed during his lifetime. Publication of *Der Illusionismus und die Rettung der Persönlichkeit. Skizze einer Weltanschauung* (*Illusionism and Saving One's Personality: Outline of a Worldview*) and *Meine Verteidigung in Sachen "Das Liebeskonzil"* (*My Defense in the Case of "The Love Council"*).

1896

Ein guter Kerl (*A Good Fellow*) and 2nd edition of *The Love Council* are published. Writes *Dialoge im Geiste Huttens* (*Dialogues in Hutten's Spirit*), self-published the following year. Released from prison August 8 and returns to Munich for two months. Renounces Bavarian citizenship in September and emigrates to Zürich in October. *Abschied von München. Ein Handschlag* (*Farewell from Munich: A Handshake*) is published, which is banned and confiscated, resulting in the issuance of a warrant for his arrest.

1897

Panizza's beloved dog, Puzzi, dies February 19. He founds a journal in June, *Zürcher Diskußionen*, and a press by the same name, to publish his journal and books. The 3rd edition of *The Love Council* and *Die Haberfeldtreiben im bairischen Gebirge* (*Charivaris in the Bavarian Mountains*) are published.

1898

The political satire *Psichopatia Criminalis* and the historic drama *Nero* are self-published. Panizza expelled from Switzerland on October 27, ostensibly for nude photography of Olga Rumpf, a fifteen-year-old prostitute. Coming a month after the assassination of Empress Elisabeth (Sissi) of Austria by an Italian anarchist in Geneva, political motives probably played a role in the decision by Swiss police to expel Panizza, a stateless anarchist with an Italian name. He leaves for Paris on November 15.

1899

Zürcher Diskußjonen continues to be published in Paris. Publication of vitriolic anti–German poetry collected in *Parisjana. Deutsche Verse aus Paris* (*Parisiana: German Verses from Paris*) results in the issuance of an international arrest warrant.

1900

Parisjana banned and confiscated, its author charged on January 30 with lèse-majesté for insulting Kaiser Wilhelm II. Panizza's entire German assets are frozen March 10 by court order. Begins to be tormented by hallucinations.

1901

Returns to Munich and surrenders to the court in April. Is arrested, spends ten weeks in jail, followed by six weeks in the Oberbayerische Kreis-Irrenanstalt, the district insane asylum where he had been employed seventeen years previously. After diagnosis of paranoia, all legal charges are dropped and assets unfrozen due to mental incompetence. Leaves for Paris immediately after his release on August 28.

1902

Final issues of *Zürcher Diskußjonen* appear, though Panizza continues writing additional articles well after publication ceases. Mounting symptoms of mental and physical distress. Spends the last years in Paris in virtual seclusion.

1903

Last major writing project is *Imperjalja*, an elaborate paranoid construct outlining a vast international conspiracy directed by Kaiser Wilhelm II.

1904

Returns to Munich in June, suffering from auditory hallucinations and other signs of growing mental disease. Briefly admitted to a private institution in July. Attempts suicide on October 9. Ten days later provokes arrest and admission to the Psychiatric Clinic by walking down a busy street dressed only in his shirt. Writes his *Autobiographical Sketch* November 17.

1905

Transferred on February 5 to St. Gilgenberg, a small private asylum in Bayreuth. Declared mentally incompetent on March 28. His brother Felix and *Justizrat* Josef Popp, an attorney and distant relative, assume custody as his legal co-guardians.

1908

Moved to Mainschloß building of Herzogshöhe sanatorium on the outskirts of Bayreuth, a luxury facility for patients suffering from circulatory and other physical ailments. Following brother Felix's death in March, Deacon Friedrich Lippert becomes Panizza's co-guardian.

1913

Reprint of 3rd edition of *The Love Council* with nine ink drawings by Alfred Kubin published in a limited edition of fifty copies by the Gesellschaft Münchner Bibliophilen.

1914

Visionen der Dämmerung (*Visions of Twilight*), collection of short stories, published with introduction by Richard Weinhöppel, afterword by Hanns Heinz Ewers and illustrated by Paul Haase.

1915

Deacon Lippert retires and moves to Bayreuth to be closer to Panizza, whose 93-year-old mother, Mathilde, dies August 13.

1921

Oskar Panizza dies on September 28 following a stroke. Two days later, Deacon Lippert conducts the author's funeral service, attended only by hospital personnel. Panizza is buried in an unmarked grave in the Bayreuth municipal cemetery.

Bibliography

Principal Biographical Monographs (Chronological)

Lippert, Friedrich and Stobbe, Horst, eds. *In memoriam Oskar Panizza.* Munich: Horst Stobbe, 1926.

Brown, Peter D.G. *Oskar Panizza: His Life and Works.* American University Studies Series 1, vol. 27, and European University Studies, Series 1, vol. 745. New York & Bern: Peter Lang, 1983.

Bauer, Michael. *Oskar Panizza. Ein literarisches Porträt.* Munich: Carl Hanser, 1984.

Düsterberg, Rolf. *»Die gedrukte Freiheit«. Oskar Panizza und die* Zürcher Diskußjonen. Europäische Hochschulschriften, Series 1, vol. 1098. Frankfurt/Main: Peter Lang, 1988.

Harder, Mathilde [Tilly, née Panizza], ed. *Die Memoiren der Mathilde Panizza.* Nieder-Olm: priv. printing [Antje and Hans-Wolfgang Redlich], 1996.

Müller, Jürgen. *Der Pazjent als Psychiater. Oskar Panizzas Weg vom Irrenarzt zum Insassen.* Edition Das Narrenschiff. Bonn: Psychiatrie-Verlag, 1999.

Books Published by Oskar Panizza (Chronological)

Über Myelin, Pigment, Epithelien und Micrococcen im Sputum. Inaugural-Abhandlung zur Erlangung der Doctorwürde der medizinischen Facultät zu München unter dem Präsidium des Herrn Professor Dr. von Ziemssen. 48 pp. + 1 illus.. Leipzig: J.B. Hirschfeld, 1881.

Düstre Lieder. 124 pp. Leipzig: Albert Unflad, 1886.

Londoner Lieder. 88 pp. Leipzig: Albert Unflad, 1887.

Legendäres und Fabelhaftes. 138 pp. Leipzig: Albert Unflad, 1889.

Düstre Lieder, Londoner Lieder, Legendäres und Fabelhaftes. 350 pp. [remainder of Unflad editions bound together in leather incl. original covers], Leipzig: Wilhelm Friedrich, 1891.

Dämmrungsstücke. Vier Erzählungen. 304 pp. Leipzig: Wilhelm Friedrich, 1890.

Aus dem Tagebuch eines Hundes. 104 pp. + 36 illus. by Reinhart Hoberg. Leipzig: Wilhelm Friedrich, 1892.

Visionen. Skizzen und Erzählungen. 298 pp. Leipzig: Wilhelm Friedrich, 1893. Remainder publ. in the same year and press as a volume in the series "Sammlung interessanter Unterhaltungsschriften."

Die unbefleckte Empfängnis der Päpste, von Bruder Martin O.S.B., aus dem Spanischen von Oskar Panizza. 108 pp. Zürich: Verlags-Magazin Jakob Schabelitz, 1893.

Der heilige Staatsanwalt. Eine moralische Komödie in fünf Szenen (nach einer gegebenen Idee). 30 pp. Leipzig: Wilhelm Friedrich, 1894.

Der teutsche Michel und der römische Papst. Altes und Neues aus dem Kampfe des Teutschtums gegen römisch-wälsche Überlistung und Bevormundung in 666 Tesen und Zitaten. Mit einem Begleitwort von Michael Georg Conrad. 310 pp. Leipzig: Wilhelm Friedrich, 1894.

Das Liebeskonzil. Eine Himmels-Tragödie in fünf Aufzügen. 78 pp. Zürich: Verlags-Magazin Jakob Schabelitz, 1895 [published 10 October 1894].

Der Illusionismus und Die Rettung der Persönlichkeit. Skizze einer Weltanschauung. 62 pp. Leipzig: Wilhelm Friedrich, 1895.

Meine Verteidigung in Sachen "Das Liebeskonzil." Nebst dem Sachverständigen-Gutachten des Dr. M.G. Conrad und dem Urteil des k. Landgerichts I. München. 38 pp. Zürich: Verlags-Magazin Jakob Schabelitz, 1895.

Ein guter Kerl. Tragische Szene in 1 Akt. Meßthalers Sammlung moderner Dramen, no. 2. 23 pp. Munich: Commissionsverlag Max Höher, 1895.

Das Liebeskonzil. Eine Himmels-Tragödie in fünf Aufzügen. Zweite, durch eine Zueignung und ein Vorspiel vermehrte Auflage. 94 pp. + 28 pp. Kritische Stimmen über *Das Liebeskonzil.* Zürich: Verlags-Magazin Jakob Schabelitz, 1896.

Abschied von München. Ein Handschlag. 15 pp. Zürich: Verlags-Magazin Jakob Schabelitz, 1897.

Das Liebeskonzil. Eine Himmels-Tragödie in fünf Aufzügen. Dritte, durchgesehene und vermehrte Auflage. 97 pp. + 42 pp., incl 35 pp. Kritische Stimmen über *Das Liebeskonzil.* Zürich: Verlags-Magazin Jakob Schabelitz, 1897.

Dialoge im Geiste Huttens. 146 pp. Zürich: Verlag der Zürcher Diskußionen, 1897.

Die Haberfeldtreiben im bairischen Gebirge. Eine sittengeschichtliche Studie. 114 pp. Berlin: S. Fischer, 1897.

Psichopatia Criminalis. Anleitung um die vom Gericht für notwendig erkanten Geisteskrankheiten psichjatrisch zu eruïren und wissenschaftlich festzustellen. Für Ärzte, Laien, Juristen, Vormünder, Verwaltungsbeamte, Minister, etc. 48 pp. Zürich: Verlag der Zürcher Diskussionen, 1898.

Nero. Tragödie in fünf Aufzügen. 107 pp. + 15 pp. Geschichtliche Übersicht. Zürich: Verlag der Zürcher Diskußionen, 1898.

Parisjana. Deutsche Verse aus Paris. Zürich: Verlag der Zürcher Diskußionen, 1899.

Oskar Panizza's Editorship of *Zürcher Diskußionen*

Zürcher Diskußionen. Flugblätter aus dem Gesamtgebiet des modernen Lebens. Ed. Oskar Panizza. Verlag der Zürcher Diskußionen, Zürich, 1897–1902.

MAJOR CONTRIBUTIONS BY PANIZZA TO *ZÜRCHER DISKUßIONEN* (CHRONOLOGICAL)

"Die Krankheit Heines: Zur hundertjährigen Wiederkehr des Geburtstages Heines." 1.1 (1897): 1–8.

"Christus in psicho-patologischer Beleuchtung." 1.5 (1898): 1–8.

Hans Kistemaecker [= Panizza]. "Die Kleidung der Frau: Ein erotisches Problem." 1.8 (1898): 1–7.

*** [= David Farbstein & Oskar Panizza]. "Christus von einem Juden." 1.9 (1898): 1–10.

"Agnes Blannbekin. Eine österreichische Schwärmerin aus dem 13. Jahrhundert nach den Quellen." 1.10–11 (1898): 1–16.

"Darlegung der Umstände gelegentlich der Ausweisung des Herausgebers der 'Zürcher Diskußionen' aus Zürich." 1.12 (1899): 6–11.

Louis Andrée [= Panizza]. "Karl Ludwig Sand: Eine biografisch-psichologische Darstellung." 2.13–15 (1899): 1–24.

Rev. of "Otto Julius Bierbaum, *Das schöne Mädchen von Pao* [Berlin 1899]." 2.16–17 (1899): 14.

"Der Anarchist Panizza." 2.16–17 (1899): 14.

"Das Denkmal für Charles Baudelaire in Paris." 2.16–17 (1899): 15.

Publication Overview of *Zürcher Diskußionen*

Volume	Issue No.	Month	Year	Page length	Article #
1	1	September	1897	8	1–2
	2	October	1897	8	3–4
	3	December	1897	8	5
	4	January/February	1898	8	6–7
	5	March/April	1898	8	8
	6	May	1898	8	9–10
	7	July/August	1898	8	11–12
	8	September	1898	8	13–14
	9	October	1898	10	15
	10–11	December	1898	16	16
	12	June	1899	12	17–19
Vol. 1 Subtotal: 11 issues				**102 pages 19 articles**	
Volume	Issue No.	Month	Year	Page length	Article #
2	13–15	September	1899	24	20
	16–17	October	1899	16	21–24
	18–19	December	1899	16	25–26
	20–21	January/February	1900	16	27–31
	22	October	1900	8	32
	23–24	November	1900	12	33–36
Vol. 2 Subtotal: 6 issues				**92 pages 17 articles**	
Volume	Issue No.	Month	Year	Page length	Article #
3	25–26	September/October	1902	16	37–42
	27	November	1902	8	43–44
	28–32	November/December	1902	40	45–50
Vol. 3 Subtotal: 3 issues				**64 pages 16 articles**	
Grand Total, 1897–1902: 20 issues				**258 pages 50 articles**	

"Vreneli's Gärtli. Eine Zürcher Begebenheit." 2.18–19 (1899): 1–14.

"Das Montmartre–Fest in Paris." 2.18–19 (1899): 15f.

Sven Heidenstamm [= Panizza]. "Juliane Déry und was sie gemordet." 2.20–21 (1900): 1–13.

Hans Dettmar [= Panizza]. "Tristan und Isolde in Paris" [poem]. 2.20–21 (1900): 13f.

"Die Verstümmelung der Fürstendenkmäler in Berlin." 2.20–21 (1900): 15.

"Bücher-Einlauf." 2.23–24 (1900), 10–12.

Hans Dettmar [= Panizza]. "Deutschland 1899" [poem]. 2.23–24 (1900), 12.

Hans Dettmar [= Panizza]. "Tristan und Isolde in Paris." 3.25–26 (1902), 1–12.

"An unsere Abonenten." 3.25–26 (1902): 13f.

Hans Dettmar [= Panizza]. "An einen Lieblosen" [poem]. 3.25–26 (1902): 16.

Hans Kistemaecker [= Panizza]. "La danse du ventre. Eine Pariser Studje." 3.27 (1902): 1–7.

Sarcasticus [= Panizza]. "Münchner Klatsch." 3.27 (1902): 7f.

Louis Andrée [= Panizza]. "Das Schwein in poetischer, mitologischer and sittengeschichtlicher Beziehung." 3.28–32 (1902): 1–34.

"Zwei Gutenberg-Gedenk-Werke." 3.28–32 (1902): 35.

"Eine Schleswig Holstein'sche Venus." 3.28–32 (1902): 35f.

"Mania anarchista progressiva." 3.28–32 (1902): 37–39.

"Neue Wörter von Eugen Dühring." 3.28–32 (1902): 39f.

J. Schabelitz Nachf. Drukerei, exterritorjale Filjale auf dem Mond [= Panizza]. "Notgedrungene Erklärung," 3.28–32 (1902): 40.

For a more comprehensive listing, see detailed descriptions in Rolf Düsterberg, »Die gedrukte Freiheit«. Oskar Panizza und die Zürcher Diskußjonen. Europäische Hochschulschriften, Reihe I, Deutsche Sprache und Literatur, vol. 1098. Frankfurt am Main: Peter Lang, 1988; and Michael Bauer & Rolf Düsterberg, Oskar Panizza. Eine Bibliographie. Europäische Hochschulschriften, Reihe I, Deutsche Sprache und Literatur, vol. 1086. Frankfurt am Main: Peter Lang, 1988.

Panizza's Contributions to Other Periodicals and Collections (Chronological)

1890

"Der Teufel im Oberammergauer Passions-Spiel: Eine textgeschichtliche Studie mit Ausblicken auf andere Mysterien-Spiele." Die Gesellschaft 6.7 (July 1890): 997–1022.

1891

"Genie und Wahnsinn." Vortrag, gehalten in der "Gesellschaft für modernes Leben." Centralsäle, am 20. März 1891. Münchner Flugschriften 1. Serie 5 & 6. Munich: Poeßl, 1891.

"Über Selbstmord." Moderne Blätter 1.3 (11 Apr. 1891): 1–4.

Publius [= Panizza]. "Zum Kapitel der Todesstrafe. Zur Beleuchtung der Frage vom Standpunkt des Juristen aus." Moderne Blätter 1.4 (18 Apr. 1891): 3–5.

Publius [= Panizza]. "Das Vergehen wider die Religion." Moderne Blätter I/5 (25 Apr. 1891): 4f.

Isarius [=Panizza]. Rev. of Die Kreutzer-Sonate des Grafen Tolstoi vom Standpunkt der Moral. Eine Entgegnung, by Josef Clemens Kreibig [Berlin: Berend & Jolowicz, 1891]. Moderne Blätter 1.5 (25 Apr. 1891): 7.

Rev. of Das dritte Testament. Eine Offenbarung Gottes, by Hanns von Gumppenberg [Munich: Poeßl, 1891]. Moderne Blätter 1.6 (2 May 1891): 6–8.

"Mister Muybridge's Moment-Aufnahmen — und die Kunst." Moderne Blätter 1.9 (23 May 1891): 1–3.

"Theater-Koups und Machinationes: Ein geschichtlicher Überblick über Szene und Konstruktion der Mysterien-Bühne, bei Gelegenheit der Oberammergauer Passions-Aufführungen 1890," Die Gesellschaft 7.5 (May 1891): 592–614 and 7.6 (June 1891): 806–829.

Rev. of Geschichte des neueren Occultismus, by Karl Kiesewetter [Leipzig: Friedrich, 1891]. Die Gesellschaft 7.6 (June 1891): 855–857.

"Unseren Mitgliedern zur Kenntniß!" Moderne Blätter 1.11 (6 June 1891): 1–4.

"Andreas Hofer: Ein schwäbisches Bauernspiel aus dem Allgäu." Die Gesellschaft 7.7 (July 1891): 885–893.

Publius [= Panizza]. "An unser aller Mutter." Moderne Blätter 1.14 (4 July 1891): 7.

"Magdalenenfest." Moderne Blätter 1.17 (25 July 1891): 5f.

"Parsifal." Moderne Blätter 1.18 (1 Aug. 1891): 1–3.

"Tannhäuser." Moderne Blätter 1.18 (1 Aug. 1891): 3–5.

"Tristan und Isolde in Bayreuth." Moderne Blätter 1.19 (8 Aug. 1891): 2–5.

"Stossseufzer aus Bayreuth." Die Gesellschaft 7.9 (Sept. 1891): 1361–1370.

"Die moderne Litteratur und die künstlerische Freiheit." Moderne Blätter 1.29 (17 Oct. 1891): 1–3.

Publius [= Panizza]. "Kirchenmoral und Staatsmoral." Moderne Blätter 1.30 (24 Oct. 1891): 5f.

"Litteratur und Kritik." Moderne Blätter 1.31 (31 Oct. 1891): 1–3.

"Zum Tag aller Seelen." Moderne Blätter 1.33 (14 Nov. 1891): 5.

Rev. of Neue dramatische Wirkungen auf Grund einer neuen Bühnenform, by Alfred Clausius [Munich: Albert, 1891]. Die Gesellschaft 7.12 (Dec. 1891): 1673f.

"Beelzebub" in Modernes Leben. Ein Sammelbuch der Münchner Modernen. 1. Reihe. Munich: Poeßl, 1891: 119–122.

"Die drei Parzen" in Sommerfest. Ein moderner Musen-Almanach. 1. Reihe. Munich: Albert, 1891: 46f.

"Das Verbrechen in Tavistock-Square." Modernes Leben. Ein Sammelbuch der Münchner Modernen. 1. Reihe. Munich: Poeßl, 1891: 109–118.

1892

Rev. of *In Dingsda,* by Johannes Schlaf [Berlin: Fischer, 1892]. *Die Gesellschaft* 8.3 (Mar. 1892): 385f.

"Hansens Menschen-Diagnose." *Das Magazin für Litteratur* 61.22 (28 May 1892): 360.

Rev. of *Frühlings Erwachen,* by Frank Wedekind [Zürich: Groß, 1891]. *Die Gesellschaft* 8.5 (May 1892): 652–655.

Rev. of *Ludwig der Bayer oder der Streit von Mühldorf. Vaterländisches Schauspiel in fünf Akten,* by Martin Greif [Stuttgart/Leipzig/Berlin: Deutsche Verlags-Anstalt, 1891]. *Die Gesellschaft* 8.7 (July 1892): 954f.

"Prostitution: Eine Gegenwartsstudie." *Die Gesellschaft* 8.9 (September 1892): 1159–1183.

Rev. of *Lieder eines Menschen,* by Ludwig Scharf [Munich: Albert, 1892]. *Die Gesellschaft* 8.12 (Dec. 1892): 1648f.

"Die Unsittlichkeitsentrüstung der Pietisten und die freie Literatur." Vortrag, gehalten von Dr. Oskar Panizza am VII. öffentlichen Abend der "Gesellschaft für modernes Leben" im großen Saal der Isarlust, 2 Dez. 1891. *Gegen Prüderie und Lüge.* Munich: Ernst, 1892: 7–25.

1893

" Stauffer-Bern." *Die Gesellschaft* 9.2 (Feb. 1893): 261.

Rev. of *Briefe berühmter Zeitgenossen an Wilhelm Freiherrn von Hammerstein, Chefredakteur der Neuen Preußischen* [Kreuz-] *Zeitung* [Zürich: Schabelitz, 1892]. *Die Gesellschaft* 9.2 (Feb. 1893): 261f.

"Prolegomena zum Preisausschreiben: Verbesserung unserer Rasse." *Die Gesellschaft* 9.3 (Mar. 1893): 275–289.

"Luther und die Ehe: Eine Verteidigung gegen Verleumdung." *Die Gesellschaft* 9.3 (Mar. 1893): 355–363.

Rev. of *Golgatha,* by M. Weißenfels [Zürich: Schabelitz 1892]. *Die Gesellschaft* 9.3 (Mar. 1893): 240f.

"Die unbefleckte Empfängnis der Päpste." *Der arme Teufel* 9.15/431 (4 Mar. 1893): 105f., 16/432 (11 Mar. 1893): 113f., 17/433 (18 Mar. 1893): 121f., 18/434 (25 Mar. 1893): 129f.

Rev. of *Lebensstücke. Ein Novellen- und Skizzenbuch,* by Anna Croissant-Rust [Munich: Albert, 1893]. *Die Gesellschaft* 9.7 (July 1893): 929–933.

"Die *Monita secreta* der Jesuiten." *Die Gesellschaft* 9.8 (Aug. 1893): 956–977.

Rev. of *Dies irae und andere Gedichte,* by Georg Schaumberg [Munich: Albert, 1893]. *Die Gesellschaft* 9.8 (Aug. 1893): 1074f.

"Ein Besuch bei den Sezessionisten in München." *Die Gesellschaft* 9.9 (Sept. 1893): 1194–1201.

Rev. of *Die Menschwerdung,* by J. G. Vogt [Leipzig 1892]. *Die Gesellschaft* 9.9 (Sept. 1893): 1218.

Rev. of *Anton von Werner und die Berliner Hofmalerei* by Friedrich von Khaynach [Zürich: Schabelitz, 1893]. *Die Gesellschaft* 9.10 (Oct. 1893): 1365.

Rev. of *Die zehn Gebote der Jesuiten. Aus den Hauptwerken der Jesuiten zusammengestellt mit genauer Quellen-Angabe,* by Adolf Brodbeck [Zürich: Schabelitz, 1894]. *Die Gesellschaft* 9.12 (Dec. 1893): 1632f.

"Heil'ge Drei König," *Moderner Musenalmanach auf das Jahr 1893. Ein Sammelbuch deutscher Kunst,* ed. Otto Julius Bierbaum. Munich: Albert, 1894: 106f.

1894

"Graf Hönsbröch." *Neue Deutsche Rundschau* 5.1 (Jan. 1894): 110f.

"Münchner Brief." *Neue Deutsche Rundschau* 5.1 (Jan. 1894): 97f.

"Die Haberfeldtreiben im bayrischen Gebirge." *Neue Deutsche Rundschau* 5.1 (Jan. 1894): 37–56.

Rev. of *Handbuch des Socialismus,* by Carl Stegmann & C. Hugo [Zürich: Schabelitz 1894]. *Die Gesellschaft* 10.1 (Jan. 1894): 133f.

Rev. of *Das Evangelium eines armen Sünders,* by Wilhelm Weitling [Munich: Ernst, 1894]. *Die Gesellschaft* 10.1 (Jan. 1894): 134f.

Rev. of *Aber die Liebe. Ein Ehemanns- und Menschenbuch,* by Richard Dehmel [Munich: Albert, 1893]. *Die Gesellschaft* 10.1 (Jan. 1894): 152.

"Der heilige Staatsanwalt. Eine moralische Komödie." *Der arme Teufel* 10.481 (17 Feb. 1894): 102f. and 10.482 (24 Feb. 1894): 110f.

Rev. of *Pierrot Lunaire,* by Albert Giraud, trans. Otto Erich Hartleben [Berlin: Verlag Deutscher Phantasten, 1893]. *Die Gesellschaft* 10.2 (Feb. 1894): 256f.

Rev. of *Der Kuß. Ein Capriccio,* by Gustav Falke [Munich: Albert, n.d.]. *Die Gesellschaft* 10.2 (Feb. 1894): 260.

Rev. of *Geschichte des deutschen Volkes seit dem Ausgang des Mittelalters,* by Johannes Janssen. Bd. 7. Schulen und Universitäten. Wissenschaft und Bildung bis zum Beginn des dreißigjährigen Krieges [Freiburg. Br.: Herder, 1893]. *Die Gesellschaft* 10.3 (Mar. 1894): 394f.

Rev. of *Feuer! Eine Klostergeschichte,* by Marie Conrad-Ramlo [Munich: Albert, n.d.]. *Die Gesellschaft* 10.3 (Mar. 1894): 682f.

"Kunst und Polizei." *Neue Deutsche Rundschau* 5.3 (Mar. 1894): 309–311.

"An einen Unterfranken." *Zum 70. Geburtstag, 19. März 1894, des alten Wotan, unseres lieben und verehrten Oberst Heinrich von Reder. Aus dem Münchner Freundeskreis.* Munich: Albert, 1894: 4f.

"Münchner Theaterbrief." *Neue Deutsche Rundschau* 5.4 (Apr. 1894): 417–419.

Rev. of *Zwischenspiel,* by Karl Henckell [Zürich: Schabelitz, 1894]. *Die Gesellschaft* 10.5 (May 1894): 685f.

"Münchner Brief." *Neue Deutsche Rundschau* 5.5 (May 1894): 519–522.

"Dr. Sigl, der Redakteur des *Bayr. Vaterland.*" *Die Gesellschaft* 10.5 (May 1894): 702–704.

"Die Frühjahrs-Ausstellung der Münchner Sezessionisten." *Die Gesellschaft* 10.6 (June 1894): 789–794.

"Die Gemälde-Gallerie des Grafen Schack." *Der Zuschauer* 2.11 (1 June 1894): 501–504.

"Kunst and Künstlerisches aus München." *Der Zuschauer* 2.14 (15 July 1894): 64–67.

"Die 'unsittlichen' Gebrüder Grimm und die neue 'Sittlichkeit' jüdisch-deutscher Verlagsbuchhändler."

Die Gesellschaft 10.7 (July 1894): 919–924. Reprinted in *Neue Bahnen* 4.4 (15 Feb. 1904): 141–144.

Rev. of *Seiner Heiligkeit Papst Alexander VI. Bulle "In rebus amoris,"* by Ludwig Scharf [Zürich: Schabelitz, 1894]. *Die Gesellschaft* 10.7 (July 1894): 956f.

Rev. of *Ultra Violett. Einsame Poesien,* by Maximilian Dauthendey [Berlin: Haase, 1893]. *Die Gesellschaft* 10.8 (Aug. 1894): 1100–1102.

"Der teutsche Michel und der römische Papst." [Excerpt] *Der arme Teufel* 10.517 (27 Oct. 1894): 388.

Das Liebesconzil. Eine Himmelstragödie in fünf Aufzügen. [Act II] *Der arme Teufel* 10.519 (10 Nov. 1894): 393f.

"Die Wallfahrt nach Andechs: Ein oberbairisches Sittenbild." *Der Zuschauer* 2.23 (1 Dec. 1894): 496–505 and 2.24 (15 Dec. 1894): 543–555.

"Pastor Johannes," *Moderner Musenalmanach auf das Jahr 1894. Ein Jahr deutscher Kunst, 2. Jahrgang,* ed. Otto Julius Bierbaum. Munich: Albert, 1894: 62–71.

"Die Haberfeldtreiben im bayrischen Gebirge." *Der Sammler.* Belletristische Beilage zur *Augsburger Abendzeitung* 63.129.

1895

"Bayreuth und die Homosexualität: Eine Erwägung." *Die Gesellschaft* 11.1 (Jan. 1895): 88–92.

Rev. of *Nemt, Frouwe, disen Kranz. Ausgewählte Gedichte,* by Otto Julius Bierbaum [Berlin: Schuhr, 1894], *Die Gesellschaft* 11.1 (Jan. 1895): 119f.

"Le Magazine International." *Die Gesellschaft* 11.2 (Feb. 1895): 280f.

"Bayreuth und die Homosexualität. Eine Erwägung," *Der arme Teufel* 11.539 (30 Mar. 1895): 147 and 11.540 (6 Apr. 1895): 154f.

Rev. of *Goethe-Brevier. Goethes Leben in seinen Gedichten,* ed. Otto Erich Hartleben [Munich: Schüler, 1895]. *Die Gesellschaft* 11.4 (Apr. 1895): 577f.

Rev. of *Varusschlacht. Ein Fastnachtsspiel in drei Aufzügen,* by Hans Merian [Leipzig: Friedrich, 1894], *Die Gesellschaft* 11.6 (June 1895): 842–844.

"Die deutschen Symbolisten." *Die Gegenwart* 47.13 (30 Mar. 1895): 201–204.

"Die deutschen Symbolisten." *Der Kunstwart* VIII/16 (May 1895), 246–249.

"Das menschliche Hirn... ." *Die Geißel* 1.17 (25 May 1895), Beilage: 9.

"Katholische Irrenbehandlung." *Das Magazin für Litteratur.* 64.25 (22 June 1895): 773–777.

"Unsere Konversationslexika von jetzt und ehedem," *Internationaler Litteraturbericht* 2 (1895): 291–293.

1896

— zz —[= Panizza]. Rev. of *Angelus Silesius,* by Otto Erich Hartleben [Dresden: Bondi, 1896]. *Die Gesellschaft* 12.2 (Feb. 1896): 272f.

— zz —[= Panizza]. Rev. of *Es fiel ein Reif. Drama in einem Akt,* by Juliane Déry [Berlin: Fischer, 1896]. *Die Gesellschaft* 12.2 (Feb. 1896): 274–276.

Jules Saint-Froid [= Panizza]. "Die geisteskranken Psychiater." *Die Gesellschaft* 12.3 (Mar. 1896): 362–367.

— zz —[= Panizza]. Rev. of M. G. Conrad, *In purpurner Finsternis. Roman Improvisation aus dem dreißigsten Jahrhundert* [Berlin: Verein für freies Schriftthum, 1895]. *Die Gesellschaft* 12.3 (Mar. 1896): 405–407.

— zz —[= Panizza]. Rev. of *Der fünfte Prophet,* by Hanns von Gumppenberg [Berlin: Verein für freies Schriftthum, 1895]. *Die Gesellschaft* 12.3 (Mar. 1896): 407.

— zz —[= Panizza]. Rev. of *Goethes Sonnetenkranz,* by Kuno Fischer [Heidelberg: Winter, 1896]. *Die Gesellschaft* 12.3 (Mar. 1896): 426f.

— zz —[= Panizza]. Rev. of *Die Freiersfahrten und Freiersmeinungen des weiberfeindlichen Herrn Pankrazius Graunzer der Schönen Wissenschaften Doktor nebst einem Anhange wie schließlich alles ausgelaufen,* by Otto Julius Bierbaum [Berlin: Verein für freies Schriftthum, 1896]. *Die Gesellschaft* 12.4 (Apr. 1896): 539–541.

— zz —[= Panizza]. Rev. of *Der Erdgeist. Eine Tragödie,* by Frank Wedekind [Paris/Leipzig: Langen, 1896]. *Die Gesellschaft* 12.5 (May 1896): 693–695.

Jules Saint-Froid [= Panizza]. Rev. of *De Profundis,* by Stanislaw Przybyszewski [Berlin: Storm 1895]. *Die Gesellschaft* 12.6 (June 1896): 781–786.

Jules Saint-Froid [= Panizza]. "Neues aus dem Hexenkessel der Wahnsinns-Fanatiker." *Die Gesellschaft* 12.7 (July 1896): 938–943.

— zz —[= Panizza]. Rev. of *Karla Bühring. Ein Frauendrama in vier Acten,* by Laura Marholm [Paris/Leipzig: Langen, 1896]. *Die Gesellschaft* 12.7 (July 1896): 970–972.

Jules Saint-Froid [= Panizza]. "Das Fronleichnamfest. Eine Verkehrsstudie" *Die Gesellschaft* 12.8 (Aug. 1896): 1068–1072.

— zz —[= Panizza]. Rev. of *Über Reform der Irrenpflege,* by Friedrich Scholz [Leipzig: Mayer, 1896]. *Die Gesellschaft* 12.8 (Aug. 1896): 1112.

Episcopus [=Panizza]. Rev. of *Die Greuel der Jesuiten! Ein Mahnwort in letzter Stunde* (anon. Pamphlet). [Leipzig: Felix Simon, 1896]. *Die Gesellschaft* 12.8 (Aug. 1896): 1110–1112.

"Mefisto." *Mephisto* 1.1 (26 Sept. 1896): 2f.

"Der Klassizismus und das Eindringen des Variété. Eine Studie über zeitgenössischen Geschmack." *Die Gesellschaft* 12.10 (Oct. 1896): 1252–1274.

"Mefisto auf Reisen." *Mephisto* 1.4 (17 Oct. 1896): 5.

"Lieben Freunde!" *Mephisto* 1.11 (5 Dec. 1896): 3.

"Richard von Meerheim." *Das Magazin für Litteratur* 65.4 (1896): 131.

"Die Gelbe Kroete." *Pan* 2.3 (Dec. 1896): 185–191.

1897

"Der Fall Miss Vaughan." *Wiener Rundschau* 1.4 (1 Jan. 1897): 147–152.

"Haberfeldtreiben. Über einen internationalen heidnisch-christlichen Kern in den 'Haberfeldtreiben.'" *Wiener Rundschau* 1.7 (15 Feb. 1897): 261–267.

"Die sexuelle Belastung der Psyche als Quelle künst-lerischer Inspiration." *Wiener Rundschau* 1.9 (15 Mar. 1897): 349–353.

"Leo Taxil und seine Puppen." *Wiener Rundschau* 1.19 (15 Aug. 1897): 742–749.

"Die Heilsarmee: Eine Studie." *Wiener Rundschau* 2.2 (1 Dec. 1897): 52–55.

1898

"Über das Küssen." *Wiener Rundschau* 2.4 (1 Jan. 1898): 129–132.

1899

"Der Papst." *Wiener Rundschau* 3.11 (April 1899): 253–255.

1900

"Brief aus Paris. Der Quatorze Juillet." *Wiener Rundschau* 4.16 (Aug. 1900): 279–282.

"Arthur Rimbaud." *Wiener Rundschau* 4.19 (Oct. 1900): 332–336.

Kalypso [= Panizza]. "Pariser Brief." *Sächsische Arbeiter-Zeitung* 11.300 (29 Dec. 1900): 1. Beilage (supplement).

1901

"Pariser Brief." *Neue Bahnen* 1.2 (15 Jan. 1901): 48–50.

"Der Goldregen." *Neue Bahnen* 1.12 (June 15 1901): 491–496.

1902

Richard Strauss. *Acht Lieder für eine Singstimme mit Klavierbegleitung.* "Sie wissen's nicht" = "Maiden and nightingale." Op. 49, no. 5. Musical score (soprano) for German poem with Engl. trans. Paul England. Berlin: Adolph Fürstner, 1902.

Republication of Panizza's Works in German (Chronological)

Das Liebeskonzil. Eine Himmelstragödie in fünf Aufzü-gen. Illus. Alfred Kubin. Munich: Gesellschaft Münchner Bibliophilen, 1913.

Visionen der Dämmerung. Introd. Hannes Ruch [Richard Weinhöppel]. Afterword by Hanns Heinz Ewers. Illus. Paul Haase. Munich & Leipzig: Georg Müller, 1914. (2nd ed. 1923, 3rd ed. 1929.)

"Der Goldregen." *Humorbuch. Deutsche Dichter aus fünf Jahrhunderten.* Ed. Richard Rieß. Munich: Müller, 1918: 281–297.

"Das Wirtshaus zur Dreifaltigkeit." *Die Welt-Literatur* 19 (1919): 1–5.

"Der operirte Jud." *Die Welt-Literatur* 19 (1919): 5–10.

"Der Mucker." *Die Weltbühne* 18.12 (23 Mar. 1922): 306.

"Der operirte Jud.'" *Münchener Beobachter.* Daily suppl. to *Völkischer Beobachter* 40.259–264 (10–16 Nov. 1927).

"Aussprüche." Erste Veröffentlichung der Panizza-Gesellschaft in Berlin, 1929.

Deutsche Thesen gegen den Papst und seine Dunkelmän-ner. Berlin: Nordland, 1940.

Aus Werk und Leben. Ed. Kurt Eggers. Berlin: Nord-land, 1943.

Die unbefleckte Empfängnis der Päpste, von Bruder Martin O.S.B., aus dem Spanischen von Oskar Panizza. Berlin: Nordland, 1943.

Das Liebeskonzil. Eine Himmels-Tragödie in fünf Aufzügen. Facsim. of 1st ed. Glücksburg (Ostsee): Petersen Press, 1962.

Das Liebeskonzil. Eine Himmels-Tragödie in fünf Auf-zügen. Facsim. of 1st ed. Berlin (West): Petersen Press, 1964.

Das Liebeskonzil und andere Schriften. Ed. Hans Prescher. Neuwied: Luchterhand, 1964.

Laokoon oder Über die Grenzen der Mezgerei. Eine Schlangenstudie. Facsim. of MS. Illus. Otto Greiner. Munich: Laokoon, 1966.

"Das Verbrechen in Tavistock Square." *Brevier des schwarzen Humors.* Ed. Gerd Henninger. Munich: dtv, 1966: 128–136.

"Der Goldregen." *Die goldene Bombe. Expressionistische Märchendichtungen und Grotesken.* Ed. Hartmut Geerken. Darmstadt: Agora, 1970: 290–301.

"Die Menschenfabrik." *Widerspruch. Lesebuch für den Deutschunterricht.* Ed. Marianne Schmitz. Pader-born: Schöningh, 1971: 205–211.

"Das Wirtshaus zur Dreifaltigkeit." *Märchen deutscher Dichter.* Ed. Elisabeth Borchers. Frankfurt/M: Insel, 1972: 14–39.

Das Liebeskonzil. Eine Himmelstragödie in fünf Aufzü-gen. In: *Theater heute* 14.10 (Oct. 1973): 13–24.

"Das Wachsfigurenkabinett." *Prosa des Naturalismus.* Ed. Gerhard Schulz. Stuttgart: Reclam, 1973.

Das Liebeskonzil. Eine Himmels-Tragödie in fünf Auf-zügen. Ed. Hans Prescher. Frankfurt/Main: Fischer, 1976.

"Das Verbrechen in Tavistock-Square." *Die rote Rose Leidenschaft.* Ed. Marie Madeleine [von Puttkam-mer]. Munich: Matthes & Seitz, 1977: 239–251.

Aus dem Tagebuch eines Hundes. Mit einem Vorspann für Leser von Martin Langbein und mit Zeichnungen von R. Hoberg. Munich: Matthes & Seitz, 1977.

Ein guter Kerl. In: *Naturalismus. Deutsche Literatur in Text und Darstellung,* vol. 12. Ed. Walter Schmäh-ling. Stuttgart: Reclam, 1977: 158–175.

Die kriminelle Psychose, genannt Psichopatia criminalis. Hilfsbuch für Ärzte, Laien, Juristen, Vormünder, Verwaltungsbeamte, Minister, etc. zur Diagnose der poli-tischen Gehirnerkrankung. Mit Vorworten von Bernd Mattheus und mit Beiträgen von Oswald Wiener und Gerd Bergfleth. Ed. Bernd Mattheus. [Incl. *Genie und Wahnsinn, Der Illusionismus und die Rettung der Persönlichkeit, Christus in psi-cho-patologischer Beleuchtung, Abschied von München*]. Kuku, vol 9. Munich: Matthes & Seitz, 1978.

"Selbstbiographie." *Tintenfisch 13.* Berlin: Klaus Wagenbach, 1978.

Dialoge im Geiste Huttens. Mit einem Vowort von

Heiner Müller, Panizzajana von Bernd Mattheus und Beiträgen im Geiste Panizzas von Karl Günther Hufnagel und Peter Erlach. Munich: Matthes & Seitz, 1979.

Abschied von München. Ein Handschlag. Erlangen & Munich: Renner, 1979.

"Über die Deutschen. Dialog zwischen einem Optimisten und einem Peßimisten." *Frankfurter Rundschau* 35.179 (4 Aug. 1979): 3.

"Der Goldregen." *Märchen des Expressionismus.* Ed. Hartmut Geerken. Frankfurt/M.: Fischer, 1979: 263–274.

"Abschied von München." *Aus Liebe zu Deutschland. Satiren zu Franz Josef Strauß.* Ed. Heinar Kipphardt. Munich: Autoren Edition, 1980: 29–35.

Das Liebeskonzil. Eine Himmelstragödie in fünf Aufzügen. In: *Dramen des deutschen Naturalismus.* Ed. Roy C. Cowan. 2 vols. Munich: Winkler, 1981: I, 645–699.

Der Korsettenfritz. Gesammelte Erzählungen. Munich: Matthes & Seitz, 1981.

"Agnes Blannbekin, eine österreichische Schwärmerin aus dem 13. Jahrhundert, nach den Quellen." *Ich habe einen Körper.* Ed. Claudia Gehrke. Munich: Matthes & Seitz, 1981: 49–75.

Das Liebeskonzil. Eine Himmelstragödie in fünf Aufzügen. Mit Materialien zum Film von Werner Schroeter [incl. "Meine Verteidigungsrede in Sachen 'Das Liebeskonzil' vor dem königlichen Landgericht München I" and "Urteil und Urteilsbegründung"]. Sammlung Luchterhand no. 388. Darmstadt & Neuwied: Luchterhand, 1982.

"Die Kirche von Zinsblech" und andere teuflische Geschichten. Bergisch Gladbach: n.p., 1982.

"Die Kirche von Zinsblech." *Die Nebeldroschke. Deutschsprachige Gespenstergeschichten.* Ed. Herbert Greiner-Mai. Berlin (East): Verlag Das neue Berlin, 1982: 315. 2nd ed. 1986, 3rd ed. 1989.

Oskar Panizza, Werner Schroeter, Antonio Salines. *Liebeskonzil-Filmbuch.* Ed. Peter Berling. Incl. screenplay, 80 color photos. Munich: Schirmer/Mosel, 1982.

"Die Menschenfabrik." *Phantastische Erzählungen der Jahrhundertwende.* Ed. Michael Winkler. Stuttgart: Reclam, 1982: 23–43.

Die Menschenfabrik und andere Erzählungen. Ed. Walter Rösler. Illus. Reinhard Zabka. Berlin (East): Buchverlag Der Morgen, 1984. 2nd. Ed. 1989.

Eine Mondgeschichte. Cotta's Bibliothek der Moderne 34. Stuttgart: Klett-Cotta, 1985.

Die kriminelle Psychose, genannt Psichopatia criminalis. Hilfsbuch für Ärzte, Laien, Juristen, Vormünder, Verwaltungsbeamte, Minister etc. zur Diagnose der politischen Gehirnerkrankung. Ed. Bernd Mattheus. [Incl. *Genie und Wahnsinn, Der Illusionismus und die Rettung der Persönlichkeit, Christus in psychopatologischer Beleuchtung, Abschied von München*]. 2nd rev. ed. Munich: Matthes & Seitz, 1985.

Neues aus dem Hexenkessel der Wahnsinnsfanatiker und andere Schriften. Ed. Michael Bauer. Sammlung Luchterhand 622. Darmstadt: Luchterhand, 1986.

"Ein Kapitel aus der Pastoralmedizin." *Das Hausbuch*

der literarischen Hochkomik. Ed. Bernd Eilert. Zürich: Haffmanns Verlag, 1987.

"Das Verbrechen von Tavistock-Square." *Der Polizeidiener in der Rattenfalle. Kriminalhumoresken aus aller Welt.* Illus. Volker Pfuller. Berlin (East): Verlag Das neue Berlin, 1987: 386.

Das Liebeskonzil. Eine Himmels-Tragödie in fünf Aufzügen. Ed. Michael Bauer. Darmstadt: Luchterhand Literaturverlag, 1988.

Pour Gambetta. Sämtliche in der Prinzhorn-Sammlung der Psychiatrischen Universitätsklink Heidelberg und im Landeskirchlichen Archiv Nürnberg aufbewahrte Zeichnungen. Ed. Armin Abmeier, Michael Farin, Roland Hepp. Munich: Belleville, 1989.

Oskar Panizzas Das Liebeskonzil. Ed. Joseph Berlinger. Munich: Kuckuck & Straps, 1990.

Das Liebeskonzil. Eine Himmelstragödie in fünf Aufzügen. Ed. Michael Bauer. Facsim. of 1913 ed. Munich: Spangenberg, 1991.

Psichopatia Criminalis. Oktav 3. Berlin: octOpus, 1991.

Mama Venus. Texte zu Religion, Sexus und Wahn. Ed. Michael Bauer. Sammlung Luchterhand 1025. Hamburg: Luchterhand Literaturverlag, 1992.

Imperjalja. Manuskript Germ. Qu. 1838 der Handschriftenabteilung der Staatlichen Museen Preussischer Kulturbesitz zu Berlin. Ed. Jürgen Müller. Hürtgenwald: Guido Pressler, 1993.

Das Schwein in poetischer, mitologischer und sittengeschichtlicher Beziehung. Ed. Rolf Düsterberg, Illus. Günter Brus. Munich: Belleville, 1994.

Eine Mondgeschichte. Gifkendorf: Merlin Verag, 1995.

Das Liebeskonzil. Eine Himmelstragödie in fünf Aufzügen. Ed. Michael Bauer. Munich: Luchterhand, 1997.

Ein Skandalöser Fall. Geschichten. Munich: Martus, 1997.

Deutsche Thesen gegen den Papst und seine Dunkelmänner. Facsim. of 1940 ed. Viöl: Verlag für ganzheitliche Forschung und Kultur, 1997.

"Ein scandalöser Fall." Herculine Barbin, *Über Hermaphrodismus.* Ed. Wolfgang Schäffner et al. Gender Studies, Edition Suhrkamp, Neue Folge, 733. Frankfurt/Main: Suhrkamp, 1998.

"Bayreuth und die Homosexualität." *Tannhäuser und andere Texte über Richard Wagner und Bayreuth.* Zur Ausstellung "Tannhäuser und Co." im Bayreuther Plakatmuseum, Sommer 2002. Bayreuth: n.p., 2002.

Der heilige Staatsanwalt. Illus. Klaus Waschk. Leipzig: Faber & Faber, 2002.

Die Menschenfabrik. Hörspiel mit Ute Springer, Thomas Gerber, Martin Engler. Ed. & dir. Christoph Kalkowski. Music by Schlammpeitziger. Berlin: Audio Verlag, 2002. CD with booklet.

Fränkische Erzählungen. Ed. Klaus Gasseleder. Bamberg: Kleebaum Verlag, 2003.

"Ein Poet, der umsunst gelebt hat" et al. Schultz, Joachim, ed. *Katalog zur Ausstellung zum 150. Geburtstag von Oskar Panizza. Hefte für angewandte Literaturwissenschaft (HAGEL) Nr.3.* Bayreuth: Bayreuth Univ., 2003.

Der teutsche Michel und der römische Papst. Altes und

Neues aus dem Kampfe des Teutschtums gegen römisch-wälsche Überlistung und Bevormundung in 666 Tesen und Zitaten. Ed. Michael Bauer. Edition Monacensia. Facsim. of 1894 ed. Munich: Allitera Verlag, 2003.

Das Rothe Haus. Ein Lesebuch zu Religion, Sexus und Wahn. Ed. Michael Bauer. Edition Monacensia. Munich: Allitera Verlag, 2003.

Das Liebeskonzil. Eine Himmels-Tragödie in fünf Aufzügen. Ed. and introd. Peter D.G. Brown. Facsim. and transcription of handwritten MS, 1st, 2nd and 3rd eds. *Meine Verteidigung in Sachen »Das Liebeskonzil«.* Munich: Belleville, 2005.

Translations of Works by Oskar Panizza (Chronological)

Tajemné príbehy. Trans. Emanuel Lešehrad. Praha: A. Hynek, 1913.

Le Concile d'amour: tragédie céleste en 5 actes par Oscar Panizza / Zürich. 1895. Trans. Jean Bréjoux. Pref. André Breton. Paris: Jean-Jacques Pauvert, 1960. 2nd ed. 1969.

"Le crime de Tavistock-Square" and "Un chapitre de la medecine pastorale." Trans. Jean Bréjoux, *La Breche: Action Surrealiste* (Paris), no. 3, 1962.

Het Liefdesconcilie: Een Hemelse Tragedie in Vijf Bedrijven. Trans. Yves van Domber, Randstad (Amsterdam), no. 7, 1964.

Concilio d'amore e Altri scritti. Trans. Enrico Filippini. Milano: Editoriale Contra, 1966.

Het Liefdesconcilie en andere vreemde geschriften. Ed. and trans. Yves van Domber. Grote ABC no. 78. Amsterdam: ABC-boeken De Arbeiderspers, 1967.

The Love Council: A Heavenly Tragedy in Five Acts. Trans. Peter D.G. Brown. Unpubl. bound script. New York: Studio Duplicating Service, 1969.

L'Immaculée Conception des Papes. Trans. Jean Bréjoux. Paris: Jean-Jacques Pauvert 1971.

Il concilio d'amore. Tragedia celeste in 5 atti. Trans. Paolo Bonacelli and Mario Missiroli. Sipario (1972), no. 310: 71–88.

The Council of Love: A Celestial Tragedy in Five Acts. Trans. Oreste F. Pucciani. Introd. André Breton. Illus. Leonor Fini. Photos by Nicolas Treatt. New York: Viking, 1973.

O concílio do amor. Trans. Luiza Neto Jorge. Lisboa: Editorial Estampa, 1974.

Le Concile d'amour. 22 original tinted dry point etchings by Leonor Fini. Genève: Grafik Europa Anstalt, 1975.

Concilio de amor: una tragedia celestial. Trans. Pedro Madrigal. Totum revolutum 5. Barcelona: Icaria Editorial, 1977.

El concilio del amor. Trans. Josep Elias. Introd. André Breton. La nave de lo locos 37. Mexico: Premia editora, 1978.

Un scandale au couvent. Trans. and introd. Jean Bréjoux. Pref. Hannes Ruch. Illus. Carlo Berté. Paris: la Différence, 1979.

"A Scandal at the Convent." *Herculine Barbin: Being the Recently Discovered Memoirs of a Nineteenth Century Hermaphrodite.* Trans. S. Wilkins. Introd. Michel Foucault. Brighton (England): Harvester Press, 1980: 155–224. Also publ. by Pantheon Books in New York: Random House, 1980.

"The Operated Jew." Trans. Jack Zipes. *New German Critique* 21 (1980): 63–80.

Journal d'un Chien. Trans. Dominique Dubuy and Claude Riehl. Paris: Plasma, 1981. 2nd ed. 1983.

Le Concile d'amour: Tragédie céleste — Zürich, 1895. Ed. Jean-Michel Palmier. Trans. Jean Bréjoux. Grenoble: Presses Universitaires de Grenoble, 1983.

Sanmi ittaitei. Trans. Suehiro Tanemura. Akashi: Nankashokyoku, 1983.

Psichopatia criminalis. Istruzioni per indagini psichiatriche e diagnosi scientifiche sulle malattie cerebrali per perizie legali. Per medici, profani, giuristi, tutori, funzionari pubblici, ministri, ecc. Trans. Andrea Chersi. Bagnolo Mella (Brescia, It.): n.p., 1985.

Psychopathia criminalis: instructions à l'usage des médecins et des profanes, des juristes, tuteurs, fonctionnaires de l'administration, ministres... Trans. Pierre Gallisaires. Paris: Ludd, 1986.

Le Concile d'amour. [Erotic comic book.] Illus. Serge Zubeldia. Adapt. Julien Grycan. Paris: Éditions Leroy, 1987.

Het Liefdesconcilie. [Erotic comic book.] Illus. Serge Zubeldia. Adapt. J.M. Lo Duca. Follies 5. Antwerp: Loempia, 1987.

Il Concilio d'amore Et cœtera et cœtera. Trans. Andrea Chersi. Introd. André Breton. Salorino, Switzerland: Edizioni L'Affranchi, 1988.

Dal diario di un cane e Altri scritti. Trans. Andrea Chersi. Salorino, Switzerland: Edizioni L'Affranchi, 1988.

Journal d'un chien. Trans. Dominique Dubuy and Claude Riehl. Collection Griffures. Paris: Editions de l'Instant, 1988.

Psychopathia Criminalis, guia para a avaliação psiquiátrica e definição científica das doenças mentais declaradas necessárias pelo tribunal; para uso de médicos, leigos, juristas, tutores... Trans. Cristina Terra da Motta and José M. Justo. Lisboa: Edições Antígona, 1989.

Un scandale au couvent: Nouvelles. Trans. Jean Bréjoux. Paris: La Différence, 1989.

Le Concile d'amour. [Erotic comic book.] Illus. Serge Zubeldia. Adapt. Julien Grycan. BD Adulte 146. Paris: J'ai lu BD, 1989.

Dal Diario di un Cane. Trans. Andrea Chersi. Trento: L'Editore, 1989.

Cuentos de un Alienista. Trans. Anke Sigerist and Agustín Izquierdo. Madrid: Valdemar Ediciones, 1989. 2nd ed. 2000.

Histoire de lune. Trans. Dominique Dubuy and Claude Riehl. Strasbourg: Circé, 1990.

La Manufacture d'Hommes et autres Nouvelles. Trans. Patrice Neau. Paris: Ludd, 1990.

Koncil o ljubavi: izbor iz djela. Trans. [*Das Liebeskonzil*, Serbo-Croation] Leo Držić. Biblioteka Zora 43. Zagreb: Graficki zavod Hrvatske, 1990.

Panittsua zenshu. [Collected works.] Trans. Suehiro Tanemura. 3 vols. Tokyo: Chikumashobo, 1991.

L'Immacolata Concezione dei Papi. Trans. Andrea Chersi. Salorino, Switzerland: Edizioni L'Affranchi, 1991.

"The Operated Jew." *The Operated Jew: Two Tales of Anti-Semitism.* Ed. and trans. Jack Zipes. New York: Routledge, 1991: 47–74.

The Council of Love: A Heavenly Tragedy in Five Acts. Trans. Malcom Green. Illus. Alfred Kubin. London: Atlas Press, 1992.

Génie et Folie: Conférence Prononcée le 20 Mars 1891, dans le Cadre des Activités de la Société pour une Vie Moderne, suivi de Psychopathia criminalis. Trans. Pierre Gallissaires. Paris: Ludd, 1993.

"The Crime in Tavistock Square." *The Golden Bomb: Phantastic German Expressionist Stories.* Ed., trans. and introd. Malcom Green. Edinburgh: Polygon, 1993: 36–45.

Le Concile d'amour. Trans. and introd. Jean Bréjoux. Pref. André Breton. Paris: Éditions Autrement, 1994.

Journal d'un chien. Trans. Dominique Dubuy and Claude Riehl. Illus. Henri Cueco. Paris: Ludd, 1994.

Écrits de prison: Un an de prison. Dialogues dans l'esprit de Hutten. Adieu à Munich. Trans. Pierre Galissaires. Paris: Ludd, 1994.

L'illusionnisme et le Salut de la personnalité, suivi de La Surcharge sexuelle de la psyché comme source de l'inspiration artistique et de Le Christ à la lumière de la psychopathologie. Trans. Pierre Galissaires. Paris: Ludd, 1995.

Le Crapaud jaune et autres récits. Trans. Pierre Galissaires. Paris: Ludd, 1996. 2nd ed. 2001. 3rd ed. 2004.

Psichopatia criminalis e Genio e follia. Trans. Andrea Chersi. Bellinzona: Edizioni L'Affranchi, 1998.

Un scandale au couvent: Nouvelles. Trans. Jean Bréjoux. Paris: La Différence, 2002.

Una storia della luna. Trans. Andrea Chersi. Brescia: Chersilibri, 2003.

Holdtörténet. ["Eine Mondgeschichte," Hungarian]. Trans. Tandori Dezső. Illus. Paul Haase. Budapest: ERI, 2005.

Diario de un perro. Trans. Luis Andrés Bredlow. Illus. Reinhold Hoberg. Logroño (Spain): Pepitas, 2007.

Imperjalja. Trans. Andrea Chersi. Brescia: Chersilibri, 2008.

Le Concile d'amour. Une tragédie céleste en V actes. Rev. trans. Pierre Gallissaires. Pref. André Breton. Marseille: Agone, 2008.

Selected Secondary Literature Concerning Performances of *Das Liebeskonzil,* 1965–2008 (Chronological)

1965

Christlieb, M. "Brisantes *Liebeskonzil.* Panizza-Lesung in der Münchner Studiobühne." *Abendzeitung* 13 Dec. 1965: 13.

1966

Stein, Ernst. "Ein grandioses Greul. Scheiterhaufen oder Denkmal für Oskar Panizza." *Die Zeit* 25 Mar. 1966: 5.

von Uslar, Thilo. "Das verbotene Konzil. 70 Jahre nach der Panizza-Affäre in München." *Abendzeitung* 18 Jan. 1966: 6.

_____. "Verhindertes *Liebeskonzil.* Ein Theologie-Professor rief nach dem Staatsanwalt." *Die Zeit* 22 Feb. 1966: 34.

1967

Kauer, Edmund Th. "Panizzas *Liebeskonzil* uraufgeführt." *Volksstimme* 3 June 1967.

Klaus, Rudolf Uwe. "Sicher nicht jedermans Sache. Neu im 'Experiment' am Lichtenwerd: Panizzas *Liebeskonzil.*" *Kurier* 3 June 1967.

Pikl, Erwin. *Das Liebeskonzil von Oskar Panizza. Eine Himmelstragödie in 7 Bildern. Szenische Uraufführung.* Theater program. Vienna: Experiment am Liechtenwerd, 1967.

Sterk, Harald. "Ein Dokument einstiger Zeitsatire." *Arbeiterzeitung* 3 June 1967.

1969

"Au Théâtre de Paris. Incidents pendant *Le Concile d'amour.*" *Le Monde* 14 Feb. 1969: 12.

Bökenkamp, Werner. "Empört—amüsiert. Oskar Panizzas *Liebeskonzil* in Paris." *Frankfurter Allgemeine Zeitung* 28 Feb. 1969.

Bondy, François. "Paris—von Panizza bis Mauriac. Neues in Theater und Buchhandlungen." *Die Zeit* 4 Apr. 1969: 19.

Dumur, Guy. "L'offense faite à Marie: Bien que le diable y soit présenté comme abominable, la pièce de Panizza a mis hors d'eux les tartufes de la presse bien-pensante." *Le Nouvel Observateur* 17 Feb. 1969: 38f.

Ferber, Christian. "Große Schau in Himmel und Hölle. Premiere in Paris: Oskar Panizzas *Liebeskonzil* mit Anspielungen auf französische Verhältnisse." *Die Welt* 20 Mar. 1969: 21.

Gautier, Jean-Jacques. "Au Théâtre de Paris: Le Concile d'amour d'Oscar Panizza." *Le Figaro* 10 Feb. 1969: 20.

Hagen, Friedrich. "Ein Skandal mit tieferer Bedeutung. Die dramatische Satire *Das Liebeskonzil* des Franken Oskar Panizza in Paris. Erotisches und Religiöses wurde auf brillianter Weise zum modernen Mysterium vermischt und provozierte Empörung." *Nürnberger Nachrichten* 28 Feb. 1969: 34.

"Incidents au Théâtre de Paris." *Le Figaro* 14 Feb. 1969: 30.

Madral, Phillippe. "Le nouveau créateur. *Le Concile d'amour* d'Oscar Panizza au Théâtre de Paris." *l'Humanité* 14 Feb. 1969: 8.

Metken, Günter. "Theater der Sinnlichkeit. Späte Uraufführung von Oscar Panizzas *Das Liebeskonzil.*" *Der Tagesspiegel* 22 Feb. 1969: 4.

_____. "Vergreister Himmel, dreiste Welt. Anmerkungen zu einer Pariser Schauspieluraufführung." *Die Presse* 19 Feb. 1969.

Vossen, Frantz. "Die Kanzel von Notre Dame bleibt leer. Tradition und Geist des Aufruhrs in der Pariser Fastenzeit." *Süddeutsche Zeitung* 27 Mar. 1969.

1970

Barber, John. "Profane Satire of 1895 drags." *The Daily Telegraph* 21 Aug. 1970: 10.

Barnes, Clive. "Sex and Blasphemy in London." *NY Times* 12 Sept. 1970.

Bird, John. "A Note on Oscar Panizza, and on the Notes." *Council of Love. Programme. Criterion Theatre.* London: Westby & Co., 1970.

Exner, Julian. "Eine himmlische Komödie. Oskar Panizzas und John Birds *Liebeskonzil* in London." *Der Tagesspiegel* 28 Aug. 1970: 4.

_____. "Scotland Yard prüft Panizza." *Frankfurter Rundschau* 27 Aug. 1970.

_____. "Vom Allmächtigen zum Strohsack." *Frankfurter Rundschau* 26 Aug. 1970.

Ferber, Christian. "Luzifer schickte die Seuche. Panizzas *Liebeskonzil*— Londoner Boulevard-Premiere." *Die Welt* 25 Aug. 1970.

Mander, Gertrud. "Der veruntreute Himmel. Oskar Panizzas Satire *Das Liebeskonzil* in London." *Stuttgarter Zeitung* 3 Sept. 1970: 30.

Spiel, Hilde. "Im Souterrain der Gefühle. Auf Londoner Bühnen: Panizza, Bolt und Pinter." *Frankfurter Allgemeine Zeitung* 2 Dec. 1970: 28.

1973

Gajewski, Alfred. "Das frivole *Liebeskonzil*. Nach 78 Jahren: Deutsche Panizza-Premiere in Hamburg." *Westdeutsche Allgemeine Zeitung* 4 Sept. 1973: 4.

Kesting, Hanjo. "Christus ist müde. *Das Liebeskonzil*." *Vorwärts* 13 Sept. 1973: 14.

Kulschewskij, Ralf. "Böse Komik. Interview mit Jorge Lavelli." *Theater heute* 10 Oct. 1973: 11.

Kulschewskij, Ralf. "Ein Pamphlet? Über *Das Liebeskonzil* von Panizza." *Theater heute* 10 Oct. 1973: 10–12.

Lange, Mechthild. "Gott? Ein müder Mann. Oskar Panizzas *Liebeskonzil* von 1894 erst jetzt deutsch erstaufgeführt." *Frankfurter Rundschau* 6 Sept. 1973: 16.

Kesting, Hanjo. "Christus ist müde." *Vorwärts* 13 Sept. 1973.

Lax, Hans-Eberhard. "Jorge Lavelli inszenierte in Hamburg Panizzas *Liebeskonzil*: Der Autor kam ins Gefängnis." *Abendzeitung* 28 Aug. 1973: 7.

Wagner, Klaus. "Höllenfarce ohne Stachel. Panizzas *Liebeskonzil* in Hamburg." *Frankfurter Allgemeine Zeitung* 6 Sept. 1973: 11.

Ziermann, Horst. "Himmelsspektakel voller Lust am Verruchten. Erstmals in Deutschland: Panizzas *Liebeskonzil*." *Die Welt* 1 Sept. 1973: 15.

1974

Müller, Christoph. "Panizza *Das Liebeskonzil*." *Theater heute* 15.8 (1974): 57.

Roesner, Winfried. "Heiße Rote von Gott Vater. Höllenabschiedsspektakel des Tonne-Ensembles. Letzte Inszenierung in Reutlingen: Oskar Panizzas *Liebeskonzil*." *Stuttgarter Nachrichten* 25 June 1974: 9.

Steinhäuser, H. and Weible, R. "Dem Kellerdasein entwachsen. *Das Liebeskonzil* ein großer Publikumserfolg — Keiner fühlte sich vom Spektakel schockiert." *Reutlinger Nachrichten* 18 June 1974.

Vollmann, Rolf. "Geile Engel. Oskar Panizzas *Liebeskonzil* im Reutlinger Theater in der Tonne." *Stuttgarter Zeitung* 19 June 1974: 7.

1975

Petzold. "*Liebeskonzil* eines Klosterschülers." *Stuttgarter Zeitung* 26 Feb. 1975: 18.

Roesner, Winfried. "Die giftige Last der schönen Lüste. Premiere im Stuttgarter Theater der Altstadt. Franziskus Abgottsponn inszenierte Panizzas *Liebeskonzil* als harmlos-frivole Gaudi." *Stuttgarter Nachrichten* 28 Feb. 1975: 13.

_____. "*Das Liebeskonzil*. Nachtnotiz." *Stuttgarter Nachrichten* 27 Feb. 1975: 25.

_____. "Nicht nur eine Dreckerei. Abgottspon inszeniert *Das Liebeskonzil* in der Altstadt." *Stuttgarter Nachrichten* 26 Feb. 1975: 7.

Skasa-Weiss, Ruprecht. "Himmelstragödie als Kammerspiel. Panizzas *Liebeskonzil* im Altstadttheater Stuttgart." *Stuttgarter Zeitung* 28 Feb. 1975: 34.

_____. "Ein perverses Mysterienspiel. Oskar Panizza im Altstadttheater." *Stuttgarter Zeitung* 28 Feb. 1975: 34.

1976

Demsky, Kenneth. E-mail to the author, 27 Dec. 2009.

"Franz Marijnen, Regisseur. Opvoering *Liefdesconcilie* blijkt nu nog een noodzaak." *Provinciale Zeeuwse Courant* [Goes, NL] 31 Dec. 1976: 15.

Hartocollis, Anemona. "Lovesick: *The Council of Love* by Oskar Panizza directed by Richard Peña at the Loeb tonight and tomorrow 8 P.M." *The Harvard Crimson* 7 May 1976.

Peña, Richard. E-mail to the author, 16 Dec. 2009.

Seidman, Gay. "Stage: *The Council of Love*." *The Harvard Crimson* 29 Apr. 1976.

_____. "Stage: *The Council of Love*." *The Harvard Crimson* 6 May 1976.

1977

Cultuurraad voor de Nederlandse Cultuur Gemeenschap. Zitting 1976–1977. Nr. 5, 15 Feb. 1977.

Stichting Toneelraad Rotterdam. "Kritieken op het *Liefdesconcilie*: een produktie van de Toneelraad Rotterdam, seizoen 1976–1977." Rotterdam: Toneelraad, 1977.

Tank, Kurt Lothar. "Himmelfahrt der Blasphemie. Franz Marijnens Gastspiel mit Oskar Panizzas *Liebeskonzil.*" *Der Tagesspiegel* 21 Jan. 1977: 4.

Wagner, Klaus. "Franz Marijnens große Wut. Panizzas *Liebeskonzil* in Hamburg." *Frankfurter Allgemeine Zeitung,* 21 Jan. 1977: 21.

1982

A. P. "Schroeter kommt mit Panizza. *Das Liebeskonzil* und der Prozeß gegen dessen Autor als Film." *Landsberger Tagblatt* 23 Feb. 1982.

Achternbusch, Herbert. "Schroeter, Panizza und 'Das letzte Loch'. *Frankfurter Rundschau* 3 Mar. 1982: 7.

"Ärger mit der Lustseuche." *Abendzeitung* 8 Feb. 1982.

"Filmfestspiele: Skandal um Schroeters Jesus-Film." *Bild,* Berlin ed., 18 Feb. 1982: 5.

Fründt, Bodo. "'Ich kann mit dem Wort *normal* nichts anfangen'. Seit mehr als einem Jahrzehnt provoziert Werner Schroeter im Kino und im Fernsehen, auf Opern- und Theaterbühnen sein Publikum mit Experimenten." *Stern* 6 May 1982: 92–96.

"Gotteslästerer und Staatsfeind. Werner Schroeter verfilmte die römische Aufführung von Oskar Panizzas *Liebeskonzil*— der gleichnamige Film läuft jetzt in den Kinos an..." *Tip* 6 (1982): 26.

Graf, Günter. "Das Liebeskonzil." *Filmdienst.* Katholisches Institut für Medieninfo. Cologne, 1982/9: 20.

Hornung, Peter. "Der Himmel als Kuriositäten-Kabinett. Werner Schroeters Film nach Oscar Panizzas *Liebeskonzil.*" *Saarbrücker Zeitung* 26 Mar. 1982: 8.

Igel, Ignaz. "Die Sache mit dem *Liebeskonzil.* Von allen guten Geistern verlassen." *Neue Bildpost* 28 Feb. 1982: 1.

Jenny, Urs. "Lästerliche Mysterien. Über zwei neue Filme von Werner Schroeter." *Der Spiegel* 5 Apr. 1982: 218.

KAHA. "Erfundene Krankheit: Das Liebeskonzil." *Berliner Zeitung* 22 Feb. 1982.

Knapp, Gottfried. "Ein göttliches Spektakel. Werner Schroeters *Liebeskonzil* nach Oskar Panizza." *Süddeutsche Zeitung* 15 Mar. 1982: 26.

Lachner, Harry. "Aus der Hand des Schöpfers. Werner Schroeters Verfilmung des *Liebeskonzils* von Oskar Panizza im Kino." *Stuttgarter Nachrichten* 22 May 1982: 32.

Niehoff, Karena. "Unnötige Aufregung. Werner Schroeters Panizza-Verfilmung *Liebeskonzil.*" *Der Tagesspiegel* 12 Mar. 1982: 4.

"Nonnen gegen *Liebeskonzil.*" *Der Spiegel* 23 Mar. 1982: 188.

Ponkie. "Neuer Film in München: Das Liebeskonzil." *Abendzeitung* (Munich) 12 Mar. 1982.

"Protest gegen *Liebeskonzil.*" *Oberösterreichische Nachrichten* 28 Sept. 1992: 19.

"Schlechter Geschmack." *Bild,* Berlin ed. 18 Feb. 1982: 2.

Schnierle, Barbara. "Was haben Sie für einen schlechten Geschmack?" *Tip* 12–25 Mar. 1982: 13.

"Schroeter kommt mit Panizza. *Das Liebeskonzil* und der Prozeß gegen dessen Autor als Film." *Augsburger Allgemeine* 23 Feb. 1982: 6.

Stone, Michael. "Schroeters *Liebeskonzil* ganz ohne Humor." *Westfälische Rundschau* 24 Feb. 1982.

"Verbotenes Buch wurde verfilmt." *Quick* 18 Feb. 1982: 94f.

Ulrich, Jörg. "Teufeleien auf Schröters *Liebeskonzil.* Noch ein fragwürdiger deutscher Beitrag bei der Berlinale." *Münchner Merkur* 23 Feb. 1982: 7.

_____. "Neuer Film: Gegen Gott und die Welt." *Münchner Merkur* 13 Mar. 1982

Wolff, Detlev. "Oskar Panizzas *Liebeskonzil.*" *Weser Kurier* 30 July 1982: 20.

1983

Phinney, Kevin. "*Council* tackles God, society in bold comedy." *Austin American-Statesman* 10 June 1983.

1984

Baumann, Günther. "Satire–Schocker um Eros, Gott und Teufel. Demnächst im Theater: Panizzas *Liebeskonzil.*" *Kurier* 31 Aug. 1984.

R.E., "Das Liebeskonzil." *Multimedia.* Bundesministerium für Unterricht und kulturelle Angelegenheiten. 1984/4: 1

Pfoser, Alfred. "Erlösungsbedürftige Menschen. *Das Liebeskonzil* von Oskar Panizza in der Wiener Arena." *Salzburger Nachrichten* 11 Dec. 1984.

Schirnovsky, Heinz. "Das 'Narrenkastel' spielt in der Arena Oskar Panizza: Noch im Scheitern ausgezeichnet." *Arbeiterzeitung* 27 Nov. 1984.

1985

Loibl, Elisabeth. "Narrenkastl inszeniert Panizzas Himmelstragödie." *Falter* 24 Apr. 1985.

1986

Bielicki, Jan. "Nur eine Affenkomödie hienieden. Panizzas [sic] eröffnet das Münchner Studiotheater auf dem Alabama." *Süddeutsche Zeitung* 30 July 1986.

Gill, Dominic. "Hell's Angels: Royal Court." *Financial Times* 8 Jan. 1986: 11.

1987

"Hummel und Hölle." *Der Spiegel* 1 June 1987:226

1988

Berlinger, Josef, ed. *Oskar Panizzas Das Liebeskonzil.* Munich: Kuckuck & Straps, 1990. [Material from Regensburg performance in 1988.]

Hammerschmidt, Ulrich. "Himmel, Hölle, Heidenspaß. Nürnberger Sommertheater: Erinnerungen an Oskar Panizzas *Liebeskonzil.*" *Theater heute* 9.88: 23.

Fander, Kurt. "Satirische Himmelstragödie. Josef Berlinger inszenierte Panizzas *Liebeskonzil* in Regensburg." *Landshuter Zeitung* 22 Jan. 1988.

Hein, Helmut. "Die Einführung der Syphilis. Berlinger inszeniert Panizzas *Liebeskonzil.*" *Die Woche* (Regensburg) 21 Jan. 1988.

Massa, Robert. "*The Council of Love.*" *Village Voice* 29 Nov. 1988: 122.

Schiller-Theater. *Oskar Panizza, Das Liebeskonzil.* Heft 76. Berlin: Staatliche Schauspielbühnen Berlin, 1988.

Skasa, Michael. "Voll Scherz und voller Hohn. Oskar Panizzas *Liebeskonzil* in Nürnberg: Blasphemical in der Kirche." *Süddeutsche Zeitung* 21 June 1988.

Stuber, Manfred. "Als die Seuche auf die Erde kam. Eine Himmelstragödie." *Mittelbayerische Zeitung* 19 Jan. 1988.

1989

Barnes, Michael. "*Council of Love* crucifies zealots with ruthless satire." *Austin American-Statesman* 20 June 1989.

Beckelmann, Jürgen. "Eine blasphemische Antiquität. Wieder einmal ein Versuch mit Panizzas *Liebeskonzil* in Berlin." *Stuttgarter Zeitung* 10 Jan. 1989.

Hammer, Wolfgang. "Bunter Abend. Oskar Panizzas *Liebeskonzil* im Schillertheater," *Frankfurter Rundschau* 14 Jan. 1989.

Hasenkamp, Johannes. "Leichtfertiges Spiel mit albernen Schocks. Panizzas *Liebeskonzil* im Borchert-Theater." *Westfälische Nachrichten* 27 Feb. 1989.

Kersten, Hans Ulrich. "In Berlin ist die Hölle los. Oskar Panizzas *Das Liebeskonzil* als Musical." *Die Presse* 12 Jan. 1989.

Luft, Friedrich. "Trotteliger Gottvater, mit Vitriol gezeichnet." *Die Welt* 2 Jan. 1989.

Maimann, Gunda. "Eine scheinheilige Familie. Wolfgang-Borchert-Theater wagte Oskar Panizzas *Liebeskonzil.*" *Münstersche Zeitung* 27 Feb. 1989.

Naumann, Cornella. "Nur bei Borchert keine Blasphemie?" Leserbrief. *Münstersche Zeitung* 3 Mar. 1989.

Rott, Wilfried. "Kein teuflischer Spaß und göttlicher Ulk. Panizzas *Das Liebeskonzil* am Schiller-Theater." *Der Standard* 2 Jan. 1989.

1990

aw. "Luzifers Hilfe wird erbeten." *Die Welt* 10 July 1990.

Böttjer, Uwe, ed. *Oskar Panizza und die Folgen: Bilder und Texte zur Wiederaufführung seines Liebeskonzils.* Brunsbüttel: Koog-Haus Press, 1992. [Documents and materials from the 1990 performance in Trennewurth.]

Hopp, Helge. "Vom grellen Schock befreit. Schüler des Monsun-Theaterinstituts zeigen *Das Liebeskonzil.*" *Hamburger Rundschau* 8 Mar. 1990.

Rusch, Jens. "*Das Liebeskonzil* von Oskar Panizza." 1990. Web. 8 July 2009. <www.jensrusch.de/id56.htm>

1991

Freitag, Wolfgang. "Lustseuche verpufft. Panizza im Ensemble-Theater." *Die Presse* 15 Nov. 1991.

hilp. "Pralles Schülertheater. *Das Liebeskonzil* in der Wilhelm-Bracke-Schule." *Braunschweiger Zeitung* 15 June 1991.

Lohs, Lothar. "*Das Liebeskonzil* und die Strafe der Lustseuche. Stephan Bruckmeiers 'Kultur der Vernichtung.'" *Der Standard* 11 Nov. 1991: Teil 3.

_____. "Gott sabbert. Stephan Bruckmeier inszeniert Panizzas *Liebeskonzil* im Ensemble Theater am Petersplatz." *Falter* 47 (1991).

Pohl, Ronald. "Österreich: Die Hölle im siebtem Himmel." *Der Standard* 14 Nov. 1991.

1992

Benedikt, Robert. "Hundert Jahre sind lang. Panizzas *Liebeskonzil* in Tirol." *Die Presse* 5 Oct. 1992.

Deppermann, Maria. "Streit um die Freiheit der Kunst. Modellfall Tirol: *Das Liebeskonzil* von Oskar Panizza." *Theater Almanach Tirol 1994. Anlässlich des 3. Österreichischen Theatertreffens in Innsbruck vom 23. bis 3. April 1994*: 14–17. [Discusses 1992 production in Innsbruck.]

Franco, Jean. "A Touch of Evil: Jesusa Rodriguez's Subversive Church." *TDR: The Drama Review* 36.2 (Summer 1992): 48–61. Reprinted in *Negotiating Performance,* Diana Taylor & Juan Villegas, eds. Durham & London: Duke UP, 1994: 159–175.

Heisz, Irene. "Pastoraler Optimismus und zementierte Hierarchien. 'Kunst, Freiheit und Zensur': Eine weitere Podiumsdiskussion im Tiroler Landestheater über *Das Liebeskonzil.*" *Tiroler Tageszeitung* 2 Nov. 1992.

Höpfel, Jutta. "Ein Theater kommt ins Gerede. Innsbruck: Oskar Panizzas *Liebeskonzil.*" *Wiener Zeitung,* 6 Oct. 1992.

ni. "Keine kleinen linken Teufel. 25 Jahre schlief Innsbrucks Theaterpublikum einen Schlaf der Seligen: jetzt krempelt ein neuer Intendant das Landestheater komplett um und wartet mit einem Skandalstück auf." *ff—Südtiroler Wochenmagazin* 3–9 Oct. 1992: 34–36.

_____. "Gotteslästerung. Der Staatsanwalt befand das Panizza-Stück im Innsbrucker Landestheater nicht der Strafverfolgung würdig." *ff—Südtiroler Wochenmagazin* 11–16 Oct. 1992.

_____. "*Liebeskonzil.* Das Panizzastück in einer Aufführung des Tiroler Landestheaters in Innsbruck." *ff—Südtiroler Wochenmagazin* 11–16 Oct. 1992.

Peters, Barbara. "Nicht mal die himmlischen Engelchen sind unschuldig. *Liebeskonzil* im Theaterstudio Olten." *Oltner Tagblatt* 15 May 1992.

1993

Heyden, Susanne. "Nachricht vom Sündenpfuhl. Traumjob für den Teufel: Schauspielstudio Maria Körber mit Panizzas *Liebeskonzil.*" *Der Tagesspiegel* 18 Dec. 1993.

1994

Braendle, Petra. "Studentenaufführung von Oskar Panizzas *Liebeskonzil.*" *taz* 8 Feb. 1994.

1996

Shirley, Don. "1894's Satirical *Love Council* Goes from Sexy to Somber." *Los Angeles Times* 6 Nov. 1996.

1997

Koslowski, Stefan. "Kann Theater Sünde sein?" *Berner Almanach. Band 3. Theater.* Bern: Stämpfli, 2000. [discusses 1997 production in Bern.]
"Schauspielschule Bern: SD wollen perverses Theaterstück sofort absetzen." *SD Pressemitteilung,* 19 Dec. 1997.

1998

von Bergen, Stefan. "Theater vor Gericht." *Berner Zeitung* 24 Sept. 1998.
_____. "Blasphemie allein ist nicht strafbar." *Berner Zeitung* 11 Dec. 1998.
Leis, Sandra. "Theater vor dem Gericht. Freispruch. Leonie Stein, Leiterin der Schauspielschule Bern, und die Regisseurin Barbara Frey haben mit der Inszenierung des *Liebeskonzils* von Oskar Panizza die Glaubensfreiheit nicht gestört." *Der Bund* 11 Dec. 1998: 9.
_____. "Kommentar: Für die Freiheit der Kunst." *Der Bund* 11 Dec. 1998: 9.
Stumm, Rheinhardt. "Gotteslästerung nicht justitiabel. Beherztes Schweizer Urteil zu Panizzas *Liebeskonzil.*" *Frankfurter Rundschau* 19 Dec. 1998: 8.

1999

Feuz, Thomas. "*Das Liebeskonzil* gerichtlich sanktioniert! Wird Blasphemie salonfähig?" *EDU-Standpunkt* 6 Jan. 1999.
was. "Donnerwolke ex machina." *Kieler Nachrichten* 11 Feb. 1999.

2000

Aigner, Hermine. "Es ist befreiend, über Gott und den Himmel zu lachen. Der Wiener Regisseur Justus Neumann inszeniert das neue Gugg-Stück." *Braunauer Rundschau* 9 Nov. 2000: 5.
_____. "Nichts ist so menschlich wie die Himmelswelt. *Liebeskonzil*— von Lust und Frust zwischen Himmel und Hölle." *Braunauer Rundschau* 11 Nov. 2000.
Hofstetter-Hambach, Heidrun. "Let's talk about sex." *Tanzaffiche* 103, Oct.-Dec. 2000.
Koslowski, Stefan. "Kann Theater Sünde sein?" *Berner Almanach. Band 3. Theater.* Bern: Stämpfli, 2000.
Kralicek, Wolfgang. "Geburt einer Tragödie. Wiedersehen mit einem alten Skandalstück: Der Choreograph Bert Gstettner inszeniert *Das Liebeskonzil* von Oskar Panizza." *Falter* 15 Sept. 2000.
stelz. "Die Himmelstragödie tanzt." *Die Presse* 11 Sept. 2000.
Suchan, Brigitte. "Von den Schwierigkeiten, einen Text tänzerisch umzusetzen." *Wiener Zeitung* 11 Sept. 2000.
wald. "Getanzter Orgasmus." *City* 38 (2000).
Werner, Oliver. "Tanz-Welt." *Neue Kronen Zeitung* 11 Sept. 2000.

2001

Nussbaumer, Wolfgang. "Lasterhöhle im Dom des Waldes. Kuluturverein spielt im Park von Schloss Laubach mit großem Elan Oskar Panizzas *Liebeskonzil.*" *Schwäbische Post* 26 June 2001.
Ullersperger, Tobias. "Himmel und Hölle schließen Pakt. Ab heute zeigt der 'Kulturverein Schloss Laubach' das Stück *Das Liebeskonzil* von Oskar Panizza." *Gmündner Tagespost* 22 June 2001: 29.

2003

Manger, Manfred. "Szenische Lesung: Oskar Panizza *Das Liebeskonzil.* Lesung bei der 'Nacht der Kultur': Sonntag, 28 September, 2003. Sieben Stunden lang Kultur häppchenweise." *Pressestimmen zu Manfred Manger.* Web. < www.manfred-manger.de/Presse. htm>.

2005

Beer, Monika. "Der Teufel spuckt Gift und Galle. [...] Für Erwachsene lockt das satirische *Liebeskonzil* von Oskar Panizza." *Fränkischer Tag* 20 June 2005.
Wunner, Horst. "*Liebeskonzil*: Opulentes Bühnenerlebnis. Theatergruppe des MGFG meistert schwierige Aufgabe bravourös. Heute Abend Podiumsdiskussion über Panizza." *Bayerische Rundschau* 20 June 2005: 9.
_____. "Von Laster und Erlösung — und wahrer Lust am Spiel. Brillante Inszenierung von Panizzas *Liebeskonzil.*" *Frankenpost* 20 June 2005.
_____. "Was darf die Kunst?" *Bayerische Rundschau* 22 June 2005: 14.

2006

Adler, Tilman. "Das Liebeskonzil — Theater von höchster Qualität am HLG." *helga. Schülerzeitung am HLG Fürth* 27 June 2006. Web. <http://helga-online.de/?pageid=10&articleid=203>.
Hänisch, Valerie. "Himmlisches Theaterspektakel." *Bayreuther Anzeiger* 21 June 2006.
Lammel, Wolfgang. "'Es geht um die Freiheit des Gedankens'. Die Studiobühne Bayreuth zeigt Oskar Panizzas 111 Jahre altes Skandalstück *Das Liebeskonzil.*" *Sonntagsblatt* 28 May 2006.
Sziegoleit, Ralf. "Die Welt ist ein Irrenhaus." *Frankenpost* 14 June 2006.

2007

Sendtner, Florian. "Der donnernde Gott und die Ruchlosigkeit auf Erden. Hans Schröck inszeniert in der Mälzerei Oskar Panizzas *Das Liebeskonzil.*" *Mittelbayerische Zeitung* 16 Nov. 2007.
_____. "'Ich wärde sie zärschmättärn!' Oskar Panizzas Himmelstragödie *Das Liebeskonzil* in der Alten Mälzerei." *Mittelbayerische Zeitung* 24 Nov. 2007.

2008

Frederiksen, Jens. "Ein Zahnarztstuhl als Thron Gottvaters — Oskar Panizzas *Liebeskonzil* in Kaiserslautern. Frechheiten von ehedem werden zum grellen Jux." *Allgemeine Zeitung* (Mainz) 17 Dec. 2008.

Schütz, Susanne. "Viel Lärm um Nichts. Oskar Panizzas antikatholische Satire *Das Liebeskonzil* am Pfalztheater Kaiserslautern." *Die Rheinpfalz* 15 Dec. 2008.

_____. "Zur Sache: Empörung im Internet." *Die Rheinpfalz* 15 Dec. 2008.

Other Selected Secondary Literature (Alphabetical)

Bandhauer, Dieter. "Bedrohliche Kunstfreiheit? *Das Liebeskonzil* vor Gericht." *Wiener Zeitung* 7 Nov. 1986.

Bauer, P. Michael. "Deutscher Prophet. [...] Oskar Panizza — nur ein 'Kultur-Kuriosum'?" *Die Zeit* 18 Sept. 1981: 55.

_____. "Oskar Panizza. Ein literarisches Porträt." Diss. Ludwig-Maximilians-Universität München, 1983.

Bauer, Michael and Düsterberg, Rolf. *Oskar Panizza. Eine Bibliographie.* Europäische Hochschulschriften Reihe 1, 1086. Frankfurt/Main: Peter Lang, 1988.

Benjamin, Walter. "E. T. A. Hoffmann und Oskar Panizza." *Gesammelte Schriften.* Frankfurt/Main: Suhrkamp, 1977: II/2: 641–648.

Berling, Peter, ed. *Liebeskonzil Filmbuch.* Munich: Schirmer/Mosel, 1982.

_____. Unpublished correspondence with the author, 1998.

Bierbaum, Otto Julius. "Oskar Panizza." *Die Gesellschaft* 9.8 (1893): 977–989.

_____. [pseud. Martin Möbius]. "Oskar Panizza." *Steckbriefe.* Illus. Bruno Paul. Berlin/Leipzig: Schuster und Loeffler, 1900: 101–104.

_____. Rev. of *Parisiana. Deutsche Verse aus Paris.* In: *Die Insel* 1.7 (Apr. 1900): 118f.

_____. Rev. of *Zürcher Discussionen.* In: *Die Zeit* 3 Dec. 1898: 157.

_____. Rev. of "Zürcher Discussionen. I. Die Krankheit Heines." *Die Zeit* 30 Oct. 1897: 77.

_____. Rev. of "Zürcher Discussionen. II Ein Capitel aus Hans Jägers Christiana Bohème." *Die Zeit* 13 Nov. 1897: 110.

Binder, Frauke. "Der zensierte Dämon." Magisterarbeit, Universität Hannover, 1995. Microf. Deutsche Hochschulschriften 2278. Frankfurt-Main: Hänsel-Hohenhausen, 1996.

Boeser, Knut, ed. *Der Fall Oskar Panizza. Ein deutscher Dichter im Gefängnis. Eine Dokumentation.* Berlin: Edition Hentrich, 1989.

Bröckers, Mathias. "Oskar Panizza. Ein extremer Dichter." *Die Tageszeitung* 19 Jan. 1981.

Brown, Peter D. G. "The Continuing Trials of Oskar Panizza: A Century of Artistic Censorship in Germany, Austria and Beyond," *German Studies Review* 24/3 (October 2001): 533–556.

_____. "Doghouse, Jailhouse, Madhouse: A Study of Oskar Panizza's Life and Literature." Diss. Columbia, 1971.

_____. "Oskar Panizza's First and Last Books: A Study in Late Nineteenth-Century Poetry." *The Germanic Review* 48 (1973): 269–287.

Brügel, Fritz. "Der kaiserliche Wahnsinn." *Arbeiter Zeitung* (Vienna) No. 211 (1926).

Burcardus, Johannes. *Diarium.* Ed. L. Thuasne. 3 vols. Paris, 1883–85.

Chiarini, Giovanni. *Vagabondi, "Sonderlinge" e marionette nella narrativa di Oskar Panizza.* Napoli: Istituto Universitario Orientale, Dipartimento di Studi Letterari e Linguistici dell'Occidente, 1989.

Coliver, Sandra [Article 19] and Schiffrin, Natalia [Interights]. *Blasphemy, Prior Restraint and Freedom of Expression: Third Party Intervention to the European Court of Human Rights in Otto-Preminger-Institut v. Austria.* London: Article 19, 14 Oct. 1993.

Conrad, Michael Georg. "Dr. Oskar Panizza." *Die Gesellschaft* 9.5 (1893): 673f.

_____. "Erklärung." *Das litterarische Echo* 1 Feb. 1900: 672.

_____. "Der heilige Staatsanwalt." *Die Gesellschaft* 10.3 (1894): 390.

_____. "Oskar Panizzas freie Auslassungen." *Die Gesellschaft* 9.4 (1893): 535.

_____. "Oskar Panizzas geniale Satire auf den Vatikanismus *Die unbefleckte Empfängnis der Päpste.*" *Die Gesellschaft* 8.5 (1893): 647.

_____. "Panizza." *Die Gesellschaft* 9.11 (1893): 149f.

_____. "*Züricher Diskussionen.*" *Die Gesellschaft* 14.9 (1898): 650.

Corrigan, Timothy. *New German Film: The Displaced Image.* Bloomington: Indiana UP, 1994.

Cziesla, Wolfgang. *Das Werk als ein unaufgeräumter Kriegsschauplatz. Oskar Panizzas Einzelkampf gegen eine übermächtige Ordnung. Ein Traktat.* Essen: Edizioni Firiwizzi, 1983.

Delincée, Susanne. "*Das Liebeskonzil.* Eine Fallstudie zur Kunstfreiheit." Diplomarbeit, Universität Salzburg, 1997.

Dietrich, Christa. "Zeichen der Intoleranz. *Liebeskonzil*—Theater erlaubt, Film verboten." *Vorarlberger Nachrichten* 24/25 Sept. 1994.

"Dr. Oskar Panizza." *Kölnische Zeitung* 2 May 1895: 1.

"Dr. Oskar Panizza." *Das Magazin für Litteratur* 2 Nov. 1895: 1434.

Eckelkamp, Hanns. Unpublished correspondence with the author, 1996–2007.

Eisner, Uli. "Aspekte einer beamteten Filmkultur: Zwischen Preis und Zensur." *Volksstimme* 4 June 1985.

_____. "Was Kunst ist, bestimmen die Richter." *Volksstimme* 16 Oct. 1985: 9.

Engel, Eduard. *Geschichte der deutschen Literatur des neunzehnten Jahrhunderts und der Gegenwart.* 4th ed. Vienna: F. Tempsky, 1912.

European Court of Human Rights, *Judgment,* Case of Otto-Preminger-Institut v. Austria, Application no. 13470/87, Strasbourg, 20 Sept. 1994. Vol. 295-A, Ser. A. Web. <http://cmiskp.echr.coe.int/tkp197/view.asp?action=html&documentId=695774&portal=hbkm&source=externalbydocnumber&table=11 32746FF1FE2A468ACCBCD1763D4D8149>

"Der Fall Panizza." *Deutsche Wacht* 12 May 1895: 2.

"Der Fall Panizza." *Deutsche Zeitung* 5 May 1895: 1f.

"Der Fall Panizza." *Der Freidenker* 1 June 1895: 183.

Fontane, Theodor. "Aus Briefen Fontanes an Maximilian Harden." *Merkur* 10 (1956): 1091–1098.

"Die Freiheit der Kunst." *Vossische Zeitung* 2 May 1895: 1.

Freud, Sigmund. *Die Traumdeutung*. Leipzig/Vienna: Deuticke, 1900.

Glantschnig, Gerd. "Innsbrucker Staatsanwalt beschlagnahmte *Liebeskonzil* — Film erregte Verdacht der Herabwürdigung religiöser Lehren." *TT* 15/16 May 1985.

_____. "Menschenrechtswidriges Verbot des Filmes *Liebeskonzil*?" *TT* 6 May 1993: 4.

Goldman, Emma. *Living My Life*. New York: Knopf, 1931.

Goldschmidt, Viktor. *Seiende und Werdende*. Leipzig: Xenien, 1912: 87–104.

Gostner, Astrid. "Die verbotene Aussage. Der Fall *Liebeskonzil*. Untersuchung auf dem Hintergrund von Michel Foucaults *Archäologie des Wissens*." Diplomarbeit, Universität Innsbruck, 1997.

"Gotteslästerung." *Badischer Landesbote* 12 May 1895: 1.

Grabenwarter, Christoph. "Filmkunst im Spannungsfeld zwischen Freiheit der Meinungsäußerung und Religionsfreiheit. Anmerkung zum Urteil des Europäischen Gerichtshofs für Menschenrechte vom 20. September 1994 im Fall Otto-Preminger-Institut." *Zeitschrift für ausländisches öffentliches Recht und Völkerrecht* 55 (1995): 128–164. Web. <http://www.zaoerv.de/55_1995/55_1995_1_b_128_165.pdf.>

Griesacker, Tina. "Die Beschwerde des Otto Preminger Institutes gegen Österreich im Lichte der Judikatur der europäischen Organe und österreichischen Gerichtshöfe zum Art. 10 EMRK." Diplomarbeit, Universität Salzburg, 2000.

Gumppenberg, Hanns von. *Lebenserinnerungen. Aus dem Nachlaß des Dichters*. Berlin: Eigenbrödler, 1929.

Haas, Willy. "Wir fordern eine 'Lex Nietzsche.'" *Die literarische Welt* 9 July 1929: 1f.

_____. "Panizza." *Die Welt* 8 Aug. 1962.

Halbe, Max. "Intimes Theater." *Pan* 1.2 (June–Aug. 1895): 106–109.

_____. "Irrlichter: II. Oskar Panizza." *Kölnische Zeitung* 8 Nov. 1933.

_____. *Jahrhundertwende. Geschichte meines Lebens. 1893–1914*. Danzig: Kasemann, 1935.

_____. "Münchner Brief." *Der Tag* 29 Dec. 1904: 1–3.

Hanstein, Adalbert von. *Das Jüngste Deutschland. Zwei Jahrzehnte miterlebter Literaturgeschichte*. Leipzig: Voigtländer Verlag, 1900.

Hasibeder, Georg. "'Ward diesem Wicht nur erst sein Maul verlötet …' Ideologiekritische Annäherung an die Zensurfälle *Lulu* (Wedekind) und *Liebeskonzil* (Panizza) im literatur-theoretischen und gesellschaftspolitischen Kontext." Diplomarbeit, Universität Innsbruck, 2001.

Hausmann, Ada. "Oskar Panizza und seine Zeit, 1853–1921." MA thesis, Hebrew University of Jerusalem, 1993.

Hawlicek, Hilde. Unpublished letter to Generalprokurator Dr. Otto F. Müller. 18 May 1987.

Hendrichs, Willi. "Oskar Panizzas Kreislauf. Interpretationen literarischer Krankenberichte." MA thesis, Freiburg, 1983.

"Ein hervorragender deutschländischer Dichter." *Der Freidenker* 2 June 1895: 4.

Heuer, Gottfried. "'Der Skorpion im Meßkelch' und 'der Teufel unter der Couch'. Oskar Panizza und Otto Gross — eine Seelenverwandtschaft." *Bohème, Psychoanalyse & Revolution. 3. Internationaler Otto Gross Kongress. Ludwig-Maximilians-Universität, München, 15.–17. März 2002*. Ed. Raimund Dehmlow & Gottfried Heuer. Marburg an der Lahn: LiteraturWissenschaft.de, 2003: 163–236.

Hildebrand, Günther. "Litterarische Zeitschriften der letzten Vergangenheit und der Gegenwart." *Die Bücherstube* 1.1. (1920): 11–16.

_____. "Oskar Panizza als Bibliophile." *Die Bücherstube* 1.3/4 (1920): 92–98.

Hoefert, Sigfrid. *Das Drama des Naturalismus*. Stuttgart: J.B. Metzlersche Verlagsbuchhandlung, 1968.

Hoevels, Fritz E. "Eine Fetischtennovelle von O. Panizza." *Praxis der Psychotherapie* 43 (1973): 205–213.

Höge, Helmut. "Sag ja zu Jes! Der Berliner Verleger und Galerist Jes Petersen stammt eigentlich aus Flensburg, wurde am 2. November im Moabiter Knast 60 Jahre alt und läuft nun wieder frei in Charlottenburg herum." *taz* 14 Dec. 1996: 36.

Holitscher, Arthur. *Lebensgeschichte eines Rebellen. Meine Erinnerungen*. Berlin: Fischer, 1924.

Höpfel, Frank. "Wie frei ist die Kunst? Zur Bedeutung des Art. 17a Staatsgrundgesetz, im besonderen für das Strafrecht." *Der Staatsbürger* (Salzburg) 8.4 (Oct. 1987): 2.

Houben, H(einrich) H(ubert). *Verbotene Literatur von der klassischen Zeit bis zur Gegenwart. Ein kritisch-historisches Lexikon über verbotene Bücher, Zeitschriften und Theaterstücke, Schriftsteller und Verleger*. Berlin: Rowohlt, 1924.

Jelavich, Peter. "Theater in Munich, 1890–1914. A Study in the Social origins of Modernist Culture." Diss. Princeton, 1982.

_____. *Munich and Theatrical Modernism: Politics, Playwriting, and Performance, 1890–1914*. Cambridge: Harvard University Press, 1985.

Kamolz, Klaus. "Verbotenes Konzil: Internationale Berichte bestätigen Österreich eine — fast — reine Weste in Sachen Menschenrechte." *Profil* 23, 7 June 1993.

Kantzenbach, Friedrich Wilhelm. "Der Dichter Oskar Panizza und der Pfarrer Friedrich Lippert, eine Lebensbegegnung." *Zeitschrift für Religions- und Geistesgeschichte* 26 (1974): 125–142.

Katzenbacher, Klaus. "Provokateur aus der Gegenwelt. Das späte Comeback des fränkischen Schriftstellers Oskar Panizza." *Nürnberger Nachrichten* 17/18 Apr. 1982: 21.

Kaufmann, Heimo. "Das Verzehren der Illusionen. Oskar Panizza und Max Stirner." Diplomarbeit, Universität Innsbruck, 1992.

Kayser, Wolfgang. *Das Groteske. Seine Gestaltung in Malerei und Dichtung.* Oldenburg & Hamburg: Stalling, 1957.

"Kein Konzils-Problem." *Oberösterreichische Nachrichten* 5 Oct. 1992: 18.

"Keinen Anwalt!" *Neue freie Volks-Zeitung* 4 May 1895: 1f.

Kistner, Ulrike. "Der wackelnde Thron: Gott, Kaiser und Vaterland bei Oskar Panizza." *Acta Germanica* 17 (1984): 99.

Krell, Max. *Das alles gab es einmal.* Frankfurt/Main: Scheffler, 1961.

Kreokowski, Ernst. "Oskar Panizza." *Das litterarische Echo* 7 (1905): 349.

_____. "Oskar Panizza." *Das neue Magazin* 3 Dec. 1904: 752–754.

Kreuzer, Helmut. *Die Bohème. Beiträge zu ihrer Beschreibung.* Stuttgart: J.B. Metzlersche Verlagsbuchhandlung, 1968.

Kristl, Wilhelm Lukas. "Armer Panizza." *Börsenblatt für den Deutschen Buchhandel.* Frankfurter Ausgabe 30 Nov. 1979: A437.

_____. "Nun mußt den Sturm du ernten: *Zürcher Diskussionen* (1897–1900) von Oskar Panizza." *Deutsche Zeitung* 26 Aug. 1961: 19.

Kunze, Wilhelm. "Dichter aus Franken. IV. Ein Poet, der umsonst gelebt hat." *Nürnberger Zeitung, Luginsland* 5 May 1928: 1.

Kürschner, Joseph, ed. *Deutscher Litteratur-Kalender.* Leipzig: G. J. Göschensche Verlagshandlung, 1893–1904.

Lahodynsky, Otmar. "Filmverbot hat Folgen." *Die Presse* 29 Nov. 1993.

Landesgericht Innsbruck. *Im Namen der Republik.* 26 Vr 1875/85, 26 Hv33/86.

_____. *Protokoll.* Nr. 32 Vr 1875/85.

Lange-Eichbaum, Wilhelm. *Genie, Irrsinn und Ruhm, eine Pathologie des Genies.* Munich: Ernst Reinhardt Verlag 1928. 7th ed. 1996.

Leixner, Otto von, and Friedlaender, Ernst. *Geschichte der deutschen Literatur.* 8th ed. Leipzig: O. Spamer, 1910.

Lepuschitz, Rainer. "Religion und Freiheit." *TT* 2 Sept. 1994.

_____. "Der Tiroler Fall *Liebeskonzil*." *TT* 3/4 Oct. 1992.

Lessing, Theodor. *Einmal und nie wieder. Lebenserinnerungen.* Prague: Mercy, 1935.

_____. *Der Fall Panizza: Eine kritische Betrachtung über "Gotteslästerung" und künstlerische Dinge vor Schwurgerichten.* Munich: Wohlfahrt, 1895.

Licha, Hans. "Freiheit der Kunst im 'heiligen Tirol' kämpft in Straßburg gegen Filmverbot. *Das Liebeskonzil* will Tiroler Ketten sprengen." *Tirol Kurier* 5 July 1991.

Lichtenstein, Jonathan D. "Perspectives on the German-Jewish Body and Mind: Analysis of Selected Works by Heine, Panizza and Thomas Mann." Senior thesis, Hampshire College, Amherst MA, May 2005.

"*Das Liebes-Konzil.*" *Die Gesellschaft* 11.1 (1895): 120.

"*Das Liebeskonzil.*" *Die Gesellschaft* 11.2 (1895): 286.

"*Das Liebeskonzil.*" *Der Kunstwart* 8.18 (June 1895): 277.

"*Das Liebeskonzil.*" *Münchner Post* 24 Nov. 1894: 3f.

"*Liebeskonzil.*" *Neue Bayerische Landeszeitung* 17 Jan. 1895: 1.

"*Das Liebeskonzil* in Tirol verboten: Beleidigung der religiösen Gefühle des gläubigen Tirolers." *TT* 13 Oct. 1986.

Lindblad, Thomas. "Oskar Panizzas Lebenslauf. Ein Versuch sein Leben zu schildern mit Hilfe seiner Tagebücher." Stockholm: np., 1969.

Linde, Winfried W. "Innsbrucker Gericht verletzte Menschenrechte. Österreich wird wegen *Liebeskonzil*-Verbot von Euro-Kommission angeklagt." *Tirol-Kurier* 6 May 1993.

Los, Lothar. "Gott sabbert. Stephan Bruckmeier inszeniert Panizzas *Liebeskonzil* im Ensemble am Petersplatz." *Falter* 47 (1991).

_____. "*Das Liebeskonzil* und die Strafe der Lustseuche. Stephan Bruckmeiers 'Kultur der Vernichtung', Teil 3." *Der Standard* 11 Nov. 1991: 12.

Lutz, Daniela. "Durchschnitt." *Tirol Kurier* 11 Oct. 1986.

Mann, Thomas. "*Das Liebeskonzil.*" *Das zwanzigste Jahrhundert: Blätter fur deutsche Art und Wohlfahrt* 5 (1895): 522.

Mehring, Walter. *The Lost Library: The Autobiography of a Culture.* Indianapolis: Bobbs-Merrill, 1951.

_____. *Die verlorene Bibliothek. Autobiographie einer Kultur.* Hamburg: Rowohlt, 1952.

Müller, Heiner. "Panizza oder die Einheit Deutschlands." *Frankfurter Rundschau* 4 Aug. 1979: Feuilleton 3.

Müller, Jürgen L. "Oskar Panizza und Emil Kraepelin. Die Wiederbegegnung der ehemaligen Assistenten Bernhard von Guddens und die Entstehung des 'Paraphreniekonzeptes' Emil Kraepelins." *Würzburger medizinhistorische Mitteilungen* 20 (2001): 319–334.

_____. "Oskar Panizza. Versuch einer immanenten Interpretation." Diss. Universität Würzburg, 1990.

Nadler, Josef. *Geschichte der deutschen Literatur.* 2nd ed. Regensburg: J. Habbel, 1961.

Neau, Patrice. "Un cas de fétichisme: L'amateur de corsets d'Oskar Panizza." *Literalität und Körperlichkeit = Littéralité et corporalité,* Günter Krause, ed. Tübingen: Stauffenburg, 1997: 209–23.

_____. *Pathologie et création littéraire chez Oskar Panizza: Étude sur les aspects pathologiques, thérapeutiques, artistiques et religieux de l'oeuvre d'Oskar Panizza.* Diss. Université Paris-Val-de-Marne, 1993. Lille: A.N.R.T. Université de Lille III, 1993.

Neumann, Christoph. "Der christliche Mythos in Oskar Panizzas *Liebeskonzil*." Diss. Freie Universität Berlin, 1991. Microform. Berlin: Mikrofilm-Center Klein, 1992.

Oberlandesgericht Innsbruck. *Beschluss.* 3 Bs 294/85, 30 July 1985.

Ohff, Heinz. "Der Moralist am Pranger." *Der Tagesspiegel* 6 Oct. 1963: 39.

Pannick, David. "When Blasphemy and Free Speech Collide." *The Times* (London) 8 Nov. 1994.

"Oskar Panizza." *Die Zeit* 24 Nov. 1894: 125.

"Oskar Panizza." *Die Geißel* 15 Aug. 1896: 3.

"Oskar Panizza." *Das literarische Echo* 1 Dec. 1904: 349.

"Oskar Panizza." *Berliner Börsenzeitung* 267 (1933).

"Oskar Panizza." *Die schöne Literatur* 22 Oct. 1921: 280.

"Oskar Panizza über Wilhelm II." *Münchner Neueste Nachrichten* 24 Mar. 1928: 2.

Otto-Preminger-Institut. "Pressemitteilung." Innsbruck: Cinematograph, 14 May 1985.

_____. "Pressemitteilung." Innsbruck: Cinematograph, 10 Oct. 1986.

_____. "Pressemitteilung." Innsbruck: Cinematograph, 8 Oct. 1987.

_____. "Presse-Info zum Fall *Otto-Preminger-Institut gegen Österreich*." Innsbruck: Cinematograph, 5 May 1993.

"Panizza." *Augsburger Abendzeitung* 1 May 1895: 6f.

"Panizza." *Das bayerische Vaterland* 1 May 1895: 2.

"Panizza." *Augsburger Postzeitung* 2 May 1895: 6f.

"Panizza." *Regensburger Morgenblatt* 2 May 1895: 3.

"Panizza." *Germania* 3 May 1895: 2.

"Panizza." *Die Deutsche Wacht* 4 May 1895: 2.

"Panizza." *Neue Zürcher-Zeitung* 9 May 1895: 2.

"Panizza." *Augsburger Abendzeitung* 10 May 1895: 5.

"Panizza." *Kölnische Zeitung* 11 May 1895: 2.

"Panizza." *Das literarische Echo* 15 Nov. 1904: 302.

"Panizza." *Das literarische Echo* 1 Feb. 1905: 638f.

"Panizza." [Todesnachrichten] *Das literarische Echo* 15 Nov. 1921: 247.

"Panizza: Umsunst gelebt." *Der Spiegel* 7 Mar. 1962: 81–87.

Panizza, Mathilde [pseud. Siona]. *Drei Brautgeschichten und Sonne, stehe still*, 3rd ed. Bad Kissingen: n.p., 1895.

_____. *Der Reichsplan Gottes mit den Menschen.* Stuttgart: n.p., 1886.

Popp, Josef. "Oskar Panizza." *Augsburger Postzeitung* 7 June 1895: 2f.

Prescher, Hans. "Die aufhaltsame Entdeckung des Oskar Panizza." *Diskurs* 12.7 (July 1962): 9.

_____. "Oskar Panizza, der ignorierte Autor." *Künste im Aufbruch. München in den 50er Jahren.* Munich: Allitera Verlag, 2006: 46–48.

_____. "Ein rebellischer deutscher Poet." *Deutsche Post* 20 July 1964: 377f.

_____. "Ein Ungebärdeter: In memoriam Oskar Panizza." *Frankfurter Rundschau* 2 Sept. 1961: 53.

Ratallack, James. "Antisocialism and Electoral Politics in Regional Perspective: The Kingdom of Saxony." Larry Eugene Jones and James Ratallack, eds. *Elections, Mass Politics and Social Change in Modern Germany: New Perspectives.* Cambridge UP, 1992.

Rösler, Walter. "Ein bißchen Gefängnis und ein bißchen Irrenhaus. Der Fall Oskar Panizza." *Sinn und Form* 32.4 (July-Aug. 1980): 840–855.

Rosner, Karl. *Damals. Bilderbuch einer Jugend.* Düsseldorf: Vier Falken, 1948.

Rost, Nico. "Oskar Panizza: Poete Maudit." *Algemeen Handelsblad* (Amsterdam) 13 June 1964: 3.

Ruiss, Gerhard. "Solidaritätsfonds österreichischer Künstler und Publizisten." Vienna: Interessensgemeinschaft österreichischer Autoren, 15 Jan. 1986.

_____. "Zum Entscheid des Obersten Gerichtshofes vom 19.12.1985 sowie weiteren aktuellen gerichtlichen und rechtlichen Einschränkungen der FREIHEIT DER KUNST." Vienna: Interessensgemeinschaft österreichischer Autoren, 24 Dec. 1985.

Rümmele, Christoph. "Die Freiheit der Kunst im Spannungsverhältnis zum Strafrecht am Beispiel des Films *Das Liebeskonzil* von Werner Schroeter (nach dem gleichnamigen Bühnenstück von Oskar Panizza)." Diplomarbeit, Universität Innsbruck, 1997.

Sailer, Anton. "Der lebenslange Amoklauf des Dr. med. Oskar Panizza." *Süddeutsche Zeitung* 30 Sept. 1971: 13.

Sandfort & Hanisch, *Begutachtung.* Juristenkommission Nr. 505, Spitzenorganisation der Filmwirtschaft, Wiesbaden, 3 Mar. 1982.

"Sauberpapst aus Polen — Out of Competition." *berlinale-tip*, No. 10, 1982: 6.

Schlaf, Johannes. "Zwei Satiriker." *Das Magazin für Litteratur* 25 Nov. 1893: 756f.

Schlawe, Fritz. *Literarische Zeitschriften, 1885–1910.* Stuttgart: J.B. Metzler, 1961.

Schöpf, Alois. "Maultrommel — Tiroler Filmverbot mit Fragezeichen." *Kurier* 16 May 1985.

Schmitz, Oskar A. H. *Dämon Welt. Jahre der Entwicklung.* Munich: Müller, 1926.

Schultz, Joachim, ed. *Katalog zur Ausstellung zum 150. Geburtstag von Oskar Panizza.* Hefte für angewandte Literaturwissenschaft (HAGEL) Nr.3. Bayreuth Univ. 2003.

Schulz, Wolfgang. *Oskar Panizza: Psichopate, Pazjent. Visionen, Halluzinationen, Dämmerungsstücke.* Würzburg: Werkstattbühne e.V., 1989.

"Schwurgericht." *Fränkischer Kurier* 1 May 1895: 2.

"Das schwurgerichtliche Urteil gegen den Schriftsteller Panizza." *Augsburger Postzeitung* 28 May 1895: 3.

Seufert, Heinrich. "Fränkische Schicksale. Oskar Panizza." *Fränkische Tagespost* 22 Nov. 1929 (1. Beilage): 1f.

Siona. See Panizza, Mathilde.

Skriver, Ansgar. *Gotteslästerung?* Hamburg: Rütten & Loening, 1962.

Soceanu, Marion. "Oskar Panizza, *Das Liebeskonzil.* Text-, Stoff- und Motivgeschichte. Interpretation." MA thesis, Regensburg, 1979.

_____. "Oskar Panizzas Kampf um den Glauben." *Colloquia Germanica* 14.2 (1981), 142–157.

"Sonntagsplauderei." *Vorwärts* 2. Beilage 5 May 1895:1.

Reiner Speck. "'Handle, wie Dir Dein Dämon vorschreibt'. Vor fünfzig Jahren starb der Arzt und Dichter Oskar Panizza." *Deutsches Ärzteblatt* 2 Dec. 1971: 3306–11, and 9 Dec. 1971: 3376–78.

Stainer, Ulrike. "Die Inquisition lebt." *Oberösterreichische Nachrichten* 21 Sept. 1994: 17.

"Steckbrief." *Münchner Zeitung* 10 Feb. 1900: 3.

Steinkeller, Anna. "Die 'Erfindung der Syphilis' brachte eine Anzeige ein." *Salzburger Nachrichten* 1 Oct. 1991: 23.

_____. "Das Stück *Das Liebeskonzil* erregt neuerlich die Gemüter — Europäischer Gerichtshof für Menschenrechte meldete sich." *Salzburger Nachrichten* 7 May 1993: 17.

Steinlechner, Gisela. *Fallgeschichten: Krafft-Ebing, Panizza, Freud, Tausk.* Vienna: WUV-Universitätsverlag, 1995.

Stobbe, Horst. *Auktionskatalog.* Munich: Horst Stobbe, 1928.

_____. *Oskar Panizzas literarische Tätigkeit. Ein bibliographischer Versuch.* Munich: Horst Stobbe, 1925.

Szilágyi, Geza. "Panizza Oskár." *Figyelö* (Budapest), 1.1 (Jan. 1905): 26–34.

Tanemura, Suehiro. *Gusha no kikaigaku* [The Machinology of a Fool]. Tokyo: Seidosha, 1991.

Trimmel, Christiane. "Religion, Sexualität und Wahnsinn bei Oskar Panizza. Eine Untersuchung anhand der Erzählsammlung *Der Korsettenfritz.*" Diplomarbeit, Universität Wien, 1996.

Tuchmann, Emil Ferdinand. "Die Lücke im Urheberrecht: Die Erben Panizzas vereiteln die Herausgabe des Nachlasses." *Die literarische Welt* 2 Aug. 1929: 8.

Tucholsky, Kurt [Pseud. Ignaz Wrobel]. "Oskar Panizza." *Freiheit* 11 July 1920: 2.

_____. "Panizza." *Die Weltbühne* 11 Sept. 1919: 321–25.

_____. "Sprechstunde am Kreuz." *Die Weltbühne* 12 Dec. 1928: 881–85.

Tuck, Susan. "O'Neal and Frank Wedekind. Part One." *The Eugene O'Neill Newsletter.* Vol. VI, No. 1 (spring 1982): 1f.

Twele, Holger. "Filmbeobachter." *Cinematographisches Calendarium 40.* Innsbruck: Otto-Preminger-Institut, May 1985: 2.

"Über Dr. Panizza." *Kölnische Volkszeitung* 11 May 1895: 1.

United Press International. "Human Rights Court Rejects Film Protest." Strasbourg, 20 Sept. 1994.

"Unterm Strich." *taz* 21 Sept. 1994: 12.

Vaget, Hans R. "Thomas Mann und Oskar Panizza. Zwei Splitter zu *Buddenbrooks* und *Doktor Faustus.*" *Germanisch-romanische Monatsschrift* 56.25 (1975): 231–37.

Vogler, Sylvia. "Wider die Religion. *Das Liebeskonzil* von Oskar Panizza in analytischer und rezeptionsgeschichtlicher Betrachtung, unter besonderer Berücksichtigung Österreichs." Diplomarbeit, Universität Wien, 1993.

Völker, Klaus. "Mehr als ein Phantast und Pamphletist. Die Schriften von Oskar Panizza werden nun neu aufgelegt." *Basler Magazin* 16 Feb. 1980: 6f.

_____. "Phantast und Gelehrsamkeitspedant. Oskar Panizza: Auf dem Weg zu einer Wiederentdeckung des Verfemten." *Frankfurter Rundschau* 19 Jan. 1980: III.

_____. "'Der Wahnsinn, wenn er epidemisch wird, heißt Vernunft'. Ein heute wieder aktueller Oskar Panizza." *Tages-Anzeiger* 26 Apr. 1980: 53f.

Walsh, Brian. "Remarks." *St. John's Law Review* 70.1 (Winter 1996): 77–100.

Wedekind, Frank. *Gesammelte Briefe.* Ed. Fritz Strich. 2 vols. Munich: Müller, 1924.

Wellershoff, Dieter. "Die Kompetenzzweifel der Schriftsteller." *Merkur* 24 (Aug. 1970): 723–735.

Wohlmuth, Alois. *Ein Schauspielerleben: Ungeschminkte Selbstschilderung.* Munich: Verlag Parcus, 1918.

Wolff, Theodor. "Oskar Panizza." *Das Magazin für Litteratur* 15 June 1895: 763f.

Wolzogen, Ernst von. "Von der münchner Dichtelei." *Das Magazin für Litteratur* 25 May 1895: 641–47.

_____. *Wie ich mich ums Leben brachte. Erinnerungen und Erfahrungen.* Braunschweig: Westermann, 1922.

Zipes, Jack. "Oskar Panizza: The Operated German as Operated Jew." *New German Critique* 21 (Fall 1980): 47–62.

"Zum Liebeskonzil-Urteil: Grüne bedauern EGH-Entscheid." *Wiener Zeitung* 23 Sept. 1994.

Radio Broadcasts

Bauer, Michael. "Oskar Panizza." Bayerischer Rundfunk. 13 Aug. 1984. 18.15h (Hereinspaziert).

_____. "Oskar Panizza." Österreichischer Rundfunk 2. Feb. 12 1983.

_____. "Ein bisschen Gefängnis und ein bisschen Irrenhaus. Der Fall Oskar Panizza." Bayerischer Rundfunk 2. 31 Jan. 1982. 22.05–23h.

_____. "Der Fall Panizza." Hessischer Rundfunk 3. 9 Nov. 1981. 22–22.15h (Bücherreport).

Benjamin, Walter. "E.T.A. Hoffmann und Oskar Panizza." Frankfurter Rundfunk. 26 Mar. 1930.

Gallissaires, Pierre. "Chroniques rebelles." Reading of *Le Concile d'amour* w. Odila Caminos (la vierge Marie), Nicolas Mourer (Satan). Radio Libertaire (89.4). 14 Feb. 2009.

Le Concile d'amour. Discussion of play. Radio Campus Lille (106.6). 21/28 Nov. 2008. http://blog.paludes.fr/public/Radio4/Panizza-LeConcileD_Amour-Critique.mp3.

Cramer, Heinz von. "Hundeleben 1892 nach O. Panizza." Bayerischer Rundfunk 2. 12 Oct. 2003. 15.15h.

Gumtau, Helmut. "Ich komme grad aus dem Gefängnis." RIAS, 24 May 1979. 22.40–23.30h.

Katzenberger, Klaus. "'Ein mäßig großes Irrenhaus'. Über den Schriftsteller Oskar Panizza." Radio Bremen 2. 29 Mar. 1980. 15.05–16h.

Kernert, Thomas. *Oskar Panizza. Eine Revue der Provokationen.* Land und Leute HF, Bayerisches Feuilleton. Munich: Bayerischer Rundfunk 2005.

Kocher, Pierre. "'...übt euch fleissig nur im Hoffen, doch sagt es hier nicht allzulaut!' Oskar Panizza, aus seinen Werken." Radio der deutschen und rätoromanischen Schweiz, Studio Bern. 20 Apr. 1982. 20.30–22h.

Müller, Thomas. *Denken ist immer eine schlimme Sache. Der Schriftstelle Oskar Panizza; ein Porträt.* 25 min. audio cassette. Leipzig: Mitteldeutscher Rundfunk, 1997.

Prescher, Hans. "Ein literarischer Beserker. Hinweise auf Leben, Werk und Wirkung Oskar Panizzas." Südwestfunk. 26 Feb. 1962. 22.30–23h.

_____. "Nestbeschmutzer und Gotteslästerer. Oskar Panizza — ein deutscher Schriftsteller zur Kaiserzeit." Südwestfunk 2. 12 May 1981. 20.30–21.30h.

Rausch, Mechthild. "Oskar Panizza: *Der Korsettenfritz.*" Bayerischer Rundfunk, TV 3. 22.40–22.50h.

_____. "Oskar Panizza: *Die kriminelle Psychose.*" Sender Freies Berlin. 4 Jan. 1979, 17.10–17.30h.

Index